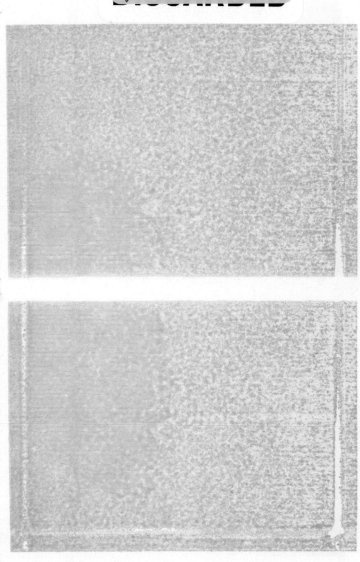

ENGLISH RECUSANT LITERATURE
1558—1640

Selected and Edited by
D. M. ROGERS

Volume 186

NICOL BURNE
*The Disputation Concerning
the Controversit Headdis
of Religion
1581*

NICOL BURNE

The Disputation Concerning
the Controversit Headdis
of Religion
1581

The Scolar Press
1974

ISBN 0 85967 162 3

Published and printed in Great Britain by
The Scolar Press Limited, 59-61 East Parade,
Ilkley, Yorkshire and
39 Great Russell Street,
London WC1

NOTE

Reproduced (original size) from a copy in the library of Stonyhurst College, by permission of the Rector. Sig. M6 recto (f. 104ʳ) has been damaged in this copy, and this page from a copy in the British Library has been substituted as an appendix, by permission of the Board.

References: Allison and Rogers 183; STC 4124.

Maſt .   *H*   *+ .*

THE
DISPVTATION
CONCERNING THE
CONTROVERSIT· HEADDIS
of Religion, haldin in the Realme of
Scotland, the zeir of God ane thousand, fyue hundreth fourscoir
zeiris.   Betuix.

The ~~pretendit~~ *Miniſteris of the deformed* Kirk
in Scotland.

OX   And,   *Jhs*

Nicol Burne Profeſſor of philoſophie in S.
Leonardis college, in the Citie of Sanctandrois, brocht vp from his tender eage in the
peruerſit ſect of the Caluiniſtis, and nou be
ane ſpecial grace of God, ane membre of
the halie and Catholik kirk.

Dedicat

To his Souerane the kingis M. of Scotland,
King Iames the Saxt.

Niſi conuerſi fueritis, gladium ſuum vibrabit: arcum
ſuum tetendit, & parauit illum. 1.
Vales ze be conuerted, God vil drau his ſuord: he hes
bendit his bovv, and preparit it
Pſalm. 7.

Imprented at Pariſe the firſt day of
October.
1581.

NEmo est qui reliquerit domum, aut Fratres, aut Sorores, aut Patrem, aut Matrem, aut filios, aut agros propter me, aut propter Euangelium, qui non accipiet centies tantum nunc in tempore hoc, domos, & Fratres, & Sorores, & Filios, & agros cum persecutionibus, & in saeculo futuro vitam aeternam. 1.

Thair sal na man leif his hous, his brethrene, or sisteris, or father, or mother, or sonis, or possessionis for my saik, and for profession of the Euangel, bot he sal resaue ane hundreth tymes als manie ma housis, and brethrene, and sisteris, and motheris and sonis and possessionis vith the persecutionis quhilk he thoillis, and in the varld to cum lyf aeternal. Marc. 10

Omnis ergo qui confitebitur me coram hominibus, confitebor & ego eum coram patre meo qui in caelis est, qui autem negauerit me coram hominibus, negabo & ego eum coram Patre meo, qui in caelis est. 1.

Quhairfor quhasouer vil confes me befoir me, I vil confes him also befoir my father in heauin: bot him quha vil deny me befoir men, I vil deny also befoir my father of heauin. Math. 10

*Vna vocis confessio, perpetua Christi
confessione honoratur.
Cyprianus de laude Martyrij.*

TO THE MAIST NO-

BIL, POTENT, AND GRATIOVS
king of Scotland king Iames the saxt.

 Indrie and vechtie reasonis
(My Sonerane) mouis me
not onlie to haue Zour M. in
gude remembrance in my
daylie prayeris, bot also to
confess my verie erneast affe-
ctione in offering my humil seruice bayth be
vord and vritt salang as the æternal God sal
prolong my dayis in this vail of miserie: This
I am bund to do alsueil be command of the
æternal God, quha inioynis to inferiore subiectis al deu obedience touardis thair Souerane pouaris. and Magistratis : as be the inæsti-
mable benefeit quhilk I receauit of zour hienes clemencie aganis the traiterous dealing of
sik malitious personis, as cruellie socht the
schedding of my innocent blude : For being
impresoned first in the Castel of Sanctandrois,
and nixt in the tolbuith of Edinburgh,
nocht for onie euil doing, bot for oppin professione of the treu and Catholik Religion,
quhilk nocht onlie al kingis and Quenis
hes euer mentenit in zour hienes impyre, bot

ã ij

thairin alſo zour M. (be the maiſt ſollicit cair
of zour darreſt mother our Souerane the
Queuis grace, ane maiſt conſtant mentenar of
the treuth) vas maid participant of the ſacramentis of Baptiſme and Confirmation : And
quhairof lykuyſe God of his infinit gudnes
granted me knaulege to my æternal ſaluatione, deliuering me out of the thraldome and
bondage of that idolatrous Caluiniſme, vith
the quhilk (alace) manie be ane blind zeal ar
fraudfullie deceauit to the lamentabil perdition of thair auin ſaulis, except be earneſt repentance ſpedelie thay returne to thair ſpiritual mother the halie Catholik kirk. This I
makand oppin profeſſion, and ſuſtenand the
ſame be plane diſputation bayth at libertie, ãd
in preſone, to the oppin confuſion of the Miniſteris coniurit ennimeis to the immaculat
ſpous of our head, and ſaluiour Chriſt Ieſus:
Thay conſpyrit maiſt cruellie aganis my lyf
firſt accuſing me be zour g. aduocat and my
Lord Iuſtice clerk, as thocht I had bene giltie
of leſe maieſtie: Bot quhen the Eſſyis var tuyſe
ſummondit, the protectore of al innocencie,
quha delyuerit Suſanna from the fals accuſa-
tione of hir ennimeis, ſcheu the richteouſnes
of my caus, and be his halie Spirit ſua mouit
zour M. hairt, that zour hienes vith ane kinglie fauore of æquitabil iuſtice receauit my
letter of humil ſupplication, hauing verie gude remembrance hou thairin I prayit our gratious God to perſerue zour M. Frõ the ſched-

ding of innocent bluid. The quhilk the king of al kingis sua infixit in zour merciful hairt, that incontinent zour grace commandit ftraitlie, that na iniuftice fould be 'exerceifed aganis zour M. auin fchollar : This vas the kinglie voce, and clemécie proceiding of Iuftice and godlines, quhilk preferuit my lyf from the bludie handis of tha cruel tygres: zit thir perfecutaris of Chriftis mébris being maift offendit, that by thair expectatione, I had obtenit fik fauore of zour hienes, and being brint vith ane infatiabil thrift of my bluid, inuentit ane neu ftratagem, propofing by zour M. vil and intelligence, to haue hungred me to death, be'debarring al accefs of freindis quha var villing to fupplie my necefsitie. And quhen extreme danger of famine conftrainit me to hing ouer ane purfe at the tolbuith vindo, to craif almous for Chriftis faik, thay perfauing the reuth and compaffió of Godlie and cheritable people, quha beftouit thair almous on me maift liberalie, caufit cut doun the purfe : And althocht thay commandit the IayVler to impefch my letteris of fupplicatione, quhairin I micht haue requirit that quhilk vas conforme to æquitie, zit God fua mouit his hairt, that he præfentit ane requeift of myne to theProuofte ãd honorable Concile of Edinburgh for licence to beg almous, quhairbie I micht be fuftenit : The quhilk albeit it vas grantit be the difcretion of the Prouofte and Honorable Concile, zit the

Minifteris obtenit ane difcharge forbidding
that I fould ask fupport in the name of ane
fchollar, or affix onie letter vpon the purfe
for fignification of my indigence:bot nochtuithftanding al thair raige conceaued aganis me, and inuie quhilk thay bure aganis my
fauoraris:Cheritabil perfonis gaif me of thair
almous maift largelie, for declaration of the
erneaft defyre quhilk thay had of the extirpa-
tion of thair feditious hærefie, and the imbraceing of the treu Catholik religion agane,
quhom I pray the Lord to recompáfe, quhen
he fal diftribut to al men according to thair
doingis in this varld. Nou becaus thir capital
ennimeis, and cruel perfecutaris of Chriftian
and Catholik men,var fruftrat of my death,
feiring that I vald haue difclofed thair erroneous doctrine gif I had remanit in the cuntrey,nocht onlie procurit my vnnatural ba-
nishment,caufing me find fouertie vndir the
pane of fyue hundreth púdis, nocht to returne, bot alfo in my abfence thay haue declairit
thair malice and inquenfibil hetret aganis my
fchaddou, laboring to bring me in contempt
be thair fals and sklanderous accufationis, as
thay do al vtheris,quha may fchau hou thay
haue collectit ane cófufit mafs of the hærefeis
quhilk hes bene condemnit be the Catholik
kirk fen Chrift and his Apoftles dayis : And
to bring me in farder contempt thay haue
fpred the brute throuch the popularis, that in
fik conference as I had vith thame in prefone

thay var altogidder victorious, and be this
and siclyk fraudful menis, detracting vtheris,
thay labore to mentene thame selfis, and
thair erroneous doctrine amang the rude
people: Bot to the effect that zour M. and al
zour G. treu subiectis, may knau hou friuole
and impertinent thair reasonis var, I haue
breiflie collectit my hail discours and disputation vith the Ministeris, and vther Protestaons in Scotland, and tane the hardines to dedicat the same vnto zour M. as ane Scholaris
taikin and signification of the perpetual remembrance of the benefeit quhilk I haue receauit of Zour Royal humanitie, Beseiking
zour M. and al zour louing subiectis to reid
the same vith sik attentiue consideration that
the reasonis of the ane, and the vther being
considerit vithout al inordinat affection, zour
G. may planelie persaue thair hæretical, and
maist pernicious doctrine to be the cause of
the loss ad tynsal of manie thousand saulis in
zour M. realme. In consideratione quhairof
zour M. sould be mair occupeit than in inlar-
geing zour temporal kingdome and dominione, as that is the onlie moyen quhairbie
zour g. may attene to æternal fælicie: And I
hoip that God hes præseruit zour hienes out
of sa monie dangeris, euin sen zour infancie
to mak zour M. ane instrument (as he maid
Iosias) to repair the ruine and destructione of
the kirk of Scotland, be iust correctione of
thame, quha, as vithout onie lauchful calling

á iiij

thay var intrudit be violence , sua laboris be the sam meane vithout repentance to arrogat vnto thame felfis the Authoritie of spiritual Pastores , maist viuelie representing to vs the tyrannie of Mahomet , and his posteritie the Turkis, quha obstinatlie defendis his diabolical and barbarous inuentione : for euin as thay knauig al poyntis of thair superstition to be contrare nocht onlie to al Godlie authoritie of halie scripture, bot als aganis al honestie of gude maneris, and ciuilitie, aganis al natural reason, and lauis of men veil constitute , vil in nauyse suffer onie man to disput , or preache aganis the same , makand oppin profession that thay vil defend it onlie be the suord and force of armore : Euin sua the Ministeris of mirknes, knauing in thair auin consciencis that thair maist vngodlie professione is contrare not onlie to the authoritie of the halie scripture , and definitionis of the General conciles , bot also to the iudgement and aggreance of al Catholik doctoris that euer hes bene sen the dayis of our saluiour : thay labore vith al diligence , that thair doctrine cum neuer in discussion , iust tryal, and examination , suppressand sa far as thay may, al bukes quhilk ar vryttin for confutatione of sik erroris. Bot albeit maist Gratious Souerane,that thay sua doand do according to thair profession , vsing proceidingis, and making progress verie conuenient to thair beginning, vrangouslie defending ane

vickie caus, and euidentlie schauing thame
selfis, the verie natural and treu offspring of
Mahomet:zit it vil nauyse becum zour M. to
imitat the Turk in mentening thair vickitnes
be zour kinglie authoritie, bot contrare to
imploy the same to the deliuerance of manie
thousand saulis of zour M.subiectis, from the
maist vnuotthie seruitude and captiuitie of
thair consciencis, causing al quhilk hes bene
maist iniustlie decreted be force and violence
in præiudice of the veritie during zour mino-
ritie to be callit agane to the iust tryal,and examination of the veritie: for nou tyme is that
zour g.enter in deip cōsideratiō as the impor-
tāce ād vecht of the mater requyris, and nocht
to beleue that Craig, Dúcansone, Lausone,and
sik vther periurit Apostatis, hes mair vndirstanding of the scripturis, nor al the learned
men quha in onie age sen Christis dayis hes
bene estemit Christianis,or that the hail varld
hes bene vithout the treu religione not imbraceing the fayth of the Catholik kitk , befoir Caluine maid defection thairfra: Quhilk
gif zour G.do, as I craif maist ernestlie of the
gudnes of God, I doubt not bot zour hienes
vil haue ane special desyre to se the prætendit
Ministeris in zour Realme confrontit vith
sum of zour G.auin subiectis,quha ar nou dif-
persit onlie for conscience caus almaist throuch al Europ,and ar maist villing to offer thair quik bodeis to the fyre , or quhatsumeuer
vther terment, vnles thay proue maist cui-

dentlie (as thay haue alreddie offerit) that the
Miniſteris ar fals ād traittorous deceaueris of
the People : God of his infinit gudnes moue
zour hieneshairt not ōlie to tak on this godlie īterpryſe, bot alſo to outred the ſame, to the
veilfare of zour M. Realme, to the glorie of
the eternal God, And zour hienes greit merite at the handis of our onlie ſaluiour Chriſt
Ieſus, quha vil recompans euerie gude vork
vpon the day of his iuſt iudgement.

At Pariſe the. 24. day of Iulij. 1581.

Zour M.

Maiſt humil, faythful ſub-
iect, and daylie Oratour.

NICOL BVRNE.

TO THE CHRISTIA-

NE REIDAR.

Thocht gude to aduerteis the Chriſtian reidar, that in the beginning of my conference, being onlie examinat be Maiſter Andro Meluine, gif I had bene groundit in the Catholik religion or nocht, I anſuerit according to his interrogationis, and ſua I haue put the mater in vritt rather in maner of ane Catechiſme, nor diſputatione, euin as it proceidit in verie deid : In the progreſs of my conference I haue brocht al the argumentis of the Miniſteris vithout onie diſſimulatione, detracting na thing from the force and ſtrenth of the ſame : As to my auin Anſueris, albeit I haue retenit the ſubſtáce of thame, zit findand greitar commoditie of buikes heir nor in Scotland, I haue ſumpairt amplifeit ád inlargeit thame, to accommodat my ſelf to the capacitie of the ruid people, quha could not be abil to comprehend ſua vechtie materis in ſua feu vordis, as I vas conſtrainit to vſe in my conference: As to the Names of the Miniſteris and vtheris quha diſputed aganis me, I haue expreſſit the names of thame quhom I kneu, and quhen I kneu

thame not, I haue vryttin in general Miniſter,
or Proteſtaon: Concerning my auin perſone,
I vas brochtup from my tender eage in the
doctrine of Caluine, quhilk of lait dayis hes
bene receauit in the realme of Scotland be
the preaching of Schir Ioann kmnox, and did
follou it vith na les affectione and zeal nor
did the reſt, quhil the tyme it pleaſed God
throuch reiding of ſum Catholik vryttaris
to illuminat my hairt, and lat me planelie vnderſtand that ſik doctrine vas nocht that, quhilk vas preachit be Chriſt and his Apoſtlis,
and hes euer bene mentened, be al Chriſtianis
ſen thair dayis: bot onlie ane collectit Maſs of
auld and condemnit hæreſeis, quhilk quhen
I vas thair preſent, I obleiſed me to defend,
and proue befoir the General Aſſemblie of
Scotland, declairing my ſelf maiſt villing to
ſuffer puneiſhment, vnles be the grace of God
I performed that quhilk I had tane in hand,
Askand of ane Miniſter callit Smeton, in Paiſlay, that I micht haue frie acceſs to thair general Aſſemblie to be conuenit in Edinburgh
ſchortlie thaireftir: To the quhilk petition
(as he him ſelf can not deny) he could anſuere
na thing bot that it vas maiſt iuſt, and promeiſt to me vpon his fayth and treuth, that I
ſould haue frie acceſs thairto: In the mentyme
ve condeſcendit to ſtand at the iudgement of
thrie maiſt learned of the Nobilitie, and thrie
of the Miniſteris choſin be him, vith thrie
Biſchopis, and thrie men of lau choſin be me:

The headdis of doctrine quhairupone ve sould haue reasoned var thir, 1. of the Calling of the Ministeris of Scotland. 2. Of the Sacramentis, and verteu thairof. 3. Of the inæqualitie of Pastores, and iudge lauchful in debait of Religion. 4. Of the definitione and causis of Iustificatione. 5. Of the definitione of Grace quhilk ve receaue be the merite of Christ. 6. Quhidder gif ane man being in grace in verie deid be inuart renouatione of his hairt, may loss the same agane or nocht? The maist honorables the Maister of Ross, The lairdis of Calduole, Blakhal, and Ihonestone quha var præsent, can beir recorde, that hauing confidence in Goddis halie spirit, I tuik in hand, that vnles, be the the iudgement of tha tuelf, (being suorne to iudge according to the reasonis of bayth the pairteis vithout feir, fead, or fauore) I prouit the Ministeris hæretikis and deceaueris of the people, I sould nocht refuse quhat puneishment thay pleased to deuyse aganis me, requiring na thing of the Ministeris, bot recantation: And for securitie that for my pairt I sould abyd'at this apoyntmét, I subscriuit thir headdis vith my hand at Paislay, in presence of the Noble men befoir mentionat: Bot my aduersare Smeton be his traittorous dealing aggreád to his profession, eftir that I had depairted fra him in peax vnto the tyme apoyntit, vithout onie varning proceidit vith excommunication aganis me, albeit I vas not subiect to his iurisdictione,

and thaireftir send to Edinburgh and procurit letteris of captione, quhairbie I vas focht
throuch the hail cuntrey, and at the laft being
apprehendit, vas vayrdit in the tolbuith of
Edinburgh fra the fourtene of October in
the zeir of God ane thoufand fyue hundreth
and fourfcoir, to the penult of Ianuar. Quhair
I had fik confort and confolation, be reafon
I fufferit for confeffion of the name of Chrift,
that I had neuer gretar in my lyf, and thocht
my felf happie gif I had obtened that grace
to haue deed in the actione: Sua the Minifteris in place to haue granted me audience at
thair general affemblie, detenit me in ftrate
prefone: Aluyfe God turnit al to the beft,
and gaif me grace to ganeftand and refel quhatfumeuer thay could obiect vnto me, as the
Chriftian reidar may efilie perfaue of this our
conference, quhilk I befeik euerie man to
reid vithout al affectione of pairteis, and vith
ane erneaft defyre to knau the treuth concerning euerie controuerfie: Confidering that
na Minifter in Scotland vil anfuer for him in
the day of Goddis dreidful iudgement, bot
that euerie man vil anfuer for him felf,
and haue na excufe gif he haue adhærit
to onie fals Prophetis, the quhilkis the fcripture commandis euerie man to auoyd vndir
the pane of æternal damnatione: And mekil
les vil the follouaris of this neu doctrine in
Scotland haue onie excufe, be reafone Maifter Iohne Hamiltone ane learned man and

verie zelous defendar of the Catholik fayth,
in name of al the Catholik Scottis mē (be thair auyſe and requeiſt) in France and vther cūtreyis, offered that thay ſould cum to Scotland
on thair auin expenſis, and diſput vith the
prætendit Miniſteris, offering thair bodeis
to the fyre, vnles thay conuictit thame to be
Hæretikis, quhilk offer (as I vndirſtude of thair priuat cōmunicationis) the Miniſteris dar
not accept: Lyk as thay durſt neuer mak onie
anſuere to the quæſtionis proponit be Maiſter
Iohne Hay Concerning thair doctrine, Eccleſiaſtical ordore, and diſcipline: feiring that
thairbie thair erroris ſould haue bene diſſit to the people. Bot not to trouble zou, gude
reidar, vith farder declaratione of the vilful
malice, ād affectat ignorāce of the Miniſteris,
albeit I haue gude hoip of ſum of the zoūg mē
quha var nocht the beginnaris of this miſcheif in Scotland, bot be ſimplicitie and ouer
facil credulitie var deceauit be ſum miſchant
Apoſtatis: And praying maiſt humelie the
eternal God, that he aſſiſt zou vith his halie
ſpirit to the treu vndirſtanding of the veritie
I vil nou vith goddis grace enter vnto our
cōference. Fairueil, At Parſie the 24. day of Iulij.   1581.

S. Paul.
2. Tim. 4.

2. Tim. 2.

2. Thes. 2.

THE tyme vil cum quhen thay vil nocht suffer healthsum doctrine, bot hauing thair earis ʒuikand, vil get vnto thame selfis ane heape of teacharis to satisfie thair luste and pleasouris, and vil turne auay thair earis, that thay vil not gif audience to the treuth, bot gif credite to fables: Thir ar thay quha albeit thay be ay learnand, ʒit thay cum neuer to the knauledge of the veritie, becaus thay resauit not the treu cheritie, that thay micht be saif. Thairfoir God vil send thame ane effectuous, and strang delusion of error, that thay vil gif credite vnto leis.

Quhair S. Paul menis be ʒuikand earis, than quha vil heir na thing of the thretning of the panes of hel, the asperitie of repetace and mortificatio of the fleshe, bot tha thingis onlie quhilk tendis to libertie, and securitie of Goddis fauore, quhatsumeuer synnis, thay commit: Sua ve may be assurit that thir ar the latter dayis quhairof S. Paul speakis, sen ve se sua monie mennis earis ʒuikand to heir of licentious leuing, and eairles securitie, and sik ane heap of fleshlie teacharis, quhilk thay haue chosin vnto thame selfis, vithdrauing thair obedience from lauchful Bischopis, and pastors, be forgit leis and inuentionis: And as experiece teachis, albeit thay be ay learnand, thay can neuer cū to the veritie: bot euerilk ʒeir bringis in sum neu phantasie, becaus thay vil not learne at the spous of Christ, that is the Catholik kirk, bot onlie at thair auin brayn and imagination: And thairfoir, as sayis S. Ierom: Quia noluerunt esse discipuli veritatis, facti sunt Magistri erroris, becaus thay vald not be schollaris of the veritie, thay ar maid Maisteris of Error.

OF IVSTIFICATION.

CHAP. I.

Meluine.

 Vhat callis thou iuſtification?
Burne. Before I cum to the
definition thairof, I think it
expedient to conſidder the
diuers eſtaitis of mankynd.
M. *Quhat be thay?*

B. The firſt is man creatit in perfyt eage, as *Gene. 1.*
Adam before his fall: the ſecund is the eſtait
of mankynd efter the fal of Adam: the thrid,
is the eſtait of childrene conceauit in original ſyn: the fourt, is the eſtait of thame quha
cúming to perfyt eage, efter the reſtitution of
grace be baptiſme, fallis in deidlie ſyn.

M. *Quhat is Iuſtification in the firſt eſtait of mankynd?*

B. It is ane operation of God, creating of na
thing in the mynd of man original iuſtice,
vithout onie mereit of mannis pouar.

M. *Quhat callis thou original Iuſtice?*

B. It is ane ſupernatural gift, creatit be God
of his auin gudnes, frelie vithout ony deſer-
uing of man, quhairby the ſaul of man is per-

A

fytlie fubiect vnto God, and the body vnto
the Saul, quhairby alfo he is abil to do thai
varkis, that leidis to lyf eternal.

M. *Vas Adam abil to haue fulfillit the commandiment, quhilk he reccauit in Paradise?*

B. It is manifeft that he micht : fen God cõ-
mandit not that quhilk vas impoffibil.

M. *It lay not in his poßibilitie to keip the commã-
dement. For gif he had keipit the fame, our Saluiour CHRIST vald not haue cũmit in the flefch
to mak fatisfaction for fin. And it vas neceffar that
he fould cum in the flefch as he did, thairfore conclude I, that the fal of Adam vas neceffar, and that it
vas impoßible, that he micht haue keipit the commandiment.*

B. Quhair ze allege, that it vas neceffar that
he fould cum in the flefch to mak fatisfactio-
ne for finI. anfuer, that it vasnot abfolutlie ne
ceffar, bot vnder condition onlie, to vit gif Ad
am fynnit, and adame fynnit nocht of neceffitie bot of his avin fre vill and electione.

M. *Let vs than cum to that fecund eftait of mankynd, efter the fal of Adam, that I may perfane
quhat thou callis his iuftification.*

B. It is ane operation proceiding of Goddis
frie mearcie, quhairby the fyn is forgeuin,
and grace (loft be breaking of the cõmand)
reftorit vithout the mereit of ony varkis pre-
ceeding according to the faying of S.Paul. ve

Rom.3. ar inftefeit frelie be his grace.

M. *Be thair na varkis requyrit before the reftitution
of this grace?*

B. Zea : to vit varkis of Repentance, proceding of the grace of God, preparing the hairt
of man thairto, Bot thir ar not meritorious
of the reſtorit iuſtice : this iuſtice efteruart
bruſtis furth in vark quhairby the frie vil being cooperant to the halie ſpreit, obeyis
Goddis cōmandementis as it is vrittin : He
quha hes my commandementis and keipis
thame, it is he quha louis me : And he that is
borne of God ſynnis not, becaus the ſeid of
God abydis in him, and he may not ſyn, bere a
ſon he is borne of God. In this reſpect that
ſame Iuſtice, quhilk is mere grace, becūmis
the fontayne of meritorious varkis. Becaus
grace quhilk is in vs, thruch the mereit of
Chriſt is the caus of al mereit, ins afar as it
vorkis, or bringis furth operations as it is
vrittin : Zea ſe thairfore that ane man is
iuſtefeit be varkis and not be faith onlie:
And in Ieſus Chriſt nather circunciſion, nather the fores kyn or genteliſme auaillis onie
thing, bot faith quhilk producis gude varkis
be cheritie,

M. Quhat callis thou that ſecund Iuſtification?

B. It is ane augmentation of iuſtice be verteu of the grace of God, and cooperation of
frie vil, as it is vrittin : he that is iuſt, let him be
zit iuſtefeit .

*M . The ſcripture ſayis that ve ar Iuſtefeit be the
meritis of Chriſt and not be ony that ar in vs.*

B. Ve ar iuſtefeit be the meretis of Chriſt,
Becaus he be verteu of his blude hes mereit

*Euang. S.
Ioan. 15.
S. Ioan. 3.*

S. Iam. 2.

*S. Paul. 5.
gal.*

Apocal. 22

A ij

vnto vs his grace, be the quhilk ve ar iustifeit before God, and quhairfra al our meritis do proceid as from the original fontayne. And thairfore our meritis (as vryttis S. August.) ar the verie giftis of God: And quhair ze allege that the scripture affirmis, that ve ar not iustifeit be our meritis: it is maist fals, zea the scripture affirmis the contrar, considdering it attributis our Iustification vnto our gude varkis, quhilkis ar na vther thing bot our meritis.

9. Confes.
c. 13.

M. *Dois thou than think that the syn contractit thruch the inobedience of Adam, is remouit in verie deid, and in place thairof, iustice inhærent in euerie mānis mynd creatit, quhairby he may compeir before the tribunal seat of God?*

Rom. 5.

B. Euin sa I mean, Becaus insafar as Christ hes maid satisfaction for syn of infinit valeur, the grace geuin be him not onlie makis the mynd abil to obey Goddis commandimentis, bot also expellis the euil disposition quhilk it receauit be propagation of Adam, as testifeis S. Iohne that Christ hes cumit for the destruction of the vark of the Deuil, that is of syn.

1. Epist. 3.

M. *The scripture testefeis that the syn contractit of Adā abydis continuallie in our mynd, and be faith in Christ is onlie not imputit, or laid to our charge, Thair is not samekle as ane iust man, thair is nane quha hes vnderstanding, thair is nane quha searchis God, al men hes past astray, thay ar altogither improffitable thair is nane quha exercesis iustice, thair is not samekle as ane: hou then sayis thou that the syn is remo-*

S. Paul. 3.

uit in verie deid, and iustice inhærent in our myndis
acceptabil vnto God?

B. This zour testimonie of scripture, and
diuerss vthers lyk vnto this is to be vnderstâd
of man before his restitution to grace, thruch
the merit of Christ, quhil as our conference
sould be of thame quha ar alreddie restorit,
and to grant al that quhilk ze desyre Gif na
man be iust, bot be the imputation of the iustice of Christ, the prophet vald not haue affirmit vniuersallie that na man vas iust, cheiflie according to zour auin meaning, quha
grantis that monie ar iust be the imputation
of Christis iustice. Then quhither ze vil or not
ze ar constranit to grant that. S. Paul meanis
of ane treu and inhærêt iustice, quhilk becaus
it could not be obtenit nather be the lau of
nature, nor the vrittin lau, as he prouis him self
in the epistle to the Romanis, bot onlie be the
faith of Christ. It follouis necessarlie that quhasoeuer ar iustifeit be Christ, ressauis in thame selfis treu and inhærent iustice.

M. *Quhat than sayis thou to the testimonie of S. Io-*   ``
hne. Gif ve say that ve haue not syn ve deceaue our   1. Ioan.3.
selfis, and the treuth is not in vs?

B. Our controuersie côsistis not in this heid,
quhither gif ane man restorit to iustice haue
onie syn or not, becaus euin the godlie committis venial synnis, quhairof the Apostle spei
kis in this place. Bot the difference consistis
in this point, quhither gif ane man restorit to
iustice thruch the mereit of Christ, remanis in

the formar vickednes, or gif thair be onie
stay quhy he sould not properlie be callit iust:
y. Ioh.3. Considering * S. Iohne testifeis, that quhasoeuer dois iustice, he is iust. And I beleue ze
dar not be sa bauld to deny that S.Iohne and
the rest of the Apostlis did iustice : quhairfore thay var treulie iust before God. And gif
ane mã be euer ennemie to God, as ze ailege ze
ar in the vrang to exhort ony to vithdrau him
self from syn, cõsiddering it is impossibie, and
also auailis na thing, sen our synnis quhilk ar
in vs impeschis not that the iustice of Christ
be impute to vs as ze zour seluis afferme.

M. *Be quhat testimoneis of scripture may thou proue
that the syn remanis not in verie deid?*

B. In special be the testimonie of S. Paul :
ve quha ar deid to syn, hou may ve leue in the
Rom.6. same heirefter? sua that gif Christ deit in verie
deid and not be iputaticn onlie as certane he-
retickis affermit, ve de to syn in verie deid, and
not be imputation onlie being baptisit in
Christ. for the apostle subionis : knau ze not
that quhasoeuer ar baptesit in Iesus Christ
thay ar baptesit to de in him ? and a litill efter
he quha is deid is iustefeit from syn : and in
the beginning of the aucht chap. Thair abydis
na condénation to thame quha being ingraft
in Iesus Christ, leuis not efter the flesch, bot
efter the spreit.

M . *Concupiscence abydis in thame quha ar rege-*
Rom.7. *nerat, quhilk be S. Paul is callit syn thaifore syn*
abydis in thame quha ar iustifeit be Christ.

B. Concupiſcence is ſumtyme interpreit ane inordinat desyre of the fleſch aganis the ſpreit of man, hauand frie vil agreing thairto quhilk is ſyn, and abydis not in the iuſtefeit man. *Gal. 5.* Becaus S. Paul teſtifeis that thay quha pertènis to Chriſt, hes crucefeit the fleſch vith the concupiſcencis thairof. In lyk maner S. Petir. Ab- *2.ep.2.* ſtene from carnal concupiſcencis quhilkis fecht aganis the Saul. In another ſignification it is tane for the inferior pairt of the mynd repugnant vnto reaſon quhilk is na ſyn except the reaſon conſent thairto as vryttis S. James. Concupiſcence efter it hes conceauit *S. Iam. cap .I.* bringis furth ſyn : and also : Let not ſyn rigne in zour mortal bodeis to obey the concupiſcencis thairof . Quhair ze ſay that in the ſcripturis it is callit ſyn : S. Auguſt. gaue anſuer to *Auguſt.* the pelagianis tuelf hundreth zèris ſyne, *de nup, &* that it is callit ſyn, becaus it proceidis of ſyn, *c onc.c. 23.* and is the caus of ſyn, gif ve reſiſt not to it, *& contra* lyk as the hand is callit the vrit that is vrittin *Iuliani.l.* be the hand: And Chriſt him ſelf is callit ſyn *6.c.5.* becaus he is ane ſacrifice for our ſynnis, And thairfore it is not callit ſyn properlie, bot be ane figurat ſpeich according to S. Paulis auin interpretation .

M . haue ve ony vther Iuſtice nor that quhilk is in Chriſt onlie repute to be ouris?

B. The iuſtice quhilk is in Chriſt is the meritorious caus of our iuſtice, according to the teſti- *Rom.5.* monie of S . Paul, as be the ſyn of ane man vickitnes come vnto al men to condénation, euin sua al men ressauis gudnes to iustificatioñ be the gudnes of ane man. Sua as be the syn of Adam not onlie be imputation bot treulie ve ar al borne in syn, sua necessarlie be the iustice of Christ, not onlie ve man be repute iust before God, bot also ve man be iust in verie deid: And thairfore zour doctrine of iustification agreis vith the heresie of Pelagius: Becaus as affirmis S. Paul, the iustice of Christ is cõmunicat vnto vs, euin as the syn of Adam is cõmunicat. And ze subsume that the iustice of Christ is not treulie cõmunicat vnto vs, bot onlie be imputation, sua necessarlie it follouis that the syn of Adam is onlie impute to vs and that ve ar not treulie borne in syn, quhilk vas the blasphemous heresie of Pelag.

M. Thou art aluyse ignorant vf the scripturis, quhilk gif thou vnderstude thou vald find na testimonie to proue iustice inhærent in vs.

B. Albeit the auctoritie before alleagit be sufficient, zit I may esilie proue the same be may. For S. Paul vryttand to the Rom. testifeis that the cheritie of God is pourit in our hairtis be the halie spreit quhilk is geuin vnto vs. And to the Corinth: my grace is sufficient vnto the. Quhairfore I vil maist glaidlie glore of my auin vaiknes that the pouar and strenth of Christ may abyd in me. In the quhilk testemonie it is euident that the grace of God quhilk is ane thing vith our iustice signifeis ane inhærent strenth, and pouar, quhairby ve may obey the desyris of the spreit

Rom.5.

2.epst.c.
12.

and concur to the operations thairof. Quhair fore ze blindit Proteſtantis ar grettumlie deſeauit, quha vil acknaulege na vther ſignification of grace, bot that quhilk is definit be the orateur Cicero, eſpeciallie in ſik formes of ſpeking : Rediit cum illo in gratiā: for the Apoſtle S. Paul callis it ane vorkand L. Coloſ. ſtrenth, pouar, efficacie, and ane neu creature. 6. Gal.

M. *Quhat than ſayis thou is requyrit to the iuſtification of zoung children conceauit and borne in original syn, quhilk thou comprehendit vnder the thrid eſtait of mankynd?*

B. Euin as the zung childrene be the firſt Adam, hes contractit original syn, ſua be the ſecūd Adam, that is be Chriſt, thay ar purgit fra it be the lauer of regeneration, as teſtifeis S. Paul, be the quhilk thay reſſaue the grace Tit.3. of God, quhairby thay ar iuſtifeit : And quhen thay cum to the zeris of diſcretion, producis varkis that meritis eternal lyf.

M. *Let vs then cum to that fourt eſtait of mankynd quha as thou ſayis fallis in deidlie syn efter reſtitution to grace thruch Chriſt. Bot firſt let me vnderſtand, quhat thou callis deidlie syn, Becaus I knau na ſik diſtinction of sin in the halie ſcripture.*

B. The diſtinction of mortal synnis, from venial quhilk ar ſpiritual diſeiſis of the Saul may be vnderſtand be comparation vith bodelie infirmeteis : for as of thame ſum ar ſa far ennemie to nature, that in ane moment thay prouok ſuddane and haiſtie death :: vthers quhairby our natural temperature of body is

vitiat, may the mair eselie be curit : Siclyk
thair is ane kynd of syn that expellis grace
quhilk is the lyf of the Saul, and the vther
kynd albeit it fyllis the Saul, zit it may consist
vith grace: This includis not manifest contempt of God, bot is onlie ane inordinat behauiour in louing of the creature proceding
of negligence, ignorance, and infirmitie. This
distinction of synmis is declarit in the euangel of S. Mat. Bot I say vnto zou quhatsúeuir
he be quha is offendit with his brother raschlie
is oblest to iugement : he quha sayis to his
brother Raha, is subiect to the cócile: and he
quha callis his brother fule, is vorthie of the
fyre of hell. Be the quhilk is vordis Christ him
self declairis, that al synnis deseruis not eternal dánation: and sua cósequentlie that al syn
nis ar not mortal or deidlie: By that it is cleir
in the scripture, that quhair deidlie syn is, the
cheritie and loue of God can not be, be rason
he quha is in deidlie syn, is in the estait of dá-
tion : and quha is in cheritie, he is heriture of
the lyf euerlesting, and zit he quha is in cheritie is not vithout al syn as testifeis S. Iohne.
quha sayis he is vithout syn he is ane lear.
Than of necessitie ve man gather, that al
synnis ar not mortal or repugnant to cheritie, bot sum venial that may consist vith cheritie as accordingto thevord of God the kirk
hes euer beleuit.

M. hou than is the fourt estait of manknd restorit
to the iustice quhilk thay ressauit be Baptisme?

S. *Mat.*5. (margin)

1. *Ioan.*3. (margin)

B. Insafar as thay losſit the grace resſauit be the abuſe of thair auin frie vil, reſtitution man be maid be the Sacrament of penitence quhairof Chriſt did ſpeik to his Apoſtlis quhen he ſaid: Quhatsúeuir synnis ze remit, thay ſalbe remittit.   1. Ioan. 20

M. *To maK ane end then of my queſtion, reherſe ſchorlie the cauſis of Iuſtification?*

B. The efficient caus is God the glorious trinitie quha creatis iuſtice in the hairt of man. The meritorious caus: is Chriſtis death and paſſion. The formal caus: is grace inherent in the mynd, as the health of the Saul reſtorit. The fenal caus is glorification, to the quhilk God hes predeſtinat his elect before the beginning of the varld.

OF PRÆDESTINATION
CHAP. 2.

M.

Vhair in conſiſtis predeſtination: and quhat be the degreis thairof?

B. Predeſtination conſiſtis in the appointment of the end, for the quhilk men and angellis var creatit, and in prouyding the meynis and cauſe quhairby thay may attene according to the propertie of thair nature to the end foreſene in goddis eternal counſal. Sua firſt he dois cal thame quhom he hes predeſtinat: tharefter iuſteſeis

thame, and laſt of al indeuis thame vith glore
and immortalitie.

M. Is not God the onlie vorkar of mãnis ſaluation
in al thir degreis ?

B. God is onlie the vorkar as the cheif and
principal caus, zit be reaſon that be his infinit
ſapience he dois gouerne and diſpone vpon
his creaturis, according to the nature of euerie ane of thame, ſen he hes maid mã to be mã
ãd not to be ane ſtok or ſtane, he requyris the
Apoc. 3. cooperatione of man as teſtefeis S. Iohne : I
ſtãd knokking at the dur gif onie mã vil heir
my voce, and opin the zet, I vil enten and of
infinit vtherplaces of the ſcripture, be the
Exod. 10. quhilk ve ar exhortit not to reſiſt to the callĩg
Act. 7. ofgod bot to obey vnto him. Be the 'quhilk
Eſaie 65. teſtimoneis the cooperation of the frie vil of
Matt. 23. man is maiſt cleirlie declarit.

OF FRIE VILL

CHAP.   III.

M.

Ald ʒe afferme that efter the fal of
Adam, man hes frie vil?

B. Sen ane man efter the fal of Adam
is not ane beiſt, he man haue frie
vil, ſua that nather is he conſtranit, nor zit
mouit of neceſſitie to do gude or euil, notuithſtanding his frie vil man be helpit vith the
grace of God gif he vald do ony thing that
deſerues euerleſting lyf, althocht in moral
actions he neid not ane ſpecial aſſiſtance of

God, as to big ane hous or not : to laubour his grund or not. And in vther siclyk actions, quhilk appertenis to the natural libertie of man. Quhairfore I acknaulege vith the halie Doctors exponand the scripturis thrie kindis of libertie, Ane natural, in al men regenerat and vnregenerat, for as al men hes reason and vil, sua in al actions quhilk ar properlie callit thairs thay haue election and fredome, quhairby thay may ather do the contrar gif thay pleis, or leue that quhilk thay do, vndone. Of this libertie spekis S. Paul : haue I not pouar to carie about vith me ane sister as vthers quhilk pouar as he schauis in that place he vsit not, bot villinglie refusit to haue onie. The secund is callit the libertie of grace, quhilk euerie man efter the fal of Adam hes not, bot onlie quha being purgit from thair synnis be the blude of Iesus Christ, resauis that gift of goddis beneuolence, quhairby vithout ony compulsio or necessitie thay ar frelie mouit vith feir and dredure to vork thair auin saluation, be assistance of this grace and Christis halie spreit. Of this libertie our saluiour spekis in the euangel of S. Iohne: Gif the sone put zou to libertie ze ar frie in verie deid. And S. Paul: Quhair the spreit of the lord is, thair is fredome & libertie. albeit thay quha ar in this libertie, may do gude varkis vithout syn, zit be infirmitie of nature thay quha standis in it, be thair auin default may fal from the same. The thrid is the libertie of

Iren. l. 4.
c. 72. clemens Alexand. l. 1.
pœda. c. 9.
Iustin.
mart. apol.
1. D. Hiero. 2. cotra
Iovin. Augst. de fide & operibus ca. 9.
10. lib. 3.
prog. lib. 1.
contra. 2.
ep. pelag.
c. 2. & de
vera rel.
c. 14.
"
"

S. Ioan. 8.
1. Cor. 3.

glore, quhilk is in gude angellis and sanctis nou glorifeit, quhilk hes adionit vith it assurance of gude doing vithout al syn.

Loufon. I vil proue that mã efter the fal of Adam hes na frie vil, *Becaus* the hail scripture testefeis that men vnregenerat ar altogither bent vnto: syn nather may thay de onie gude thing accordiug to the saying „ of our maister Christ : vithout me Ze may do na „ thing.

B. Gif zour allegeance var maid in forme of argument, the reason alleagit sould in verie deid be knauin maist sophistical, and imperti nent. Becaus I demand not quhidder gif a man vnregenerat may do thaj varkis be the pouar of his frie vill vithout special grace qukilk leidis to lyf eternal, bot onlie gif the vil in ane vnregenerat man be frie or not.

L. Be reason the vil of man vnregenerat is abill to do euil onlie, I can not vnderstand hou it may haue fredome, sense frie vil hes pouar to do ather gude or euil.

B. Ze ar deceauit be ane vitious definition of frie vill to vit quhilk may ather do gude or euil: for gif ze grant this definitiõ sufficient ze salbe cõpellit to deny that god or the gud an gelles haue frie vil becaus nather god nor the gude ágellis cã do euil. The vil thairfore is frie, Becaus quhen al thingis requesit to the operation thairof, ar present it may ceis from vorking gif it pleis him quha sould performe the vark. And thairfore I am assurit, that as sathan

is anthor of al euill, sua hes he craftelie sauin
in zour hairtis this erronious opinion to
clok zour vickednes quhairby ze refuse all
kynd of reprehension. For being rebukit
according to zour doctrine ze may ansuer I
micht not do vtheruyse: sua consequentlie ze
transfer the caus of zour transgression to God
making him the author of syn and affirming
that al thing cūmis of absolut necessitie.

Farder the grund quhilk ze haue laid, to vit
that ane vnregenerat man may do euil onlie,
is not sure, becaus ze acknaulege not ane distinction of gude varkis to vit in gude varkis,
quhilk by reason thay proceid from grace
thruch Christ Iesus thaj deserue lyf eternal.
And in gude varkis moral quhilk may be in
the vnregenerat, as quhen thay honor thair
parentis, quhen thay do thair deutie touart
thair nichtbour, or thair cōmonveil, quhen
thay giue almous vnto the pure, and in vther
siclyk actions he the quhilk varkis ze vil not
say that thay deserue eternal dānation, by that
becaus that be the help and special assistāce of
god thay may repét of thair synnis, and turne
thame selfis vnto god thay haue frie vil, and
remanis in thair former lyf, not be necessitie
as ze maist falslie allege, bot maist frelie of
thair auin election, Becaus thay vil not follou
the motion and instinction of the halie spreit
be the quhilk thay ar valknit and callit to
Repentance. Thairfore zour argument is

vicious in al pointis in denying ane thing
quhilk is maist cleir and euident in the self
quhair in ze follou the futesteppis of Symon
Magus and the Manicheans, opponing zour
selfis to al ancient vryttaris quha euer in ony
eage hes florishit in the kirk as zour maister
and Idol Iohne Caluin is constranit to
grant.

Clémens li.3. recog. Aug. de si-de contra Manichæ cap.9. & Caluī insti.lib.1. c.2.sect.4.

M. *thou maruellis that ve afferme that al thingis
cūmis of necessitie, sen thou can not escaip to grant
the same. Considering God hes the foresicht of al
thingis before thay cum, the quhilk foresicht being
iusallibill, It is necessar that all thingis cum euin sua
as thay ar foresene be god.*

B. This zour argument is sufficient to deceaue the pure ignorant people, bot quhen it is
examinat as it aucht to be, it is fund maist
vane and sophistical, zea repugnant to zour
seluis. Becaus ze confes that Adam quhen he
vas creatit be God had fre vill and zit ze can
nocht deny bot god had the foresicht of al
thingis quhilk Adam vas to do, then the frie
vil of man and foresicht of god ar not repugnant to thame selfis, zea gif zour argument
var gude god him self vald not haue frie vil,
bot vald be constranit of necessitie to do al
thing that he dois, for ze can not deny bot
god foreseis al thingis quhilk he is to do: sua
according to zour argument he dois all thingis of necessitie, quhilk is ane blasphemie. Gif
ze had imployit zour tyme better in the schu-
llis, ze vald haue learnit that quhilk S. Augustin

Iustin.in dial. cum tryph. hye-ron.in 26. cap. Iere. Athanas. in libr. de pass. Chri-sti Chryso. hom.60.

halie Doctors vryttis : that ane man is not to
be euil, becaus god hes forekuanin that, Bot
becaus he vas to be euil god forekneu the same quha can miſknau na thing to cum. And
the proper caus quhairfore he vas to be euil
is his auin frie vil, Becaus he vald not obey the
vil and cōmandement of god. Thairfore
ane man ſould not reiect the caus of his auin
euil and vickednes to the preſcience of god,
bot to him ſelf and his auin inobedience,
Bot ze in this follou the futſteppis of all the
vicked men quha euer hes bene in the varld,
quha to defend thame ſelf caſtis the caus of
thair vickednes on god and vpon ane fatal
neceſſitie.

OF THE VERTEV OF THE SA-
SACRAMENTIS.   CHAP.   IIII.
M.

Q*Vhat is a Sacrament of the Chriſtian and euā-*
gelical lau?

B. It is ane ſigne inſtitute and ordenit be
Chriſt, quhilk be his inſtitution is ane inſtrument quhairby his grace is cōmunicat vnto
vs.

M. Think is thou then the doctrein of the ſcolaſtik
theologiens treu, quha teachis that in the adminiſtra-
tion of the Sacramentis of the euangelicall lau grace
is geuin ex Opere operato, as thay ſpeik, vnles the reſ-
ſauer be incredulite max impediment.

B. I think I aucht to giue alsmekle credeit to
the ſcholaſtik Doctors as to zou and zit that

B

the sacramentis geuis grace ex opere operato is not onlie thair Doctrene as ze appeir to say, bot the doctrein of Christ him self, quhilk becaus peraduenture ze vnderstand not I vil declair it: I afferme then vith the hail catholik kirk, that the Sacramentis ar the caus of grace not be verteu of the resauer, nor be verteu of the geuar, bot be the verteu of the blude of Christ quhilk vorkis be thame in vs, to our sanctification, sua that quhen ze deny that the sacramentis hes thair strenth ex opere operato, ze deny the strenth and efficacie of Christis institution and blude and denyis his eternal preistheid, sence it perteñis to it not onlie tohaue payit our ranson, or to haue sched his blude for vs, bot also to apply the said ranson vnto vs, quhilk cheiflie he dois beverten of ye Sacramentis.

Ephes. 5.

Of the nüber of the Sacramentis.

M. *hou monie Sacramentis be thair?*

B. Seuin: to vit Baptisme, Confirmation, Penitence, The Sacrament of the altar, Extreme vnction. Mariage, and Ordour.

M. *Quhat grund hes thou to estableis seuin sacramentis, sence ve acknaulege bot tuay?*

B. It is na gret mater that ze acknaulege bot tua, sence the Catholik kirk hes acknaulegit seuin, euer sen the dayis of the Apostlis, and zour maister Caluin acknaulegis thre.

Caluin li. 4. cap. 9. sect. 18 instit.

Of Baptisme.

M. *Quhat sayis thou is requyrit in the sacrament of Baptisme?*

B. As in al vther sacramentis ane lauchful minister hauing the auctoritie of Christ vpon the face of the earth is requyrit, quha ioning to the element as the material caus the formal caus, to vit the deu forme of uordis requesit, quhairby the grace signeseit be the sacrament is geuin, sua in Baptisme is requyrit valter, quhilk according to the vse of the kirk sould be hallouit, representing that quhilk vith blude sprang furth of the voundit syd of our saluiour Christ vpon the croce, according to the saying of S.Iohne Thair be thre thigis quhilk geuis vitnes in earh, the spreit, the valter, ād the blude, ād thir thre ar bot ane thing. Sua that the administration of Baptisme is proper lie callit the vesching of the saul contenand the caussis of the purification of the same, and is groundit vpon this promeis of Christ : he quha sal beleue, and be baptesit, salbe saif. the necesitie thairof vnto all mankind is denuncit be the threatning of Iesus Christ : Except ane man be borne of valter and the spreit, he may not enter in the kingdome of God.

S. Iohne 5.
chap. ep. 1.
"
"

S. Marc.
16.
"
"

M. *Baptisme is not necessar, becaus Paul. vryttis that the childrene of the faihful ar sanctefeit.*

S. Ioan. 3.

1. Cor. 7.

B. Gif ze vnderstand be thair sanctification that thay ar borne vithout syn, ze repugne to S.Paull quha sayis that vé ar al borne the sönis of vraith. and ze fal in the heresie of Pelagius affirming vith him that the infantis ar not borne in original syn. Attour, S. Paul in that same place quhilk ze allege for zou

Ephes. 1.

sayis that the vnfaithfull vomã is sanctefeit
be the faithful man, and zit ze vil not say, that
scho obtenis thairby remission of hir synnis,
sua zour obiection is of na strenth. The same
argument vas proponit be the Pelagianis
aganis S. Augustine, quha ansuerit that sanctefication in the scripture is tane sindrie vayis
and that thair it sould not be tane for remission of synnis as ze vald afferme, Bot that the
infantis ar sanctefeit, becaus thay ar in the
vay of sanctefication, euin as the vnfaithful
ar sanctefeit be the faithfull. And S. Ierome
aganis Iouianinus, ansueris in the same maner, And lang before thame baith Tertullian
quha sayis that S. Paul could not vnderstand
thair be sanctification that the infantis ar sua
sanctifeit that thay ar deliuerit from syn, sen
he could not misknau the vordis of Chrst:
Except ane man be regenerat vith valter and
the halie spreit, he may not enter in the Kingdome of heauin Quhairfore ze se that this
interpretation proceidis of zour auin brayne
aganis the meaning of S. Paul and al the ancient fathers vryttand on this place.

*Aug. lib. 2
de nupt. et
concup.*

*Hier. cõ-
tra Iouin.
lib. 1.*

OF HALIE VALTER
CHAP. V.

M.

VAld thou mak distinction of valteris, calling
the ane Hallouit the vther cõmune, as gif thay
had diuerss operations, sence ze haue na grund for sik

distinction in the vrittin vord ?

B. The craftie inuention of the Deuil, hauing
pouar of the elementis, lyk as S. Paul callis
him prence of the air, hes raisit vp fals prophettis to deny all hallouing quhairby his pouar is aboleist, for na gude Christian doubtis,
bot the valter quhilk vith blude sprang furth
of the syd of Christ vpon the croce hes mair
excellent verteu, nor common valteris, and
farder the example of Naaman quha vas curit
of his leprosie be vesching him self seuin tymes in the valter of Iordane at the command
of Elisæus prouis manifest distinction of
valteris, quhilk proceidis of the institution
of God, and his vord in thame quha ar lauchfullie promouit to be preistis in his kirk. And
gif the meat quhilk ve eit as S. Paul sayis, be
sanctefeit be the vord of God, quhat doubt
can thair be bot be verteu of the inuocation
of the name of Christ vpon the valter, the
craft and subtelitie of the Deuil is vinqueist
and ouercum ? as Christ gaue to his apostolis
pouar ouer the deuillis quhilk pouar vil euer
remane ito his kirk vnto the end of the varld,
as the Deuil vnto the end of the varld vil not
desist to trubill aud molest his kirk, sua ve
aucht to be assurit that the prayers of the
kirk, and inuocation of Chtistis name vpon
the valter hes sik stréth that thairby the craft
of the deuil is esilie brokin, and be verteu of
this inuocation that he is chassit out of thay
places quhair before he vas, sua that he can

Ephes. 2.

S. Ioh. 19.

4. Reg. c. 5.

1. Tim. 4.

Matt. 10.
Ephes. 4.

Clemens
lib. 8. con-
stit. apost.

not abyd the valter, on the quhilk the name
of Chriſt is inuocat to aboleis his vicked ope-
rationes and thairfore the greik vord quhilk
S. Paul vſis, quhen he ſayis that our meat is
Sanctifeit be oreſon ἐντευξις ſignifeis ane im-
ploration of help aganis thaj thingis quhilk
may hurt, quharby ve ar inſtructit, that be
the ſanctification of the valter the help of
god is implorit aganis the pouar of the vicked ſpreittis. Bot as the doggis feir the batons
quhairby thay vſe to be dung, ſua the deuil
and his follouaris be reaſon that be halie valter thay ar oftymes ſtayit from thair vicked
operations, ſua do thay maiſt grettúlie feir it
and lauboris to aboleis the vſe thairof ſua far
as thay may, quhairof it is maiſt eſie to produce vnto zou ſindtie examplis of the maiſt
,, learnit and ancient vrytters. Epiphanius vryt-

Epiph. li.
1.tom. 2. in
hareſi ebio
nitarum.

tis hou that Cõſtantinus magnus had geuin
charge to ane Ieu quha vas bapteſit to beild
and erect ſum kirkis, qu'ha villing to fulfill
his charge did prepare ane gret quantitie of
lyme. Bot be the vorking of the deuil the natural operation of the valter quhilk vas caſ-
ſin on the lyme vas impeſchit on ſik maner
that it could not be vrocht, the quhilk being
perſauit be this chriſtiã man, for ane maiſt ſouerane remeid did hallou valter, and mak the

S. Paull
Gal. 6.
Coloſſ. 2.

ſigne of the croce vpon it, and ſtrinkle it vpõ
the lyme, quhairby the pouar of the Deuil vas
incontinent impeſchit, and the lyme thairef-

ter in ane maiſt eſie vay vas vrocht In the eccleſiaſtical hiſtorie I reid of the lyk exampil,
hou quhen Theodoſius the empriour commandit to burne ane temple of Apollo, the
deuil did impeſch the operation of the fyre,
quhil the tyme that the halie man Marcellus
Biſchop of Apamæa did mak halie valter, and
caſt it in the fyre, quhairby the vorking of the
Deuil vas alluterlie ſtayit, and the ſaid temple of Apollo vas incontinent turnit into aſſ.
S. Ierome deſcriuand the lyf of Hilarion vryttis hou that the deuil did moleſt ane certane
ſtabil quhairin vas ane núber of horſs be hor
ribil, ſpectaclis and viſions, ſua that the horſs
did becum inrageit: And hou the godlie man
hylarion did mak halie valter, and ſtrinkle it
ouer the ſtabil, and thairefter the deuil had
ña pouar to moleſt onie mair. And the maiſt
learnit vrytter Theodoret, vrittis in lik maner
in the lyf of the halie man Aphrates, hou that
the deuil did induce ſterilitie in certane landis, and impeſch thame alluterlie to produce
fruict, quhilk being ſignefeit to this halie mã
for ane maiſt ſouerane remedie aganis the
vark of the deuil, he did mak halie valter and
ſtrinkle it ouer the landis, and thairefter thay
var reſtorit to the ſame fertilitie quhilk thay
had before. And to cum to our auin Ile, quhen
S. Germain the Biſcop of Auſer vas ſend to cõ-
fute the hereſie of pelagius in Ingland the deuillis to hinder his maiſt godlie interpryſe rai-
ſit ane vehement ſtorme vpon the ſea, ſua that

Theodoret.
li.5.ca. z'1.

Hieron. in
vita hyla-
rionus.

Theodoret.
in vita A-
phratis.

B iiij

he vas brocht to extreme dainger, quha as he
vas ane halie man, vnderstanding sik ane hy-
deous tepest to be raisit be the inuy of sathan
had recourse to the ordinar remedie of the ha
lie kirk aganis the pouar of the ennemie, that
is the haly valter, quhilk being cassin in the
sea, the storme cessit, and the sea become cal-
me as it vas afore. And quhen he come to land
the deuil be the mouth of ane possessit persone confessit that he vas the caus of that tem-
pest, as vitnessis the venerable ād godlie Beda.

Beda li. 1.
historiæ
Anglorum
cap. 17.
Of thir exemplis except ze be blind, ze may
se the force and strenth of the benediction of
God, and hou the valter is sanctefeit and hallouit thairby. I vil vith silence pretermit monie vther lyk examplis, bot this I can not pretermit, hou that ze tak the baldnes vpon zou,
to reproue the hallouing and sanctification
of valter, quhilk euer hes bene obseruit in the
kirk sen the Apostlis dayis, And ze zour selfis
confes that Alexāder the first, Bischop of Rome quhilk vas fourscore zeris onlie immediatlie efter the death of our saluiour, makis
mention thairof, quhom ze confes also to haue bein ane martye, and aue treu member of
Christ. sua that ze sould be eschamit to be sa
bauld as to condemne ane haly martyr in this
point, and all Christian men that euer, sen his
dayis, hes agreit vith him, as he did na thing
bot that quhilk he had learnit of thame quha
var before him.

OF CONFIRMATION.

CHAP. VI.

M

Qvhat is Confirmation, and the effect thairof?

B. It is ane sacrament nixt follouing the sacrament of Baptisme in ordor, Be the quhilk the grace that ve haue ressauit be baptisme is augmétit in vs, and ane speial force and strenth, for the métenance and defence of our faith, geuin: sua côueniétlie thairto. The element of this sacrament is oyle and baulme mixt togither, to signifie that thairby ve becum campions of Christ. The fotme of this sacramét consistis in the vordis, quhairby the exhibition of the graces, and giftis, of the halie ghaist is signefeit, quhilk be thir seuin in speial sapience, intelligence, science, counsall, strenth, feir, and piete, heirof ve reid in the haly scriptute: Mairouer it is God quha confermád vsvith zou to attene vnto Christ, quha hes anointit vs, quha also hes markit vs, and geuin to vs the atlis pennie of the halie spreit in our hairtis. And, Bot quhé the apostisrémanádin hierusálé hard that samaria had receauit the vord of God, thay séd Petir and Iohné to thame, quha efter thay had passit doun, thay prayit for thame that thay micht ressaue the hadie spreit, for nane of thame had ressauit the same as zit, bot thay var onlie baptesit in the name of Iesus: Then thay laid thair hádis vpó thame, and thay ressauit the halie spreit. Quhair of it is maaifest, that in the premitiuekirk

S. Paul. 1. Cor. 1.

"

Act. 8.

"
"
"
"
"
"

Euseb. lib. 6. hist. cap. 35.

this vas ane sacrament maist necessar, the administrator heirof being ane Bischop sik as var S. Petir and S. Iohne. Eusebius vryttis that the heresiarche Nouatus vas possessit vith the deuil, and did fall in heresie, Becaus he had not resauit this sacrament. And Theodoretus testefeis that he vas the first quha denyit Confirmation, quhais futsteppis ze appeir to follou, opposing zour selfis to the hail ancient doctors, quha euer hes flurischit in the halie kirk, sen the dayis of our saluior Iesus Christ.

Theodoret. in libr. haret. fab.

Ambro. 2. de sacram. cap. 7.
Aug. li. 2. côtra petilianũ. cap. 104.
Orig. ho. 9. in leuit.
Cyprian ep. 70. & de vnctione charis. & aliis sacram.

Aemil. cateches. 3. Basil. de spir. sancto. cap. 21. Hieron. contra luciferianos. Ambros. de his qui myst. init. & lib. 1. de spiritu sancto. cap. 6. August. lib. 5. de Baptis. contra Donat. cap. 19. & 20. tract. 6. in epist. D. Ioan. Leo magnus epist. 88.

OF PÆNITENCE.
CHAP. VII.

M. *Quhat gude testemoneis hes thou to proue that Penitence is ane sacrament?*

odo. in ?. her.

?. mat. 18.
S. Ioh. 20.
Ambro. in lib. de pœnit.
Aug. de Ciui. Dei li. 20. c. 9.

B. It is prouin maist cleirlie be the vordis of S. Matthew : Quhatsumeuir ze bind vpon earth salbe bund in heauin, and quhatsumeuir ze louse vpô the earth, salbe lousit in heauin, and quhais synnis ze remit ar forgeuln to thame &c. according to the meaning and vnderstâding of all ancient vrytters, quha haue florischit in ony eage sen the dayis of the Apostlis vnto this present. And gif ze haue red the antiquitie, ze can not mis knau this, and in speciall hou that Nouatus vas con damnit as ane heretik becaus he denyit this sacrament as ze do. And gif Christ hes institute ane sacrament for the remission of original syn, and vther synnis quhilk ve may commit before ve be regenerat: it is na les assurit bot he hes institute ane sacrament, quhairby ve may obtene the remission of thai synnis, that ve commit efter that ve be maid members of Christis body: or ellis our estait and condition var maist miserabill. Sua that ze quha denyis this sacrament, and consequentlie substractis the benefeit thairof from the people, hauelargelie amplefeit the kingdome of sathan, and tane away a maist souerane remedie for all spirituall diseasis frō the mēbers of Christ Iesus.

M. Thair apperis na outuard signe in that zour sacrament of Repentence.

B. Ze appeir to misknau quhat is ane outuard signe, considdering ze persaue cleirlie hou in the administration of this sacrament the absolutiō of the preisthis is ane signe that is persauit be our earis, and signefeis the inuart absolutiō quhairby our saulis ar absoluit and deliuerit from the burding of syn. And siclyk on the pairt of the penitent, the cōfession and satiffaction ar taiknis of the vorking of the halie spreit thruch the mereit of Christis passion in the hairt of the absoluit synner.

M. Nou haue I curage to lauch sence thou art not eschamit to pronunce that opin blasphemie, saying that ane preist may giue absolution of synnis.

B. Sir it is na maruel, for zour maner and custume is to lauch at al thing that ze vnder-

Cyprianus lib. 1. ep. 2.

Hyeron. epistv. ad Hesiod.

ftand not: Bot prayſit be god, my faith is
not groundit von zour lauchter, bot vpon
Chriſtis vord quha ſaid to his Diſciplis, as the
father hes ſend me, ſua ſend I zou, quhais
ſinnis ze forgiue ar forgeuin to thame. Gif
Chriſt come in the varld for remiſſion of
ſynnis, he ſchauis, that he hes geuin pouar
to his Apoſtlis, and thair ſucceſſors to remit syn alſo. Quhilk he declaris in thaj
vordis: Quhais synnis ze forgiue ar forgeuin to thame, thairfore ze ar maiſt ingrait to
the benefeitis of Chriſt, quha vald ſubſtract
that pouar fra his apoſtlis quhilk he confeſſis
vith his auin mouth to haue geuin thame
ſua lauch alsmekle as ze pleis, I vil anſuer to
zou as did S. Ambroiſe to the Nouatians
The preiſtis (ſayis he) quhen thay giue remiſſion of ſynnis be the ſacrament of pænitence
thay vſurp na auctoritie vnto thame ſelf, bot
vſis onlie the auctoritie that god hes grantit
vnto thame, and addis: Gif thay giue remiſſion of ſynnis be the ſacrament of Baptiſme,
Quhy blaſpheme ze to say that thay haue not
pouar to remit synnis in the Sacrament of
Penitence.

M. Bot I can not vnderſtand be quhat teſtimonie
of the vritten vord thou may proue the Auricular
confeſſion.

B. Thair be monie vther thingis attour that,
quhilk ze vnderſtand not, aluiſe the mater is
maiſt cleir: Becaus it is aganis reaſon that abſo
lutiõ be geuin, and pænitence inioynit, vnles

S.Ioã.20.

Ambroſ.
in lib de
pænitent.

Ambroſ.
Lib.1.de
pœni.ca.2.
& 3.

the Iuge, to vit the Preiſt, quha is in the place *Matt. 18.*
of Chriſt haue knaulege of the ſinis committit, *Ioan. 20.*
quhilk he may not vndirſtand vithout auricu
lar confeſſion, quhairby the preiſt may vndirſtand all the ſinnis of the pænitét, ather in pu
blik or ellis in priuat, ſua that Clemens diſci- *Clemens*
ple of S. Petir in his epiſtle direct to S. Iames *epiſt. 1.*
the Apoſtle vitneſſis planelie this to be the
treu tradition of S. Petir, that it behouis al
Chriſtian men villiug to be abſoluit to confes *Diony. ad*
thair euil thochtis before the preiſtis of our *Demoph.*
ſaluiour Chriſt. And S. Dioniſe Diſciple to S. *lib. 4. ep. 2.*
Paull teſtifeis the ſame to haue bene practiſit *Pacianus*
in his dayis, And ſik hes bene the cuſtome euir *epiſt. 3. ad*
ſen the beginning of Chriſtis kirk, vnto this *rumum.*
preſent. And ze zour ſelfis experimentis hou *Epiphan.*
monie kynd of abhominabill ſynnis ar re- *hæreſ. 69.*
gnand in this cuntrie ſen the tyme that ze haue diſpenſit vith the conſciencis of men that
thay neid not to mak confeſſion of thair ſynnis quhilk vas ane maiſt cheif ſtay and brydil
to vithdrau men thairfra.

M. *Quhy affirmit thou before that ſatisfaction is*
ane pairt of Panitence conſidering the ſatisfaction
quhilk our maiſter Chriſt hes maid is ſufficient for
all our offencis.

B. The ſatiſfaction of our ſaluiour Chriſt is
ſufficient indeid for the ſynnis of the hail
varld, Bot zit it is applyit to thame onlie quha
thruch the grace of his ſatiſfaction reſſauit,
dois the varkis of Pænitenee, as teſtifets S. *Rom. 8:*
Paull. ve ſuffer vith him that ve may be glori-

feit togither vith him that the temporal pane
quhilk vevillinglie suſtein for our ſynnis com
mittit, is in this reſpect callit ſatisfaction to
the iugement of God. Becaus heirby the paſſion of Chriſt is maid ouris be aſſiſtance of
his grace and halie ſpreit, quha performis this
" ſatisfaction in vs. Of the quilk S. Paul vryttis
2. Cor. 7. to the Corinth. This that for the offéce of god
" ze haue bene ſorifull, hou gretcairfulneſhes it
ingenerit in zou zea hou gret ſatisfactió, hou
gret indignation, hou gret feir, hou gret deſyre, hou gret emulatione, hou gret reuégement?
And this I. reid to hauebene the mening of the
vniuerſall kirk ſen the beginning as Caluin
zour maiſter himſelf cã not diſſimble: And tha
Caluin in- irfore ſayis in plane vordis that the hail anciét
ſtit. lib. 3. fathers hes bene deceauit in this point. Bot be-
cap. 4. caus as apperis al zour felicitie conſiſtis in de
licat cheir and treating of zour ſelfis, and zour
fair vyſſis, this doctrine of ſatisfaction or Pænitence can nocht enter in zour hairtis.

M. *Is it neceſſar that euerie man, quha hes commit-*
tit ſyn ſuſtene temporal pane that heirby he may ha-
ue participation of the ſatisfaction quhilk Chriſt hes
maid for ſin?

B. I. maruel of zou quha callis zour ſelf à
maiſter in Iſraël, hou ze can doubt that eſter
the remiſſion of ſyn ye aucht to vnderly ſum
2. Reg. 12. temporal payne: ſen ze reid that Dauid the halie prophet notuithſtanding he had gottin remiſſion of his ſyn zit he vas verie hauelie pu-
Gene. 3. neiſt be god. And Adam him ſelf eſter god

had forgeuin him the giltenes of his syn, zit
he saidvnto him: maledicta terra in opere tuo:
Cursit be the earth in thy vark. And ve vnto
this present thole diuerse trublis for the syn of *hold*
Adam. The syk may be confirmit be innumerabill testimoneis of the hail scripture. Sua I
ansuer vnto zou maist resolutlie with the vniuersal kirk that the satisfaction of Christ is
not applyit vnto vs, except that ve indure sik
temporal payne ather in this varld, or in the
varld to cum. And I let zour self consider, gif
it be according to reason, that Christ quha vas
our heid vas crounit vith the croun of thorne,
and drank the bitter coup of the croce : And
ve quha professis our selfis to be his members
sould be euer in ryattousnes and plesours of   2. *Tim.* 2.
this varld : sen the hail scripture exhortis vs sa   1. *Pet.* 2.
oft to conforme our seluis to our heid, and to
thole and indure vith him gif ve vald be par-
takaris of his glorie.

OF PVRGATORIE.
CHAP. VIII.
M. .

B E this thy meaning I collect, that thou vald approue the auld papisticall purgatorie.

B. Thair is na doubt bot sindrie depairtis out
of this varld quha enterris not in heauin im-
mediatie, nather zit, ar thay condénit to euer- "
lesting pane as prouis the example of Lazarus "
quha had lyin four days in the graif, for gif he   S. *Mat.* 25
had bene in ioy eternal, he ressauit na benefeit   S. *Ioan.* 11
"

to haue bene brocht thairfra to this vale of
miserie: and gif ze vil afferme that he vas in
hel, ze at condenit be the manifest vordis of
the scripture out of hel thair is na redeption.
Quhairfore I agrie to the determination of
the halie kirk, and doctrine of the maist god
lie teachers thairof, exponing sindrie passa-
gis in the halie scripture of purgatorie, as in
special the thrid chap. of the first epistle of S.
Paull to the Corinth Euerie mannis vark salbe maid manifest, for the day of the lord sall
schau it quhilk is reuelit in fyre, and the
fyre sall try euerie mannis vark. for of the
vordis follouing, it is manifest, that he meanis
not samekle of the Doctrine of the teachers,
as of the maners of thame quha ar teachit
saying : knau ze not that ze ar the temple of
god, and the spreit of god duellis in zou.
Gif ony man prophane the temple of god,
god sall destroy him, siclyk our lord him self
sayis : Al man salbe seasonit vith fyre, and all
sacrifice salbe seasonit vith salt, quhairby he
meanis that lyk as the salt is appointit to con-
serue ony thing from corruption, sua god hes
appointit ane fyre quhairby the corruption
quhilk the Saul contractis of the body is consumit, and sen na inquination can enter in
the kingdome of heauin. And according to
the common fragilitie of man thair is feu bot
hes sum spot sa lang as thay leue in this varld,
hou dar ze deny that thair is sum purgation
efter this lyf, vnles ze debarre al men from the
kingdome

S. August.
in 103.
Psal.
Basil. de
spir sanct.
cap. 15.
Ambros.
in Psalm.
117. Orig.
hom. 6. in
Exod.
1. Cor. 3.

S. marc. 9.

Apoc. 21.

S. Ioh. ep.
1. chap. 1.
S. Iam. 3.

kingdome of heauin ? and quha of zou ar sa
bauld that dar say that quhen zour Saul depairtis, from zour body, it is aluterlie clene
vithont al spot of syn, cheiflie sen in the confeſſion of zour auin faith ze profeş maiſt planelie that sa lang as ze leue in this varld thair
is na thing into zou bot syn ? sua sen thair is
na purgation efter thisvarld ze remaning per-
petuallie in zour synnis, ar condēnit for euer.
And quhat can be mair cleir nor that quhilk
is in the buikis of the machabæis quhair Iudas Machabæus cauſit offer ſacrifice for the
ſynnis of thame quha var dead ? the quhilkis
buikis thir tuelf hundreth zeris and mair hes
bene reſſauit for Canonikis as vitneſſ S. Auguſt. And ſik hes bene euer the cuſtume of
the Ieuis, from the beginning of the ſynagogue, and is zit kepit to this day: ſua that I maruel amang the reſt that in zour neu byble in
zour note vpon this place of the Machabeis
ze haue sua impudent a leiſing as to ſay that
the ſynagogue of the Ieuis vſis not to pray
for the dead. As to the vſe of the chriſtian
and Catholik kirk, gif ze haue red ony thing
of the antiquitie, ze can not misknau hou
this cuſtume euer hes bene Keipit as vitneſſ
Dioniſius Areopagita diſciple to S. Paul Tertullian, Chryſoſtome Auguſtine, and the reſt.
I knau zour maiſter Caluine ſayis that the
haill ancient Doctors thir threttene humdreth
zeris hes errit, and bene deceauit in this point
Bot I think it als liklie that M. Iohne Cal-

2. Mac,12

Augu.li.2.
de doctr.
Chriſt.c.8.

dioniſ.c.7.
ecl.hierar.
Tertul. de
cor. mil.
Chryſoſ.l3
ad Phi·ip.
Aug. in li.
de cura pro
mort.ag

Caluin in-
ſtit libr. 3.
c.5.ſect. 10

C

uine sould haue bene deceauit as sua monie
learnit godlie vrytters, quha thir threttene
hundreth zeris hes floreist in Christis kirk.

OF THE INDVLGENCIS.

CHAP. 9.

M.

AR not Zour indulgencis the inuention of the
Pape, quairby he may vin syluer?

B. Ze sirris quha raillis sua oft aganis the Paip
and papistis as ze cal thame vse to tribute
the inuention of monie thingis to the Pape,
bot quhen ze ar demandit in particular from
quhat Pape sik inuentions did proceid ze becum al dum, and hes na thing to speik. As
quhen ve demand zou quhat Pape inuentit
the sacrifice of the Messe, the Inuocation of
sanctis, Praying for the deid, and vther heidis
of religion quhilk ze haue callit in doubt. Sua
I desyre that ze proue that thing quhilk ze
say, and schau quhat Pape vas he that inuentit
the indulgencis, quhilk ze vil neuer be abil to
do. Nou becaus ze say that the indulgencis ar
na thing bot the inuention of man, I vil declare that ze ar manifest impostors before tha
me all quha ar heir present. I scheu before be
goddis vord that quhen the syn is remittit ve
aucht to vnderly sum téporal pane the quhilk
vsis to be inionit efter a man haue maid confession of his synnis. Nou sen Christ hes geuin pouar to his kirk to bind and louse, euin
as pastors hes pouar to inioyne penance to

Marginal notes (left): velulgences eye p mben d by the vc, nor by say tan.

Marginal notes (left, lower): Genes. 3. 2. Reg. 12. S. Mat. 18 S. Ioh. 20.

men for thair synnis, sua thay haue pouar to
relax thair penance vnto thame, vtheruyse the
pastoris vald haue gretar pouar to bind nor
to louse, quhilk is cōtrare to the mearcie and
gudnes of God. And thairfore S. Ambroise
monie hundreth zeiris syne in his buikis de
pœnitentia aganis the Nouatians, did obiect
vnto thame, that thay did onlie bind men,
and na vayis lousit, aganis the ordinance and
institution of Christ. Zea S. Paul him self as is
manifest in the secund to the Corinth. did giue sik indulgence to him, quha had committit the horrible cryme of incest, saying : Giue I
haue pardonit zou onie thing, I haue appar-
donit zou bering the persone of Christ Iesus.
Be the quhilkis vordis he testifeis maist cleirlie thir be the pouar and auctoritie grantit vn
to him be Christ he did relax sum pairt of
that Pænitence quhilk before vas inionit for
the said cryme of incest. And gif ze had plesit
to haue red the ancient vrittaris ze vald haue
persauit maist cleirlie hou in the tyme of the
persecutiō of the Romā emperoris as Decius,
and vtheris, this vse and custume vas keipit in
the kirk, that be the intercessiō of the Christia
nis quha var impresonit for thair faith, and religione the bischopis and pastoris of the kirk
vsit to relax the pænitēce quhilk thay had inioynit for ony gret and vechtie crime. Of this
ve haue monie epistlis in S. Cyprian, threttene
hūdreth zeris syne and mair: zea thay quha fol
louit the heresie of Mōtanus did reproue the

Ambrof. in
lib.1. de pœ
nit.ca.2.

2. Cor. 2.
"
"
"

Cyprian,
li 3. ep. 15.
& 16.

the Papis of Rome that thay did grant sik indulgencis to adulteraris, and vther siclyk synners thruch the intercession of martyrs impresonit. Quhairof I produce to zou as ane sufficient vitnes Tertullian quha vrait before fourtene hundreth zeiris. Sua the indulgencis is na Papis inuention as ze maist falslie preach to the people. Bot the ordinance' of Christ Iesus (practesit be his Apostlis and the vniuersall kirk euer vnto this present) groundit vpon the meritis of his maist ptecious death and passió quhilk ar applyitvntovs, for the satisfactió of our synnis and to supplie our vaiknes and imbecillitie in that pairt : for quhat thing can be thocht mair according to reason, nor that the ful and perfyt satisfaction of the head supplie the vai knes and imbecillitie of the mébers, zea euin the satisfaction of ane member may supplie the satisfaction of ane vther, conforme to our beleif I beleue the communion of sanctis. Bot ze sirris, as ze haue na thing amág zou bot syn according to zour auin cófession, It is na maruel that ze deny the communion of sanctis. M. The Apostlis and Martirs ressauis glore aboue the merit of al thair temporal afflictionis, Becaus as vritis S. Paul: I esteme not the afflictiou of this present tyme equal to the glore quhilk salbe reuelit in vs. And farder thair is na truble quhilk man efter the fall of Adam may sustine bot his syn hes deseruit the same and rather mair, sua that the sanctis ar scarcelie sufficient or abill to dispone thame selfis that thay may

Tertul. li. de pudici-tia.

S. Paul Gal. 6.

Rom. 8.

haue participation of that satisfaction quhilk Christ hes maid.

B. The gude varkis, and paynis quhilk the Apostlis, and martyrs haue tholit ar considerit in ane vay, as meritorious, proceiding from grace thruch Christ be the operation of the halie ghaist. And in this respect the Apostlis and Martyrs hes ressauit glore according to thair varkis: vtheruyse ve considder the trublis quhilk thay sustinit, as satisfaction for syn, In the quhilk respect thair meritis may be applyit to vther membris of the kirk, seing sindrie of thame (as Ieremie quha vas sanctifeit *Hier. 1.* fra his mothers vambe) sustinit monie maj temporal paynis in this lyf, nor vas requyrit to mak satisfaction for ony synnis be thame comittit. Syclyk S. Iohne the Baptist, and Innumerable vther martyrs, quha thoillit gret paynis in thair lyf quhilk vas aluyse vithout gret syn, as the halie and pacient Iob in his vexatio *Iob. 6.* sayis: vald god my synnis quhairby I haue de- "
seruit goddis vraith var veyit in ane ballance "
vith the calamitie that I suffer, for my truble in compareson of thame is hauiar as the sand of the sea. And insafar as thir paynis and pacient suffering of aduersite for goddis caus being varkis maist acceptable vnto god, vrocht be the halie ghaist, thruch the grace of Christis satisfaction, can not be in vane, It is necessar that thay be applyit to vther membris of the kirk quha hes mister of the same : sua that heirby the grace thruch Christ comuni-

cat vnro the faithful is cōmendit infafar as
be the fame that quhilk inlaikis in ane member, may be fuppleit be another, for vnto
this dois appertine the communiō of fanctis,
quhairby the gude varkis of ane ar proffitable to vthers, according to the maift ex
pres vordis of S. Paull: that zour aboundance may fupplie thair indigence, and thair aboundance m ay fupplie zour pouertie. as he vald
fay, euin as ze be zour riches do fupplie thair
pouartie in vardlie guddis, fua thay quha ar
rache in gude vai kis may fupplie zour pouartie thairin , fua that according to the maift
expres vord of God, ve fould navyis doubt,
bot that the panefull induring of the martyrs
and vther halie men may be applyit vnto vs,
and fulfill that quhilk inlakis of our fatiffac
tion. For euin as the Eey dois fe not onlie to
the felf bot the hail body as it is ane member
of the fame, fua as ve ar all mēbers of the kiı k,
the varkis of euerie ane, ar proffitable to vthers. As to zour laft obiection, I maruel gret
tumlie hou ze ar fa forzetfull of zour felf as to
admit manifeft cōtradiction, for at fum tyme
ze deny altogither that efter the fyn is remittit, thair be ony temporal payne quhilk
fould be fuftinit for it, and nou ze affirme
that ve fuftine al trublis and pane for the O-
riginal fyn, quhilk ve contract of Adam. I
anfuer thaifore, that feing be baptifme, thruch
the merit of Chrift al our fynnis ar alluterlie
aboleift , fua that be the iuftice of god, ve

ar obleist to na satisfaction for the same,
and verie monie sustinis gretar pane temporal, nor thair synnis deseruit efter grace
ressauit in Baptisme, as is manifest in the
halie martirs quha for confession of the name of Christ sufferit al kynd of tormentis
that could be deuysit be infidel Princis:heirof
it is euideut that thair paneful induring of
troubillis may be applyit to supplie the
satisfactione of vtheris.

OF THE VARKIS OF SVPE-REROGATION. CHAP. X.

M.

Qvhat dois thou call ane vark of Supererogation?

B. It is that quhairto ane man is not obleist
and gif he leue it vndone he incurris not the
syn of omission,or neglecting his bund deutie , as the vark quhilk Christ gaue the zung
man counsal to do,saying: Git thou vald be
perfit,sell al thaj thingis that thou hes, giue
thame vnto the pure. Cum follou me, and
thou sall haue ane threasor in heauin. And
the passionis quhairof S. Paul vryttis in this
maner. Nou I reiose in my afflictions for zou
and I supplie in my flesch that quhilk inlaikis of the afflictons of Christ, for his body
quhilk is the kirk. And it is maist certane,
that the Sanctis and martyrs sufferit monie
and gret afflictions to the quhilk thay vas

S.Matth.
19.
„
„

1.Coloß.
„
„

C iiij

nocht obleist as S. Paul testifeis of him self,
that he vas not obleist to indure the paynis,
and laubour to vyn his meat be the vark of
his auin handis, quhilk notuithstanding he
did villinglie indure. Sua quhither ze vil or
not ze man confes sum varkis of supererogation : I agrie indeid in that, that amang
zou, quha callis zonr selfis ministers of goddis vord, thair is na varkis of supererogation,
except it be to vissie all the bancattis that ar
maid in the tounis, quhair ze ar, to the quhilk
ze ar, not obleist be the command of god.
Albeit the pnre people that in the mean tyme
deis of hungar hes litill vantage of siclyk supererogation.

*M. Is it not blasphemie to say that Christis passi-
on is not sufficient for the synnis of the varld, and
that it inlaikis perfection?*

B. Quhen hard ze euer ony Catholik man
say that the passion of Christ is not sufficient?
This is zour maner quhairby ze vse to decea-

Heb. 5. ue the people. Thairfore I say vnto zou that
the passion of Christ is sufficient, not onlie
for ane varld bot for ane thousand : zea not
onlie his passion bot the leist drop of his blude. zit I say lykuyse vith S. Paul that he is
onlie the caus of saluation to thame quha
obeyis his commandimentis, and quha con-
formis thame vnto him, sua that his passion
auaillis not bot to thame, to quhom it is applyit be sik meanis as he hes apoynted. As to

the present mater his satisfactione is applyit
vnto vs, and maid ouris quhen ve conforme
our selff to him , to thoill and indure vith
him, to the end, as sayis S. Paull that ve may 2. *Tim.* 2.
in lik maner be glorifeit vith him. Thairfoir
sayis the halie Doctore prosper mening of *Prosper in*
the passione of Christ the coup of immorta- *sent.*
litie is preparit to al men, bot it is profitabile
to thame onlie quha drinkis of the same.

OF THE FASTINGIS OF THE
KIRK. CHAP. XI.

M.

ZE that ar Papistis forbiddis meattis quhilk God
hes created for the sustentatione of man, aganis
the expres vordis of Christ, quha sayis that na thing, *Matt.* 19.
quhilk enteris in the mouth sylis the saull, and of S.
Paull quha affirmes that na thing aucht to be refu-
sed quhilk is tanevith thankis geuing, and thairfoir I. *Tim.* 4.
he propheceis of zou maist cleirlie , that in the latter
dayes thair sall ryse vp men, quha sall forbid meattis
quhilk God hes created, quhais doctriue he callis, the
doctrine of the deuillis.

B. I meruall that ze ar noth eschamed to follou the futstoppis of Iouinianus, and vtheris
codemnit heretikes: sen Iouinianus as vitnessis S. Hierom vreittand aganis him did obiect *Hier. lib.*
that sam argument to the Catholiques in tha I. *contra*
dayes quhilk presentlie ze obiect vnto me, *Iouinian.*
ze the Manichæanis to colore thair auin per-

uerſed and vicked doctrine, vſed alſo aganis
S. Auguſtine and vther Catholiques that ſam
ſelf argument as vitneſſis S. Auguſtine aganis
fauſtus the Manichæane. I vill thairfoir anſuer
to zou na vther thing bot that quhilk Auguſtine, Hierom, Ambroſe, Chryſoſt, and vther
ancient doctoris hes anſuered beſoir me, that,
that place of S. Paul aucht to be vndirſtãd aganis the Marcionitis, Tationitis Manicheanis
and vther heretikis, quha did forbid meattis
becaus thay var vnclene of thair auin nature,
and created nocht be God bot be the deuill
as thay affirmeid. And thairfoir S. Paull callis
this the doctrine of the deuill, and affirmes
that God hes created all meattis, and that all
the creaturis of God ar gud, and vreittand to
the Romanis I knau and am perſuadit be the
lord Ieſus, that thair is nathing vnclene of it
ſelf, and vretand to Titus, all thingis ar clene
to thame that ar clene. Sua that the mening
of S. Paul is that it is ane peruerſed and vicked
doctrine to abſtene from meattis as giſ thay
var vnclene, or defylit in thame ſeluis, or created be the deuill, as the Marcionitis and Manichæanis maiſt planelie affirmed. Bot to abſtene from certane meattis noth becaus thay
ar euill of thame ſelfis, bot for faſting peniten
ce and dantoning of the fleshe it is nauyſe
condemnit be S. Paull, bot gretumlie appro-
ued be him, and be all the prophetis and halie
men quha euer hes floriſhed in the kirk of
Chriſt. Of the quhilk S. Paull ſayis that ve ſuld

Aug. Lib.
20. contra
fauſt.cap.5
& 6.

Amb. in 4
cap. preoris
ad timot.
Chryſoſt
ibidem.

Rom. 14.

Tit.1:

2.Co6.r.

behaue our selfis as seruandis of God in mekill patience, and afflictionis, in fasting, and
sua furth. And in the actis of the Apostlis, it is   Act. 15.
commandit be the Apostlis thame selfis that
the gentiles quha var conuerted to the fayth
suld abstene fra certane kyndis of meatis.
Thairfoir sayis S. Augustin, Christiani nō here   Aug. lib. 30
tici sed Catholici, edomandi corporis causa,   Contra
propter animam ab irrationalibus motibus   faust cap. 5.
amplius humiliandam, non solùm à carnibus,
verumetiam à quibusdam terræ fructibus ab-
stinent, vel semper sicut pauci, vel certis die-
bus, atque temporibus sicut per quadragesi-
mam fere omnes, vos autem Manichæi ipsam
creaturam negatis bonam, & immundam di-
citis, & quod diabolus carnes operetur ex fœ-
culentiore materia mali. The Christianis sayis
he, nocht the heretikis, bot the Catholikis to
dantone thair bodie, and to vithdrau thair
mynd from vnressonabill motionis, abstenis
noth onlie from fleshe, bot from sum fructis
of the erd also, ather ay, as ane feu nomber, or
at certane tymes and vpone sett dayis, as almaist all men in he tyme of lenterne, bot ze
quha ar Manichæanis denyis that the creature is gud, and sayis that it is vnclene, and that
the flesh is maid be the deuil of the grosest
pairt of the mater of euill. And a lytill eftir   Aug. ibi.
he sayis, Thair is ane greit differéce betuix thame quha abstenis from meattis for ane halie
signnificatione, or the chastising of the bodie,
and thame quha abstenis from meattis quhilk

God hes created, saying that God hes noth
created thame, for the quhilk caus, that is the
doctrine of the prophetis and Apostlis, bot
this is the doctrine of leing deuillis. Heitof
euerie man may persaue that this place of scri
pture is alluterlie peruerted be zou, and falslie
applyit to the Catholique kirk, quhilk neuer
did forbid onie kynd of meate as gif it had
bene euill, and defylit of the self. Considering
that quhilk is forbiddin vpone ane day vsis to
be eattin vpone ane vthir, bot forbiddis certane meattis for the datoning of the fleshe, that
ve may be mair abill to prayeris and vther
godlie exerceisis. For the quhilk caus as vreit-
Basil hom. tis S. Basil quha euer hes excellit in onie kynd
de Ieiunio. of verteu , thay haue bene mekill geuin to
prayer, fastig, and datoning of thair fleshe. Experience prouis the same of S. Iohne the ba-
Petr. mar. ptiste and innumerabill vtheris, albeit zour
in 7. Iud. halie Prophete Petrus Martyr is nocht eschamed to condem Basile, Gregorius Nazianze-
nus, and vther halie men becaus thay var mekill geuin to fasting, and dantoning of the
fleshe, and var nocht of the flock of Epicurus
vith him and monie of zou, ministeris this day
in scotland. ze may thane esilie persaue hou
vranguslie ze obiect this place of S. Paull aganis me. And hou I for my defence haue all the
learned and halie men that euer hes florished
in Christis kirk. Zour vther obiectione that
quhilk eteris in the mouth fylis nocht the saul
hes the lykvanitie, and calunie coioynitvithit,

sen na catholique hes euer teached that the
fleshe dois defyle the saull, bot that the inobedience and breiking of the command
quhilk proceidis out of the hairt, dois defyl
the saull. As quhen Adame eated the Apill in *Gene. 2.*
paradise, it vas nocht the apill quhilk defylit
his saull, bot the breking of the command.
Thairfoir S. Augustine sayis ansuering to heretikis lyk zou. Memineruut Catholici omnia munda mundis, & non quod intrat per os
coinquinat animam, itaque non reiiciendis
generibns ciborum quasi pollutis, sed concu-
piscentiæ domadæ inuigilat omnis industria.
The Catholiques rememberis veill that all
thigis ar clene to thame quha ar clene, quhair
for thay beftou nocht thair trauel on reiecting of kyndis of meatis as gif thay var vnclene bot onlie abstenes fra certane meattis
to dantone and subdeu the fleshe and concupiscence of the sam.

OF THE SACRAMENT OF THE
altar, and reall presence of Christis bodie, and blu-
de in the same vnder the formes of braid and vyne.

CHAP. XII.

M.

Qvhat is contined in that quhilk thou callis the
sacrament of the altar?

B.   In verie deid and reallie the precious and
glorious bodie of Iesus Christ our saluiour,

vndir the forme of braid, and his blude quhilk
vas sched vpone the Croce vndir the forme
of vyne, efter the vordis of cósecratione deulie pronunced, quhilk noth onlie signifeis as
the vordis of man, bot hes vorking pouar, insafar as thay var pronunced be our saluiour
him self, and ar, or salbe deulie pronunced be-
thame quha hes lauchfull authoritie of him.

M.   *Thou appeirs to grond thy fayth vpone thay*
vordis (hoc est corpus meum) and dois nocht vndirstád
that thay suld be tane figuratiuelie, as quhen Christ
callis him self ane dur, or ane vay, and Paull callis
Christ ane rok. And the paschall lamb is callit Pha-
se or the pasouer, quhilk maneris of speiking may
nocht be tane, bot be ane figurat and sacramentall
loquutione, euin sua (hoc est corpus meum) suld be in-
terpret figuratiuelie as ve do in our reformit Kirkis.

B.   I am sorie to se the pepill deceauit be sik
vane argumétis as ze vse, for the force of zour
argument consistis in this, Christ is callit impropirlie ane dur, Thairfoir quhé he sayis this
is my bodie thir vordis suld be tane impropirlie. The quhilk argument as onie man may
esilie vndirstand, is of na strenth. Becaus vith
lyk probabilitie the Arrian micht haue said,
Christ is callit ane Rok impropirlie, thairfoir
he is callit God impropirlie, and the Nestoria-
ne micht haue argumented in lyk maner
Christ is callit the vay impropirlie, thairfoir
thir votdis. The vord is maid flesche, suld be
tane impropirlie. Ze suld be eschamed to propone sik ane sophistical argument in ane ma-

S. Mat. 26
S. Ioh. 10.
S. Ioh. 14.
I. Cor. 10.
Exdo. 12.
Matt. 26.

S. Ioh. 1.

ter of sua grete consequence, considering that
for our pairt ve haue the maist cleir and express vordis of God This is my bodie: Sua gif *Matth.26*
ze may not schau be als cleir and euident scripture that thay vordis suld be tane in aue im-
propir significatione, it is ane thing aganis all
reasone to mistrust the vord of God, and grūd
our sayth vpone the consait, and brayne of ane
mortall mā, as Zuinglius, or Caluin quha hes
inuentit this neu glose and interpretatione.
Mairatour gif ze vill considder all the circū-
stancis of the text bayth befoir and behind,
quhairof the treu mening of tha vordis
suld be gathered, thair is na thing at all,
quhairof onie sik motiue is offered vnto vs.
For first Christ did abrogat the paschal lamb
quhilk vas the figure of his bodie, and fulfilled that thing quhilk vas præfigurat Sua
necessarlie according to his auin vordis, that
quhilk he gaue to his disciples vas nocht the
figure of his bodie as vas the paschall lamb
bot his auin verie bodie. In lyk maner he did
abrogat the figure of his blude quhilk vas in
the auld testament, and institute the coup of
the neu testament, quhilk he could not haue
done giff in the coup that he gaue to his discipillis, na thing had bene contened bot vyne
Cheiflie sen the blude of brutall beistis, that
vas in the auld testameut did mair perfytlie
represent the blude of Christ nor vyne can
represent the same. Secundlie this vas the last
thing quhilk Christ befoir his death vas vill-

ling to recommend vnto his beſtbeloued
diſcipilles, and quhilk he vald thay did in remembrance of his deth and Paſſion quhil
his cumming agane to iuge the hail varld,
ſua he did ſpeik maiſt cleirlie and planelie
vnto thame as al men vſis to do, quhen thay
ar to declare thair latter vill, quhilk Chriſt
as he forkneu all thingis to cum, and louit
his diſciples maiſt tenderlie, vithout al doubt
hes done at his depairtíng, to the effect that
the Apoſtlis micht mair euidentlie knau his
latter vil, and na contention nor ſtryf ryſe
amang thame thairanent, quhairby ony of
thame micht miſknau the ſame, The mater being of ſa gret importance to all men as
it is: for experience it ſelf teachis quhat debait
is riſſin ſen ze haue begun to interpreit his latter vil of zour auin brayne, be ane figuratiue
loquntion, and hes put the varld in ſik per-
plexite, that ane gret pairt thairof is in doubt
of the ſame. And it is impoſſible that euer
ony reſolution may be tane thairin, except
that it be laid for ane ground that the vordis
may not be tane bot in the proper ſignification, for vtheruyſe it vil euer be doubtſum gif
thay ſould be tane properlie or improperlie,
And ſua ve vill neuer haue ony aſſurit reſo-
lutiõ thairof, quhilk is aganis baith the promeis of Chriſt, and the loue and cheritie quhilk
he bearis to his kirk. Thridlie Chriſt in the
latter ſuppar, did inſtitute ane of the maiſt che
if and principal myſtereis of our faith and religion

ligion, bot the mistereis of our faith, as thay
sould be beleuit be al men, sua aucht thay to
be declarit in maist cleir and plane vordis
vtheruyse the vordis being obscure(as thay vse
to be in figuratiue loqutions, ve vald euer be
in doubt quhat ve sould beleue, considering
thruch the obscuritie of the vordis euerie
man vald drau thame to his auin phátasie and
opinion. And thairfore as obseruis S. Augusti-   *Augu.de*
ne, quhē ony misterie of our faith is proponit   *doc. christ.*
be ane figuratiue loqution, in vther places   *lib. 3.*
of the scripture it vsis to be declarit in maist
cleir and plane termes. Zit as concerning this
misterie ve find na sik declaration bot sa oft
as the scripture makis mention thairof, ve
find it euer callit the bodie of Christ, and ne-   *Matt. 26.*
uer ane figure or bare signe of his bodie. Four-   *Marc. 14.*
tlie, quhensocuer ony commād is geuin in the   *Luc. 22.*
                                                   Ioan. 6.
scripture as Augustine, and vther vrytters ob-   *Augu. de*
seruis, it vsis euer to be declarit in plane and   *doct. Chri*
proper termes : for gif it var obscure, that   *sti libr. 3.*
thing quhilk is commandit could not eselie
be knauin, and consequentlie vald not be fulfillit: Bot Christ in his latter suppar, gaue com *Matt. 26.*
mand to his Disciples to do that thing quhilk   "
he did, sua it behouit thame to vnderstand the
vordis of Christ, according to the proper sence and signification of thame. I pretermit manie vther thingis that seruis grettumlie to the
same purpose : as that our saluiour Christ did
lift vp his eyis to the heauin and gaue thankis "
to his father for the gret benefeit that he vas "

D

to giue vnto the varld. Bot gif he had not geuin his body, it had bene na vnaccuſtumat benefeit: zea Manna, quhilk vas geuin to the fathers of the auld teſtament, vas ane gretar benefeit, nor ane pece bread, gif he gaue navther thing to his Apoſtlis as ze allege : zea he had abrogat ane maiſt excellent and perfyt figure as vas manna and the paſchal lambe, and in place thairof had ordanit ane vther figure mair obſcure, and of les perfection, quhilk is aganis the nature, qualitie, and cõditiõ of the neu teſtament, it beand the veritie, & the auld teſtamẽt the vmbre and ſchaddou onlie. And thairfore that ve ſould haue na doubt in this heauinlie miſterie, as thai thingis quhilkis of thame ſeluis apperit to be verie hard and incredible, and var of greteſt conſequence, vſit to be promeſit before to diſpoſe men to faith and to the reſſauing of thame, quhen thay ſould be offerit, ſua Chriſt promeiſt to his Diſciples that he ſould giue thame his bodie to eat, and his blude to drink, quhilk promeis he fulfillit in his latter ſuppar, quhen he ſaid (This is my bodie quhilk is geuin for zou) Declairing thairby that it vas not ane figure of his bodie bot his treu bodie, as it vas not the figure of his bodie that deit on the croce for vs, for this pronoume, hoc, or, hic, quhen it follouis vpon ane promeis of God, it declairis the Reall exhibition, and repreſentation of the thir g promeiſt be God, As quhen the father of heauin ſaid : (Hic eſt filius meus dilec-

Marginal notes:
Exod. 16.
S. Paul.
2. Cor. 3.
S. Paul.
Heb. 10.
S. Ioan. 6.

tus: quhilk signifeis the treu exhibition of
the sone of God as he vas promeist to the fathers. And sua be reason Christ promeist that
he sould giue his bodie to be eatin, quhen he
sayis. (Hoc est corpus meum) He declaris the
Reall exhibition of his bodie. Considder ze
vith zour selfis, gif he had geuin onlie ane
morsel of bread to his Disciples, gif it had bene necessar to haue promeist this afore hand,
or gif it had bene ony gret misterie, quhilk he
had left vnto vs in the latter suppar: To conclude for my pairt I haue not onlie the plane
vordis of Christ, bot also the vniuersall consent of all ancient vrytters, quha being mair
nar to Christ and his Disciples, nor ze, hes vn-
derstād the meaning of his vordis better nor
ze may be abill to do, as thay quha ar neirar
the sone, resauis greatar influence thairof,
nor thay quha ar farder fra the same.

*M.   Thou leis in that point, and thou can not be abill
to schau ony Doctor before Thomas, and Scotus that
euer defendit that opinion.*

B. Iustine martyr, quha vas afore Thomas
and Scotus ane thousand zeris and mair teachis in maist plane termis, that euin as Christ
had flesch and blude, sua he gaue his flesch ād
blude to his Disciples. And Irenæus in lyk
maner: that be the coniunction of the bodie
and blude of Christ, vith our bodeis, the same
rysis to immortalitie according to Christis
vord in the 6. of S. Iohne: he that eittis me sall
leaue be me and I sall rais him vp on the latter

S. Ioh. 6.

Iustin.
apol. 2.
ad Anton.
Iren li. 4.
contra hæ-
res. ca. 32.
,,
,,
,,

day: In the quhilkis vordis he attributis thē
force of the vprysing of our bodeis to immortalitie, to his body quhilk ve eit. And
Tertullian aganis the marcionitis prouis that
Christ had ane treu body, and treu blude, becaus according to his auin vord he gaue his
body and his blude to his disciplis in the lar-
ter suppar. And S. Cyprian sayis that not onlie
our saulis, bot euin our mouthis ar sanctifeit
be the bodie and blude of Christ. And Optatus Mileuitanus for that caus, callis the altaris
the seat of the bodie and blude of Christ. And
Gregorius Nyssen. Euin as the meat quhilk
ve eit is chaingeit in our flesch thruch our natural operation, Sua be the vord and opera-
tiō of God the breid is chaingeit in his body.
And Cyrillus Bischop of Ierusalem, vnder the
forme of Breid the body of Christ is geuin,
And vnder the forme of vyne his blude. S. Am
brose : the bodie that ve cōsecrat in the sacrament is the body that is borne of the vergin,
And that same flesch quhilk vas crucifeit for
vs and bureit. S. Hylare, of the veritie of the
body and blude of Christ thair can be na
doubt sen he hes said, It is his flesch ād his blu
de. And thairfore be the participation of this
sacrament, ve ar conionit vith Christ not onlie be faith and chetitie, bot also naturallie
and corporallie. And Cyrill Bischop of Alexandria vryttand aganis Nestorius, quha affermit that Christ vas onlie man and not God,
be this sacrament prouis that he is baith God

*Tertul. li.
4. contra
marcion.*

*Cyprian.
serm. 5.
de lapsis.*

*Gregorius
nyss. in ca-
tach.*

*Cyril. ca-
tach. 4.
mysta.*

*Ambro. de
iis qui
myst. initi.
c. 9. Hyla.
8. de trini.*

and man, Becaus his flesch quhilk is geuin to
vs to be eatin, could not quickin vs gif it var
onlie the flesch of ane man, not conionit vith
the diuinitie, according to Chriſtis auin ſaying   *S. Ioan. 6.*
The flesch proffetis na thing, it is the ſpreit
that geuis lyf. And concludis as afore did Hy-   "
larius, that ve ar naturallie and corporallie cō-
ionit vith Chriſt, And thairfore Chryſoſt. cryis   *Chryſoſt.*
vith a gret exclamation, O miracle! O gude-   *libr. 3. de*
nes of God! he that ſittis at the richt hand of   *ſacerd.*
the father in that ſelf ſame moment is tuichit
be the handis of men, and geuis him ſelf to be
eitin be al thame that vil reſaue him. The reſt
of the doctors confermis the ſame, quhairof
ze may reid Garetius ane Catholik vryttar,
quha hes collectit the teſtemoneis of cheif
Catholik vrytters quha hes florishit ſen Chriſt
vnto thir dayis.

M. *As to Zour doctoris ve man examine thame*
be the tuicheſtaine quhilk is the vord of god, Thair-
foir let vs not depairt from goddis vord, Nou thou
may noth deny bot thir vordis quhairbie Chriſt ſpa-
ke of his blude ſaying This coup is the neu teſtament,   "
in my blude, ſuld be tane as ane figurat loquutione,
for thou may notht ſay, that the coup is propirlie the
neu teſtament, ſua euin in lik maner, thir vordis
this is my bodie, ar to be vndirſtand as ane figurat
loquutione.

B. giff ze vill examine the vrittinis of the
fatheris be the tuicheſtane, ze man proue
zour ſelfis to be fineuris, lapideris, and gold-
ſmythis, and declair at quhat maiſteris ze

D iij

learned zour craft, for euerie man hes not that
skill suppofe he haue the tuicheftane to examine the treu gold , bot he quha maid zou
gouldfinithis in this cace, maid lykuyfe fou-
ters fchipmen, Attour gif ze vil tak vpon zou
to examine the vrittingis of the fathers be the
tuicheftane, Do ze not think it als refonable
that theFathers examine zour opinions be the
tuicheftane, quhilk thay haue done before ze
var borne, and condēnit zou all for heretikis.
Bot to cum to zour obiection ze fould haue
fchauī that Chrift callit that quhilk vas in the
chalice, his blude be ane figurat loquution,
and then ze vald haue prouin fum thing : Bot
fen ze can no: fchau this of ony place in the
hail fcripture, zour reafon is impertinent: becaus albeit the chalice is tane improperlie for
that thing quhilk is contenit thairin , zit the
blude is tane properlie, and according to that
quhilk I fpak before , this figurat loquution
(This coup is the neu teftament in my blude)is declarit be ane proper, and plane loquution baith be S.Marc, and S. Mattheu , this is
my blude quhilk falbe fched for zou and for
manie . And fua the chaleis is callit the neu
teftament in Chriftis blude , becaus it contenis in it the blude of Chrift, quhilk is the blude of the neu teftament . And thairfore of
that figuratiue loquution ze fould rather haue gatherit that the treu blude of Chrift is in
the chalice.my reafon is, becaus that na vther
reafon maj be geuin, quhy the chalice fould

Marc. 14.
Matt. 26.

be callit the neu testament in the blude of Christ, bot that it contenis in it the blude of the neu testament, for gif it contene na vther thing bot vyne, as ze allege, it could not be callit the coup of the. neu testament, mair nor the coup quhairin vas contenit the blude of beistis that vas ane figure of Christis blude could be callit the coup of the neu testamér, quhilk is ane gret blasphemie, and makis Christ inferior vnto Moyses, and derogatis to the estait ád perfectió of the neu testamét: zea quhilk is maist horribill of all, makis Christis vord to be fals, quha in place of the blude of the auld testamét and of the coup quhilk côtenit the same, assurit his Disciples that he did giue thame his auin blude in côfirmation of the neu testament. And this may be maist cleirlie prouin of the vordis follouing. Becaus he sayis that this coup quhilk he gaue, sould be sched for vs, and in na vther meaning the coup maj be sched for vs, bot becaus that quhilk is in the coup is sched for our synnis, sua gif that quhilk vas sched for the remission of synnis vas his auin blude, it follouis necessarlie that it vas his auin blude quhilk vas in the chalice: the quhilk argument is sa cleir and manifest that zour paraclet Theodore Beze is constranit to deny this pairt of the scripture, and to say that it vas eikit to the text.

Beza in com. in luca 22.

M. *Quhill as thou grantis the Real presence of Christis bodie in the sacrament thou vilbe compellit to deny the article of the beleif anent our maisters sit-*

ting at the richt hand of the father, quhilk of thir then vil thow afferme sence thay mai not bayth be treu.

B. Infafar as ze refer the sitting of our halie faluioris bodie at the richt hand of his father, to ane difpofition of place, and corporal fituatiō as ve haue in the earth, zour blind imagination in that behalf proceidis of zour ſtupeid ignorance, as thocht god the father, quha is ane maist fimple fpreit, had ane richt or left fyd, o r ony fleſchlie hand lyk vnto mortal men. Quhairfore gif ze vil to auoid this incommodite, expone the article of the beleif concerning his fitting at the richt hand of the father, of the honor quhairunto Chriſt Iefus in his manlie nature is exaltit, It is ane better argument: Chriſt is at the richt hand of the father, thairfore he is reallie prefent vith men, noriſching thame be participation of his glorious bodie to immortalitie, nor be the vrangus expofition of this article to collect the cōtrar. Bot becaus ze haue brocht me in rememberance of the beleif, I fall fchortlie be inductiō proue that the fals prophettis of zour deformit kirk, denyis all the articlis heirof. And firſt of all quhill as ze giue na credeit to the faithfull men, quha haue vrittin the miraclis that god hes vrocht be his halie fanctis for confirmation of the treu faith fen the firſt fondation of the Chriſtian religion: And ficlyk quhil as ze doubt, hou may our halie faluioris precious bodie be reallie present in the sacrament, and in heauin at anis, or the accidentis consist vithout actual inherence, quhilkis ar als credible, as that god hes maid the heauin and earth of na thing, quhat do ze vther bot deny god to be almichtie, makar of heauin, and earth?

As to the secund persone in diuinitie concerning his assumption of manlie nature, quhil as ze beleue not the halie kirk saying: that our saluior vas borne vpon the tuentie fyue day of December, I vald glaidlie vit at zou, giue ze beleue he be borne or not, and gif ze vald say that he is borne, Be quhat moyen knau ze or may knau the same, bot be thame quha sayis that he vas borne on sik ane day, quha as thay giue testimonie that the buikis of the neu, and auld testament ar canonik, quhairin it is vrittin that he vas borne: siclyk thay afferme constanlie as thay haue resauit of thair fathers, that he vas borne vpon the tuentie fyue of december, sua quhil as ze dout on this, and lyk infidel paganis callis in controuersie, quhither he vas borne in symmer or vynter, geuand the people occasiō to suspect, that thay ar bot fablis quhilk ar spokin of his Natiuitie, thairby taking auay the memorie of the same from zour miserable Disciples and voful flock, ze deny altogither the secund article of the beleif.

TheodoreBeze quhais sayingis ze resaue as oraclis of the halie ghaist, affermis planelie that Christ vas borne of his mother as vther

Beza contra Brent.

childrene ar borne of thair mothers quha ar
na virgenis, sua that in his birth the integritie
of his mothers virginite vas not conseruit.
Qnhat is this vther bot to deny that Christ
vas borne of the virgin Marie?

Qnhair as the visdome of the halie ghaist
in the kirk, appointit four cheif festual dayis
quhairby the people of god micht be retenit
in obedience, and confession of thair faith a-
nent Christis Natiuitie, Passion, Resurrection
and Ascesion, ze brekers of al gude and godlie constitutions refusand the obseruation of
thir dayis makis plane protestation that ze
beleue not thir articlis, be reason all Christians sen the Apostlis dayis quha beleuit the
same, neglectit not the obseruation of thir
halie dayis, as vitnessis the halie martyr Ignatius Disciple of S. Iohne the Euangelist, vryttand to the Christian people in ane of his epistlis: [Festiuitates ne spernite,] neglect not
the keiping of the halie dayis.

*Ignatius
epist. 4. ad
Philipp.*

Zour Idol Iohne Caluin in his catechisme, quhilk ze read our of zour pulpittis for
canonik scripture, denyis planelie that Christ
efter his death past doun vnto hel, bot referris this article to signefie the agonie of death
quhairin Christ vas quhe he said:My god,my
god quhy hes thou left me?

As to iugement on the latter day, quhil as
ze deny baith meritorious varkis,and frie vill
ze haue left na place thairto atall: Becaus the
forme of Iugement pronucit be our saluiour

aganis the vicked for thair demeretis vilbe: « Depairt from me vnto the fyre of hel, that « is preparit for the Deuil and his angellis. *Matt. 25.* Quhilk sentence could not iustlie be pronúcit gif synners had not frie vil, quhairby vith the assistance of grace thruch Christ, frelie offerit to euerie man, and vilfullie reiectit be euerie condamnit persone, thay micht haue escheuit the synnis, for the quhilk thay demereit to heir this feirful sentence of condénation.

To cum to the last pairt concerning the halie ghaist and Catholik kirk, ze deny the same maist impudentlie, quhil as ze spulzie the halie ghaist of his principal operation, quhilk consistis in the gouernement of the kirk, and instructió of the general conceilis of the kirk, in making definition of the treuth and declaration of fals doctrene, sua that thay maj not erre, for ze teache that the general conceillis hes errit, And siclyk denyis, that the kirk of our saluiour Christ is Catholik halie and visible vpon the face of the earth.

As to the communion of Sanctis, and lyf eternal, quhil as ze teache that the prayers of the blissit vergin Marie, of Sanct Michael, of S. Petir. S.Paul, and al the glorious Angellis, and sanctis proffittis vs nathing quhat place haue ze left to the communion of sanctis, or ony lyf efter this?

Ze deny inlykmaner the remission of synnis quhil as ze obstinatlie defend that the

syn is neuer remouit in verie deid be grace
thruch Chriſt applyit to vs be adminiſtration
of the ſacramentis, bot onlie not imputit.

And laſt of all infafar as ze deny the Reall preſence of the glorious bodie of Chriſt
Ieſus in the ſacrament, and Conſequentlie
the reall coniuction of our mortal fleſch vith
the immortal bodie of our ſaluior, be taking
auay this ordinar meane appointit be god,
quhairby our bodeis may ryſe agane, nather
may ze beleue the reſurrection of the bodeis
to immortalitie, nor hoip for ony ſik beneſeit . Quhairfore it is maiſt manifeſt that in
verie deid ze deny all the articlis of our beleif, to zour auin condenation, albeit ze vald
appeir to confes thame in vord.

*Blacuod. Zour doctore Auguſtine exponing the dra-
me of Pharao quhairof mentione is maid in Geneſis*
Gene. 17. *vitneſſis that thir tua places of ſcripture (ſeptem*
Matt. 26. *ſpicæ, ſeptem anni ſunt) and (hoc eſt corpus meum)*
ar figuratiue loquutionis, hou than may thou defend
the reall preſence of Chriſtis bodie in the ſacrament,
gif, as heir planelie vitneſſis Auguſtin , quhais da-
ctrine Ze imbrace, the vordis be nocht tane in the pro-
pir ſignificatione.

B. Ze cite S. Auguſtine maiſt falſlie, becaus na
ſik thing is to be fund in him as ze allege. The
firſt that euer exponit thir vordis of the ſcrip-
Matt. 26. ture (this is my bodie) be the vthir place (the
Gene. 17. ſeuin ſtalkis ar ſeuin Zeiris) vas zuinglius quha
ſayis that hauing ane greit deſyre to expone
tha vordis (hoc eſt) this ſignifeis, and finding

this expofitione to be verie hard, that ane
Angell appeirit vnto him, bot he kneu not quhidder he vas quhyt or blak, and said to him,
feir not, and propofed the vther place of fcripture (the seuin stalkis ar seuin zeiris) that is,
fignifeis: fua in lyk maner (this is my bodie)
aucht to be interpreit this fignifeis my bodie:
And thaireftir he had na feir, bot propofed bauldlie vnto all men this neu glofe, that he had
refaued from the hand of the angell, euin as
Mahomet reffauit his Alcoran from the hand
of God. I remember that S. Auguft vreittis
of ane callit Vincentius ane Ptifcillianift quha
affirmir in lyk maner that ane Angell had a-
peirit vnto him, and learnit him the richt interpretatione of the fcripture, to quhom he
anfuerit vitht S. Paull, that albeit ane Angell
of heuin teueill onie thing attour that quhilk
is preched, ve aucht not to beleue the fam.
Bot that ze be efchamit to cite S. Auguftine
in tymes cumming, I vil propofe vnto zou
thre, or four places maift cleir, and manifeft for
the confirmatione of the treu, and Catholik
doctrine. The firft is, out of his expofitione of
the threttie thre Pfalme, quhair he fayis that
suppofe it be impoffibill that onie mortall
man beir him felf in his auin handis, that
Chrift notuithftanding buir him felf in his
auin handis, quhen he faid (this is my bodie:)
gif he bure onlie ane figure of his bodie as
ze allege, euerie man micht haue done alfine-
kill as he: The fecund is vpone the nyntie

Zuingli li subfidii de cœna domi ni.

Auguft contra vincent.

S. Paul. gal. 1.

Aug. i, pſ. 33

August in
psal.98.;
aucht Psalme, quhair he sayis that Christ left
vs that same self flesche, quhairin he valkit
in this varld, and that na man eitis of that
flesche except first he adore the same. The
thrid, is in the thrid buik of the Trinitie, qu-

Aug. lib. 3
de trinit.
cap. 10
hair he vryttis in this maner: gif it var proponit to ane chyld be sik authoritie as he behouit to beleue, quhais bodie and quhais blude ve tak in the Sacrament, gif the chyld had
neuer vndirstand in quhat maner and liknes
Christ had apperit in the earth, he vald beleue
assuritlie that Christ had appeirit in sik forme as he is schauin in be the handis of the preist, and that it quhilk is in the chalice, had
sprung out from the vound of sik ane bodie.
The fourt is in the tuentie buke of the Citie

Aug. lib.
20 de ci-
nit. Dei.
cap. 17.
of God, quhair he sayis that the bodie of
Christ, quhilk is nou offerit in the sacrifice of
the kirk, and geuin in the sacramét to all quha
resauis it, vas præfigurat be all the sacrifices of
the auld lau. Considder vith zour self gif the
sacrifices of the auld lau, var figuris of ane figure, and nocht of the treu bodie of Christ, i
micht cite monie vtheris gif I pleised, bot thir
ar sufficient to schau zour impudence: that albeit ze neuer red S. Augustine, zit ze ar nocht
eschamit to cite him in zour præchingis, and
impose tha thingis vnto him quhilk he neuer
thocht.

M. *Thair is na poynt of our beleif contrare the conclusione of ane demonstratione lyk vnto this, All natural bodie is in ane propir place, and may not at anis*

be in ma nor ane, bot Chriftis glorious bodie is ane na-
tural bodie, thairfoir it is in ane propir place, and
may not be in ma at anis, and confequentlie Chriftis
bodie can nocht be in heuin, and reallie prefent in the
facrament at ane tyme.

B. Heirby al men may perfaue zour deceat,
that albeit ze allege that ze teache na thing,
bot the pure vord of God, and alfo that zour
doctrine is not groudit vpone natural reafo-
nis, bot vpone the omnipotent pouar of God
zit zour practicque is aluterlie contrare, for
nou to vithdrau men from thair faith, ze produce not the plane vord of god, bot as all
men may fe ane natural reafone, inuentit be
zour auin brain, quhilk ze call ane demonftratione, albeit in verie deid it be nane at al:
fence the firft and cheif propirtie of ane demonftratione is, that the propofitionis thairof be fua treu, cleir, and euident that na man
indeuit vith the natural licht of vndirftanding, may deny the fame, quhilk inlaikis in
this zour demonftration : Becaus Ariftotil
him felf prouis that zour propofition in this
zour præten dit demonftration is fals, feing
that the heauin quhilk is ane verie natural
bodie is not contined in ane propir place. And
it is als liklie that ane bodie be in diuerfs places, as that maj bodeis be in ane propir place,
Bot ze ar compellit to grant that ma bodeis-
may be in ane propir place, vnles vith the heretik Iouinianus ze deny that Chrift vas borne of his mother as of ane virgine. Vnles ze

deny lykuyse that Christ come in, quhair his
*S. Ioh.*20 discippillis var, the durris being close, as sum
of zour brethrene dois, quha affirmis that
Christ com in at the chimnay heid : And sua
ze at constranit alsua to grant, that be the
omnipotent pouar of god, ane bodie may be
in ma places, this being na mair repugnant
at the lest to the groundis of natural philoso-
sophie: Considering euin as the philosophou-
ris teachis that euerie bodie suld be in ane
place, sua thay teache that euerie bodie aucht
to haue ane place æquall vnto it self, in sik
maner that the place be nather of les, nor mair capacitie, nor the bodie quhilk is contined
thairin: Bot be the omnipotent pouar of god
aboue nature ane bodie may be in ane les place nor the natural dimensionis of it requiris,
*S.Ioh.*20. as quhen tua bodeis occupeis ane propir place, thay requirand of thair auin nature ane
mair place, quhairin thay may be comprehendit. Than be the lik pouar ane bodie may
occupie ane far greittar place nor the nature
of the dimensionis thairof requiris, quhilk is
na thing els, bot that ane bodie may be in mo
nie places. Bot suppoise I vald grant zou the
propositione treu that euerie natural bodie as
natural, is in ane place, sua that it may not be
in monie, it seruis na thing for zour purpose:
Becaus Christis bodie is substātiallie present,
not contined in the sacrament as in ane place,
bot in ane incomprehensibill maner, insafar
*Ioan.*6. as it is glorious, and conioynit vith the diuinitie

nitie, quhairbie it surpassis the maner and cō-
ditione of pure, and natural bodeis : for sen
the occupatione of ane place, euin according
to the menig of the philosophoris, is nocht of
the nature or substance of ane bodie, vnles ze
be infidelis, ze can nocht deny, bot God be his
omnipotēt pouar may separat Christis bodie
from the occupatione of ane place, it being
onlie ane accident of the same. And gif ze
ground all zour fayth on naturall reasonis, I
feir that ze dout not onlie of this mysterie of
the real presence of Christis bodie in the sacrament of the altar, bot also of the Natiuitie
of Christ of ane virgine: of the Resurrectione
of thir sam self bodeis eftir thay ar resolued in
dust : of the Trinitie of distinguised personis
in ane indiuisibill substance of the Godheid,
Becaus the lyk, ze strenthiar demonstrationis
may be brochraganis the treuth of thir mystereis: And this I can nocht prætermit that ze
gif me greit occasione to suspect, that be siclyk vther reasonis ze ar mouit pairtlie to dout
of the mysterie of the Trinitie. Becaus I neuer
hard zou in onie of zour sermonis speik onie
thing of that mysterie : sua that gif this verse
Glore to the father, and to the sone, and to the
halie gaist var abstracted from the end of the
psalmes, quhilk aucht to be done according
to zour doctrine, sen ze admit na thing bot
that quhilk is expreslie vreittin in sa monie
bukis of the auld and neu testamēt as ze pleise
to admitt : And this verse vas nocht adiected

E

Platina in vitis pontificum. be the vtryittar of the psalmes, bot be the raip Damasus sensyne, I dout not bot ze suld altogidder glaidlie forzet this mysterie.

OF THE TRANSVBSTANTIA-
tione of the breid, and vyne in the bodie and blude of Christ Iesus.

CHAP. XIII.

M.

THe scripture callis that quhilk is geuin in the lordis suppar breid, as quhen *Paull* sayis, the breid, quhilk ve brek, is it nocht the participatione of Christis bodie? And in the actis of the Apostlis it is vrittin, that the faythful did perseueir in the breiking of breid, and in vther sik places, quhy than affirmis thou vith the papistis, that the breid remanis not, bot is changit in the bodie of Christ?

S. Paul. 1. Cor. 10.

Act. 2.

B. Gif ze had conferred thir places vith vther places of the scripture, zevald haue fund maist esilie ane solutione to zour obiectione, Christ him self in the saxt of S. Iohne declairis in quhat sens the name of breid suld be tane in thir places alleged be zou, sayand, I am the breid quhilk is cummit out of heauin, and the breid quhilk I sall giue zou is my fleshe, that salbe geuin for the lyf of the varld: for as the maist commone and principal nuriture is breid, sua the fleshe of Christ being the nuritur of our saulis, and bodeis to immortalitie, is callit breid be him self. Efter the quhilk maner of speiking his Apostlis, and the Euā-

Ioan. 6.

geliſtis callis alſo his fleshe, breid . And thairfoir, as quhen Chriſt ſaid I am the breid, quhilk is deſcedit from heauin, it follouis nocht
that he vas corruptibill or material breid , ſua ₁ *Cor.*10.
quhen in the ſcripture his fleshe is callit breid, *Act.*2.
as in the places alledged be zou, it follouis
not, that the vord ſignifeis corruptibill or material breid, becaus efter the maner of ſpeiking of the hebreuis, quhilk Chriſt and his
diſcipiles follouit, quhatſumeuer nuriture, in
the hebreu tourg is callit generalie חֶם, that
is breid, ſua, as ze may eſilie perſaue, zour argument is of na ſtrenth, ze the ſcripture it ſelf
geuis vs ane ſufficient argument that thai
zour alleged places ſuld nocht be vnderſtand
of material breid, ſeing S. Paull ſayis that the
breid quhilk ve brek is the communication
of Chriſtis bodie, gif it be material breid, it
may not be the communicatione of Chriſtis
bodie, And in that ſame place ve ar all ane
breid, and ane bodie, quhaſoeuer ar maid participant of ane breid, and ane bodie. Quhairof
it follouis that the ſelf ſame breid and body is
geuin to vs all, vtheruyſe ve could not be ane
breid and ane bodie mair be the participation
of this ſacrament, nor be the eitting of commone breid, quhilk is expres aganis the mening of S. Paull . ſua gif it var ane material
breid that ſame ſelf could not be geui tovs all,
as ze that ar heir in Ediburgh reſſaues not that
ſelf ſame breid in zour comunion, quhilk thay
reſſaue that ar in Sanctadrois ze amang zour

felfis euerie ane of zou reſſauis his auin mor-
ſell of breid, Bot ve quha ar Catholikis according to ſanct Paulis doctrine reſſauis all that
ſame ſelf breid , that is that ſame fleſch of
Chriſt quhilk vas offerit on theCroce to mak
ſatisfaction for the ſynnis of the varld, and ſua
ve ar all ane breid be the coniunction quhilk
ve haue vith the heuinlie breid quhilk is the
bodie of Chriſt : for the quhilk caus vreittis

Chryſ. ho-
mil.8.in
2. cor.

the godlie and lerned doctor Chryſoſtom
(Non ſicut in vetere lege partem quidem po-
,, pulus, parte ſacerdos comedebat, verum om-
,, nibus vnum corpus proponitur & vnum po-
,, culum)not ſayis he as in the auld lau the pepill
eated ane pairt of the ſacrifice , and the preiſt
ane vther, bot euerie man reſſauis ane hail bodie, and ane coup or chalice: Mairouer becaus
Chriſt vas to giue his fleſch in the place of
Manna, quhilk amag the Ieuis vas callit breid,
he affermit that he vil gif thame another
breid, not that he vas to giue thame ane material breid , bot according to the common
maner of ſpeiking that he vald giue thame
ane nuriture mair perfyt ad excellent nor vas
Mana, quhilk he declaris to be his auin fleſch.
Nou ſuppoſe I vald grant zou that thai places
of the ſcripture ſould be vnderſtand of the
material breid , zit ze var not nerar zour purpoſe, becaus according to the phraſe of the
ſcripture, quhen ane ſubſtance is chaingeit in
another , it vſis to keip the name of the formar ſubſtance , as quhen the vand vas turnit

in ane serpent, the serpent neuertheles is callit
ane vand in Exod. quhair it is vrittin, that the *Exod. 7.*
vand ef Moyses deuorit the vandis of the Ma-
giciés. And Adam becaus he vas formir of the
dust of the earth, is callit dust in the scripture, *Genes. 3.*
sua be the lyk phrase the body of Christ is
callit breid, becaus the breid is chaingeit thair
in . Thairfore baith the scripture and the fathers of the primitiue kirk , to the effect that
this sublime and heich misterie sould not be
prophanit be the Gentilis , in quhais handis
thair vrittingis micht fall, vsis sindrie tymes to
call this sacrament breid, quhairby thay var
vnderstand be the faithfull, and thair mistereis var keipit hid and secreit from the infidellis according to Christis command. Cast not *S. Mat. 7.*
precious stanis before suyne. For the quhilk *S. August.*
caus S. Augustine oftymes in his sermons vsis *in psal. 33.*
this circumloqution. (Sacramentum quod "
norunt fideles , the sacrament quhilk the
faithfull knauis. (Et Christus accepit in mani- "
bus, quod norút fideles &c.) And Christ tuke
it in his handis, quhilk the faithfull knauis,
And sik vther maners of speiking. Ze the gentilis thame selfis be reason of this misterie *Tertul.*
quhilk thay vnderstude to be amang the Chri *Apolo. ad-*
stians, albeit thay atteint not to the perfyt in- *uersus gé-*
telligence thairof, zit thay vsit to obiect vnto *tes.*
thame that thay eat mennis flesch, as amang *Iustin* *mart.*
Vthers vitnesis Tertullian, and Iustin martyr, *Apol. 2*
Vthers did obiect that thay vorschippit Ceres *ad Anto-*
and Bacchus, that is the goddis of breid and *nis.*

Augu. 18.
cōtra Fau
stum.

Aug. epist.
13.

Augu. de
symbhol. ad
cathec.

Basil. lib.
de spiritu-
sāēt.c. 37.

Chryso. in
liturgia.

vyne, as vitneß S. Augustine vryttand aganis Faustus Manichæus: vthers as vitneß also Augustine for this caus vsit to demand at the Christians, quhat ane God vas that, quhilk thay feinzeit thame self to se in thair sacrificis and assembleis? zea the Manichæas obiectit in plane termes to the Christianis, that thay did vorschip breid and vyne. And vther siclyk obiections var vsit, be reason of the gret profunditie of this misterie, quhilk not onlie vas not maid manifest vnto the gentilis, bot vas hid also euin fra thame quha var callit Catechumeni, that is quha var techit and instructit in the rest of the mistereis of the Christian religion, bot zit had not ressauit the sacrament of baptisme, for the quhilk caus it vas not lesum to thame, as vitnessis S. Augustine, Basile, Chrisostome, and vther anciét vrytters to be present in the kirk during the tyme of the sacrifice, bot incótinent efter the Euangel vas red, before the preist did cum to the consecration of the sacrament, the Deacon vsit to cry vith ane loud voce, (Exeant Catechumeni.) And S. August. for the same caus spek and of this sacramét sayis: [nesciunt Catechumeni quid accipiant Christiáni:] Thay quha ar callit cathechumeni, knauis not quhat the Christians do ressaue. Gif that quhilk Christ gaue to his disciples var na thing bot breid and vyne as ze allege, aganis his auin expres vord, the Christians vald not haue trauellit samekle to haue hid the mater from the gentilis, and infidel-

lis,and from thame quha var inſtructit euin of
the miſterie of the Trinitie , and incarnation
of Chriſt, as var thaj quha var callit catechumeni,nor zit vald not haue geuin occaſion to
the gentilis to haue maid ſik obiections to
thame as thay did mak, nor zit vald haue tholit death,becaus quhē thay bure the ſacramēt
vith thame thay vald not diſcouer it vnto the *Venerabi-*
gentilis, conſidering it vald haue bene na mi- *lis Beda*
ſterie at all. For quhat miſterie is it to beleue *logio.*
that Chriſt gaue breid and vyne to his diſciples,ſen that is eſilie done be euerie man,and
ane thing ſua eſie of it ſelf, that na man hes
miſter of gret faith to beleue it, bot to beleue that he hes geuin his auin bodie vnder the
formes of breid and vyne, that is ane verie
ſublime and heich miſterie, quhilk requyris
ane gret ſubiection,faith and obedience vnto
God,to beleue that thing quhairof ve haue na
argument nor ſenſible perſuaſion , bot rather
apperis to be repugnāt to our ſenſis, and natu
ral vit,onlie becaus God hes ſpokin it.For the
quhilk caus.S.Chriſoſto. Ciril,Ambroiſe,and
vthers exhorting vs to beleue the vord of god
in this miſterie albeit it appeir repugnāt to our
ſenſis,becaus our ſenſis and vit may deceaue
vs,ſay thay, bot his vord may not deceaue vs.
ſua ſayis the halie vryttar Chriſoſtome . Sen *Chryſo.ho.*
Chriſt hes ſaid, This is my body, let vs on na *mil.83. in*
vyſe dout,bot vith ane maiſt certane and aſſu *Matth.*
rit faith beleue that it is euin as he hes ſpo- *Cyril. lib.*
kin. And Ciril ſayis:ſence he hes ſaid. This *cap.15.*

Ambr.li.6
de sacram.
cap. 1.
is my blude, quha dar be sa bauld, as to doubt
heirof, and say, that it is not his blude? hou,
maj ze then purge zour seluis of plane infidelitie and atheisme, sen ze giue na credeit vnto
goddis vord, bot in place thairof hes setfurth
ane neu vord of zour auin, quhilk vas neuer
acknaulegeit for the vord of god before zou?
And hou maj ze purge zour seluis to be maist
miserable and vnhappie men, quha perseuis
me sa rigorouslie, becaus I Beleue the vordis
of Christ to be treu, That is becaus he said
(This is my body) I beleue that it is his bodie
And euin as he did nurissh Helias the space of

of the kin
gis 3.chap.
19.
Exod. 16.
fourtie dayis vith ane breid baikin vnder the
Assis, quhil he come to the montane of god
Horeb, And the Israëlitis vith the maist precious Manna, that raynit out of heauin, quhil
thay come to the land of promission, sua I beleue maist surelie that he dois nurishe the treu
Christians vith his auin precious body quhilk vas prefigurat be Manna, quhill thay cum
to the land of promission, to vit the assurance
of the lyf euerlesting. This vas also prefigurat
be the brunt offering of the Israëlitis in the
auld testament, quairof na thing remanit except the skin, to signefie that the hail substance of the breid is chaingeit in Christis body,
and that the skin onlie, that is, the exteriour
forme and accidentis of the breid remanis.
And euin as the first miracle quhilk Christ did
S.Iohne.2 vas the chaingeing and couersion of valter in-

to vyne, sua the laſt quhilk he did before he
vas betraiſit, vas the chaingeing and cōuerſi-
on of breid in his auin body as be his auin
vord, and the vniuerſal conſent of the hail
kirk is maiſt manifeſt and cleir.

M. Be quhat teſtimonie of ſcripture mai thou pro-
ue the tranſmutation of the nature of the breid, in
the ſubſtance of Chriſtis glorious body?

B. I vil produce thir inuincible argumentis
quhilk Sathan zour maiſter and ze ſall neuer
be abil to refel. The firſt dois conſiſt in thir
vordis: My fleſch is verie meat, and my blude *S. Ioan. 6*
is verie drink. This fleſch and blude quhair-
of he ſpeakis in thir vordis ar reallie geuin to
vsin this ſacramēt, or ellis thay maj not be the
verie fude of our ſaulis. Bot thay may not be
reallie geuin in the ſacramēt, gif the ſubſtance
of the bread, quhilk is bot corporal fude and
maj not nurish the Saul, remane vnchainge-
it, Quhairfore tranſubſtantiation in this ſacrament is neceſſar. The ſecund argument
conſiſtis in thir vordis: As the leuing father "
hes ſend, me and I leue be the father, euin ſua *S. Ioan. 6.*
he quha eatis me, Sal leue be me alſo. Bot "
the ſone in diuinitie proceidis of his father in
ſik ſort that he reſſauis his hail ſubſtance of
him, and is of ane indiuiſible ſubſtance vith
his father: Quhairfore neceſſar it is, that be eating of this ſacrament according to the meaning of Chriſt, ve ar maid ane ſubſtance vith
his manlie nature, hauing our hail ſubſtance
of him inſafar as it is inmortal. The thrid ar-

" gument is contenit in thir vordis, Not as
S. Ioan. 6. zour fathers eatit Manna, and deit, for the
difference aſſignit in this place conſiſtis ather
in the diſtinction of the nature of that quhilk is geuin in the ſacrament of the altar, and
the ſubſtance of mána that the ane hes pouar
to aboleis death, quickin, and giue lyf: The
vther had not the ſame:or ellis this difference
is nane, Becaus gif the ſubſtance and nature
of the ſacrament be corruptible, lyk as the
vnbeleuaris in the auld lau deit efter thay had
eatin Manna, and the beleuaris leuit be faith
onlie, and not be verteu of eating of Manna,
ſua ſal ve ſay of thame quha eitis Chriſtis body, quhil as the contrar heirof is manifeſtlie
" prouin be this teſtimonie. The fourt is, that
Chriſt quhen he tuk bread in his handis, he
S. Matth. bliſſit it be thir vordis:(This is my body,)the
26. quhilk bliſſing not being in vane, bot hauing efficacie and ſtrenth to do that thing quhilk it ſignifeis, it behouis of neceſſitie that
the breid be chaingeit in his body:Bot ze quha acknaulegis na thing in this ſacrament bot
onlie breid, ar maiſt iniurious vnto Chriſt, taking auay the verteu and ſtrenth of his benediction. The fyſt is that thir vordis . [hoc eſt
Corpus meum] being tane in thair proper
ſenſe and ſignification as thay ſould be, con-
uictis neceſſarlie the tranſubſtantiation of the
breid in Chriſtis bodie, becaus that this pro-
noune (hoc) quhilk is demonſtratiue of ane
ſubſtance, ſould neceſſarlie be referrit to that

substance, quhilk Christ gaue to his disciplis, that can not be the substance of breid, Considering it can not be treu : This breid is my body, Than it vas not breid quhilk Christ gaue to his Disciples, bot his auin body, and sua consequentlie, the substance of the breid remanit not. Quhairfore zour maister Caluin prouis necessarlie aganis Vestphalus the Lutheriā, that gif the bodie of Christ be in the sacrament, It can not be bot be trransubstantiation. And the same is prouin be zour paraclet Beze aganis Hessusius, Mairouer I propose the vniuersal consent of thaj godlie Doctors quha ar resauit be all Christians sen the Ascension of Christ vnto this day, that this is the treu exposition of the vordis of Christ. Iustinus : Euin as Christ had flesch and blude, sua be his vord the breid and vyne ar chaingit in his body and blude S. Cyprian : The breid be the omnipotencie of god is changeit in the flesch. Cyrillus hierosolomitanus : Gif Christ being in Cana of galilie turnit the valter in vyne, hou can ve doubt bot in the latter suppar, he turnit the vyne in his blude, sen he said him self in his latter supper, This is my blude quhilk is sched for zou S. Ambrose: Gif god hes creatit all thingis of na thing, quhy maj he not turne ane substance in another, and change the breid and vyne in his bodie and blude? Quhairfore ve aucht fermelie tō beleue, that albeit our sensis persaue the accidentis of ane corruptibill creature,

Caluin. cōtra Vesph.

Beze a contra H-ssus.

Iustin. Apol. 2 ad Antonin.
Cypria. de cœna domini.
Cyrill. cach. 3.
"
"
Ambros. ca 9. de iis qui myst. initiātur.

Zit vnder the couerture thairof is contenit the heauinlie, spiritual, immortal, and impaſſibil body of Chriſt Ieſus, profferring his vord to our ſenſuall Iugement quhilk may not attein to the profunditie of ſik hid miſtereis.

M. Our maiſters body at the ſuppar vas mortal and paſſibil, hou then ſays thou that he could giue the ſame to his Diſciplis vnder the forme of breid, as immortal and impaſſibil?

B. Becaus our lord and ſaluiour Chriſt foreknauing all thingis that he vas to ſuffer for mankynd, and hauing a feiling thairof as teſtefeis thaj droppis of ſueat lyk blude quhilk iſſuith from him quhē he prayir, villinglie , and maiſt glaidlie acceptit all paynis before he ſufferit, he had the mereit equal vith that, quhairuith he raſe vpon the thrid day out of the graif: Quhairfore at his latter ſupper geuing thākis vnto God, he gaue efter conſecration , his body, in ane impaſſibil and glorious maner vnder the forme of breid. This is confermit be the transfiguration of his bodie before his death aboue the natural eſtait of ane paſſibil body, ſchauin to his Diſciplis in the montayne, quhen his face ſchynit lyk the ſone, and his clething vas quhyt lyk licht: Sua it vas maiſt eſie vnto Chriſt , to giue his bodie in ane impaſſibil and glorefeit maner , euin as in ane glorefeit maner he apperit vnto his Diſciplis before his paſſion : And quha of zou ar ſa bauld to deny that Chriſt micht do it ? or produce me onie ſcripture gif ze cā that he micht

Luc. 22.

Matt. 17.

not do the fame. Sua it apperis zd at not content to limitat the pouar of kingis, Quenis,
Bifchoppis, and all eftaitis, bot ze vil limitat
the pouar of god him felf. And in al this difputation ze haue propofit na vthet argumentis aganis me, except it be, hou can god do
this, or that? euin as ze var on the fecreit coun-
fal of god, and had compaffit al thingis in zour
phantaftical braynis, quhilk ar in the incom-
prehenfibil pouar of the infinit vifdome and
fapience of god. As to me I am content vith
his vord, not fekand ony farder affurance.
And thairfore fen he hes faid, (This is my body) I vil beleaue him and fearche na farder.
And vil giue mair credeit to his fimpil vord,
then to al zour reafons and probations, thai
being onlie fophiftical, captious, and inuentit
be zour auin braynis.

M. *I vill proue be ane Inuincibill argument that in
the lordis fuppar the fubftance ef the breid and vyne
remanis aluyfe vnchangeit, becaus the accidentis as
the colore, quantitie, and taift of the breid and vyne
ar perfauit be our fenfis quhilk deceauis vs not, and
thir may not confift vithout the fubftance quhairin
thay haue inhærence, hou than fayis thou that Chriftis bodie is prefent in the facrament be tranfubftan-
tiatione?*

B. Albeit Luther, as he confeffis in his diá-
bolical buke de Angulari Miffa, be the ftrenth
of this argument proponit be his father Sathan vas ouercummit. Zit ane faythfull man
vill efilie beleue, that tranfmutatione being
maid of ane corruptibill creature in ane fu-

Luther
lib. de an-
gularimiſ-
ſa.

pernatural and immortal bodie, the accidentis
tholand na corruptione reſſauis verteu actiue
and paſſiue in thame ſelfis quhairbie thay may
conſiſt euin as giue thay var inhærent in thait
auin ſubſtance : And this beneſeit is granted
vnto vs of the greit mearcie of god, becaus ve
at vnabil to abyd the preſence of Chriſtis real
bodie in proper forme as it is nou gloriſeit,
As amang vtheris vreittis the halie doctoris
Ambroſe, Damaſcen, and Theophilactus, bot
Ambro.li. ze ar maniſeſt blaſphemaris aganis goddis
4. de ſacra omnipotent pouar, quhil as ze ſay that god
men. may not caus the accidentis haue exiſtence
Damaſc. vithout the auin proper inherençe : Conſi-
lib. 4. c. 14. dering that god, quha is the caus of conſerua-
Theoph. in tion of al thingis, and miſteris not the concur-
Luc. c. 14. rence of his creaturis, euin as he coſeruis the
accidentis be the ſubſtance as ane ordinar me-
ane, ſua he maj conſerue the accident be his
omnipotent pouar vithout the ſubſtance, or
ellis it behouit him neceſſarlie to haue miſter
of ane creature for conſeruation of another,
quhilk is ane maiſt horrible blaſphemie. Mair-
attour the philoſopheurs thame ſelfis tea-
this that the ſubſtance and accident ar tua
thingis Reallie diſtingueiſt : Quhat then maj
be mair eſie to god, nor that he be his omnipotent pouar ſeparat the ane from the vther?
eſpeciallie ſence it is als neceſſar according to
the ordinar courſe of nature, that ane ſubſtance, haue the auin ſubſiſtance, as that the accidentis haue thair inherence. Bot ze ar conſtra-

nit to grant: that ane substance maj be vithout the natural subsistance thairof, as in the incarnation of Christ, thair vas treulie the humane nature, and zit it vas denudit of the proper subsistance, vnles ze grant vith Nestorius that in Christ, lyk as thair is tua naturis, sua thair is tua subsistencis or personagis. Quhairfore the accidentis in lyk maner may be vithout inherence, sen as teachis the maist learnit scolemen: the nature of the accident consistis not in this, that it hes actual inherence, bot that it may haue inherence in ane substance. As the accident is oftymes definit vithout the actual inherence thairof, quhilk could not be gif it var of the nature of the same: As quhen the mathematicians definis thair quantiteis and figuris, as Aristotle him self teachis, thay mak ane abstraction from al inherence, and zit neuertheles thay cumpas the nature of the accident quhilk thay define. And I meruel of zou, quha professis zour seluis philosophors, that ze vil not grant that thing to the omnipotencie of god, quhilk manie learnit philosophors grantis sum tyme to be agreable to the natural ordour of thingis appointit be god, as amang vthers manie of the quhilkis Aristotle makis mention in the fourt buik of the phisikis quhais opinion Philoponus that vas ane Christian man and ane maist learnit philosophour follouis, and S. Basile in the secund homilie of his hexameron affermis: that the licht quhilk vas first creatit

Philoponus in 4. Phys. Basil. homil. 2. in hexam.

be god, had na substance quhairin it had inherence, and adionis thairto that god may
mair eselie separat reallie the licht frō the substance quhairin it hes inhærence, nor ve may
separat the ane from the vther in thocht and
cogitation. Simplicius also ,and Ammonius
quha var gret philosophors,in the declaration
of Aristotle sayis : that ane accident may pas
out of ane substance to another, quhilk is al
alyk according to the grund of Metaphisik,
as to be seperat from ane substāce.And suppose I could not atteine to the vay hou the accident may be separat from the substance, zit I
vald grund my faith vpon the speiking of god
him self, quha is infallible treuth , and vorkis
for the confort of man thai thingis,that he is
vnable to conceaue,not regairding zour diffi-
dence, proceding as ze think of natural rea-
sons,quhilk being veil tryit,ar fundin na vther
thing bot phantastical captions and illusions.
For gif Abraham had benę mouit be natural
reason , quhen he vas commandit be the Angel to offer his onlie sone Isaac in quhom god
had maid vnto him the promeis of the benediction of all nations , and mnltiplication of
his seid,he vald haue collectit that it vas impos
sible, giue Isaac var offerit in ane brunt sacrifice, that the promeis of god sould be treu,
And sua vald haue becum inobedient, Zit be
faith that euer leadis reason captiue, and brin
gis it in obedience,quhen it apperis to improue the votd of god , he collectit the contrare,
that

Genes.22.

Genes.17.

S. Paul.
2. Cor. 10.

that it vas gude to obey the commandiment
of god vith al reuerence, sen he vas abil to rase
vp Isaac agane quik out of the ass of his bodie efter he var consumit vith fyre : And vnles men follou this example of Abraham in the
hie mistereis of our faith, thay vil neuer haue
tranquillitie of mynd.

OF THE SACRIFICE OF THE
MESSE. Chap. XIIII.

M.

A Pprouis thou the institution of that Idolatrie,
quhilk the Papistis callis the Messe , seing thair
is na mention maid thairof in the vrittin vord?
B. I acknaulege the offering of Christis bodie vnder the forme of breid and of his blude   *Luc. 22*
vnder the forme of vyne , as ane propiciator
sacrifice for the quick and the deid , as he deit   *Rom.14*
for saluation of thame bayth, quhilk is callit
the Messe, for this vord Missah signifeing ane   *Deut.16*
voluntar offering as ve reid in the 16 of Deut
is retenit be the Christian Doctors, lyk as sindrie vthers, Alleluia, osanna, Amen. &c.
M. *Hou prouis thou that Christ offerit his body in*
the latter suppar?
B. It is manifest be the Euangelist S. Luc. quhair our saluiour commandit S. Petir and S.   *S. Luc. 22.*
Iohne his Disciplis to prepare ane hous quha-
ir he sould eit the Paschal lamb , quhilk [as is
is thair testefeit] vas offerit before it vas eitin,   *Exod.12*
according to the institution of god as ve reid

F

in the tuelf chap of exod. Quhairfore it behouit our saluiour Iesus Christ to eat the Paschal lambe vpon ane Altar, insafar as itvas ane
figure, maist lyuelie representing the offering of his bodie and eiting of the same, that
the treuth micht be correspondent to the figure, it vas necessar that Christis bodie (als re-
alie eitin in the latter suppar vnder the forme
of breid, as the body of the lambe) sould be
first offerit vnder the same forme vpon the Altar quhairupon before vas offerit the body of
the lambe, being the figure nou aboleist be
substitution of the treuth. Insafar then as thir
foisaidis be manifest, It is necessar that the
euangelical preistis hauing the Auctoritie of
Christ, and assistance of the halie ghaist, vpon
altaris offer Christis bodie and blude, quhilk
vas sched vpon the Croce for the synnis of
Hebr. 13. monie. for as vryttis S. Paul, ve haue ane altar
of the quhilk it is not leisum to thame to eit
quha seruis in the tabernacle meaning of this
sacrifice, considering thair is na vther sacrifice
except this quhairof it is not lesum to thame
to eit quha seruis in the tabernacle. In lykma-
Genes. 14. ner ve reid hou Melchisedec the heich preist
of God did offer breid and vyne as ane figure
Psal. 109. of this sacrifice, sua Christ being ane preist efter the ordore of Melchisedec, it behouit that
he offerit ane clene and vnbludie sacrifice or
ellis the figure had not bene fulfillit be the veritie. Nou schau me quhen he did offer ane
vnbludie sacrifice efter the ordor of Melchise-

dec, gif he did not offer it in the latter suppar.
Sua ze denying this tak auay the eternal preistheid of Christ efter the ordour of Melchisedec, and consequentlie makis the vord of God,
and prophecie spokin of him to be alluterlie
fals. For confirmation heirof I may produce
to zou the hail ancient fathers as, Iræne quha
sayis that Christ in his latter suppet did institute the sacrifice of the neu testament, the
quhilk the kirk hauing ressauit from the
Apostlis offeris euerie quhair vnto God. Arnobius vryttand vpon the hundreth nyne
psalme sayis that the sacrifice efter the ordor
of Melchisedec, quhilk vas institute be Christ
i the suppar is nou offerit thruch the hail yard.
And. S. Cyprian, Melchisedec sayis he, offerit breid and vyne, quhilk sacrifice our saluiour
did fulfill in his latter suppar, quhen he offerit
that quhilk vas presfigurat be Melchisedec, to
vit, his bodie and blude. And. S. Hierom in
his epistle to Marcella: Gif thou vil cum (sayis
he) to Ierusalem, thair vil thou se the Citie of
Melchisedec, quha in prefiguration of the sa-
crificie quhilk is nou offerit be the Christianis
in the bodie and blude of the Lord, did offer
breid and vyne. S. Augustine vryttand vpon
the threttie thrie psalme: The preisteid (sayis
he) efter the ordor of Aaron is tane auay, and
nou euerie quhair thair is ane sacrifice offerit
efter the ordor of Melchisedec. In lik maner
the Prophet Malachie did forespeik of this
sacrifice saying: In euerie place fra the sone ry-

*Ireneus
lib. 4. cotr.
Valent.
cap. 32.*

*Arnob. in
psal. 109.*

*Cyprian.
ep. 1. c. 9.*

*S. Hieron.
ad Mar-
cel.*

*August.
in psal. 33.*

*Malachie
1.*

sing to the going to of the same, thair salbe
offerit to my name ane clene sacrifice, The
quhilk according to the interpretatione of
the haill ancient fathers is vnderstand of the
sacrifice of the bodie and blude of Iesus Christ,
quhilk is offerit euerie quhair. And I vald desire zou to schau me of quhat vther sacrifice
the prophet could meane: he could not meane of the sacrifice of prayer, becaus that sacrifice vas before in the auld testament, sua
that it could not be ane sacrifice of the neu
testament: And the sacrifice of payer to pretermit that it isnot properliecallit anesacrifice:
according to the lau of nature, it man be necessarlie in al religion, sua it had bene na prophecie to haue forespokin that sik ane sacrifice sould haue bene amang the Christians.And
ze zour seluis teachis that al our prayers, and
quhatsumeuir varkis ve do, ar syn in the ficht
of God and vnclene in thame selfis, sua the
prophet could not forespeik euin according
to zour meaning, of payers or ony vther varkis quhilk sould proceid of vs, nor zit could
he mean of the sacrifice of Christon the Croce, becaus that sacrifice vas offerit onlie in ane
place, and this sould be offerit euerie quhair:
Then necessarlie ar ze constranit to acknaulege ane vther sacrifice efter the ordor of Melchisedec, baith according to the Doctors of
the synagogue of the auld testament before
the cumming of Christ,and al thame that hes
flurischit in ony eage sen Christ, as Iustine

Iustine

martyr, Iræne, Tertullian, Arnob. Bafile, Na-
zianzene, Chrifoftome, Hylare, Ierome, Ambrofe, Auguftine and the reft, the quhilk is fa
cleir and euident, that zour maifter and Idole
Iohne Caluin confeffis that the hail ancient
Doctors ar aganis him, and that thay interpreit the prophecie euin as ve do, gif ze haue
red him ze can not misknau his vordis. [Ar-
ripiunt tritam iftam Malachiæ fententiam, In
omni loco offeretur nomini meo oblatio mu-
da, obiiciunt locum iftum fic exponi ab Iræ-
næo : oblationem Melchifedec fic tractari ab
Athanafio, Ambrofio, Auguftino, & Arno-
bio : Breuiter refponfum fit, veteres iftos fcri-
ptores tam ridicule per panem interpretari
corpus Chrifti, vt ratio & veritas cogat nos
diffentire] Thay tak for thair defence this oft
vfed fentence of Malachie, In al place thair fal
be ane clene facrifice offered to me, Thay obiect that this place is fua exponit be Irenæus,
Thay fay that the oblatione of Melchifedec is
itraitted in fik maner(that is applyit to the efta
blifhing of the mefs) be Athanafius, Ambro-
fius, Auguftinus, and Arnobius, lat thame haue this anfuer in feu vordis, That the ancient
yreittaris fua fulishlie interpreitis the breid to
be the body of Chrift, that reafon and the
treuth compellis vs to difagrie from thame.
And a litil efter he addis : that thay var al
iniutious to the Paffion of Chrift, and concludis on this maner. [Quod ad veteres atti-
net, non eft quod in eorum gratiam ab infle-

Mart. dia
lo. cu try-
phone.
Irene li. 4.
cotra Va-
lent.ca.32.
Tertul. de
corona mil
arnob. in
pfal. 109.
Bafil de
fpiritu an-
cto. Na-
ziazen in
carminib.
Calu.li.de
reform. ec-
clef.
Chryfoft.
in 9. ad
heb. Hyl.
8. de Trin.
Ierom ad
Marcel,
Ambrofe
de facram.
lib.6.Aug.
lib.17.de
ciust.cap.
20.

xibili Dei verbo recedamus.] As tuiching the ancient Doctors, thair is na caus quhairfore ve sould pas from the inflexibil vord of God for thair pleasure. Considder the proudnes and arrogance of this vnhappie and ignorant man, quha dar preser his auin daft iugement in interpretation of goddis vord, to sa mony learnit and halie men, zea to the interpretatió of the vniuersal kirk of god. Zea sirris quha assistis I desire zou to iuge, gif ze think that I sould rather follou the vordis of the scripture, interpreit be sa monie learnit and goddie fathers before, and efter the cúming of Christ, to the interpretation of ane filthie Sodomeit, quha in the hail progres of his lyf hes neuer schauin ony signe or demonstration that he vas mouit be the spreit of god, bot manifestlie hes euer declarit that the spreit of Sathan did rigne into him, as being the author of bludeschedding, of breking of all halie lauis and ordonnancis, pulling doun of kirkis, and vther halie placis, buyldit to the honor of god, of inducing subiectis to oppres and douthrau thair maisters and sik vther horribil crymes.

M. Gif I vald grant for disputations caus, that our maister Christ offerit his body at his latter suppar, hou vil thou proue, that the pastores succeiding sould offer the same inlykuyse? Becaus in the epistle to the hebreuis ve reid, that he hes maid thame persyt for euer, be ane oblation quha ar sanctifeit, for gif euerie preist offerit Christü bodie, it is necessar to grant pluralitie of sacrificis.

Paul heb.
10.

B. That the preiſtis of the Euãgel ſucceiding to the Apoſtlis ſould offer Chriſtis glorious body, it is manifeſt be his expres cõmandimẽt: Do ze this in remẽberance of me. Quhairin is includit the hail inſtitution of this ſacrifice to be continuit in his kirk to his cũming to iugement, as S. Paul him ſelf, interpreitis thir vordis: hou oft ze ſal eit this breid, and drink this coup, ze ſal declare the death of the lord vnto his cũming. As to the teſtimonie of the ſcripture quhilk ze cite aganis me, ze appeir to miſknaü the meaning of S. Paul in his e-piſtle to the Hebreuis, quha from the end of the ſacrificis of the auld lau, and the imperfe-ction of the ſame, prouis that the benefeit of the Meſſias cõſiſtis cheiflie in that, that Chriſt being God and man, as ane perfyt mediator hes reconcelit the varld be his death, and de-ſtroyit the varkis of the deuil, to vit ſyn and iniquitie, quhilk is ſa perfyt of the ſelf that the force and ſtrenth heirof abydis continual-lie vithout onie iteration of his death, vthe-ruyſe it behouit him to de ofter nor anis, and his bludie ſacrifice to be iterat, lyk as var the ſacrifecis of the auld lau, quhilk proceidit of thair imperfection and in this mening ſayis S. Paul, That Chriſt be ane oblation hes maid thame perfyt for euer quha ar ſanctifeit, the quhilk is gatherit baith of the expres vordis of S. Paul him ſelf, and of the interpretation of the vniuerſal kirk of God.

Nou to cũ to zonr obiectiõ, I anſuer maiſt

S. Math. 26.

S. Paull. I.

Cor. II.

S. Paul Heb. 10

directlie that be the onlie sacrifice of the Croce, the ranson for our synnis is sufficientlie
payit, that ve mister na vther oblation, or sacrifice to pay the ráson of our synnis to God.
And gif the sacrifice of the Messe var offerit
to that end, it vald be iniurious to the death
and passion of Christ, Bot suppose our ranson
be sufficientlie payit be the said sacrifice of the
Croce, zit it is necessar, that it be applyit vnto
vs, or ellis as I haue said, it vald auail vs na
thing: thairfoir the sacrifice of the mess is na
thing ellis bot ane lyuelie and perfyt representation of the sacrifice of the Croce, thruch
the quhilk the strenth and verteu thairof is
zet and pourit in our Saulis, as testefeis S. Paul
hou oft ze eit this breid, and drink this coup,
ze sal declare the death of the Lord vnto his
cúming. And Chryso. exponing that same place quhilk ze haue allegeit for zou, makis ane
obiection to him self in this maner: Quhat
then (sayis he) haue ve na sacrifice? he ansueris,
That ve offer that same self thing quhilk
Christ offerit; Bot ve offer it not as he did, bot
in rememberance or commemoration of his
death and passió: I in lykmaner do, is speik the
hail ancient fathers, as I haue schauin before,
Quhairof ve may se, that this place of scripture allegeit be zou seruis na thing at al to zour
purpose, and that al zour reasonis and argumentis tendis to na vther end, bot to aboleis
al rememberance of the passió of Christ. And
this cheiflie quhilk is maist perfyt and proffi-
tabill of al. Quhairin ze declare zour seluis the

Chrysost. in
cap. 10. epi.
ad Heb.

Disciplis of the Antichrist quhais cheif laubor, as is propheceit be Daniel, salbe to aboleis the continual sacrifice of the kirk: quhy ar ze sa ingrait vnto Christ that ze vil not represent his death in offering of this sacrifice commemoratiue, as he commandit in the latter suppar, and as the kirk hes euer done to this day for ane maist certane confirmatione of the treu fayth in the Messias and saluiour of the hail yarld, and oppin protestatione befoir the haill varld that Christ deed, and sched his blud for the redemptione of synnaris, and thairfoir as vreittis the halie doctor Prosper vpone that passage of scripture [Vox sanguinis fratris tui clamat ad me de terra, the voce of the bluid of thy brother cryis to me out of the earhe. Cayn figurabat Iudaicum populum terrenis desideriis inhiantem : Abel Christum pastorem ouium ab eo populo occisum : nullus iam ambigit Christianus cuius sacrum sanguinem omnis terra excipiens clamet Amen, hoc est verum : vt neganti Iudæo quod occiderit Christū, recte à Deo dicatur, vox sanguinis fratris tui clamat ad me de terra] Cayn præfigurat the people of the Ieuis, hauand thair hairtis intent on vardlie desyris. Abel præfigurat Christ the pastore of the scheip slane be that people: Nou na Christiane man douttis quhais halie blude al the earth resauand Cryis Amen, that is treu, sua that to ane Ieu denyand that he hes slane Christ, it may be ansuerit be God maist instlie, the blud of thy brother

Daniel. 12

Prosper de prædictionibus parte I. cap. 6.

cryis to me out of the erthe, quhy spulzie ze
the Chriſtianis of this maiſt ſtrenthie argument aganis the Ieuis and the Antichriſt, that
Chriſt hes deed, Becaus he hes left vs in his teſtament his blude quhilk vas ſched vpone the
erth, for ane infallibill argument of his deth,
and bitter paſſion? And quhy aboleis ze ane
gret part of the office of ane perfyt mediator
frō Chriſt, cōſidering the deutie of ane perfyt
reconciliator and peax makar is not onlie to
pay the ranſon of thame that ar in captiuitie,
bot mairouer to apply the ſaid payment, and
reconciliation vnto thame? Bot ze vil that
Chriſt haue onlie payit the ranſon, and not
applyit the ſame vnto vs. The vniuerſal kirk
hes euer acknaulegit Chriſt as ane perfyt mediator, that not onlie he hes payit the ranſon
for vs, bot alſo that he hes applyit the ſaid
ranſon to vs, cheiflie be the ſacramentis and
halie ſacrifice of the Meſſe, for the preiſtis in
this behalf ar onlie his miniſters, and he the
cheif preiſt and ſacrificator him ſelf, as amang
Chryſoſtó. vthers vryttis the maiſt learnit Doctor Chri-
hom. 83. in ſoſtome: Qui ſanctificat & tranſmutat ipſe eſt,
Matthe. nos miniſtrorum tenemus ordinem, that is, he
(mening Chriſt) quha ſanctefeis and chaingeis
to vit the elementis, ve ar in the rank of his
miniſters and ſeruandis. And in this reſpect he
is callit ane preiſt for euer efter the ordor of
Melchiſedec. ſua that the ſacrifice of the Meſſe
makis vs participant of the fructis and bene-
fetis of the gret pouar and efficacie of the ſacrifice of the Croce. Quhairfore ze ſould be

eſchamit to deceaue the people ſa rudelie
ſaying that this ſacrifice dois obſcure the benefeit of the ſacrifice of the Croce. Bot as al
zour doctrein proceidis of ignorance, ſua dois
this pairt of it. Quharfore I pray zou opin
zour eyis in tyme cūming, or at the leiſt deſiſt
to leadythers thevay quhilk ze knau not zour
ſeluis, incace ze being blind, fall baith togither in the pit of condemnation.

*M.   Gif the Meſſe be ane ſacrifice propiciator for the
quik and the dead inſtitute be Chriſt, quhat is the
caus that the Euangeliſtis, and Apoſtlis makis not
als oft mention of Chriſtis ſacrifice vith his Diſciplis,
vnder the formes of breid and vyne, as of his ſuppar?*
B.   Thay not onlie mak als oft mention of
his ſacrifice as of his ſuppar, bot far ofter. For
the inſtitution of Chriſt at his latter ſuppar
contenis the formes of ſpeiking, quhilk pro- ["] *Luc. 22.*
perlie pertenis to ane ſacrifice, as (This is my
body quhilk is geuin or offerit for zou. This
is my blude quhilk is ſched for zou) Mairouer *Heb. 7.*
it is manifeſt be the Doctrene of S. Paull, that
baith the ſacrifice according to the ordor of
Aaron, and according to the ordor of Melchiſedec quhilk vas diuers, for the ane had beiſtis
that var ſlane, the vther breid and vine, var figuris of Chriſtis ſacrifice. Quhairfore be reaſon he ſubſtitute the treuth, and aboleiſt all figuris, he behouit in his ſacrifice be the omnipotent pouar of the halie ghaiſt, turne the
breid and vyne in his body and blude: vtheruyſe it had bene bot the ſame figure, quhilk

vas before quhen Melchifedec maid oblation.
For na religion, nor lau can be vithout facrifice it being the cheif vorfchipping of God,
fua that the auld being chaingeit in the neu,
it is neceffar that in the place of the auld facrificis, ane neu facrifice fould fucceid, quhilk
fould left fa lang as the lau leftis. Thairfore S.

Aug. li. 17
de Ciuit.
Dei c. 20.

Auguftin fayis that in place of al the facrificis
of the auld teftament this facrifice of the body and blude of Chrift efter the ordor of Melchifedec fucceidis. And the halie vryttar Cy-

Cyprian.
de can. do.

prian, The Capernaitis (fayis he) beleuit that
thay fould haue eitin the body of Chrift in
fik maner that thay fould haue confum it the
fame, quhilk vas ane thing impoffibill. Becaus
it vas neceffar, that as the lau of Chrift fould
indure to the end of the varld, fua it fould haue ane perpetual facrifice quhilk could not be,
gif his bodie and blude had bene anis confu-

Leo. ferm.
7. de paff.
dons.

mit. And Leo vryttis that Chrift in the mean-
tyme quhen the Ieuis var thinking to betray
him, did ordane the facrifice of his bodie and
blude, to the end that the Chriftian religion
fould haue ane perpetual facrifice, quhilk it
micht offer to God. I micht cite zou manie
vthers gif I pleifit of the ancient vryttaris to
the fame purpofe, var not I feir it fould turne
to zour damnation, quha vil trou na thing
bot that quhilk ze find in zour maifter and
idol Iohne Caluin. Quhairfore it is neceffar
that the fucceffors of Chriftis halie Apoftlis
haue ane outuart facrifice vith ceremoneis,

contenand the treuth and licht for the schaddouis of the auld lau. Becaus as ve reid in the Actis of the Apostlis, the primitiue kirk had thair liturgia, quhilk Erasmus (quhais interpretation ze imbrace) exponis to be ane sacrifice, for thair it is vrittin λειτουργέντων δὲ αὐτῶ τῶ κυρίω: That is quhen thay var making sacrifice to the Lord. *Act.13*

And S. Augustin exponing the beginning of the secund chap. of the first epist. of Paul to Timothie, sayis that the vordis, deprecatiõs, obsecrations, interpellations, and thankisgeuing ar referrit to the diuers thingis quhilk ar done in the sacrifice of the Messe. As to the prayers quhilk precedis the consecration of Christis bodie and blude, to the prayers quhilk follouis thairefter, and the Benediction quhilk is geuin to the people: I knau that zour maister Caluin callis the interpretation of S. Augustin, ane bairnlie exposition. Bot I beleue Caluin vas als gret ane barne as S. Augustin. Chrisostome, Basile, and vther ancient vrytters hes left vnto vs the formis of the auld liturgeis quhilk var vsit amang the greikis, and arvsit this day in the Catholik kirk, quhairin al thingis ar to be fundin that pertenis to the sacrifice of the Messe, alsueill concerning the nature and substance of the sacrifice, as concerning the ceremoneis quhilk ar ordanit to the reuerence of the same, and to excitat the deu deuotion of the people thairto, quhilk ar not of lait dayis inuentit be the Ca- *Augu. ep.*

Caluin in 2. ca. & 1. ad Timoth

Leiturg. Chrysost. Leiturg. Basil.

tholik and Romane kirk, bot euer sen the beginning hes bene vsit be all treu Christianis: Quhairof S. Paul him self makis mention: Cætera cum venero disponam. The rest I sall put to ordor at my cuming, vpon the quhilk place S. Augustin vryttis in this maner: Becaus it vas ouer lang to haue vrittin al thingis that sould be in the ministration of this sacrifice, the Apostle S. Paul differis that to his auin cuing to the Corinthianis. Zour maister Caluin vill say that S. August. in this point did raue, as before he said he vas ane bairne; Bot I becaus I am ane fule, vil hald me daft vith S. Augustin, and sa monie halie Doctors of the kirk of Christ Iesus.

M. Hou can thou deny bot the Ceremoneis of the Messe ar tane from the Idolatrie of the gentelis, for euin as ze say, Ite Missa est, sua the Greikis concludit thair sacrifice uith thir vordis λαοῖς ἄφεσις *quhilk is al ane thinge, to pretermit manie vthers quhairof sum of our faithful brethren hes vrittin at gretar lenth.*

B. In this obiection as in manie vthers, ze declair zour auin ignorance, for it follouis not that becaus siclyk thingis hes bene vsurpit be the Gentelis, the Christien men thairfore hes borrouit thame fra thair vse and accustume, for as vryttis Iustime Martyr, Tertullian, and vther ancient fathers, the gentilis vsit to baptise thame quha come to thair mistereis and to mark thame in the forrer, And also to mak ane sacrifice of breid and

1. Cor. 11.
"
"
August.
Episto. 18.

Iustin
Martyr
dialo cum
Tryphon.
Tertul. de
cor. mil.

vyne,zit I beleue ze vil not say that the Christianis hes ressauit thair baptisme or sacrifice
quhilk thay offer in thair kirkis, from thame.
The greikis feinzeit, Campos Eliseos, for the
gude efter this lyf, and loca tartarea, for the
vickit: sall ve say thairfore that the Christianis
hes learnit of thame thay thingis quhilk thay
beleue of the glore of Paradise, and paynis of
hel: The Gentilis had templis, preistis, and
sacrificeis, and zit thair vil na man be sa fulish
as to think that the Christianis hes learnit to
haue sik thingis at thame. Ze se to quhat end
and impietie this zour argument dois tend,
that is, that not onlie ve reiect the ceremoneis of the Messe, bot ve refuse lykuyse to beleue thay thingis quhilk the Christianis tei-
chis of Baptisme, of heauin and hel, to the quhilk infidelitie ze haue brocht manie in Scotland alreddie be the preaching of zour neu
Euagel: Gif ze had red the ancient vrytters
ze vald haue learnit, hou that the Deuil, quha
aspyris euer to be lyk vntoGod, desyris maist
cheislie to be vorschippit in that sam self maner, quhairin he seis god vorschippit, that is
vith lyk ceremoneis and sacrificis, as maist
cleirlie testefeis Tertullian. [Diabolus res *Tertul. de*
sacramentorum in Idolorum mysteriis æmu- *scrip.hære*
latur, tingit ipse qnosdam vtique credentes
& fideles suos, signat in frontibus milites su- "
os, celebrat panis oblationem, habet & vir-
gines, habet & continentes, Denique in Romanis illis Sacerdotalibus officiis, insignibus,

& priuilegiis morositatem illam Iudeæ imitatus est.] The deuil sayis he lauboris to haue thaj thingis quhilk ar contenit in the sacramentis, In the mystereis of the Idollis, he veschis or baptesis sum as his beleuaris and faithful Disciplis, he markis his suldartis in the forret, he celebratis the offering of breid and vyne, he hes virginis, he hes continent personis: to beschoit he hes follouit that cummersum number of the Iudical ceremoneis, in thaj officeis, bages, ad priuilegis of the Romane preistis, meaning of thame quha var institute be Numa Pompilius. And S. Augustin maist learnitlie ansueris to zour obiection that the Ceremonie or sacrifice is not euil, becaus it is vsurpit be the gentelis and infidellis, bot becaus it is vsurpit be thame to ane vrang and peruersit end, to vit for the honoring of thair Idollis, sua that the self same thing being applyit to the honor and seruice of god, is gude and louabill, [Qui Christianas literas vtriusque testamenti legunt, non hoc culpant in sacrilegis ritibus paganorum quod construant templa, & instituant sacerdotia, & faciant sacrificia, sed quod hæc Idolis & dæmonibus exhibent]. Thay quha reidis the Christian vryttingis of the neu and auld testament, reprouis not this in the sacrilegious ritis of the paganis, that thay big kirkis and institutis preistis, and makis sacrificis, bot becaus thay do all thir thingis to honor Idollis and the Deueillis. And in the same place.

August. epist.49

cc.

ce. [Cum hæc exhibentur Deo secundum "
eius inspirationem atque Doctrinâ, vera reli- "
gio est: Cum autem demonibns secundum
eorum impiâ constitutionem, noxia superstitio.] Quhen thir thingis ar geuin to god, or
dedicat to his seruice, according to his inspira-
tion and doctrine, it is treu religion, Bot quhen thay ar dedicat to the Deuillis accordig to
thair vicked constitutiõ, it is verie hurtful superstition. And S. Ierome, [Sicut ergo virgini-   *Hiero.lib.
tati veræ nõ preiudicat imitatio virginû dia-   *2, contra*
bolicarũ, nec veris Ieiuniis, Coßorum, Isidis, &   *Iouin.*
Cybeles ; & sicut signa quæ faciebat Moyses "
imitabantur signa Aegyptiorum, sed non erãt "
in veritate, ita per omnia quæ in æmulatio- "
nem Dei facit diabolus, non nostræ Religio-
nis superstitio, sed nostra arguitûr negligentia
id facere nolentium, quod bonum esse etiam
sæculi homines non ignorant:] Thairfoir as
the Imitatione of the Virginis of the Deuill,
preiudgesna thing treu virginitie, nor zit the
fastingis quhilk var institute in the names of
the Idolis Coßi, Isis, and Cybele, And as the
miraclis of the Aegiptianis, var lyk the miraclis that Moysesvrocht, bot var not miraclis in
verie deid, Euin sua our religione is not conuict as superstitious be all thay thingis quhilk
the Deuil dois throuche æmulatione of God,
bot rather our negligence is rebuke d becaus
ve vill not do that quhilk the men of this
varld misknauisnocht to be gude: Sua ze may
persaue hou vane this zour obiectione is

G

quhilk ze setfurth to the pure pepill as ane
maistsure and infallibil argument to vithdrau
thame from the halie sacrifice of the Mess.

OF THE PRAYING IN LATI-
NE.   Chap.   xv.

M.

Giff the Mess in substance aud ceremoneis contene the maner hou God suld be vorshipped institut be Christ, as the Papistis sayis, quhy say thay
not thair Messis in the vulgar tounge that the simpil
pepill quha vnderstandis not latine may be edifeit
thairbie: for it vas bot ane mocKing of God that ignorant pepill sat done befoir god babling in ane strange
langage tha thingis quhilk thay vndirstud not, seing
it is vreittin, gif I pray vith my toung, my spreit
prayis, bot my mynd vantis the fruit: quhat than?
sal I pray in spreit? bot I sall pray in my mynd also:
And hou sall he quha suppleis the place of the Idiot,
ansuer Amen to thy benedictioue, gif he vndirstand
the not?

S. Paul. 1.
Cor. 14.

B. Thair be tua Kynd of prayeris in the kirk,
the ane is priuat, quhilk euerie man sayis be
him self: the vthir is publik quhilk the preistis sayis in name of the hail kirk: As to the
priuat prayeris, na Catholik denyis, bot it is
verie expedient that euerie man pray in his
auin toung, to the end he vndirstand that quhilk he sayis, and that thairbie the interior
prayer of the hairt may be the mair valkinnit,
and conseruit the bettir, and gif onie man

pray in ane vther toung, it is alſo expedient
that he vnderſtand the mening of the vordis
at the leſt. For the quhilk cauſ in the Catholik kirk the parentis or godfatheris ar obleiſt,
to learne thame quhom thay hald in baptiſme
the formes of prayeris, and Beleif, and in-
ſtruct thame ſufficientlie thairin, ſua that thay
vndirſtād the ſame: Albeit the principal thing
quhilk god requiris is the hairt, that ſuppois
he quha prayis vndirſtand nocht perfytlie the
vordis quhilk he ſpeikis, zit god quha lukis
in the hairt, vill nocht lat his prayer be in vane. As to the publik prayeris of the kirk, it is
not neceſſar that the pepill vndirſtand thame,
becaus it is nocht the pepill quha prayis, bot
the preiſtis in the name of the hail kirk, and
it is aneuche that thay aſſiſt be deuotione liſt-
and vp thair myndis to god or ſaying thair
auin priuat oraeſonis, and that be thair deuotione thay may be maid participant of the
kirk: As in the ſynagogue of the Ieuis, the
peopill kneu not, quhat all thay cerimoneis
ſignifeit, quhilk vas keipit be the preiſtis and
vtheris in offering of thair ſacrifices, and vther
vorſhipping of God, and zit thay did aſſiſt vnto thame, ze ſum of the preiſtis thame ſelfis
miſkneu the ſignificatione of thir cerimoneis: Than gif it vas aneuche to the pepill to
vndirſtand that in ſik ane ſacrifice conſiſted
the vorſhipping of god, ſuppois thay had not
ſua cleir ane vndirſtanding of euerie thing
that vas done thairin, ſua in the catholik kirk,

quhen the people affiftis to the facrifice of the Mefs; thay acknaulege that thairbie god is vorfhippit, and that it is inftitute for the remembrance of Chriftis death, and paffione, Albeit thay vndirftãd nocht the Latine toung zit thay ar not deftitut of the vtilitie and fruit thairof: And it is nocht vithout greit caus that as in the infcriptione and titil quhilk Pilat fixed vpone the croce of Chrift Iefus, thit thre toungis var vrittin latine, Greik, and Hebreu, fua in the facrifice, and publik prayeris of the kirk, thay ar cheiflie retenit, for the conferuatione of vnitie in the kirk, and nationis amãg thame felfis: for gif al thingis var turnit in the propir lãgage of euerie cuntrey, na man vald ftudie to the latine toung, and thairbie al com municatione amangis Chriftiane pepil vald fchortlie be tane auay, and thaireftir greit barbaritie infeu. Mairatour fik publique prayeris and feruice ar keipit mair perfytlie in thair auin integritie vithout al corruptione: for gif ane natione vald eik, or pair onie thĩg, that vald be incontinent remarkit, and reprouit be vther nationis, quhilk culd not be, gif euerie natione had al thai thingis turnit in the auin propir langage, as ze may fe be experience, gif ze vald confer the prayeris of zour deformit kirkis, togidder vith the innumerabil trãflationis of the pfalmes, quhilk ar chaingit according to euerie lãgage in the quhilk thay ar turnit. It is not than vithout greit caus, and ane fpecial inftinctione of the halie Ghaift

that thir toungis foirspokin hes bene retened
as thay vil be retenit to the end of the varld.
And quhen the Ieuis fall imbrace the Euágel,
than fal the facrifice, and vther publik prayeris be in the hebreu toung, according to that
quhilk I faid befoir, that on the Croce of
Chrift thaj thrie toungis onlie var vrittin, to
fignifie that the kirk of Chrift fuld vfe thay
thre toungis cheiflie in his vorshipping, as
the neu, and auld teftament ar in thir thre toungis in greitaft authoritie amangis al pepill.
Nou to cū to the firft pairt of zour obiection,
ze proue na thing except onlie that he quha
prayis fuld nocht be aluterlie rude or ignorát
of that toung in thequhilk he prayis, quhilk I
do alreddie grát to zóu, As to the vthir pairt of
zour argument, I confeſſ indeid that that place aucht to be vndirftand of the publique
prayeris of the kirk, bot zit it feruis nathing
to zour purpofe, bot is rather repugnant to
the fame, and prouis that the cōmon feruice of the kirk vas nocht than in the vulgar
langage quhilk euerie man vndirftude, bot in
ane vthir langage quhilk vas nocht fua commone to euerie man. For the vndirftanding
of this I reid in Chryfoftom, and vther anciẻt
vryttaris that amangis vther giftis quhilk vas
in the primitiue kirk, thair vas alfo the gift of
prayer, quhilk cōfifted in this, that quhen the
Chriftianis var gathered togidder, thay quha
var indeued vith this gift kneu quhat thing
vas maift expediẻt to be afked at God, quhilk

Chryfoft.
in 14. prio.
ad cor.

thay craued in name of the haill kirk. Nou becaus it vas expediét to the haill kirk to vndirstand that quhilk thay prayed for, S. Paul desyris him quha reſſauis this gift, to craue a God the grace of the interpretatióe of the ſame, for the quhilk caus he ſayis that he quha ſpekis vith ane toung, he ſpekis to God, ád nocht to men, ád eftiruart, ᴎe quha propheceis is gretar nor he quha ſpekis vith toungis except that he interpreit him ſelf, that the kirk may be edifeit. Nou ſen this gift of prayer remanis nocht zit in the kirk, bot all thingis quhilk ve craue of God ar put in certane formes of oraiſonis, it is nocht neceſſar that he quha prayis in name of the kirk, declair his prayer at that tyme to the pepil, Bot it is aneuche that it be declairit be ordinar ſermonis and exhortationis, and vther ſik menis, to the effect that the pepill be inſtructed quhat ar thay thingis quhilk the kirk in hir publique and ordinar prayeris crauis at God, quhilk is done at all tymes in the Catholique kirk. As in the tyme of Paſche the pepill knauis that all the prayeris tendis to louing and thankeſgeuing to god for the benefeit of the redemptione of the varld. At Vitſonday, that the praying tédis to the inuocatione of the halie ſpirit, and ſua furth of the reſt of the ſeaſonis of the hail zeir. Nou that S. Paul forbiddis nocht the publique ſeruice of the kirk to be done in ane toung quhilk is nocht vulgare to the haill pepill, ze vill eſilie vndirſtand gif ze pleis to note diligentlie

S. Paull.
1. Cor. 14.

this diſtinctione that almaiſt in euerie natione thair vſis to be ane vulgar toúg quhilk eue
rie man ſpeikis, and ane vther toung quhilk is
nocht commone to all bot to the maiſt learned, as teſtifeis S. Hierom in his commentaris
on the epiſtle to the Galatianis that the Galatianis had thair auin vulgar toung, and by
that the greik toung, and throuche the haill
Orient albeit thair vas ane greit nomber of
vulgar toungis, zit the greik toung vas commone to thame all. And Beda in the deſcri-
ptione of Britanie vryttis that thair is fyue
toungis in it, the Ingliſhe toung, The Britonis
toung, the Scottis toung, the pichtis toung,
and the latine toung, not that the latene
toung vas vulgare to onie pepill of Britanie,
bot becaus it vas commone to thame all: and
for that caus it is callit thair toung: Sua Sanct
Paull quhē he vill that the ſeruice of the kirk
ſuld nocht be in ane ſtrange toung, he menis
that it ſuld nocht be in ane toung quhilk is
alluterlie ſträge and barbar, bot in ane toung
quhilk is nocht aluyſe vnknauin to the pepill, as throuche the haill Orient vas the greik
toung, and the hail Occidēt the latene toung:
The quhilk interpretatione is gathered maiſt
cleirlie, becaus that euin in S. Paulis dayes
throuche all the Orient the publique prayeris
and ſeruice of the kirk, vas in the greik toúg
Albeit thair vas innumerabill vulgar toungis
amangis ſa monie pepill, and thair is na probabilitie that euerilk cuntrey did thane turne

S. Hierom cont. in ep. ad Gal.

Beda in deſc. Brit.

G iiij

the scripture quhilk vsed to be red in the publik seruice of the kirk in thair auin vulgar
toung, not zit can thair be onie argument
produced that sua hes bene done. In lyk maner in the Occident sen the fayth vas first plá-
ted, ye find na vther toung to haue bene vsed
in the publique prayeris of the kirk bot the latene toung, Albeit euerie natione by the latene toung quhilk is commone to all, haue
thair auin vulgar toungis. And S. Augustine
Auguſt. testifeis that in his dayes throuch al Afrik the
epiſt.11. commone seruice of the kirk vas in the latene toung, and hou be the changeing of ane
vord quhilk befoir vas accustumed ane greit
sklander, and tumult of the pepill did vpryse.
Mairatour quhen S. Paull sayis, he that suppleis the place of the Idiot hou sall he ansuer
Amen, to thy benedictione, gif he vndirstand
the nocht, he schauis that sic benedictiós vas
not accustumed to be in the vulgar toúg cósi-
dering S Paul callis him ane Idiot quha vnderstandis onlie his auin vulgar toung, And
o vnact requiris, or rather supponis that in the ser-
...ls only uice of the kirk thair suld be ane vthir to sup-
owne plie the place of the Idiote, that is that suld
par ...nne haue farder vndirstanding and intelligence
ne idco4 of that toung in the quhilk the seruice of the
...t oy s kirk is said. Bot giff the seruice had bene do-
... ne in the vulgar toung, thair mistered na man
to haue suppleed the place of the Idiot: Than
Sanct Pauli schauis maist cleirlie that sic seruice vas not exercised in ane vulgar toung,

bot in ane vther quhilk vas not commone
to the haill pepil, sik as is the latine toung, as
said is, in Scotland, and throuch the hail Occident: Albeit it vas not in the contrare ex-
tremitie strange, or barbaruse. Bot sen ze haue
euer mair this place in zour mouthe, and dissa-
uis thairbie the pure peopil, I am constranit
to schau that in zour neu deformed kirk it is
alluterlie peruerted be zou, and the rest of the
ministeris, becaus quhair the greik and latene
text hes, He quha suppleis the place of ane
Idiote hou sall he say Amen, zour ministeris
of Geneua in monie of thair Bybilis, hes turnit
it maist deceatfullie and malitiouslie, he that
is ane Idiott hou sall he say Amen: euin as gif
thair var na difference betuix ane Idiot and
him quha suppleis the place of ane Idiot.
Mairouer the benediction to the quhilk S.
Paull sayis Amen, suld be ansuered, is nauyse
practised in zour deformet kirkis and nather
zour Idiotis, nor thay that suppleis the place
of zour Idiotis Ansueris Amen, as Sanct Paul
vill haue ansuered, bot ze hane turnit Amen in
So be it, quhilk is plane repugnant to his mening, and the practeise of the haill kirk, sen ze
can not excuse zour selfis to say that S. Paul
vrait to thame quha spak the Hebreu toung,
as Amen is Hebreu considering he vraitt to
the Corinth. quha had thair publique seruice
in greik, and not in hebreu, geuing vs ane
sufficient argument, that that vord Amen
aucht to be retened in al langages, as it hes

euer bene retenet befoir zou amang all Chriſtian men. And as the Euangeliſtis quha vreit in greke and thay quha turned the Euangelis out of grek in latene hes in lykmaner retened it, zea, ze zour ſelſſis in zour bybillis ſumtymes perſauing that vtheruyſe ze vald be mockit be all men, ar compellit to retene it, as in the verſione of the fourtene chaptour of the firſt to the Cor. He quha ſuppleis the roume of the vnlearned hou ſall he anſuere Amen, giff ze had turned hou ſall he anſuere Sobeit all the vatld vald haue lachin at zou, And quhat thing can be thocht mair vane nor to turne tha vordis of Chriſt Amen Amen dico vobis, Sobeit Sobeit I ſay vnto zou : Thairfoir ze aucht to beleue that it is nocht vithout ane greit myſterie that S. Paul and the Euangeliſtis hes euer retened this vord Amen, and that nane vther ſen thair dayes hes bene ſua bauld as to turne it in onie vther langage, In-

Aug. epiſt.
188. & 2.
de doctrina
Chriſt.
cap. 10.

ſafar that the maiſt learnet S. Auguſtine vryttis that it is nocht leſum to turne Amen in onie vther vulgar langage vithout the ſklander of the hail kirk. Hou may ze than purge zour ſelfis, bot in the turning of Amen in zour neu [Sobeit] ze vald appeir to haue bene vyſar nor S. Paull and the Euangeliſtis, and that ze haue ſklanderit the haill kirk, nocht being mouit thairto be onie reſſone, except onlie to mak profeſſione that ze ar ſchiſmakis, and vill haue na thing commone vith

Christis kirk:For as concerning the vndirstã-
ding of the pepill quhilk ze allege for zour
defence, Thay vnderstud [Amen] als veill as
nou thay do sobeit, and albeit thay had nocht
vndirstand it, zit thay var nocht of sua grose
ane spirit, bot thay micht haue learned it in
les not half ane zeir. Bot to cõclud the mater I
vil discouer the craft of Sathane be the quhilk
he hes induced zou to turne, Amé in zour Sobeit. In all the prayeris of the vniuersall
kirk in quhatsumeuer pairt of the varld to
our dayes, at the end of all oraisonis and benedictionis vsed euer to be ansuered Amen,
quhilk is ane hebreu vord, to signifie that the
Ieuis at the end sall imbrace the Christiane
religione, and that in thame the militant kirk
in ane certane maner sall be concludit, and
endit: quhairof ve mak ane daylie professio-
one, quhen for the conclusione of all our prayeris ve vse euer to say Amen, And protestis
that the prophecie of Christ salbe accomplished of ane scheipfald and ane pastore: And
that the Ieuis albeit thay be reiected for ane
tyme as vrytis S. Paul, zit thay sal nocht be *ad Rom. 11*
reiected for euer, bot at the last salbe gathered in the scheipfald of Christ: Bot ze, as ze
haue denyed the fulfilling of the prophecies
of the calling of the gentiles, and the vniuer-
salitie, and visibilitie of the kirk and kingdome of Christ, sua be the turning of, Amen, in
Sobeit ze protest that the prophecie sall not

be compleit of the calling of the Ieuis, and conuersione of thame to the Christiane fayth this is the craft of Sathan in zou, quhairbie he laboris to mak all thingis fals, quhilk hes bene foirspokin of Christ ād his eternal kingdome, that he may thairbie estableis the kingdome of the Antichrist. God grant zou grace to acknaulege zour blindnes, and to deliuer zour self out of the snare of sathan be vnfenzeit repentance. Amen.

M. Bot quhairsoir reseruit the Papistis the Bybil in ane langage vnknauin to the people, quhairbie thay var defraudit of thair saluatione, and of the confort quhilk thay micht haue had be reiding of the sam, and turnit it not in thair auin Mother toung, as ve haue done in our reformit kirkis?

B. I se in zour deformit kirkis the Bybil, be priuat men not hauing commissione of the kirk nor knaulege of the scripturis, turnit in the inglishe toung, peruertit in infinit places: Albeit it aucht to be referrit to the deliberatione of the hail kirk Catholik, and aduyse of the halie ghaist, quhidder it suld be translated in al langages or not? be ressone thre onlie, to vit hebreu, greik, ana latine var vreittin vpone the Croce of Christ Iesus be instinction of the halie ghaist. Thair ar lykuyse monie formes of speiking maist propir and sententious in the hebreu, greik, and latine toungis, quhilk ather tynis the grace, or ane greit pairt of the strenth, gif thay be translated in vthir mair rude langages, or ellis requi-

ris lang circumſcriptionis, quhilk be diuerſs
interpretoris vil euer be changeit vith greit
danger of the loſſing of the treu mening of
the halie ſpirit : Bot the vay quhairbie ze haue deceaued the people drauing thame from
obedience of Chriſtis halie kirk, ſaying that
ſcho hid from thame the buke of lyf, quhilk
gif thay red, thay ſuld be als learned as ather
the Preiſtis, or Freiris, vas maiſt Iyk the firſt
tentatione of Eua in Paradiſe, quhairbie ſcho   *Gen.3.*
vas puſt vp vith deſire of knaulege to brek
goddis commandiment : Becaus Iyk as ane
vnlichted candel ſchauis not to onie man in
ane mirk nicht the danger of the vay, albeit
he beir it in his hand, ſua the vryttin buke in
his hand quha hes not the ſpecial grace of
god to expone the ſame vithout errore, makis
not the vay manifeſt quhilk leidis to ſaluatione: And do ze not think that it is als vnſeimlie
ane thing, that ane vyf quha ſuld be occupeit
vith the Rok, or ane Soutar, or Skynnar ſuld
reaſone quhidder the general Concile of the
vniuerſal kirk, and hail Clergie of Chriſtiani-
tie hes interpreit the vord of god treulie, as
that Sardanapalus ſat amang vemen doing
tha thingis quhilk apertenit to thair vocation
onlie, ſua the greit abhominationis committit be the gentilis in ſenſibil erroris, at nou
committit ſpiritualie be zou laſt riſſin vp He-
tetikis. And it is knauin hou in Almanie ſum
be the exemple of Lot, vald haue committed
inceſt, vith thair auin dochteris, becaus thay

fand that vryttin in the bybil: And Lauter him
self published, that euerie man eftir the exemple of Abrahame, as thay red in the scripture
micht ly vith thair auin hyre vemen in place
of thair vysis, pronuncing his maist notabil
sentence agreable to the libertie of his neu
Euangel [si non vult vxor, veniat ancilla] Reid
Staphylus, and ze vil find, quhat abusis hes cūmit in the cuntrey of Almanie, sen euerie mā
had libertie to reid the Bybil in his auin vulgar langage : As quhair ze say that the people
vas defraudit of the vord of lyf, and treu fude
and nuriture of thair saulis, zea abuse zour auditoris, becaus the mystereis of our fayth, and
the commandis of God var declairit, and maid manifest vnto thame mair esilie be preaching and teaching, nor be reiding of the Byble: Vtheruyse thay quha can not reid culd
not attene to saluatione: And gif it var necessar that al men suld reid the Byble, thay suld
not reid it in the Inglishe or onie vulgar toung, bot rather in the Hebreu, or Greik toung in the quhilk it vas vreittin: becaus in the
reading of it in another toung thay man repose thame selfis vpone the fidelitie of him
quha hes turnit it in sik ane toung, and sua can
neuer haue onie certane assurance, cōsidering
he quha hes turnit it, hes bene bot ane man,
and micht haue faillit : Quhairof necessarlie
I conclude that ather the people man repose
thame selfis on the instructione of thair
pastoris, or ellis gif thay vil not be content

Lauterlib.
de voto &
continent.

vith the inftructione of thair Paftoris, except thay reid the Byble, thay man al begin to ftudie to Hebreu, and Greik, to the effect that thay may reid the Byble in thaj toungis, quhairin, thay ar affurit, thay var vryttin yithout onie errore.

OF THE APPAREILL AND OR-NAMENTIS OF THE KIRK.
CHAP   XVI.

M.

BOt *quhair reidis thou that it is lefum to the Papiftis to adorne thair altaris fa fumptuouflie vith precious ftanes, vith fa monie touallis, and to haue fic confecrat chalices of Gold and filuer, quhilk vas abufed be the preiftis and freris to the greit hurt of tre commoneveill, And hou can thou deny bot the Papis of Rome hes borrouit from the gentiles the fuperftitious maner of adorning kirkis vith gold filuer and precious ftanes, quhilk God hes not commandit nor apoynted in the vrittin vord.*

B.   Suppois in the Dayes of the Apoftlis, and during the greit perfecutione of the Emperoris of Rome, the Chriftianis could nocht haue tyme to buyld fua notabill kirkis as thay vald haue defyrit, nor zit to adorne thair altaris vith ornamentis of gold and precious ftanis, being oftymes conftrainit to fle out of ane place to another, and to lurk in couis vndir the erd, and thair to vfe the exerceis of thair religione, zit quhen it pleafed

God to tak auay the persecutione, and illuminat the hart of the Emperore Côstantinus
Magnus to imbrace the Chriſtian religioṇe
and to be ane inſtrument of the furthſetting
of it, than as the Chriſtianis began to big maiſt magnificẗ templis, ſua began thay to adorne thair altaris vith gold and preꞇious ſtanes,
and to cleyth thame maiſt richelie. and to mak
Chalices of gold and ſiluer in mair quantiꞇie
and aboundance nor befoir. For lang afoir
Conſtantinus Magnus the Chriſtianis in thair
ſacriꞇices vſed to haue Chalices of gold as a-
mangis vtheris vitneſſis the learnet Poer Prudentius deſcryuand the persecutione of Deci-

*Prudent in
Laurent.*

us, [Soletis (inquit) conqueri, ſæuire nos iu-
ſtò amplius, quum Chriſtiana corpora, plus
quam cruentè ſcindimus: abeſt atrocioribus
cenſura feruens motibus, blandè & quietè
efflagito, quod ſponte obire debeas: hanc eſſe
veſtris orgiis, moremque & artem proditum
êſt, hanc diſciplinam fæderis, libent vt auro
Antiſtes, argenteis ſcyphis ferunt fumare
ſacrum ſanguinem, auroque noꞇturnis ſacris
adſtare fixos cereos] ze vſe ſayis the cruell
EmperoreDecius to complane that ve ar mair
cruell than becummis vs, quhen ve caus ryue
and deſtroy the bodeis of Chriſtiane men vithout mercie, ve vil nocht vſe ſa exorbitât and
horribil crueltie, ve craue vith pleſandnes
and tranquilitie, that quhilk ze ſuld do villinglie: Thay ſay that this is the maner and
faſſone of zour ſacrifices thay ſay this is the

Diſcipline

difcipline of zour couenant, that the Bifchopis makis facrifice in vefchelis of gold, that
the halie and confecrat blude is offerit in
coupis of filuer, and that in the euening
or nichtlie feruice the torchis ar fet in chan-
deleris of gold. Reid gif ze pleis Ruffinus, and *Ruff.lib.9*
thair ze vill find hou Conftantinus Magnus
did erect fa monie notabill templis and adorne thame vith all kind of rich and pretious ornamentis, ze vill find hou that the halie voman Helena his mother did decore the Altaris
vith maift riche touallis and pretious ftanes,
and chalices of gold and filuer. Reid S. Chry- *Chrifoft*
foftome, and thair ze vil find alfo hou that the *homil.51*
in Math.
altaris vas vont to be ornit with veluot, and fil- *opt.lib.2.*
kis ād vith touallis of clayth of gold and vith *contra par-*
chandelaris of gold: And Optatus Mileuitanus *me.*
vritand aganis the heretik Parmenianus the
kirk fayis he, hesmonie ornametis of gold and
filuer: and obiectis to the donatiftis, that thay *Opt.lib.6.*
had cōmitted ane maift horribill cryme that
thay had brokin the chalices quhilk did cōte-
ne in thame the blude of Chrift and diffoluit
thame in peces, fua that the gentiles did by
thame to mak vefchellis in the quhilk thay
micht offer facrifice to thair Idolis, ô, fayis
he, ane cryme quhilk vas neuer hard befoir,
to tak from God, and to giff to ane Idole. *August*
And S. Auguftine vrittis that ve haue monie *in pf. 113.*
vefchellis, and inftrumentis quhilk ve vfe in
the adminiftratione of the facramentis, the *S. Ambrof.*
2. de offic.
quhilkis ar confecrat and halie, becaus *cap. 28.*

H

of the halie ministerie to the quhilk thay serue: And S. Ambrose vrittis that in sum caices
ve may breke and sell euin the halie veschellis quhilkis ar cōsecrat and hallouit: The kirk
hes gold sayis he, nocht to keip it, bot for the
necessitie of the pure (Tunc enim vas Domi-
nici sanguinis nosco , cum in vtroque video
redemptionem vt calix ab hoste redimat,
quem sanguis ab hoste redemit) that is than
I acknauledge the veschell that contenis the
blud of the lord, quhen in thame bayth I behald the pryce of redemptione, that the Chalice may redeme him from the ennimie, quhom the blude hes redemit from the ennimie.
And Athanasius vryttand of the persecution of the Arrianis , vitnessis that the Arrianis had tane auay all the vestimentis,
and vther ornamentis of the kirk : And that
thair persecutione and violence vas sua greit
that thay prophaned the halie veschelis and
Chalicis be the polluted handis of the gentiles: And Gregorius Naziázenus being accused
be the Arrianis, schau me sayis he, quhais blude I haue mixed vith the blude of Christ? mening of the Arrianis quha in the tyme of the
sacrifice vas the caus of sa monie murtheris in
the kirk, and of the spilling of Christis blude
out of the Chalices, in the quhilk it vas offerit
sua that the blude of thame quha var slayne
vas mixed vith the blude of Christ be thair
persecutione , schau me sayis he, quhair I
haue exposed the Chalices quhilk ar depute

Ambros,
lib. 2. de of
ficiis c. 28.

Athana.
in epist. ad
Marcum.

Athana.
in vita An
tonii.

Nazian.
in oratione
de Arrianis
& seipso.

to the sacrifices, quhilk, it is nocht lesum, to
the pepill to tuiche, to be tuiched and contaminat be the handis of the infidelis, as ze haue
done? ze quha callis zour selfis Protestantis ze
se quhais sutstoppis ze follou in breiking of
the Chalices, and spulzeing of the kirkis. And
vnles ze cum to repentance, ze may be assured
of na vther reuard, nor the Arrianis, and infidelis hes gottin befoir, quhilk is the inquens-
hibill syre of hell. And in this varld ze vill
nocht eschaip the vraith and iust iudgement
of God mair nor vtheris quhais sutstoppis ze
follou. Victor Vticensis descryuand the persecutione of the Vandalis vrittis that Ginseri-
cus king of the Vandalis did send ane callit
Proclus to spulzie the kirkis, quha obeying
his masteris commādiment tuke the couerin-
gis of the altaris, and maid vnto him self of
thame sarkis and hoise: bot a lytill estir he did
eate out his auin toung, and de be ane maist
filthie and horribil death. Theodoretus vrittis in lyk maner of ane callit Phymelicus ane
danser quha had bocht ane halie vestiment of
gold and silk, the quhilk Constantinus had
genin to the kirk of Hierusalem, and did put
this vestimēt vpone him and danse in it, quha
did fall incontinent to the erd and de maist
miserabillie be the iust iudgement and punitione of God: quhairof I counsal zou to tak
exemple in tyme: And sen the Ieuis in the auld
testament be the command of God, had sua
coistlie and riche apparellis in the tempill of

Victor Vti.
lib. 1. de per
secutione
vandal.

Theod. li. 3.
cap. 37.

Hierusalem quhilk vas bot ane schaddou and vmbre, hou can ze eschaip to be iniureous vnto Christ, sen ze vill that the kirkis quhilk ar dedicat to his honore be alluterlie destitute of all precious and riche apparell, and that zour auin priuat housis be mair magnifict nor the house quhilk is dedicat to the honoring and vorshipping of god. Ve haue nocht learned the maner of the apparelling of our kirkis of the infidell Gétiles as ze say, bot rather the infidelis hes lerned that from the pepill of god, as Numa Pompilius did learne ane greit pairt of tha thingis quhilk he ordinit in the Citie of Rome for the vorshipping of the Idolis out of the bukis of Moyses. Ze of the lau of nature it self, all nationis hes vniuersalie learned that the tempillis quhilk ar dedicat to the vorschipping of god, aucht to be decored vith greit magnificence, and exteriour apparell, nocht that god hes mister of onie sic thing, bot for declaratione and testificatione of our deuitie and subiectione vnto him, and als to excitate, and valkin our dull nature be sik exteriore thingis as ar subiect to our eis to deuotione and pietie, And euin as the kirk militant is ane certane image and liknes of the kirk triumphant, sua according to our vaiknes and imbecillitie, be the exteriore ornamétis of gold, precious stanes, and vther thingis, quhilkis ar in our kirkis ve do declair the greit affluence and aboúdance of all Ioy and consolatione quhilkis ar amang the halie san-

&is, and angellis of heuin, quha triumphis in glorie, sua ze appeir to me, mair rude and barbare, nor at the gentiles thame selfis, considering ze vill that thair be na differenee betuix zour kirkis, and als monie noult saldis, as experience it self dois teache. Nou that this decoring and apparelling of kirkis, hes euer bene accustumed be all Christiane pepill, it is maist cleir and manifest to all thame quha pleisis to reid the ancient vrittaris as Ruffinus quha vritttis as said is that Constantinus Magnus, hauing obtened victorie ouer the tyrane Macétius did imploy him self to buyld maist suptuous and magnifict kirkis exornād thame vith al kynd of apparell as also his mother Helena quha gaue sindrie veschellis of gold decored maist richelie vith pretious stanis. Reid Theodoret, and ze vill find hou richelie the tempillis in that aige vas accustumed to be apparelled. The sam is testifeit be S. Hierom vrittand to Heliodorus. Be Paulinus, be S. Chrysostom, be Optatus, be Ambrose, be Gregorius Nissenus, be Athanasius, be Gregorius Nazianzenus, be Prudétius, and all vther ancient vrittaris. And, as is manifest of thir said authoris, ze in spulzeing, and taiking auay the ornamentis of the kirk, follou the futstoppis of Iulianus the Apostat, of the Arrianis, and of the Donatistis, quha did tak auay the veschellis of gold, and vther pre-

Ruffin. li, 9 cap. 10.

Theod. li. 8 de curandis gracanicis affectionibus.
S. Hiero ad heliodo.
Paulinus i natali fœlicis.
Chryso. ho. 51. in Mat.
Nissenus in laudibus Theodori martyris, Athana. in

episto. ad Marcum de Arrianis, Nazianzenus in orat. de & seipso Prudentius in Laurentio. *Arrianis*

cious ornamentis of the kirkis euin as ze do,
albeit ze surpas thame sum parte in sic impietie, hauand maid gretar prophanatione of all
sic thingis nor euer thay did, as is cleir to all
thame quha plesis to copair thair vorkis vith
zouris: I desyre that ze schau me of onie anciet
historie, that in onie aige the Christian men
hes had sik kirkis, as ze haue nou in the realme of Scotland, That is the bair vallis destitute of all kynd of ornament, vithout dure, vindo, or ruffe. I am assurit ze vill neuer be abill
to schau onie sic thing: hou can ze thane profes zour selfis treu vorshipparis of god, quha
vses sua manifest contempt of thai places quhilk ar cheiffie dedicat to his honore and
vorshipping.

OF THE DEDICATIONE
of kirkis and altaris.
CAP. XVII.

M.

AR not the Papistis maist lyk the idolatrous na-
tiones quha dedicatis thair Kirkis to men, and
vemen, euin as the gentilis did thairis to Diana,
Apollo, and Iupiter.

B. As in zour formar obiectionis ze haue declarit zour selfis to be Gentiles follouing the
exemple of Iulianus the Apostate, Porphyrius, and vtheris, sua in this ze declair zour selfis to be Manichæanis : for as testifeis S. Augustine, the Manichæanis did obiect the sa-

Aug. li. 20 cotra Faustum.

myn argument to the Catholiques in tha day
is , and that thay had maid goddis of thair
Martyris and erected templis vnto thame,
To quhom S.Auguftine did aufuer that our
tempillis and kirkis ar onlie côfecrat to god,
as to god onlie facrifice aucht to be offered,
albeit thay be confecrat in memorie of the
Martyris , to the effect as he fayes , that ve
thank God of the victorie , quhilk he hes
granted to thame , and that throuch the remembrance of fic places, our cheritie may be
kendilled touard god, and his halie Martyris
and that ve may be helpit be thair prayeris,
and be maid pairtakaris of thair merites :
vtheruyfe ve vald be Iudged ingrate giff ve
did nocht thank god of the greit benefeittis quhilk he hes granted to thame , thay being membirris of ane bodie vith vs : cheiflie
fen thair victorie dois proceid from the
ftrenth and efficacie of Chriftis blude: Thairfore quhen ve dedicat tempilles vnto god in
the quhilk the memorie of Martyris, and fanctis fuld be obferuit and keipit, ve do ane maift fpeciall honore vnto god, extolling the victorie of the croce, quhairthrouche the Martyris and Sanctis hes triumphed ouer thair
ennemeis: As ze be the contrare in taking a-
uay all fic memorie, vill not acknaulege the
victorie of the Croce, and obfcuris it fua mekill as ze may : Sua ve call nocht the kirk of
Paull or of Petir , becaus that it is dedicat to
Petir or Paul, bot becaus it is dedicat vnto
                    H iiij

god for memorie and honore of Petir and
Paull , as ve call nor ane altar of Petir or
Paul , as Augustine teachis in the same place
becaus that ve offer onie sacrifice to thame,
for as he sayis to Faustus theManichæane, quhen hard thou onie preist sayand I offer vnto
thePetir or Paull? bot ve offer onlie vnto god,
albeit ve offer vnto him for the memorie and
honore of S.Petir and Paull: sua zour obiectione proceidis of plane ignorance, sen ze
impugne the Catholique religione befoir ze
vndirstand it , That this vse and custume hes
euer bene keipit sen the beginning of the
kirk, it is maist cleir and manifest of all historeis, Aurelianns Discipill of Martiall, ane of
the seuintie tua Discipillis vrittis that he
did caus buyld ane kirk to the honore of S.
Stephane the first Martyr, in Limoges ane toune of France , quhilk kirk standis vnto thir
dayes: Abdias in the lyff of S.Iohne the Apostle testifeis hou that in the toune of Ephesus thair vas ane kirk buyldit to the honore
and memorie of S.Iohne: And Anacletus quha
vas neir the Apostlis dayes testifeis that Marcus in the toune of Alexandria caused buyld
an tempile dedicat to the honore and memorie of S.Petir: And clemens S Petirris scol-
lar vitnessis hou that ane nobill man in the
toune of Rome callit Theodosius did mak a-
ne kirk of his anin hous to the honore also
of S.Petir : And Damasus testifeis hou that
Calixtus quha vas in the aige of Tertulliane

Aug.lib.
20. contra
Faustum,

Aurelia.in
vita mar-
tialis.

Abdias in
vita S.Io-
annis.

Damasus
in vitis pō-
tificum.

did erect ane kirk in the toune of Rome to
the honore of our Ladie : And Cóstantinus
the Emperour as vitnessis Sozomenus did the
lyk in Constantinopill. And hou that be the
help of our Ladie that toune at sindrie tymes
hes bene deliuerit from dangeris. I micht pro
duce vther innumerabill exemplis gif I plai-
sed as of Helena, Pulcheria, Iustinianus and
vtheris: Sua ze suld be eschamed to impugne
that quhilk according to goddis vord hes bene established be all Christiane and godlie
men befoir zou. And zit zour Centuriatoris
of Almanie ar nocht eschamed to say, that in
place of the goddis, quhilk vas vorshipped be
the Ethnictis, ve do bring in in our kirkis
our Ladie and the Sáctis to be vorshipped be
the Christianis, Euin as the Gentiles and Manichæanis vas vont to obiect: Ze Beza zour
paraclete pronoúcis bauldlie his sentence, quhilk I am assurit all Christian mennis eiris vill
abhore, That the kirk of our Ladie of Lauret
is euin' lik the tempill of Diana Ephesiorum,
And that the lyk superstitione is vsed in thame bayth, sua gif zour Paraclet Beza had bene in the dayes of the primitiue kirk , quhen
the gétiles obiectit vnto the Christianis, that
in place of Diana and the rest of the goddis,
thay brocht 'in our Ladie and the Sanctis : he
vith the rest of his ministeris of Geneua vald
haif bene maist fauorabill vnto thame ád vald
haue approuit thair maist blasphemous calú
nie to the quhilk the Christiáis did ásuer maist

Sozomen̄ lib. 7. ca. 5.

Centur. 7. cap. 6.

Beza cō; in Act. 19.

constantlie as amangis vtheris Theodoret, that our Martyris and Sanctis ar of gretar puissance and strenthe nor ar thair goddis, becaus our Martyris, and Sanctis albeit thay be nocht goddis, hes eiected thair goddis out of thair tempillis, and for Iupiter, Bacchus, and vther goddis, ve haue Petir, Paul, and Thomas, be quhais names the tempillis ar named, quhair befoir thay var named be the names of Iupiter, and Bacchus: And thairfoir giff ze pleis to reid the ancient vrittaris as Augustine, Hierom, and vtheris, ze vill find that thay vse to call the kirkis be the names of Petir, Paul, Iames, and vtheris, As Augustine in his first buke of the Citie of God quhen he vrittis, that the Gothis did forgiue al thame quha vsed to flie to the kirk of S.Petir for girth: And in the tuentie tua buke he callis the kirk of his auin toune, the kirk of S.Stephane: And S.Hierome de viris illustribus makis mentione of the kirk of S. Clement in the toune of Rome: and all vther ancient vrittaris geuis in lyk maner testimonie to this vse of dedicatione of kirkis to the glorie of god, for memorie of Christis halie sanctis and martyris. Zour Centuriatores sayes that this maner of the buyldig of kirkis begane at Cóstantinus Magnus, bot thay ar conuict to be learis of that quhilk is said befoir: And the vniuersall consent of all nationis vill euer be ane sufficient argument for the condemnatióne of zour impietie: For to pretermit vther

Theodoret lib.8.de cu rādis græcanicis affe ctionibus.

Aug.lib.1. de Ciuita. Dei, Aug. libr. 22. de ciuit. Dei.

Hierom. de viris illustribus.

Cēturia 1. lib.2.c.10.

cuntreyis als lang as the memorie of Chrīst
fall left in the Realme of Scotland, salang thair salbe the memorie of sum sanctis, for qū-
hais memorie sindrie of the kirkis vas dedicat to the seruice of God, As S. Petirris kirk
(in the toune of Megill) The kirkis of S. Geill,
S. Duthes, S. Ringane, S. Mongo, S. Padie, S.
Leonard in S. Leonardis colledge, and vtheris:
Quhilk names it vill pas zour pouar euer to
abolishe, except that as ze ar deliberat to
cast doune the thrid part of all the kirkis in
scotland as I heir reported, sua vith procefs
of tyme ze be resolut to cast thame all doune,
and aboleise alluterlie the name of Chrīst Iesus out of the realme of Scotland.

OF EXTREME VNCTIONE
CHAP. XVIII.

M.

BE quhat testimonie of scripture may thou proue
extreme vnctione to be ane sacrament?
B. Nocht onlie in the Euangel of S. Marc, Marc. 6.
quhair it is said that the Apostlis obeying the
command of Chrīst eiectit deuillis, and oyn-
tit monie seik vith oyle, and haillit thame:
bot also in the epistle of S. Iames all thingis
requirit to ane sacrament, ar maist lyuelie des-
cryuit, to vit ane lauchfullie callit Pastore, ane
Preist of the kirk, be quhais administratione
it is geuin, the external element to vit oyle,
representing the inuart grace of consolatione

geuin be the halie Gaift, vith expres mentione
of the effect of ane sacrament, to vit remif-
fione of synnis, vith the forme of vordis per-
tening to ane sacrament, to vit, prayer in the
name of the lord (For thair it is vryttin gif,
thair be onie seik amangis zou, lat him cal for
the Preiftis of the kirk, and lat thame pray
vpone him, oyntand him vith oyle in the name of the lord, and the obfecratione of fayth
fall haill him quha is seik, and the lord fal rai-
fe him, and gif he be in synnis, thay salbe remitted vnto him): Bot ze, becaus ze haue reiected this sacrament, and refufis the confola-
tione of the halie Ghaift, quhilk be the verteu
of it, he vfis to gif to the faythful, aganis the
maift horribil tentationis of Sathan, in the
extreme hour of zour lyff, ze de for the greitaft pairt, in defperatione: Iohne Caluine con-
fefsis him felf that in the tyme of the Apoftlis
it vas ane treu sacrament, bot that nou it is
na sacrament: Be the lyk reffone he micht haue tane auay Baptifme, and zour Suppar from
zou. Frere Martine Lauter zour foirgrandfchir
paffed mair cannelie to vorke and did deny
that euer S. Iames vrait ane epiftle, or maid
mentione of this sacrament, bot he micht haue denyit alfueil the Euangell of S. Iohne: hou
can ze than purge zour felfis of maift intole-
rabill ingratitude to Chrift, that vil nocht ref-
faue fua healthfum and profitabil ane sacrament, as he hes left vnto treu Chriftianis?

M. *Thou hes alledgit in thy Anfuere tua thingis,*

S. *Iames* 5.

*Caluin in
lib. de refor
ma. ecclef.*

quhilk in my iugement ar disagreand from the spirit
of god, first that Presbyter, in the primiture kirk, vas
ane preist, and leuit as ane kirk man, quhill as accor-
ding to the signification of the greik vord, it is callit
ane elder, sik as ve chuse Zeirlie in our reformit Kir-
kis. The secund is, that Ze vald retene that vn-
ctione, quhairof the Apostle spekis, the verteu thai-
rof to vit corporall health, nou ceissing.

B. As to the first, it is manifest that in the primitiue kirk (Presbyter) vas nocht tane for ane
Soutar, Tailzeour, or Merchand hauand ane
mechanik vocatione, zeirlie chosin, as ze do
in zour deformit kirk, bot for ane Pastore
beíg anoyntit. For S. Paul vryttis to Timothie *Tim. 1. epi. chap. 5.*
[qui bene præsunt Presbyteri duplici honore
digni habeantur, maxime ij qui laborāt in ser-
mone & doctrina] Lat the Preistis quha reulis
veill, be estemit vorthie of doubill honore,
cheiflie thay quha trauellis in preching of the
vord and teching, quhilk in nauyse can agrie
to zour idiotEldaris: And in the first chapter of
the epistle to Titus, he callis the Bischop Presbyter, quhair he sayis, for this caus I left zou
in Creta, that ze may amēd tha thingis quhilk
inlaikis, and apoynt in euerie toune, Presbyte-
ros, that is, Bischopis, as I haue ordinit zou to *Tit. 1.*
do, gif thair be onie giltles: for vnles Sanct
Paull be [Presbyter] and (Episcopus) vndirstude ane thing he vald nocht subioyne as
ane caus of the former sentence, [Oporret
enim Episcopum irreprehensibilem esse] It
is necessar that ane Bischop be vithout falt,

&c. And gif ze vil reid bayth the greik, and latine vryttaris in Chriſtis kirk, ze vil find that ,preſbyter, amangis the greikis is callit [ἱερεύς] quhilk ſignifeis ane preiſt or ſacrificatore, and amangis the latinis is callit (ſacerdos) and that na man befoir zou did acknaulege ſic Eldaris, as ze do, or that onie ſic office at onie tyme hes bene in the kirk of god: ſua I vald inquire of zou the caus, quhy in zour vrytingis in lating, ze vſe nocht this vord, Sacerdos, to ſignifie him that miniſteris the ſacramentis, as euer al vryttaris and latiniſtis hes done befoir zou, quha euer hes tane, preſbyter, and (ſacerdos) fot ane thing? As to the ſecund I meruel gretumlie of zour vilful ignorance, quha confundis the externall mirakil, vith the effect of this ſacrament, quhilk is inuiſibil and ſpiritual. For in the primitiue kirk to côfirme the fayth of thame quha reſſauit this ſacrament, thair vas at the adminiſtratione thairof ane mirakil ſchauin, lyk as in the reſt of the ſacramêtis: becaus thay quha al men kneu to be neiraſt approchand to deathe, vithout reparatione of health be onie kynd of natural medicine, vas reſtorit to bodelie health, quhilk vas lytil les miraculous, nor gif thay had bene raiſed fra dede to lyff: Quhairfoir gif ze deny the verteu of this ſacrament, becaus the mirakil hes ceiſſit, ze ſal deny inlyuyſe that Baptiſme is ane ſactament: For as ve reid in the Euangel of S. Marc. Thay quha beleuit and var baptized in the primitiue

Marc. 16.

kirk reſſauit ſic pouar that be the name of
Chriſt thay eiectit Deuillis, thay ſpak vith
ſindrie toūgis, thay handillit ſerpentis vithout
onie hurt, quhilk verteu, as experience prouis, euerie baptized perſone dois nocht reſſaue in thir dayes,

OF MARIAGE.
CHAP. XIX.

M.

MAy thou lauchfullie alledge onie teſtimonie
of the vritten vord to proue Mariage to be
ane ſacrament?

B. Sen Mariage contenis ane outuart ſing
of the inuart grace, quhilk God omnipotent
creatis in the hartis of thame quha ar mareit
for the procreatione and educatione of Childrene, and is apoyntit, and ordinit be god
thairto: I meruel hou ze deny it to be ane
ſacrament, cheiſlie ſen S. Paull mening of *Epheſ.5.*
Mariage, ſayis, It is ane gret Sacrament: or
hou can ze beleue that Mariage hes na grace
nor prerogatiue amangis the Chriſtianis: the
quhilk it hes nocht amangis the Ieuis and gé-
tilis, or that the Chriſtianis ar nocht ſanctifeit be the halie band of Mariage to produce
Childrene vnto Chriſt, aganis the mening of *Auguſt.*
S. Paul in his epiſtle to the Epheſianis? Thair- *Lib. de bo-*
foir S. Auguſtin ſayis that Mariage in the ha- *no con. cap.*
lie citie of god, may in nauyſe be diſſoluit, *24.*
becaus it is ane ſacrament: and as Chriſt can

nocht be separat from his kirk, bot is consoy-
nit vith hir be ane insolubil band, sua the
band of Mariage can not be dissolued: Of
this ze may persaue the lesing of zour maister Caluine quhair he sayis, that na man acknauledgit Mariage to be ane sacrament befoir Gregoris dayes, sen ane lâg tyme befoir S.
Augustine acknauledgit the sam: Bot nou I
vndirstand quhat hes mouit zou to deny
that Mariage is ane Sacrament, becaus ze
nocht onlie grant that our halie saluiours
spous the kirk hes errit, as diuorcit from hir
housband, bot ze celebrat also the bâd of Mariage betuix men and vemen diuorcit, And sua
approuis adulterous Childrene for thame that
ar begottin in the honorabil band of Matri-
monie expres aganis the testimonie of our
saluiour Iesus Chrift, quha nather permittis
the man, nor the voman diuorcit to contract
agane vndir the pane of breking the lau quhair it is vrittin : Thou sall nocht commit
adulterie: for albeit diuorcemeut may be maid
from bed speche, and burde, zit as to the dis-
solutione of the band of Mariage, thay may
na mair be separat, nor the Saul from the bodie vithout death, As vitnessis S. Paul to the
Cor. Bot thame quha ar mareit I command
nocht I bot the lord, lat nocht the vyf be separat from hir housbâd, bot gif scho be separat,
lat hir abyd vnmareit, or ellis be reconcilit
vith hir housband, and lat nocht the housband put auay his vyff, quhair it is to be vndirstand

Calu. li. 4.
inst. ca. 16.
sect. 34.

S. Paul. 1.
Cor. 7.

stand lykuyse, gif he leue his vyf, he aucht
ather to be reconcilit vith hir agane, or ellis
abyd vnmareit.

M . *As to the testimonie of Paul, it seruis not* Eph̄e.5.
to Zour purpose becaus he callis nocht Mariage [Sa-
cramentum .] *bot* (μυϛήελον).

B. Do ze nocht think that S. Hierom, quha
vas author of the vulgar translatione, ressaued
be the Kirk, ād as zit imbraced euerie quhair,
had sufficient knauledge to expone the vers
of the greik text, in latine or nocht ? Bot
ze appeir to desyre that S. Paul vryttand in
greik suld haif spokin latine, and callit it (sacram ētum) zea the name (sacramētum) amang
the latinistis signefeis mair impropirlie that
quhilk ve call ane sacrament, nor dois the
vord (μυϛήελον) amangis the Greikis.

OF THE VOV OF CHASTITIE

CHAP. XVIII.

M.

ZE that ar Papistis albeit Ze can nocht Keip the
commandis of God, Zit as thocht the keiping of
thame var nocht sufficient, Ze charge Zour selfis vith
the vou of chastitie, aganis the expres vordis of Paul
lat euerie man haue his auin vyf to auoyd fornicatione, Zea Paul dois planelie foirspek of Zou saying 1.Cor.7.
that in the latter dayes thair sall vpryse sum quha
sall forbid men to marie quhilk is maist planelie ful- 1.Tim.4.
fillet amangis Zou, sen Ze vill nocht that it be lesum
to Zour Preistis Freris Monkis and Nonnis to marie.

B. Zour argument is full of calumnie and
deprauatione of goddis vord, sen ze can nocht

I

be abill to schau that euer onie Catholique teached that the fulfilling of the commandimentis vas nocht sufficient to atteine to the lyf euerlasting, quhilk at nocht impossibill, as ze allege, sen the scripture teachis vs, that thay ar maist esie saying, his commandimentis ar nocht hauie. Bot to cum to zour obiectione the vou of chastitie is nocht aganis the scripture as ze allege, bot maist conforme thairto, ze consaled be Christ him self, quhen he sayis thair be sum quha hes chastiseit thame seluis for the kingdome of heauin, quhairbie he declaris that thay astrict thame seluis to perpetual continecie and chastitie. And S. Paul vrytand to Timothie sayis, that the vidouis quha eftir thay ar dedicat to the seruice of the kirk dois marie incurris damnatione, becaus thay haue brokin thair first promeis quhilk vordis can not be vndirstand bot of the promeis and vou of chastitie, sen vtheruyse be mariage thay vald nocht haue incurrit damnatione. The quhilk place is sua cleir that Caluine him self albeit he labour mekil to interpreit it in ane vther sense and mening, zit he is constrainit to grant that it vas nocht lesum to thay vidouis to marie, and that thay quha vald marie did incur damnatione, quhairbie also he is constrainit to confes that thay had sum vou and obligatione of chastitie, vtheruyse mariage had nocht bene vnlesum to thame, sua the vou of chastitie is nocht aganis goddis vord as ze maist falslie allege, bot veray conforme thairto, and maist acceptabil vnto God. As

Ioan. epi. cap. 5.

Matt. 19.

1. Tim. 5.

Calu. libr. inst. 4. cap. 13. sec. 18.

sanct Paul testifeis maist planlie he quha is
mareit is cairfull for the thingis of the varld,
hou he may pleise his vyf, and he quha is vnmareit is cairful for the thingis ot the lord,
hou he may pleis the lord : teachand vs thairbie that as thay quha ar consecrat to the seruice of God, and ministrie of the kirk aucht
to be onlie cairful hou thay suld please God,
sua thay suld nocht be mareit, according to
that quhilk euer hes bene practised sen the
beginning of the kirk to thir dayes, as is maist
manifest of all ancient vryttaris: And I meruel
of zou that ze do nocht reid zour maister
Caluine mair diligentlie in this poynt, quha
spekand of the vidouis that var dedicat to the
seruice of the kirk sayis [Ego verò illis mini-
mè nego viduas quæ se suásq; Ecclesiæ operas
addicerét, perpetui cœlibatus legem simul su-
scepisse, non quia in eo religionem aliquá sta-
tuerent, vt postea fieri cœptum est, sed quoniá
nisi sui iuris, iugo maritali solutæ, functionem
illam sustinere non possent] I deny nocht to
thame that the vidouis quha addicted thame
selfis and thair haill trauel to the seruice of the
kirk, to haue subiectit thame self to the lau of
perpetual chastitie, nocht making onie religione in doing of that, as eftiruart begá to be
done, bot becaus thay micht nocht fulfil that
charge, vnles hauing ful pouar of thame selfis,
thay var fre from the zok of mariage. Gif the
vidouis quha hes bot lytil, or ná thing ado in
the kirk in cóparesone of the ministeris, can

I ij

I. Cor. 7.
"
"
"
"

Basil. in
lib. de vir-
ginit.
Amb. ad
virg. lapsá
ca. 5. hiero.
I. contra
Iouinia.

Cal. inst. 4
cap. 13. sec.
18.
"
"
"
"

nocht fulfil thair charge except thay remane vnmareit, as Caluine fayis, hou can
it be poffibil that the Minifteris being mareit can fulfil thair charges ? hou can ze
than clenge zour felfis bot ze repugne to S.
Paul, and to the practeife of the vniuerfal kirk
ze to zour auin maifter Iohne Caluine, and
that ze all, for the maift pairt fen ze haue profeffed chaftitie, incur the fentence of condemnatione pronunced be S. Paul aganis the Vidouis, quha efter the promeis of chaftitie did
marie? As to the places of fcripture quhilk ze
allege for zou, The firft is finiftrouflie inter-
preted, for the mening of S. Paul is nocht that
euerie man fuld be mareit, vtheruyfe he vald
be repugnant to him felf quha being vnmareit defyris al men to be lyk vnto him, and in
the beginning of the chaptoure fayis, It is gud
to ane man nocht to tuiche ane voman, bot as
vryttis S. Hierom amangis vther quæftionis
quhilk vas propofed to S. Paul be the Corint.
this vas ane, quhidder gif thay quha var mareit, to vaick on oraifone and prayer, fuld leue
thair vyfis or nocht ? he anfueris that thay
fuld nocht leue thame, bot euerie mã fuld keip
his auin vyf, quhilk is the mening of tha vordis neuertheles to auoyd fornicatione lat
euerie man haue his auin vyf, and euerie voman hir auin houfband.

The fecund place aucht to be vndirftand of
the Tatianitis, Marcionitis, and the Manichæanis quha cõdemnit Mariage as vnlefum, and
affermit that thair vas na difference betuix

S. Paul. 1.
Tim. 5.

1. Cor. 7.

D. Hiero. lib.
1. contra
Iouinia.

1. Timo. 4.
Clemens
libr. 6. con-
ftit. apoft.
ca. 8. Aug.
heref. 25.
epipha. 46.

Mariage and fornicatione, the Catholiques affirmes na sic thing, ze thay afferme the contrare, thatMariage is ane honorabil bād, and halie sacrament ordinit be Chrift for the procreatione and educatione of childrene: Thay afferme that it is nocht lesum to marie eftir the vou of chaftitie, quhairin thay condem nocht mariage bot condemnis thame quha brekis thair vou, and promeis maid vnto God, as S. Paul dois the Vidouis quhairof I haue spokin befoir. Thairfoir S. Bafil sayis that gif ane Virgine marie eftir the vou of chaftitie scho committis adulterie, becaus hir housbād is zit on lyf that is Chrift. And S Ambrose vrytand to ane Virgine that had fallin, sayis that scho had committed adulterie. And S. Hierom callis it nocht onlie adulterie bot alfo inceft. And ze can nocht misknau hou that Iouinianus vas condemnit for ane hæretike be reffone he vas the caus that Monkis and Nonis did Marie as vryttis S·Auguftine, sua ze suld be eschamet of sua manifeft prophanatione ād deprauatione of goddis vord,: Bot as ze ar deftitute of all spiritual consolatione, and delyttis onlie in the sensuall pleasoris of the fleshe, sua almaift quhat euer ze reid in the scripture, ze vreift it to zour fleshlie libertie, and hes na vther places of scripture in zour mouthis, bot thai quhilk be zour corruptit Iudgemét appeiris to cloik zour sensualitie. As [crescite & multiplicamini: Melius eft nubere quá vri: Vnusquisque propter fornicationem vxo-

Bafil. de virg.
Ambrof. ad virg. la pfam ca. 5

Hierony. lib.1. cōtra Iouinianū.

Aug. haref. 82. ad quoduulf deum.

rem suam habeat, vir vxori debitum reddat, non est bonum homini esse solum, faciamus ei adiutorium simile sibi: volo iuniores viduas nubere, filios procreare, an non habemus potestatem mulierem sororem circumducendi? oportet Episcopum esse vnius vxoris virum: vtere modico vino propter stomachum: vinu exhilarat cor hominis, spiritus tristis exiccat ossa : nihil quod intrat per os coinquinat hominem, omne quod in macello vænit manducate, nihil interrogantes propter conscientiam: omnia munda mundis: exercitatio corporalis ad modicum vtilis est] and sua furht of the rest, deny gif ze can bot thir and siclyk places of the scripture ar euer in zour mouthis, bayth in zour prechingis and familiar conuersatione. And as to the places quhilk tendisto mortificatione and dantoning of the fleshe ze mak na mentione at al, bot vald haue al sic places forzet and aluterlie vnknauin to the peopil, persauing maist cleirlie that gif thay kneu thame thay vald incontinent abhore zour maist sensual and adhominabil lyf, and vald knau perfytlie that it is nocht conforme to godis vord. For exemple I micht produce monie siclyk places quhilk I neuer hard zit cited be zou nor zit as I beleue, onie of the peopill, vnles by zour intent thay had chancit in zour otdinar textis, as for example, [It is gud for ane man nocht to tuiche ane voman : Thair ar sum quha hes maid thame self chast for the kingdome of heuin. Art thou

1. Cor. 7.

Matt. 19,

loufed from ane vyf:feik nocht ane vyf, I vald
haue zou vithout cair:the vnmareit cairis for
the thingis of the lord, hou he may pleafe the
lord: bot he quha is mareit cairis for the thingis of the varld hou he may pleafe his vyf: He
quha geuis his virgin to mariage dois veil, bot
he quha geuis hir nocht dois bettir. Refufe the
zoûgar vidouis for quhen thay begin to vax   1. *Timo.* 5
vantone aganis Chrift, thay vil marie incur-
rand damnatione, becaus thay haue brokin
thair firft promeis: It is bettir to vaik on orae-   *Tobie.* 12.
fone vith fasting and praying than lay vp-
threaforis of gold: Nou thairfoir fayis the lord   *Ioel.*
turne to me in all zour hairtis, in fasting, in   *Matt.* 6.
yeiping and murning: Bot quhen thou faftis,
oynt thy head and vefch thy face, that thou
appeir not vnto men to be faftand, bot to the   *Marc.* 2.
father of heuin in fecreit, The dayis fall cum
quhê the brydgrome falbe tane from thame   1.*Cor.* 7.
and than thay fal faft. Lat not ane of zou fub-
strač the deuitie of Mariage from the vther
except for ane tyme that ze vaik on fasting   1.*Cor.* 9.
and praying: I chaftife, my bodie, and bring it
vndir obedience, left quhen I haue præched
the Euágel to vtheris, I my felf be fund in the
nomber of the reprobat: It var tædious to cite
the thrid pairt of the placis of the fcripture
quhairin ye at exhortit to fasting and al kynd
of dantoning of the flesh, and zit in all zour
fermonis and conference, thair is nane of thir
mair hard, nor gif thay had neuer bene vryttin.

OF ORDOVR
CHAP. XIX.

M.

Vil thou lyKuise approue the seuint Papistical Sacrament quhilK is callit Ordour?

B. It is nocht vithout gret caus that Hæretikis lyk zou, at al tymes hes bene maist offendit that Ordour, quhairbie is geuin the grace of lauchfull calling, and administratione of the sacramentis, suld be reuerenced as ane sacrament: Becaus this being granted it vil euidentlie appeir, that thay ar na Pastoris, bot Volsis, and Toddis, quha hes nocht cú in at the dur, bot as ze, haue violentlie done brokin the dyk of the scheipfald : zit al the treu Doctoris in the kirk of god hes acknauledgit Ordour to be ane Sacrament, of the quhilk S. Paul makis mentione vrittand to Timothie *1.Timo.4.* neglect nocht the gift of prophecie, quhilk is geuin to the be the onlayig of the hádis of the preistheid: in the quhilk testimonie thay quha ar nocht villinglie blind, may collect al thingis requesit to the definitione of ane sacrament. *Calu.li.4.* Zea Caluin zour maister conuict *cap. 19.* be the stréth and euidence of the veritie, qu- *sect.31.* hilk is sua expreslie contenit in goddis vord, is constranit to grant that Ordour is ane treu and lauchful sacrament, vith the quhilk al thay aucht to be indeuit, quha exerceisis the preaching of the vord, and administratione

of the sacramentis: albeit in thir feu vordis he
cuttis his auin throt, and declaris maist cleirlie that he being deftitute of the said sacrament, is na minifter of goddis vord, bot ane
fals Prophet, quha vithout al calling hes
ftart vp at his auin hand: And as to zou quha
denyis this sacrament, ze nocht onlie contra-
vene the manifeft vord of god, the practife
of the vniuerfal kirk euer sen the Apoftlis
vnto this present: and zour maifter Iohne
Caluine: Bot mairouer ze induce sic ane confufione amang zour selfis (sen ze mak it lefum
but onie lauchful calling to vsurp the office
of ane minifter) that the lyk vas neuer hard
nor fene in the varld befoir: and gif I vald
fay that I var ane Minifter, and had als gret
pouar to preache, and adminiftrat the facramentis as ze haue, quhat argument can ze
haue aganis me? For I am als abil to schau quha gaif me pouar, as Iohne knox vas abil to
fchau, quhen he vas demandit of his authoritie: fua ze may fe be taking auay of this facrament, hou ze put the pure flok of Chrift in
perpetual vauering, hauing na reul to difcern betuix the lauchful fcheipherd, and the
volf.

M. Vil thou approue al the degreis of Ordore in the
Papifticcal Kirk, as thocht thai var inftitute be our
Maifter and Apoftlis, sence our reformatione allouis
nane of the fam?

B. Gif ze can propone onie scripture, or determinatione of onie general Concile, or zit

the practeiſe of the vniuerſal kirk, aganis ſik
diſtinctione of ordoris, I vil do gude vil to
anſuere zou: bot I am aſſurit ze can do na ſik
thing: As to zour reformationes it is hard
to mé to groúde my faith vpone thame, becaus thay conſiſt cheiflie in pulling doune,
and denying of thaj thingis quhilk beſoir hes
bene vniuerſalie eſtablished, and thairfoir I
tak lytill head of zour argument, quhilk lea-
nis onlie vpone zour deformationis: For I
think for my auin part, I haue als gret authoritie as ze or onie miniſter of Scotland, and
am mair aſſurit of the aſſiſtance of the halie ſpirit nor ze ar: Bot to conclude I meruel
na thing that ze grant nocht the diſtinctione
of the degreis, and offices of kirk men, quha
hes thair ordináce of the halie Ghaiſt ſpeikád
in the halie kirk, quhilk is the piller and
groúde of treuthe: For gif ze grant the ſame,
as al gud Chriſtian man dois: ze ſe manifeſtlie
zour auin arrogance and condemnatione:
Becaus the laſt general Concile conuocat be
the authoritie of Chriſt our ſaluioure, as Heiche Preiſt in the Pape, hes denuncit al zour
venemous doctrine maiſt peſtiferus, and hæretical.

i. Tim. 3.

OF THE PAIPIS AVTHORITIE.
CHAP. XXI.

B*Alcanqual. Quhat authoritie grantis thou*
vnto the Paip?

B. Gifonie controuerſie of religione ſal aryſe betuix Chriſtian men being of learning
and eſtimatione, being abil to mak ane greit
diuiſione, vnles the Concile of the general
kirk be conuocat: The biſcop of Rome quha is Paip, hes pouar and authoritie to aſ-
ſembil his Concile of the quhilk he is Preſident as Vicar of our ſaluiour Chriſt vpon the
earthe, and vithout quhais cõfirmatione the
ſame hes na effect.

*Bal. Our maiſter Chriſt is onlie head of the kirk,
quhairſoir the authoritie of the Paip is vſurpit, and
tyrannicall.*

B. Zour proudnes lattis zou nocht vndirſtand the veritie : for Chriſt indeid is onlie
head of the kirk fra quhom all grace and ſpi-
rituall giftis dois proceid throuche the haill
bodie of it, lyk as from the head, the mouing
and vital ſtrenth proceidis in the reſt of the
bodie. And in this maner nather the Paip, nather zit onie mortal man can be head of the
kirk: bot as to the exterioure gouernement
ãd adminiſtratione thairof Chriſt, nocht beïg
vith vs in ane corporal and ſenſibil maner,
to quhom ve may haue our recours in al materis and difficulteis, he hes left vs ane Vicare
in his place, quhom in this reſpect ve cal the
heid of the kirk as ſubordinat vnto Chriſt,
and depending on him : quhairin he hes ſchauin his gret luſe and Cheritie touardis his
ſpous the kirk, and touardis hir pure flok, leuing thame in his place ane to quhom thay

mycht euer haue recurse, quhatsumeuer dif-
ficultie micht occur: And thaifoir sayis S.
Ambrose, speking of S. Petir (Christus reli-
quit nobis Petrum, tanquam vicatium amoris
sui)that is, Chrst hes left vs Petir in his place
as vicare of his lufe touardis vs, quhom he
constitute cheif pastore vndir him selff, saying
Sathan desyrit to riddil zou as quheit, bot I
prayit for the Petir, that thy fayth inlaik
nocht : Of the quhilk ze may vndirstad esilie,
that suppose Christ be head of the kirk, zit
that it is na vyse repugnant that he haue ane
Vicar in his place for the exteriore gouernement as said is : lyk as the king is head of his
realme, suppoise he haue ane lieutenet vndir
him : zour argument than as ze may persaue,
is of na strenth, for in ane maner Christ is
callit head of the kirk, and in ane vthir maner
the Paip is callit head of the sam, lyk as
ze zour selfis do cal zour ministeris, Pastoris
of four kirkis(suppoise thay feid thame veray
euil) and zit ze vill nocht deny bot Christ is
Pastore of thame: For it is all ane thing to be
callit pastore of the kirk, and head of the kir-
ke, considering the pastore man gyde and gouerne his floke: quhilk is the propir office and
devtie of the head in respect of the rest of
the bodie.

Bal. Is nocht this ane sufficient argument to say,
Christ onlie v us head of the kirk , thairfoir Petir in
nauyse micht be heid of the sam, nor be consequece his
successoris?

Luc. 22.

B. Gif this be ane sufficient argument, it follouis alsueil Christ is onlie Pastore of zour four kirkis, thairfoir ze ar nocht pastoris of thame: gif be this argument ze proue that the Paip is nocht head of the kirk, ze may proue lykuyse that ze ar nocht pastoris of zour four kirkis, quhilk I trou be veray treu: Becaus ze can schau na authoritie of goddis vord, apoyntand ane minister to four kirkis.

Bal. Our Maister Christ in the Euangell of Luc. Denyis, that thair suld be onie head or Prince amang Luc.22. *the Apostlis, as is in ciuil policie. For thair it is vryttin. Thair arase ane contentione amang the Disciples quhilk of thame appeirit to be greitast, bot he said vnto thame, The kingis of the nationis hes dominione ouer thame, and thay quha hes pouar ouer thame ar callit beneficent, Zit Ze ar nocht sua: Bot he quha is gretar amang Zou lat him be as he quha is les, and he quha is Prince lat him be seruand to the rest.*

B. This is ane commone place, quhairfra ze souke sophisticall argumentis to dissaue the ignorant pepill: to vit quhen as in onie place of scripture, the abuse of ane gud thing, (sic as is the authoritie of he preistheid quhairbie vnitie is conseruit in the kirk of Christ) is reprouit, to collect that the gude thing, is altogidder denyit to haue onie profitabil vse in the societie of mankynd, as in this place ze do maist manifestlie. For our maist halie saluioure Iesus Christ denyis nocht in this place, that thair suld be ane amang the rest of the Apostlis, eftir his departing, of gretar Authoritie

nor ane vthir, bot onlie inſtructis him quha
ſal reſſaue this præeminent Authoritie, that
he Ioyne nocht thairuith pryd, ambitiõe, and
lifting vp of his hart, thinkand that throuche nature, merite, or operatione of his auin,
he is mekil mair vorthie, nor the reſt of his
brethene : for ſaying [he quha vald be Prince
amang zou, lat him be as he quha ſeruis] it
is neceſſar that ve grant ſum of the Apoſtlis
to haue bene Prince, or ellis the inſtructione
var ſuperfiuous, quhil as na man is inſtructit:
This is mair manifeſt be the exeple tane from
his auin humilitie, becaus thair is na dout bot
he vas Prince amang his diſcipillis, zit he did
veſche thair feit, and reſſonis in this place,
quhilk of the tua is gretar, quhidder he that
ſittis doun, or he quha ſtandis, and makis
ſeruice ? bot I am in the middis of zou as he
quha makis ſeruice : Sua as he vas head of
the Apoſtlis and did ſerue vnto thame, in lyk
maner he requiris that his Vicar and lieutenēt
ſuld be ane ſeruand to the reſt, And that his
ſuperioritie ſuld nocht tend to his auin propir glore, and vantage: bot onlie to the pro-
fite and vtilitie of his flok: abyding his reuard nocht fra his flok, bot fra Chriſt, quha
did apoynt him thairto : And thairſoir gif
ze vil conſidder the ſtylis of Emperouris, and
kingis of the earthe, ãd of the Papis of Rome
Vicaris to Chriſt, ze vil find thame mekil diſ-
ctepant : As the ſtyle of the Emperoris is na
thing, bot titillis of honore , Imperator, Do-

minator, Triumphator: The Paip ſtylis him
ſelf maiſt humlie Seruus ſeruorum Dei, hauing gud remembrance of the vordis of
Chriſt quhilk ze haue maiſt faſlie cited for
zour purpoſe.

*Bal. Gif thou think that Petir vas Prince of the
Apoſtlis, eſtir the aſcenſione of our Maiſter Chriſt,
thou art conuict be manifeſt ſcripturis, quhairin
ve reid that Paul reprouit Petir at Antiochia, and
ſayes that he vas na thing inferiore to the Cheifaſt
Apoſtlis.*

B. Zour argumēt is of na ſtrenth,Sanct Paul
reprouit S.Petir, tharfore Sāct Petir vas nocht
head of the Apoſtlis, Becaus the reprouing
of Sanct Petir, apertenis nocht to his office
quhidder it vas mair heich and excellent in
dignitie, nor Sanct Paulis or nocht : bot
onlie to his perſone inſafar as ane particular
membir of the kirk, bund to the obſerua-
tione of the Chriſtian lauis quharin he micht
als ſone fail as onie of the reſt of the Apoſtlis, and ſonar,becaus Sathan is maiſt reddie
to procure the fal of thame, quhilk may be
gretaſt ſklander and caus of ruing to monie:
Siclyk ane ſingular and ſimpil preiſt may reproue the maneris of the perſone, quha is
lauchfullie promouit to be head of the kirk,
hauingthe authoritie ofChriſt vpone the face
of the earth. For the command of fraternal
correctione is general and dois comprehend
al men in quhatſumeuer eſtait or degrie thay
be:For euin as men may failzie: ſua aucht thay

to be subiect to correctione, and admonition: Porphyrius (as testifeis S. Hierō in this place) suppois he vas ane Apostat frō the Christiane religione, zit vas nocht sua blind as ze, bot gatherit albeit vrāgustlie, that S. Paul vas ane arrogāt man, becaus he interprysit to reproue S. Petir quha vas his head: The mater of the supreme Authoritie of S. Petir vas thā so cleir and manifest in the self, that euin amang the Apostatis from the Christian religion, it could nocht be denyit: As to the vthir part of zour obiectione, quhair ze say that S. Paul thocht him na thing inferiore to the maist gret Apostlis: That testimonie seruis na thing for zour purpose, becaus as the Ancient vrittaris interpretis that place, Sum vald haif persuadit the Corinthianis, that S. Paul vas onlie ane discipil, or schollar of the Apostlis, and nocht of the sam rank vith the rest: For the quhilk caus he vrittis, that he vas ane Apostil alsueil as thay var, chosin thairto be god immediatlie, ād hauīg pouar to preache throuch the hail varld as thay had, and that he had laborit alsmekil for the setting furth, and plāting the Euāgel as thay had: and zit nothuithstāding he acknauledgit S. Petir as principal, and cheif head of the rest: Zea in the epistle to the Galatianis he testifeis him self, that he passit vp to Hierusalem to confer vith S. Petir, vthervyse al his preaching had bene in vaine the quhilk sanct Hierom exponand sayis that the preaching of sanct Paul had bene of

na au-

Hiero. in 1. ad Galatas.

2.cor.11.

Gal.2.

na authoritie, except it had bene confirmit
be the authoritie of fanct. Petir: And S.Aug.
vrittis in plane vordis that gif S. Paul had
nocht fund the Apoftlis in lytt, vith quhom
he micht haif conferrit his Euangel, the kirk
vald haue geuin him na credeit at al: quhairof
ze may perfaue that S.Paul acknauledgit the
Authoritie of S.Petir, v theruyfe it had nocht
bene neceffar, for to get authoritie to his doctrine, to haue conferrit vith S Petir.

*Bal. Thou that pretēdis the vndirſtanding of Dia-
lectiк maк me ane forme of neceſſar cōcluſione groundit vpone onie place of the vrittin vord, quhairbie
thou may praue that S. Petir vas head, and grounde
of the Кirк quhilк thou callis bayth ane thing.*

B. Quhat mifteris me to mak onie argument to proue that Petir vas the ground of
the kirk, fen Chrift him felf, callis him the
groude, faying:(vpone this rok I vil buyld my
kirk)?Gif ze culd fchau the lyk teftimonie of
fcripture that the kirk fuld be groundit vpone Iohne Caluin, or that Iohne Caluine fuld
haue bene callit the rok, vpone the quhilk
Chrift fuld buyld his kirk, I trou ze vald
cry loudar for the defence of the kirk of Geneua'nor ve do for the kitk of Rome:Bot thākis to god thair is na vord in the fcripture nather of Caluine, nor zit of knox.

*Bal. Chriſt him ſelf vas the roк, as vitneſſis
Paul, thairfoir Petir vas nocht the roк vpone the
quhilк the kirk ſuld be buyldit.*

B.Ze beir greit inuie to S.Petir,For fen Chrift

him self, callis him the Rok vpone the quhilk
his kirk suld be buildit, ze may persaue zour
argument to be maist vane: euin as gif onie
man suld say: Chrift vas the licht of the varld,
according to that teftimonie of scripture I am
the licht of the varld, thairfore the Apoftlis
vas nocht the licht of the varld quhilk repugnis expreslie to the fcripturis [Ze ar the licht
of the varld:] Chrift is callit Petra becaus he
is the principal grounde on the quhilk the
hail kirk dependis, and reffauis fubfiftence:
Petir is callit be Chrift the rok, nocht as the
principal grounde, bot as dependent from
Chrift, to quhom all the membirris of the
kirk aucht to be conioynit, gif thay vald be
membirris of Chrift, as I haue fchauin maift
cleirlie be goddis vord, and al the hail anciét
vrittaris dois teftifie: As amangis the reft,
S. Hierõ vrytand to Damafus Paip of Rome,
Quha euer fayis he, is nocht conioynit vith
the, he is feparat from Chrift: And Optatus
Mileuitanus vrittand aganis the hæretik Parmenianus, thou can nocht misknau fayis he
that Petir vas head of the kirk: and fua making ane enumeratione of all the Papis of
Rome vnto Siricius, quhilk vas in his dayes:
vith Siricius fayis he, ve ar cõioynit in vnitie
of doctrine: producing that as ane infallibil
argument of the cõiunctione vith Chrift, and
befoir thame bayth the ancient vrytar Tertullian in his buke, quhilk he callis de Præfcri-
ptionibus Hereticorum, quhair he callis Petir

Math.5 (margin)

Hierõ in epiftola ad damafum. (margin)

Optat 2. cõtra Parmenia. (margin)

Tertul. de. prefcriptio (margin)

the Rok of the kirk and confermes thame
to be in treu doctrine quha ar conioynit vith
the treu fucceffours of Petir : And befoir him
alfo Ireneus fpeking of the kirk of Rome
aganis the Valentinianis, To this kirk fayis he
it is neceffar that all vther kirk aggrie, becaus of the authoritie quhilk it hes aboue the
reft: And to be fchort vith zou,zea can nocht
be abil to fchau in onie eage fen Chrift that
euer thay quha hes bene conioynit vith the
kirk of Rome hes bene eftemit for hæretikis,
or thay quha hes bene feparat from it, for
treu Chriftianis, or Catholiques: And fua be
ane fufficient inductione, I may conclude that
ze quha hes feparat zour feluis from it, ar
heretikis, as euer al ancient doctoris hes concludit befoir thir dayes. And as ze aggrie
not vith the fuccefforis of Petir, fua ze ar
nocht conioynit vith the Rok vpone the quhilk Chrift did buyld his kirk faying: (Tu es
Petrus & fuper hanc Petram ædificabo Ec-
clefiam meam.) Thou art ane rok and v-
pon this rok I fal buyld my kirk, for the Hebreu text of Sanct Mattheu hes tuyfe Ce-
phas vithoutfic chágeing as is in *ælęys* and *miles*.
Dene. Durie. Thou knaw nocht quhat our maifter
Chrift vnderftude be the roke in that place, for it is
the faith and confeßione of Petir, fua that al faythful
Brethrene, confeßand Chrift to be the fone of the le-
uing god, is equal to Petir be verteu of this teftimonie,
and grounde of the kirk na les nor he.
B. I vat nocht in quhat fcripture ze haif fund

that the rok is callit the confessione of the
fayth of S. Petir : And suppois it var callit sua,
it seruis nocht sua mekil to zour purpose as
ze beleue, becaus the confessione of the fayth
of S. Petir aucht nocht to be separat from Petir, bot that the kirk suld be groudit on Petir
as ane faythful membir of Christ, vith quhais
fayth the rest of the membirris suld aggrie:
Nou schir that al Christianes ar nocht equal
to S. Petir be verteu of this testimonie, of the
vordis immediatlie follouing it is maist manifest. Becaus our maist halie saluiour sayis vnto him (to the I sal gif the keyis of the kingdo
me of heuin) quhilk ze vil nocht grant to ap-
pertene to euerie man indifferentlie : And gif
al Christianis in safar as thay confes Christ to
be the sone of the leuing God, be the ground
of the kirk: than vald I demad of zou, quhair
in dois consist the rest of the buylding?

*D D . Thou art ane obstinat, stifnekkit Papist, and it
var almous to hang the fals theif knaif.*

B.   Schir gif al papistis merites to be hangit
ze vald haue bene hanged lang syne, and zour
Coule vpon zour head.

*Bal.   Quhy geuis thou nocht credite to Gregore ane
Bischop of Rome, quha refused the name of ane vniuersal Bischop, saying, gif onie man vald be callit ane
vniuersal Bischop, he is the foirrunnar of the Antich.*

B.   I meruel that ze ar nocht eschamit to cite
S. Gregore, sen in his hail Epistles he schauis
maist cleirlie hou he dois succeid to S. Petir,
and hes Authoritie aboue al vther Bischopis.

as amang the reſt, reid the epiſtle to Auguſtine quha vas ſend to Ingland for conuerſione
of the cuntrey, in the quhilk he geuis diſpenſatione to contract mariage in certane degreis
forbiddin be the kirk: and in ane Epiſtle vryttin to Scotland concerning the obſeruation
of Paſche day, amangis vther thingis, he ſayis,
he meruellis hou that Scotland being bot ane
nuke of the varld, dar vſurp to celebrat paſche
day, at ane vther tyme nor the vniuerſal kirk
dois? Reid his Epiſtlis to the Biſchopis bayth
of the Orient, and Occident: And I am aſſurit
that ze vil be confundit of zour impudencie,
as to tha vordis quhilk ze cite for zou, ze haue neuer red nor conſiderit the mening of
thame: Becaus he callis him ane vniuerſal Biſ-
chope, that dois ſua vſurp to him the name of
ane Biſchop, that he vil na man be biſchop by
him, in the quhilk maner quhaſoeuer callis
him ſelf ane vniuerſal Biſchop he is ane foir-
rūnar of the Antichriſt ſuppoiſe in ane vther
maner ane vniuerſal Biſchop may be callit
he quha hes authoritie ouer the vniuerſal kirk
and hes pouar to gather the vniuerſal kirk
togidder, as in the general Cōcilis, the quhilk
pouar S. Petir, and al Biſch. of Rome, euer had,
and practiſed ſen the beginning to thir dayes.
*Bal. Ze lay euer for ane grounde, that Petir vas biſ-
chop of Rome, bot I afferme that he vas neuer in Rome,
and thairfoir he culd nocht be Biſchop of it.*

B. And I affirme, he vas in Rome, bringand
for me al ancient vryttaris, that euer hes vryt-

Egeſip a
exciðio
Hieroſoly.

tin of this mater, quha teſtifeis that he vas nocht onlie in Rome, bot ſched his blude in it, as Egeſippus: Irenæus lib. 3. contra Valentinos.cap. 3. Tertullian de præſcriptionibus Hæreticorum: Optatus lib.2. contra Parmenianú Auguſtin in ane thouſand places , as aganis the Donatiſtis, Creſconius grammaticus, Parmenianus, and in his 165.Epiſtle: S Hierom de viris illuſtribus, quhair he teſtifeis that in the ſecund zeir of Claudius, he did cum to Rome: This ſaù teſtifeis Euſebius , and al the reſt. Nou ſchau me ſamekil as ane, of onie Authoritie, quha teſtifeis that S. Petir vas neuer in Rome. Bot indeid I mã lauch at zour greit ſubtilitie : Sanct Petir vas neuer in Rome, thairfoir he had nocht Authoritie ouer the kirk of Rome: for ſuppoiſe the antecedent var treu, the concluſione dou na thing , as gif ze ſuld ſay, the Quene of Ingland vas neuer in Irelád, thairfoir ſcho vas neuer Quene of it, or as ze vald ſay, to cum neirar to zour purpoſe , the miniſter hes nocht viſeit ane of his four kirkis, , thairfoir he hes na authoritie aboue thame.

Bal. Petir vas Biſchop at Antiochia, thairfoir he vas nocht Biſchop of Rome.

B. Egeſippus the ancient vryttar teſtifeis that be ane reuelation maid vnto him, he chan git his ſeat out of Antiochia to Rome , ſua he did conſtitute Rome his ſeat, in the quhilk he did ſit as heid of the hail kirk, and in the quhilk he did ſched his blude, for the Euangel.

Egeſip. de excidio hierofoly. Iren.lib.3. cap. 3. Tertu.lib. de praſcri. hæretici. Opta 2.cõ tra Parm. Aug. epiſtol.63. Hiero. de viris illuſt.

Egeſivp. de excidio hie roſoly.

M.

Thou hes neuer sene na thing of the antiquitie,
quhilk gif thou had done, thou vald haue red
hou that the fatheris of the saxt Concile of Carthage
quhair Augustine also vas present opposed thame selfis
to the Paip Bonifacius, And quhen Faustinus quha
vas the Paipis legate, for to defend his maisteris vsurpit authoritie did produce ane decreit of the Concile *Cõcil. Car-*
of Nice, that it suld be lesũ in al ecclesiastical materis *thag. 6.*
to mak appellatione fra all vther bischopis and ordi-
nar iudges to the bischop of Rome, The fatheris of the
said Concile did conuict him to be ane lear, and did
schau cleirlie that na sic thing vas to be fund in that
Concile, hauing conferred sindrie exemplaris of it,
quhilkis thay had gottin pairtlie out of Alexandria,
partlie out of Constantinopil, sua thou may se that it
is nocht ve onlie, that hes ganestand the tyrannie of
Zour Paip, bot Augustine also him self, and all the
fatheris quhilk vas in the Concile of Carthage.

B.   Zour obiectione to gather it in feu vordis consistis in tua poyntis, the ane is that the
Bischopis of the saxt Concile of Carthage
vald nocht permit that onie appellatiõe suld
be maid out of Aphrik to the Bischop of Rome, The vther is that Faustinus the Papis legat
did falslie allege the Concile of Nice for his
pairt. As to the first, befoir, I cum to the ansuere of zour argument, I vil schau hou in al

aiges bayth befoir, and eftir that Concile, it
hes bene practised to mak appellatione to the
seate of Rome, As in the zeir of God ane hundreth fourtie and tua Marció in Pótus, being
Epiph.hæ- excommunicat be his Bischop com to Rome
res. 42. to be absoluit. And in the zeir of God tua
húdreth fyftie tua Fortunatus and fælix being
Cyp.lib.1. deposed be S.Cypriane did saill to Rome that
ep. 3. thay micht be absoluit be Cornelius. And a lytil eftir Basilides and Martialis Bischopis of
Spanzie being deposed, maid thair appellatione to Stephanus than Bischop of Rome,
and desyrit to be restored be him. And in the
zeir of God thre húdreth and fourtie, Athanasius being deposed be the Bischopis of the
Orient, maid his appellatione to Iulius than
Theod. li. Bischop of Rome, zea Iulius keipand the or-
2. cap.4. dinar discipline of the kirk commandit, that
tha Bischopis quha had deposed Athanasius
suld cum vnto Rome, and that thair the hail
Sulp.lib. caus suld be intraitted. And nocht lang eftir
2. hist. Priscillianus being deposed be the Bischopis
of Fráce appélled to Damasus Paip of Rome.
Greg. tu- And in the four húdreth zeir of God, Brixius
ron.de reb' the Bischop of Touris being deposed be the
gest. Frác. Bischopis of France also, maid his appellatio-
Lib.10. ne to the Bischop of Rome, be quhom he vas
Chrisost. restored agane. And about the sam aige Chry-
ep.1. et 2. sostome being deposed from the seate of Có-
ad Inno- stantinopil be Theophilus and vtheris, maid
cent. his appellatione to Innocentius than Bischop
of Rome, and be him vas restored to his di-

gnitie agane. In the zeir of God four hund
reth fourſcoir or thairtie, Theodoretus being *Theod.epi.*
depoſed, maid his appellatione to Leo , be *1.ad Leon.*
quhom he vas alſo reſtored agane. S.Baſil vryt *S.Baſ.epi.*
tis to Athanaſ. that letteris be directed to the *3.*
Biſchop of Rome that he may Iudge of the
hail côtrouerſie quhilk vas amang thair hâdis,
and for that caus that the Biſchop of Rome
deput ſum to viſſie the hail kirkis of the O-
rient. And Athanaſius him ſelf vryttis that the *Athana*
biſchopis of Grece paſſed to Iulius,and deſy- *apol.2.*
rit to be abſolued be him. And Epiphanius,
that Vrſatius, and Valens paſſed to Rome for *Epi.here.*
the lyk caus. And Theodoretus teſtifeis that *68.*
Damaſus Paip of Rome depoſed Flauianus
the patriarche of Antiochia,and albeit Theo- *Theo.li.5.*
doſius the Emperour , did defend Fla- *cap. 27.*
uianns pairt , zit he ſend him to Rome to
trait and defend his auin caus. And Socrates *Socra. li.5*
vitneſſis hou that Theophilus Biſchop of Ale- *cap. 15.*
xandria ſend his legat vnto the Biſchop of
Rome to mak interceſſione for Flauianus,
And this maner of Appellation vas ſua commone that euin the infidelis acknauledgit the ſame , quhairof I produce to zou the
exempil of Paulus Samoſatenus quha being
iuſtlie condemnit for hereſie, and being commandit to depairt our of the ſeat of Antiochia *Euſeb.lib.*
vald nocht obey,bot had recourſe to Aurelia- *7. hiſt. ec-*
nus the Emperore, quha vald nocht tak the *cleſiaſt.*
iudgemét vpone him,bot cômâdit him to pas *cap.24.*
to the Biſchop of Rome, quhom he kneu veil

aneuche, albeit he vas ane infidel to be his ordinar Iudge. And eftiruart quhen the Donatistis var códemnit in Afrik thay maid thair appellatione to Conftantinus Magnus, quha vald nocht iudge in the mater, bot commandit thame to pas to Melchiades Bifchop of Rome, that he as lauchfull iudge micht difcerne vpone thair caus, the quhilk mater being fullie intracted be S. Auguftine, he declairis planelie that Melchiades had pouar to Iudge on thame albeit thay had bene iudgit befoir be the Bifchopis of Aphrik. Of thir and vther lyk exéplis, quhilk I micht produce, It may be maift cleirlie pfaued, hou bayth befoir ád eftir the Concile of Carthage the authoritie of the Bifchop of Rome, hes bene acknauledged to the hail varld. Victor that vas neir the Apoftlis dayes, ane Bifchop of Rome, ane maift halie man, ád martyr for the treu fayth of Chrift, for confirmatione of his iurifdictione did excommunicat al the kirkis of Afia, becaus thay aggreit nocht vith the Romane kirk in the keiping of Pafche day. And na man reproued him of onie vfurpit iurifdictióe in that poynt. Tertull. aganis Praxeas teftifeis that Zephyrinus did excommunicat the kirkis of Afia, be reffone thay folloued the herefie of Montanus. Zonaras in the lyff of Iuftiniane vryttis hou that the Bifchop of Rome did excommunicat the Bifchopis of Dardania, And Innocentius excommunicat thame quha had iniuftlie condemnit Chryfo-

Auguft. epif.162.

Socr. lib.3. cap.7. Syn. calcedoné. act.7

Eufeb. li.5. ecclef. hift. cap.4.

Tertul. cótrapraxeá.

Zonaras in vita Iuftinian.

ſtome. Celeſtinus lykuyſe excommunicat
Neſtoriᵉ:finalie al vther hæretikis almaiſt hes
bene excommunicat, and condemnit be the
biſchop of Rome, as Symon Magus be S. Pe- *Irenæ.li.3.*
tir. Valentinus and his diſcipillis be Higinus *contra Va-*
and Pius. Cerdon and Marcion be Anicetus. *lent. cap.3.*
The Montaniſtis be Zephirinus, Blaſtus and *Tertul. con*
his factione be Victor. The Nouatianis be *tra Praxeā*
Cornelius. The Sabellianis be the Paip Dio- *S.hiſt.cap.*
nyſius. The Donatiſtis be Melchiades. The *25.26.27.*
Atrianis be Sylueſter. The Macedonianis be *6.cap.36.*
Damaſus:The Pelagianis be Innocentius,Zo- *In Con-*
zimus, and Bonifacius, and ſua furth of the *cil.Nicen.*
reſt, to Leo the tent quha condemnit Lauter *In Concil.*
and all his ofſpring as Caluiniſtis, Zuinglia- *Conſtant.*
nis, Anabaptiſtis, and vtheris. Farder for ac- *Auguſt.*
knauledgeing of this iuriſdictiōe, ve reid hou *epiſt.162.*
that the biſchoppis of Rome had thair ordi- *Leo cp.84.*
nar lieutennentis in the Orient,and in Afrik,
in France,and vther pairtis,as Leo the firſt had
Anaſtaſius biſchop of Theſſalonica his lieutē- *Leo ep.78.*
nent throuche the haill Oriēt. And in the cūtrey of Aphrik he had for his lieutennent ane *Hormiſda*
biſchop callit Potentius. And Hormiſda maid *ad Saluſt.*
Saluſtius the biſchop of Suilzie his lieutennent in Spanzie. And Gregorius the firſt had *Gregor.li.*
the biſchop of Arlis his lieutennent into Frā- *4.epiſt.52.*
ce,aluyſe thay reſerued euer the gretaſt and
maiſt difficile materis to thame ſelfis, for the
quhilk reaſone thay vſed euer to haue the maiſt learned men about thame, As in the tyme
of Damaſus S.Hier. vas callit for that caus vn-

to Rome to help the said Paip Damasus in resolutione of al materis bayth cōcerning the Oriēt, and Occidēt, as he testifeis him self. And S. Augustine vas imployed to help the Paip Zozimus in resolutione of the Ecclesiastical materis in Afrik, and had command of the Paip for that caus, to pas to Cæsarea, as vryttis Possidius his discipill : Nou albeit aganis sua monie plane testimoneis of thir maist learned and halie vrytraris quha hes florished in diuerse aigis, be the quhilk the Paipis Authoritie is maist manifestlie declarit, ze micht produce for zour part in the contrare the opinione of sum certane bischopis gathered togidder in that prouincial Cōcile of Carthage, al men of richt iudgemēt vald think vith thame selfis, that zour caus suld nocht be gretúlie thairbie auanced, sen the priuat opinione of sum bischopis can nocht preiudge the vniuersal consent of the haill kirk. Zit that ze haue na occasione to gloir, I vil schau that euin the Fatheris of that Concile at alluterlie repugnant to zou, and all zour proceidingis: first, thay bischopis callit not the Paip the Romane Antichrist, nor zit separat thame selfis from the cōmunione vith the kirk of Rome, as ze do, nor zit denyed that the bischop of Rome had authoritie and Iurisdictione aboue al vther bischopis, as is cleir of S. August. quha vas thair present as deput be al the bischoppis of Numidia, quhen he vryttis in this maner. (In ecclesia Romana semper Apo-

ftolicæ Cathedræ viguit principatus] In the *Auguft.epi*
Romane Kirk fayis he, the fupreme Chyre and *162.*
Authoritie hes euer bene keipit, And vrittand to Innocentius vith the fatheris of the
Mileuitane Concile (quia dominus te gratiæ *Auguft.*
fuæ præcipuo munere in fede Apoftolica col- *epif. 102.*
locauit &c. Paftoralem diligentiam quæfu-
mⁿ adhibere digneris:) That is becaus that god
be ane fpecial gift of his gudnes, hes placed the
in the Apoftolik chyre, ve befeik the to beftou
the deutie, and diligence of ane paftore touard
vs, Heir S. Auguft. vith fa monie vther fatheris
acknauledges the bifchop of Rome for thair
paftore, thay being in Afrik and he in Italie.
And vrittand to Bonifacius he declairis pla- *Augnft.li.*
nelie, that the cure of the vniuerfal kirk aper- *1. ad Boni-*
tenisvnto him, and that he is put as in the vat- *fac.cap.14*
che, to aualk ouer the hail kirk: Sua the quæftione vas nocht amangis thame of the authoritie of the bifchop of Rome, Bot becaus ane
preift of Afrik callit Appiarius being iuftlie
condemnit be the bifchopis of Aphrik, had
paffed to Rome to Paip Zozimus, and geuin
him vrang informationis, the faid bifchopis
thocht it nauyfe profitabil for the ordour, añd
difcipline of rhe kirk, that fik appellationis
fuld be maid in tymes cumming, Bot thay beleuit, that the authoritie of the bifchop of
Rome being euer granted to him, it vas
nocht profitabil for the kirk that the preiftis
and inferior clergie efter thay var condemnit
iuftlie be thair ordinar iudges fuld be per-

mitted to mak appellatione to Rome, be reafone thair caufes micht be mair perfytlie decer
nit in thair auin cuntrey, as hauing in it thair
vitnes prefent, and monie hauing infpectione
of the haill caus, quhairbie all fraud and de-
ceptione micht efilie be auoydit, and that the
grace of the halie Spreit, vald nocht be denyed to the Bifchopis, and ordinat iuges to decerne fufficientlie in fik caufis: As amangis the
Romanis it vas nocht lefum to mak appellatione fra thame quha var callit Præfecti prætorio to the Emperour, becaus that thay quha
var put in fik offices var iudgit to be indeuit
vith fik qualiteis, that thay vald nocht iudge
vtheruyfe nor the mater requyrit, And zit it
var ane veray euil argument to proue heirfoir
that the Emperoris had na iurifdictiõe aboue
thame quha var callit Præfecti prætorio : the
quhilk maner of reffoning ze vfe prefentlie.
Mairatour to cloife all zour mouthis they beleuit nocht generallie that na appellatione
fuld be maid to Rome as ze vald falflie allege,
bot onlie that the preiftis and inferior clergie
fuld not vfe onie fic appellatione : As to the
Bifchopis Archebifchopis and vtheris it vas
nocht callit in dout bot it fuld be lefum vnto thame to haue recurfe, and mak appellatione to the feate of Rome. For probatione
of this, I produce vnto zou the Actis of the
Concile it felf, and the maift plane vordis of
S. Auguftine, and the hail Concile to Bonifacius [tuæ venerationi infinuare debemus quæ

Auguft.
epif. 101.

.vtrorumque concordia terminata sunt,vt Romam liceat episcopis prouocare,&vt clericorum causæ apud suarum prouinciarum episcopos finiantur]that is,Ve aucht to mak intimatione to zourvorship of tha thingis quhilk ar decernit and aggreit on be bayth the parteis, that the bischopis may mak thair appellationis to Rome, and that the causes of the inferiore clergie be finalie decidit be thair auī Bischopis:quhat thing can be mair cleir ād manifest aganis zou for the acknauledging of the Papis authoritie ? Gif ze follou the fut stoppis of the fatheris of this Concile, as ze vald appeir to do, quhy suffer ze not zour bischopis quhom ze condem iniustlie,mak appellatione to the Paip of Rome , as did the fatheris of this Concile? Last of al, gif thay bischopis of Aphrik did onie thing quhilk micht do præiudice in quhatsumeuer poynt to the Authoritie of the seate of Rome,efteruart thay changed thair opinione, and condemnit quhatsumeuer had bene done quhilk did derogat to the priuilegis of that seate, as is manifest of the Epistle of Bonifacius the secund to Eulalius.And this far concerning the first part of zour obiectione.As to the secund pairt of it, quhair ze say that Faustinus quha vas Bonifacius legate,did produce for his part ane canon of the Concile of Nice ,that appellatione suld be granted from al bischopis to the bischop of Rome, and that he vas conuicted to be ane lear, ze schau zour self to

*Bonifa.ep.
ad Eula-
lium.*

haue lytil regard vnto the veritie, sua that ze
may say onie thing quhilk may derogate to
the Authoritie of the Paip of Rome: first Faustinus vas nocht conuicted to be ane lear, bot
the fatheris of that Concile ansuerit to him
vith all modestie, that thay did find na sik
thing in the Concile of Nice. And in that
sam forme vreit to the Paip of Rome desyring
the mater to be inquirit, and schauand thame selfis villing to obey thairto, gif it culd be
fund in the said Concile: Aluyse the questione
being as said is, nocht general of all appellatione, bot onlie of the appellatione of the inferiore clergie. Farder I say vnto zou, that the
Paipis legat Faustinus vas nocht dissauit nor
zit producit onie thing falslie, bot that the
fatheris of that Prouincial Concile, becaus
thay had nocht perfyt exemplaris of the Co-

Athanas.
*Apol.*2.
Theod.lib.
2.*cap.* 4.
Soz.om. li.
3. *cap.*8.
Iul.epi.ad
*Orien.*1

cile of Nice, var begylit becaus that the exe-
plaris of the kirk of Costatinopil and Alexa-
dria var corrupted be the Arrianis, as is manifest of Athanas. in his secud Apologie, and of
Theodoret. Socrates, Sozom. And Iulius, quha vas bot tuentie zeiris estir the Concile of
Nice, vreitand to the bischopis of the Orient
dois cite that self sam decreit of the Concile
of Nice, that in all gret materis, appellatione

Athana-
sius epis.
al Mar.

may be maid to the seate of Rome, the quhilk Canon, Zozimus esteruart did allege vry-
taand to the bischopis of Aphrik: and Athanasius lamentis gretumlie that the Canonis of
the Concile of Nice var corrupted be the Arrianis

rianis, and deſyris the Paip to ſend him ane
treu exemplar of thame quhairof it is maiſt
cleir that the haill Concile of Nice vas better
keipit in Rome nor in Alexandria or Conſtantinopil, and that Iulius quha vas tuentie
zeiris eftir, kneu better the decreis of the ſaid
concile nor the biſchopis of Aphrik quha vas
monie zeiris eferit, kneu the ſame: It being nauyſe liklie that Iulius vald haue cited
falſlie onie decreit of that Concile, cheiſlie
ſen Athanaſius, and monie vtheris var zit leuand quha had bene thair preſent, and be quhom he vald haue bene eſilie conuicted, ſua
Fauſtinus vas nauyſe deceauit, as ze falſlie allege, hauand in reddines to produce the Canon of the Concile of Nice, in the quhilk the
Paip of Rome is acknauledged for ſucceſſor
of Petir, and to haue authoritie, to diſpone
vpon quhatſumeuer materis that apertenis
to the diſcipline, and ordour of the kirk, and
to change al thingis quhilk be not veil conſtitute be inferioris. The vordis of the concile ar thir [Conſideret Patriarcha ea quæ ar-
chiepiſcopi, & epiſcopi in ſuis prouincijs
faciunt, & ſi quid reperiat ſecus quam oportet, immutet & diſponat prout ſibi videatur,
ſiquidem ipſe eſt Pater omniam, & illi Filij
eius, ſicut ille qui tenet ſedem Romæ, caput
eſt, & princeps omnium Patriacharum, & illi
data eſt poteſtas in vniuerſam Eccleſiam
Chriſtianam, & quicunque contradixerit, à ſy-
nodo excommunicetur] Lat the Patriache

Cõc. Nic.
Canõ. 39.

L

confidder tha thingis quhilk the Archebifchopis And Bifchopis dois in thair prouincis, and
gif he find onie thing vtheruyfe done than
becummis, lat him change, and difpone it as
he thinkis gude, becaus he is the father of thame al, and thay ar his fonis, as he quha occupeis the feat of Rome, is head and prince of
al the Patriarchis, and pouar is geuin him ouer
the hail kirk of Chrift, and quhatfumeuer he
be that ganefayis lat him be excommunicat be
this affemblie: Sua ze fuld be efchamed of zour
Maifter Caluine, quha throuch plane ignorance, and malice, hes brocht zou in fua greit,
darknes of volful ignorance that nou being
conuicted ze vat not quhat to fay, quhairof I
meruel not mekil fen zour Maifter him felf
being brocht in vauering be his auin proud
and arrogant iudgement, vas na les perplex in
this mater nor ze ar: As is manifeft to thame
al quha reidis the feuint chapture of the fourt
buk of his inftitutions, for thay vil perfaue
cleirlie that he vattis not quhat he fayis, becaus in the nynt fectione he vrittis that Zozimus Paip of Rome quha fend Fauftinus to
that Concile of Aphrik to defend his vfurpit
authoritie maift mifchantlie, and impudentlie cited the Concile of Sardis, for the Concile
of Nice, quhairin firft he leis and fecundlie he
vald malicioullie deceaue the reidar, I haue
fchauin his lefing afoir be produceing the
vordis of the Concile of Nice quhilk Zozimus did allege: he deceauis the reidar becaus

Caluin.ca.
7.lib.4.
Inftitut.

Sect.9.

hevald appeir to mak the Concile of Sardis
of na Authoritie, quhill as the self sam fatheris, quhilk vas at the Concile of Nice, var present in the concile of Sardis, insafar that thay
tua conciles ar estemed as ane, becaus at it thair vas na neu decreit maid, bot the decreit tis
of the Concile of Nice onlie confirmed be
the sam fatheris quha var at the Concile of
Nice: Sua Caluine geuis sufficient testimonie
aganis him self that the fatheris of the Concile of Nice acknauleaged the Authoritie of the
seat of Rome, and that appellatione suld be
maid to that seat from al vther bischopis, the
vordis of the Concile ar thir [Si episcopus Iu-   *Canon. 3.*
dicatus fuerit, & putauerit se habere bonam   *& 4.*
causam, vt scribatur ab his qui causam exami-
nauerunt Romano pontifici, vt si indicauerit
renouandum esse iudicium, renouetur, & det
iudices, & vt alter episcopus ante determina-
tionem litis in illius Cathedra non constitu-
atur] .1. Gif ane bischop be condemnit, and beleue that he hes ane richteous caus that vrittingis be direct be thame quha hes tryit the
caus to the bischop of Rome, that gif he
think that the iugement be reneuit, it may
be reneuit, and he may apoynt iudges, and
that na vther bischop be placit in his chyre,
befoir the decisione of the pley: Deny nou gif
ze can, bot zour Maister Caluine is ane manifest deceauer, and that ze, and he bayth
opposes zour selfis to the determinatione
of thay Fatheris quha var first gathered at the

L ij

Concile of Nice, And thaireftir at the Cōcile
of Sardis quhilk as Caluine him felf grātis did

Cal.lib.4. acknaulege the Authoritie of the Bifchop of
inftit.cap. Rome aboue al vther bifchopis. In his feuīte-
7.fect.17. in fectione, he affirmes that Phocas the Emperor did mak Bonifacius the thrid, head of
the kirk, quhilk authoritie Gregori' his præ-
diceffor vald nocht defyre, confidder hou
this aggreis vith that quhilk he faid befoir
that the Concile of Sardis aknauledgit the
bifchop of Rome to be head of the kitk or to
haue authoritie aboue al vther bifchopis, ād
nou that his authoritie did begī at Phocas the
Emperour, quha vas a lang tyme eftir the faid
concile: Thir ar the Oracles of zour neu fpirit quha infpyrit Iohne Caluine to repugne
fua manifeftlie vnto him felf, and vnto the
maift manifeft veritie. For monie Emperoris

Eufeb.li 7 befoir Phocas acknauledget the kirk of Ro-
ecclef. hift. me to haue authoritie aboue alvthir kirkis, As
cap.24. Aurelianvs and Cōftantinus as I haue fchauin
Lib.1.de befoir: And Gratian, Valentinian, and The-
fummaTri odofius qua declaris in thair lauis, that thay
nitate,& vil al men imbrace that religione, quhilk is
fide catho- imbraced be Damafus bifchop of Rome (Om-
lica. nes quos clementiæ noftræ regit imperium in
religione Damafi effe volumus) Ve vil al tha-

Iuftin.in me quha ar gouernit be the impyre of our
ep.ad Ioā- clemencie to be of that religione quhilk Da-
nem Pont. mafus profeffis. And Iuftinian the Emperour
Rom.& vrittand to the bifchop of Rome, [Omnes
in principio facerdotes, & Epifcopos orientis veftræ fan-
authent.

&itati vnire, & subiicere properamus , quæ
caput est omnium sanctarum Ecclesiarum] ve
at haistand vs to Ioyne in vnione and subiectione al the preistis and bischopis of the orient to zour halines quhilk is head of al the
halie kirkis. And in ane vther place, (sumi pō-
tificis apicem apud Romanam Ecclesiam esse
nemo est qui dubitet) Thair is na man quha
douttis bot the supreme authoritie of the hie
preist abydis in the kirk of Rome. And Valē-
tinianus, and Martianus vryttand to leo than
Biscop of Rome (tuam sanctitatem principa-
tum in Episcopatu diuinæ fidei possidentem
literis in principio iustum credimus esse allo-
quendam.) Ve think it iust in the beginning
tovrit to zour halines quha hes the principali-
tie inthe estair of bischopisquha makis profes
sione of the treu fayth: It vas nocht Phocas
than , quha maid the Bischop of Rome head
of the kirk as Caluine maist impudentlie affermes. Mairatour quhen Caluine sayis, that
the bischop Gregorius quha vas befoir Bonifacius desyrit not sik authoritie to be granted
vnto him, he leis na les impudētlie nor he did
befoir , it being maist certane that he professed him self to haue pouar , and authoritie
aboue al vthir bischopis , as is manifest of his
seuintie nynt epistle, (Quæ sine Episcopo Romano in Conciliis decernuntur irrita sunt,) r.
Al thingis quhilk ar decernit be the Concilis
vithout the bischop of Rome , ar vithout effect. And (omnes arduæ quæstiones ad sedem

*Valētinia-
nus &
Martian⁹
epist. ad
Leonem.*

*Greg.
ep. 79.*

Apostolicam sunt referendæ] al difficilquæ-

Greg.li.2.
epist.46.

stionis aucht to be referrit to the Apostolik seat: And he threatnes the pane of excommunicatione, gif onie do vtheruyse. And agane, (Nescio quis Episcopus non sit subiectus sedi Apostolicæ vbi culpa inuenitur.)i.I knau not quhat bischop is not subiect to the Apostolik

Lib.2.ep.
64.

seat, gif onie fault be fund in him. And Petrus Martyr him self vas cōstranit to grant that as cōcerning Iurisdiction, Gregorius had pouar

Petrus
Martyr in
cap.8.Ind.

and authoritie aboue al vther bischopis, albeit he vald not tak to him self the name of ane vniuersal bischop: Quhairof ze may vndirstand hou zour Prophetis aggreis amang thame selfis, and hou impudentlie zour maister Caluine leis, quhen he sayis that the Authoritie of the bischop of Rome began at Phocas the Emperore, and that Gregorius ascryuit not to him self authoritie aboue al vther bischopis: to be schott vith zou I prætermit monie vther thingis of the discourse of zour maister Caluine cōcerning this mater, quhairbie I micht esilie schau maist manifestlie his proudnes, malice, and ignorance, as quhen he sayis that the Concile of Nice vas haldin vndir the Pape Iulius, quhilk is ane manifest lesing, and repugnāt to al treu historeis, sē it vas haldin vnder Syluester, as is cleir of the Concile it self, and of the letteris of Athanasius to Marcus bischop of Rome, and of the Concile of Rome, quhilk vas haldin be Siluester eftir the Concile of Nice, sua gif Siluester quha præceidit Iulius leuit eftir the Concile of Nice, the Cócile of Nice could not be haldin vnder Iulius, as he affermes. In lyk maner quhen he vryttis that Athanafius vas præfident in the Concile of Nice, he leis na les than befoir, becaus as is manifeft of the actis of the Concile, Hofius vas præfident of it in the name of Siluefter, hauand vith him Vitus, and Vincentius. And Athanafius vas not bifchop at that tyme, bot ane feu zeiris thaireftir fucceidit to Alexander Bifchop of Alexandria: Quhen he affermes that the Concile of Nice did not acknaulege the authoritie of the bifchop of Rome, nor zit the Concile of Conftantinopil, he leis alfo, becaus of the actis of bayth the Conciles the contrare is manifeft : for the fatheris of the Concile of Nice defyris confirmatione of Siluefter, and the Concile of Cóftátinople acknauleged Damafus for the head of the kirk. Quhen he fayis that the Conciles of Calcedon, and Ephefus acknauleged the authoritie of the bifchop of Rome aboue al vther bifchopis, bot that the bifchopis of Rome did obtene that be ambitione or ane certane priuilege, he affirmes that quhilk he can not be abil to proue, and repugnis to al hiftoreis : And albeit the bifchopis of Rome had bene ambitious as he alleagis, zit it vald haue bene verie hard to thame to perfuade the hail Orient to acknaulege thair authoritie except it had bene lauchful, and euer acknauleged befoir : To pretermit that Leo Magnus quha vas acknauleged in the Concile of

Cal. lib. 4. inft. cap. 7. fect. 1

Caluin ibid.

L iiij

Calcedon vas ane maist learned , and halie
man,as his vrytingis teſtifeis , and al the vryttaris of that aige , quhais halines God him ſelf
did miraculouſlie confirme , as quhen Atila,
quha callit him ſelf (ſlagellum Dei) did exerceiſe maiſt horribil crueltie in ſindrie pairtis,
and vas deliberat to come to the toune of
rome to deſtroy it, Leo Magnus than biſchop
cled in his Pontifical vithout onie kynd of
armore, albeit the tyrane vas aluterlie inraged
did meit him at the valter of Po, and commä-
dit him to gang abak, quhilk incontinent he
did becüming forzetful of his accuſtumed rage and crueltie, quha eſtiruart being asked of
ane of his companie quhat moued him, quha
had dantoned ſa monie people to feir ſamekil
ane vnarmed preiſt , he auſuered that he ſau
vith Leo Magnus ane Angel, and ane ſuerd in
his hand quha boſted to ſlay him gif he myn-
dit to pas onie farder, ſua na man euer befoir
Iohne Caluine accuſed Leo of ambitione.
And as to Celeſtinus vnder quhom the Concile of Epheſus vas haldin,hou lerned, and halie ane man he vas it may be knauin of ſanct
Auguſtine,quha vrait vnto him,and of Cyrillus Alexandrinus quha vas præſident of the
Concile in his name, And of Proſper Aquita-
neus quha vas his ſecreitar : and ve for our
pairt haue ane ſufficiét teſtimonie of the cair,
and ſolicitude quhilk he had of vs that ve ſuld
not be corrupted be the hereſie of Pelagius,
for the quhilk caus he ſend to vs the maiſt

halie and learned Palladius, as prosper vitnes- *Prosper cō-*
sis : And zit Iohne Caluine takis on him the *tra collat.*
bauldnes to accuse him of ambitione, quhilk
na man euer did befoir him : Not being content to haue falslie accused the halie men Leo
and Celestinus of ambitione, he taxis also of
the lyk cryme the maist godlie man Innocen- *Caluin li.*
tius quha preceidit thame bayth, Albeit S. Au- *4. inslit.*
gustine, and al the fatheris of that aige did ho- *cap. 7. sect.*
nore him vith al reuerence, and desyrit that *15.*
he suld confirme the decreis, quhilk thay had
established in thair Conciles. And gif Innocentius var leuand this day , he vald meruel
mekil to se zou , quha ar his natiue cuntrey
men, he being ane Scottisman borne as ze ar,
to be sua addicted to the priuat iudgement,
and opinione of Iohne Caluine, and to haue
left that religione quhilk vas taucht in the
realme of Scotland quhen he vas borne in it,
and quhilk he mentened as cheif pastore, and
head of the vniuersal kirk, being chosin thairto not be ambitiō, he being borne sua far from
the toune of Rome, bot be his singular verteu,
and halines of lyf. And this far I haue spokin
being constranit be the importunitie of zour
Prophete, and maister Iohne Caluine : gif ze
haue onie vther thing to say aganis the Iurisdictione of the Paip of Rome, produce it.

M. *Thou art sua addicted to the Pape, that it is*
bot tint tyme to vse onie farder ressone aganis the,
Zit sence thou speikis sua bauldlie I vil propose
ane cleir, and manifest argument aganis the Iuris-

dictione of the Pape: Quhen the Donatistis maid their appellatione from the Bischopis of Afrik to the Emperore Constantinus Magnus, and being remitted be him to Melchiades Bischop of Rome, albeit the bischop of Rome had pronunced the sentence aganis thame, Zit thay maid ane new appellatione to the bischop of Arlis in France, quhilk thay vald not haue done, gif the Bischop of Rome had had supreme authoritie aboue al vther Bischopis.

B. This is ane of the great gunnis of zour Maister Iohne Caluine, To the quhilk S. Augustine, Optatus Mileuitanus, and vther ancient vryttaris hes ansuered monie húdreth zeiris sésyne, that the Donatistis did peruert the ordore and discipline of the kirk be thair importunitie, And that eftir the decreit of Melchiades thair vas na farder iudgement on the earth to be lukit for: sua as vryttis S. August. the Emperor being ouercummit be thair importunitie, and hauing ane greit desyre of thair returning to the kirk agane, grantit to thame that the bischop of Arlis vith vther bischopis of France micht iuge of thair caus. Gif thay had maid thair appellatione to onie reformed kirk lyk zouris quhilk at that tyme had not acknauleged the authoritie of the bischop of Rome aboue al vther Bischopis, zour argument vald haue appeired perchance of sum probabilitie, bot ve reid of na sik thing in onie historiographore : Nou as to the bischop of Arlis, he arrogat not vnto him self to Iuge of that thing, quhilk had be-

Cal.lib.4. cap.7.sect. 10. Aug.epi. 162.Optatus Mileuitan⁹ lib. 1. & 2.cótra Parmenianum.

ne decreited befoir in Rome, bot onlie be
commãd of the bischõp of Rome, and hauing
hoip of the conuersione of the Donatiſtis,
zit thay var not content of his iugement bot
maid ane neu appellatione to the Emperore:
Sua gif zour argument hes onie force, The
Emperore ſuld be supreme iudge to al controuerſie of Religione, quhilk is repugnant to al
ſcripturis, to al antiquitie, and to al reaſone,
zea to zour doctrine alſo, quha vil haue na
vther Iuge bot onlie the vryttin vord, quhilk
can nather heir nor ſpeik.

OF THE CONTINVAL SVC-
ceſſione of the Paipis.

CHAP. XXII.

B Ran d. *Quhat ſayis thou than of the ſcho Paip
Ioanna quha buir ane chyld being in proceſſione
of the quhilk Platina quha vrait the Paipis lyuis
makis mentione, had ſcho lauchfull authoritie and
iuriſdictione ouer the vniuerſal Kirk,*

B. I. perſaue it is treu quhilk the ancient
vryttar Naziãzenus teſtifeis, that hæretikis ar
lyk the Fleis, quha vſis to pas by al tha partis
quhilk ar healthſum, and quhair thay find
onie corruptione thair thay vſe to repoſe thame, euin ſua do ze, that in al thing quhilk
Platina hes vryttin, ze trou na vther thing, bot
onlie that quhilk is vryttin of the ſcho Paip:
And ſuppoſe it had bene ſua, ze ſuld nocht

skar at the mater, becaus ze haue ane ſcho Paip
beſyd zou for head of the kirk of Ingland:
Nou ſuppois that it vat treu quilk ze alledge,
I vat nocht quhat ze vald gather thairof: Becaus it is maiſt eſie to anſuere that during
that tyme, the ſeat of Rome hes vakit be reſſone that ane voman is nocht capabill of ordore, nor gouernement of the Kirk: Zit I
anſuere to zou that is maiſt fals, that euer ſik
ane voman ſat in the ſeate of Rome, quhilk
I vil ſchau to zou be manifeſt demonſtratio-
ne: firſt becaus he quha vas author of that fa-
bil callit Martinus Polonus, quhom Platina
did follou, vryttis the hiſtorie in ſik maner,
that in it ſelf it contenis maiſt manifeſt con-
trarieteis, ſua the hiſtorie it ſelf ſeruis for ane
ſufficient proue of the vanitie thairof, firſt he
vryttis (Ioanna Angla natione, nata mogun-
tij,) that is as ze vald ſay in ſcottis, Ionet ane
ingleiſs voman of natione, borne in heiche
Almanie, in ane toune callit Moguntium hou
could ſcho be ane Ingliſs voman and borne
in Almanie? he paſſis forduart that ſcho ſtu-
deit in Athenis, and becom ane veray lernit
voman, In the quhilk tyme thair vas na profeſſione of letteris thair at al, the toune of A-
thenis being alluterlie deſtroyit: thaireftir he
vrittis that ſcho come to Rome, and vas
choſin, Paip, Euin as the Italianis had bene
ſua blait, that thay culd nocht diſcerne betuix
ane man and ane voman: And that the Papis
vat choſin ſua eſilie vithout inquiſitione of

thair cuntreyis,andvithout gret experience of
thair maneris, and behauiour in all thingis:
And to pretermit all thir thingis Confidering
the bifchop of Rome vfis to confecrate bifchopis to difpenfe in fum lauis, and exerceife
fik vthir actis of iurifdictione, gif euer thair
had bene ane voman in that feate, eftir hit
deathe, the mater being difcouerit, thair had
follouit ane greit confufione in the kirk,and
al thingis had bene annullit, quhilk fcho had
done: Be reffone that ane voman hes nocht
pouar to exerceife onie fik iurifdictione, bot
of this ve find na mentione at all, fua the hail
mater is prouin to be fals : And to put zou
to filence in tymes cumming, Platina and
vtheris quha vryttis of this,fayis,that fcho vas
in the zeir of God 850, or thairby betuix Leo
the fourt and Benedictus the thrid . Bot
Anaftafius Bibliothecar of the kirk of Rome,
quha vas than prefent, vryttis that eftir the
death of Leo the fourt, ane greit conuention
being maid, Benedictus the thrid vas chofin
immediatlie eftir him,fua that zour Ionet hes
na place quhair fcho may fitt. And I remember I red in fum Catholique vryttaris, that in
fum bibliothekis, as in the bibliothec of the
duke of Florence,quhair thair is auld vryttin
bukis of the fucceffion of the Paipis of Rome,that in thame efter Leo the fourt , immediatlie is fund Benedictus the thrid : This
appeirandlie is fufficient to the refutatione
of zour fcho Paip : And zit I meruel of zou

that ar ministeris, quha ar sua rigorus in this part, For ze micht haue vsit this argument to proue that the ministeris suld haue vyffis, becaus thair could nocht ane voman haue place in the kirk of Rome, vnles scho had bene the Papis vyff, Bot nou gif ze sal heir patientlie I vill mak ane Catalog of al the Paipis, quhilk hes bene in Rome, desyring zou to schau me the interruptione of the continual successione of ane to anoher, thay all being men: sua that zour impudent leing may be knauin to the varld, quha alvayis laboris to brig zour miserabill floke in hetret of the Authoritie of the bischop of Rome, quha hes condemnit al hereseis vnto this day including zouris vith the rest.

PONTIFICES SVMMI, THE PAPIS
Iesus Christ the onlie head of the kirk.

S. Petir, Apostle and martyr, the vicar of Iesus Christ.

S. Clemés martyr the lauchful successor to sanct Petir.

S. Linus mart.

S. Cletus, mart.

ritur LLB S. Anacletus, mart.

S. Euaristus, mart.

Anno Domini. 100.

S. Alexander. 1. mart. 121

S. Sixtus. 1. mart.

S. Thelesphorus, mar.

S. Higinus, mart.

S. Pius. 1. mart.

S. Anicetus, mart.

S. Soter, mart.

S. Eleutherius, mart.

S. Victor. 1. mart.

S. Zephirinus, mart.

Anno Domini. 200.

S. Calixtus. 1. mart.

S. Vrbanus.1. mart.
S. Pontianus,mart.
S. Antherus, mart.
S. Fabianus,mart.
S. Cornelius,mart.
S. Lucius.1.mart.
S. Stephanus. 1. mart.
S. Sixtus.2.mart.
S. Dionysius.1.mart.
S. Fælix.1.mart.
S. Eutychianus, mart.
S. Caius,mart.
S. Marcellus, mart.

Anno Domini. 300.

S. Eusebius, mart.
S. Melchiades,mart.
S. Siluester.1.
S. Marcus.
S. Iulius.1.
S. Liberius. *354*
S. Fælix.2.
S. Damasus.
S. Siricius.
S. Anastasius.

Anno Domini. 400.

S. Innocentius. 1.
S. Zozimus.
S. Bonifacius. 1.

S. Celestinus. 1.
S. sixtus. 3.
S. Leo magnus. *vixit 452*
S. Hilarius. *vixit 464*
s. Simplicius.
S. Felix. 3.
S. Gelasius.1. *vixit 492*
S. Anastasius. 2.
s. Symmachus.

Anno Domini. 500.

S. Ioannes.1.mart.
S. Fælix. 4.
    Bonifacius 2.
S. Ioannes 2.
s. Agapetus.
s. Syluerius mart.
    Vigilius.
s. Pelagius 1.
s. Ioannes 3.
s. Benedictus 1.
s. Pelagius 2.
s. Gregorius magnus. *vixit 586*

Anno Domini. 600.

Sabinianus.
s. Bonifacius 3.
s. Bonifacius 4.
s. Deusdedit 2. Boni-
    facius.5. Honorius 1.

seuerinus.	Paschalis. 1.
Ioannes. 4.	Eugenius. 2.
Theodorus. 1.	Valentinus.
s. Martinus. 1.	Gregorius. 4.
s. Eugenius. 1.	Sergius. 2. Leo. 4.
Vitalianus.	Benedictus. 3.
Adeodatus.	Nicolaus. 1. *vixit 862*
Domnus	Adrianus. 2.
Agatho.	Ioannes. 8.
s. Leo. 2.	Martinus. 2.
Benedictus. 2.	Adrianus. 3.
Ioannes 5. canon	stephanus. 6.
vixit 688 Sergius. 1.	Formosus.
	Bonifacius. 6.
Anno Domini. 700.	stephanus. 7.
	Theodorus. 2.
Ioannes. 6.	Ioannes. 9.
Ioannes. 7.	Benedictus. 4.
sisinnius.	
Constantinus.	*Anno Domini*. 900.
s. Gregorius. 2.	
s. Gregorius. 3.	Leo. 5.
Zacharias. 1.	Christophorus. 1.
stephanus. 2.	Sergius. 3.
stephanus. 3.	Anastasius. 2.
Paulus. 1.	Lando.
stephanus. 4.	Ioannes. 10.
Adrianus. 1. Leo. 3.	Leo. 6.
	Stephanus. 8.
Anno Domini. 800.	Ioannes. 11. Leo. 7.
	Stephans. 9.
Stephanus. 5.	Martinus. 3.
	Agapetus

Agapetus. 2
Ioannes. 12.
Leo. 8.
Ioannes. 13.
Domnus .
Benedictus, 5.
Bonifacius, 7.
Benedictus, 6.
Ioannes, 14.
Ioannes, 15.
Ioannes, 16.
Gregorius, 5.
Siluester, 2.

Anno Domini. 1000.

Ioannes, 17.
Ioannes, 18.
Sergius, 4.
Benedictus, 7.
Ioannes, 19.
Benedictus, 8.
Gregorius, 6.
Clemens, 2.
Damasus, 2.
Leo, 9.
Victor, 2.
Stephanus, 10.
Nicolaus, 2.
Alexander, 2.
Gregorius, 7. vixit 107.
Victor, 3.

Vrbanus. 2.
Paschalis, 2. vixit 1106

Anno Domini. 1100.

s. Gelasius, 2.
s. Calixtus.
s. Honorius, 2.
s. Innocentius, 2.
Celestinus. 2.
Lucius, 2.
Eugenius, 3.
Anastasius, 3.
Adrianus, 4.
Alexander 3.
Lucius, 3.
Vrbanus, 3.
Gregorius, 8.
Clemens, 4.
Celestinus, 3.
Innocentius, 3. vixit 1200

Anno Domini. 1206.

Honorius, 3. vixit 1216
Gregorius, 9. vixit 1226
Celestinus, 4.
Innocentius, 4. vixit 1244
Alexander, 4.
Vrbanus, 4. vixit 1262
Clemens, 4.
Gregorius, 10.

M

Innocentius *5 vixit 7.* Alexander, 5.
Adrianus 5.　　　　Ioannes, 22. *vixit :320*
Ioannes, 20.　　　Eugenius, 4. *vixit 1413 1437*
Nicolaus, 3.　　　Nicolaus, 5.
Martinus, 4.　　　Calixtus, 3.
Honorius, 4.　　　Pius, 2.
Nicolaus, 4.　　　Paulus, 2.
s. Celeſtinus, 5.　　Sixtus, 4.
Bonifacius, 8.　　　Innocentius, 8.
　　　　　　　　Alexander, 6.

　　　Anno domini. 1300.

　　　　　　　　Anno Domini, 1500.

Benedictus, 9.
Clemens, 5. *vixit 1304* Pius, 3.　　*Gregorio 14.*
Ioannes, 21.　　　　Iulius, 2.　　*Innocentio 9*
Benedictus, 10.　　　Leo, 10.　　*Clemente 8*
Clemens. 6. *? 6*　　Adrianus, 6.　*Leo XI*
Vrbanus, 5　　　　Clemens, 7.　*Paulus V*
Gregorius 11.　　　Paulus, 3.　　*Gregori: 15*
Vrbanus, 6.　　　　Iulius, 3.　　*Vrba: 8*
Bonifacius, 9.　　　Marcellus, 2.
　　　　　　　　Paulus, 4.
　　Anno Domini. 1400.　Pius, 4.
　　　　　　　　Pius, 5.
Innocentius, 7.　　　Gregorius 13.
Gregorius, 12.　　　*Sisto, 5.*
　　　　　　　　vrbano, 7.

Quha is Paip this day. And this is the continual ſucceſſione of the biſchopis of Rome
from S. Petir to our dayes, quhilk as vryttis
S. Auguſtine, and vther ancient Doctoris, al
hæretikis notvithſtanding thay haue euer

Auguſt. de vtilita-te credédi.

bene barking aganis it, culd never ouertum it
in onie vay: Bot be the contrare thay haue
euer bene vincused and suppressed, as ze vith
the rest vil.be sum day, ad nochtuithstáding al
zour railling and crying out aganis the Roman Antichrist, zit the Paip remanis euer stil
in Rome, and hes als gret, ze gretar iurisdictione nor he had the first day that Lauter
begane to preache: quhat gif ze culd schau the
lyk successione in the kirk of Geneua? Bot
thankis to God al zour successione ather in
the kirk of Geneua, or vthir kirkis hes euer
bene inuisibil to our dayes: And I hoip in
God that vithin ane schort space of tyme, it
sal be maid als inuisibil agane, as gif it var in
the gróude of the loche of Geneua.

*B. It behouit the nocht enlie to haue schauin the
tótinual successione of ane Paip vnto another, bot alse
that ane succeidit to another in lyk puritie of doctrine, and halines of lyf vith his predicessore, quhil as be
the contrare thay haue al bene vickit men, sum ma-
giciaunis, sum adulteraris and polluted vith al kynd
of vyces.*

B. As to the puritie of doctrine it is manifest to al thame quha ar not altogidder ignorant of the Ecclesiastical historeis that, the có-
tinuance thairof hes bene conioynit vith the
continual succession of Paipis lauchfullie ordinit and promouit be verteu of Christis promeis to S. Petir, and his successoris in name of
the hail kirk: Farder the successione of lauchful pastoris, according to the custume and vse

of the Romane Kirk, and vther anciēt kirkis, hes neceſſarlie conioynit vith it the ſucceſſion of doctrine in lyk maner, becaus that this vas ane ancient cuſtume maiſt diligentlie obſeruit, that the names of thame onlie quha had conſtantlie to the end remanit in the profeſſion of the fayth, had thair names keipit in the commone tabillis of the kirk (quhilk be the greikis var callit δίπlυχα) bot as the experience teachis vs, al the names of the biſchopis of Rome hes bene inrollit in the ſaid commone tabillis of the kirk of Rome, quhairof it is neceſſarlie gatherit, that thay haue al profeſſit ane doctrine, and that quha euer hes bene choſin in that kirk, hes approuit the doctrine and religione of his prediceſſore: vtheruyſe he vald nocht haue confentit that the name of his prediceſſore ſuld haue bene inrollit in the ſaid maner, nor zitvald haue acknauled git him ſelf as ſucceſſor to him, quha had maid profeſſione of fals doctrine : As be exempil Maiſter Iohne douglas vald nocht ſay that he ſucceidit to the biſchop of Sanctandrois, quhilk vas befoir him, nor vald nocht acknauledge him as ane lauchful biſchop : Nor zit Maiſter Iames Boyd vil ſay that he ſucceidis to the biſchop of Glaſgou : Nor Maiſter Dauid Cunynghame to the Biſchop of Abirdene, bot thayvil ſay that euerie ane of thame is the firſt lauchful biſchop that euer ſat in tha ſeattis: quhairbie ze may perſaue maiſt cleirlie that the ſucceſſione of perſonis can nocht be

keipit in ſik maner, as it hes bene keipit in the
Romā kirk. vithout ſucceſſione in doctrine:
gif ʒe haue red the ancient vryttaris, ʒe can
nocht misknau, hou that in the kirk of Con-
ſtātinopil, he quha follouit Macedonius, vald
nocht acknauledge him ſelf as ſucceſſore to
him, and hou that in the tabil of the kirk of
Conſtantinopil, the name of Macedonius can
nocht be fund amang the biſchoppis of that
ſeat, nor the name of Paulus Samoſatenus in
the tabillis of the kirk of Antiochia, nor the
name of Dioſcorus amangis the biſchoppis
of Alexandria: and in ſindrie vthir kirkis of
the Orient, in the quhilk the Arrianis, and
yther hæretikis did ſit, thair names var neuer
put in the commone tabillis of the kirk. I re-
mēber of the hiſtorie of Chryſoſtome quhais
name his ennimeis throuch inuie vald nocht
permit to be inrollit in the foirſaid tabillis
of the kirk of Cōſtantinopil, and quhat ſtryf
and contentione vas for that caus, and ʒit the
veritie did preuail, for his name vas vryttī vith
the names of the reſt of the biſchopis miracu-
luſlie: Quhairof ʒe may vndirſtād quhat ſtryf
vald haue bene in the Roman kirk for the in-
rolling of the Biſchopis, gif thay had nocht al
euer perſeuerit in ane doctrine of fayth: Mairouer ʒe ſpeke verie bauldlie that the biſchopis of Rome hes corrupted the treu doctrine,
bot in particular nather ſchau ʒe, nor can ʒe
be abil to ſchau onie Paip that euer inuentit
ane particular head of Religione, or euer

maid defectione from that fayth quhilk his
predicessoris had professed befoir him : And
nou I desyre the maist learned of zou to
schau me this in particular gif ze can, and con
sidering I haue proposed to zou al the bischopis of Rome, to name me ane of thame quha
euer maid defectione from his predicessoris,
or that euer inuentit ane particular head of
religione, and gif ze can noch: , for my pairt
I vil esteme zou to be maist impudent learis
and impostoris: And to mak zour pane schor-
tar, becaus ze vse to plenzie that the cair of
zour Childrene and familie, Lttis zou nocht
luke ouer zour bukes as ze vald, I vil tak ane
pairt of the paine on me. Caluin zour Maister
in the secund chapter of his fourt buke, confessis, that quhil Augustinis dayes, thair vas na
thing changit of the Religione of the Apostlis, euin in the kirk of Rome: Schau me that
efter S. Augustinis dayes onie thing hes bene
chágit, or that Gregorius the threttent, quha
is nou bischop of Rome, professis onie vther
fayth bot that quhilk Innocentius, Zozimus,
Bonifacius, Celestinus quha var bischopis in
in S. Augustinis dayes, professed ? I am assurit
ze vil bleir out al zour eis, or euer ze can be
abil to schau onie sik thing : Cheiflie sen the
Catholikes in France hes offerit zou be vryttin bukes , to stand at the religione quhilk
vniuersalie vas professed throuche the hail
varld in Augustinis dayes , and ze durst neuer
zit accept the offer, sua that ze condemn zour

maister Caluine, and geuis ane sufficient proue, that the doctrine quhilk is professed nou
in the kirk of Rome, is that sam self quhilk
vas professed in Augustinis dayes, and vas
euer professed befoir him. As to the maneris
of the Paipis, sence the first xxxij. almaist vi-
thour exceptió vas maist cruellie martyrit for
confessione of the name of Christ, by exceiding gret núber of thame quha succeidit eftir,
maist godlie and learnit men resistâd al heresie
and vicious leuíg: suppois sum of the number
as particular mébirris of the kirk, hes bene vicious, zit it folouis nocht that thair authoritie
vas ather vnlauchful, or inlaikit deu executió:
vtheruyse I vald demand of zou, quhidder ze
think that the minister kelloche eftir he had
murdreist his vyf, tint his authoritie or nocht?
or that the bairnis quhilk he baptized, suld be
baptized agane: quhair as ze allege that sindrie
vas Magicianis âd adulteratis, quhilk ze aucht
nocht to beleue, becaus it is nocht expreslie
vryttin in the Byble, albeit I vald grât it treu, I
ansuer to zou vith S. Augustine in his 165. epistle, that albeit in the seat of Rome, thair hes
bene sum euil men, zit that dois nocht pre-
iudice to the veritie, considering God commandis vs, to do according to that quhilk the
pastoris teachis vs, and nocht as thay do thame seluis: Bot I meruel that ze suld nocht be
eschamit to obiect sic crymes vnto vs, ze zour
seluis in sa feu zeiris being contaminat vith
siclyk, ze and mair horribil crymes, quhilkis

August.
epist. 165.

M iiij

nocht to offend the reidaris earis, I vil pretermit vith silence: As for the practeis of ma-
gict I micht obiect vnto zou willox, quhais
sone raised the deuil zour doctor, in Arthu-
ris seate, quhair ze maid zour first preachingis, And Iohne Kmnox zour first Apostil, quha
caused ane zoung vomā in my lord Ochiltreis
place, fal almaist dead, becaus scho sau his
maister Sathan in ane blak mannis liknese
vith him, throuche ane bore of the dure: quha
vas also ane manifest adulterare, bringand
furth of Ingland bayth the mother and the
dochter, quhom he persuadit, that it vas lesum to leue hir housband, and adhere vnto
him, making ane fleshe of him self, the mother, and the dochter, as gif he vald conioy-
ne in ane religione, the auld synagoge of the
Ieuis, vith the neu fundat kirk of the Gentiles: I leue Paul Mephuen that Palliard Apostle, quha vas conuoyit throuche the cuntrey
on horsbak (in ane viddieveil) armit vith pistolattis, to slay the pure folkis hennis, to
mak gud cheir on frydayes: As for the practeise of bougrie and sodomitical syn, I remit
zou to the verse of zour Paraclet Theodore
de Beze, quhilk he makis preferrig the zoung
man Audebertus, to Candida another mannis vyf, hauing gretar plesure in satisfeing the
inquensibil fyre of his concupiscence vith
ane man aganis nature, nor vith ane voman:
for testimonie heirof I produce not ane vthir
mannis speiking quha vas of the number of

his aduersaris, bot his auin verse out of the
buk of epigrammes quhilk he him self maid.

THEODORVS BEZA DE SVA
in Candidam & Audebertum
beneuolentia.

ABest Candida, Beza quid moraris?
Audebertus abest, quid hic moraris?
Tenent Parisij tuos amores,
Habent Aurelij tuos lepôres,
Et tu Vezelis manere pergis
Procul Candidula, amoribusque,
Et leporibus, Audebertulóque:
Immò Vezely procul valete
Et vale pater & valete fratres,
Namque Vezelis carere possum
Et carere parente, & his, & illis,
At non Candidula, Audebertulóque.
Sed vtrum rogo preferam duorum?
Vtrum inuisere me decet priorem?
An quemquam tibi Candida anteponam?
An quenquam anteferam tibi Audeberte?
    Quid si me in geminas secem ipse partes?
Harum vt altera Candidam reuisat,
Currat altera versus Audebertum.
At est Candida sic auara, nuui,
vt totum cupiat tenere Bezam,
Sic Bezæ est cupidus sui Audebertus,
Beza vt gestiat integro potiri:
Amplector quoque sic & hunc & illam
vt totus cupiam viuere virumque,

Theodo-
rus Beza
lib. epi-
gramm.

Integrisque frui integer duobus,
Præferre attamen alterum necesse est,
O duram nimium necessitatem!
Sed postquam tamen alterum necesse est,
Priores tibi desero Audeberte,
Quod si Candida fortè conqueratur,
Quid tum ? Basiolo tacebit imo.

THE TESTIMONIE OF THEO-
dore Beze the neu Pseudoprophet and pretendit reformator of the varld concerning
his Sodomitical Bougorie vith the zoung
man Audebertus, And adulterie vith Candida, ane vthir mánis vyf, quha is his harlet
zit for the present, composit be him self in
Latine.

B*Eza quhy bydis thou, quhy dois thou stay?*
Sen Candida and Audebert ar baith auay?
Thy loue is in Pareis, in Orleanis thy mirth,
Zit thou vald veZel keip to thy girth,
Far from Candida lust of thy cor-s
Far from Audebert thy gret plea-sors
  Fair veil veZel veil mot Ze fair,
Fair veil my brethering quha du-ellis thair
I may spair veZel, my father, and Zou,
Bot nather Audebert, nor Candidais mu.
Then quhilk of thir prefer sould I ?
Quhilk sould I vissie first or espy?
  Candida may onie he deirar, nor thou?
Or Audebert ony preferrit to Zou?
Quhat gif I cuttit my bodie in tuay?
And giue the ane half to Candida gay?

The vther t'Audebert: Zit Candida nei-die
Vald BeZa haue hail scho is so gre-die:
And Aude-bert vald BeZe haue hail
So couetous is he for to pre-uail.
Bot I vald so thame baith imbrace
To be al hail vith baith in a place
Hir vith hir ~~—~~ him vith his ~~—~~,
And I betuix vith ane ~~———~~:
  Zit th'ane sould I prefer indeid
Bot ô hou hard a thing is neid!
And sen the ane man be preferd
My fore-quarters sal be con-ferd
To Aude-bert for Bou go-rie
The cheifest of my vo-luptie
Bot Candida gif scho com-plaine
I sal hir ~~—~~ kiss laich a-gane.

Siclyk Caluïn vas markit vith the flour de-
lise vpone his schuldir for the hörribill syn
of Sodomie: And this is the halines of zour
kirk, quhairin ze gloir, reprouing euer the
auld Romane kirk (in the quhilk sa monie
halie mé and Martyris hes florished) of sik cry
mes quhilk ze can nocht be abill to proue:
and albeit zour accusatione var treu, it seruis
na'thing to zour purpose.

CHAP. XXIII.

M.

THe Papiſtis makis ane Idol of the Paip, ſaying that he may nocht err, quhilk is proper to god onlie: vil thou defend this error vith the reſt?

B. Gif ze think it ſtrange to beleue that ane man may nocht err, ze vil be compellit to grant that Sanct Paulis epiſtlis ar nocht treu, becaus he vas bot ane man : Bot the mening of that propoſitione is, that the Paip inſafar as he ſittand in his Chyre in place of Chriſt in the fleſch adherent to his Concile, lauchfullie conuocat, agreand in vnitie of ſpirit, be the band of pace (as ſpekis S. Paul) erris nocht in making definitione of treuth, and condemning hereſie : becaus the halie Ghaiſt promiſed be Chriſt at his departing ſpekis in thame repreſenting the Catholik kirk, quhilk is the pillar of treuth : ſua that the definitione of treuth promulgat be the general Cócile in the name of the Paip, as Chriſtis vicar, is nocht the inuétion of the brayn of mã, bot ane declaratione of the mening of the halie Ghaiſt : zit inſafar as the particular perſone quha hes the Authoritie of the Paip, hauing conuerſatione vith men, is ſeparat from his Concile, he may ſyn, and ſiclyk ſynnis in him

haue bene, and ſuld be reprouit vith cheritie
and ædification, he may alſo as ane particular
méber of the kirk, haue ane fals ſentéce concerning onie head of Religione, and zit be
the firſt, quha ſall condem the ſam errore, quhen he ſittis in iudgement for examinatione
of the ſam : Quhair ze cal vs Papiſtis ze iuſti-
fie our caus, that ve ar no heretikis, becaus
that the Paip ſignifeis no ane particular man,
that hes inuentit onie religione, bot is the
name of him, quha hes ane publict office
and authoritie in the kirk, on quhom Chriſt
promiſed to buyld his kirk, and to quhom he
promiſed the keyis of the kigdome of heauin : bot ze ar callit Caluiniſtis, from Iohne
Caluin quha vas the firſt inuentar of zour
doctrine and religione, as befoir him ze can
ſchau na man, that euer profeſſed it in al poyntis.

*Proteſtant . Paphnutius reſiſtit vnto the decreit of
ane general Concile, maid concerning the Chaſtitie of
Preiſtis: thairfoir the general Concilis may err.*

B. ze ſchau that ze haue neuer côſiderit that
hiſtorie, quhilk gif ze had done, ze vald nocht
haue ſpokin ſua impudenlie as ze do, foi fiiſt
the quæſtione vas nocht, quhidder gif preiſtis
ſould marie or nocht ? it being maiſt certane
amangis al Chriſtianis, that ettir thay var anis
preiſtis, thay ſould nocht marie, to the end
thayſould nocht bevithdrauin vith the cair of
the varld fra the ſeruice of god, to the quhilk

thay ar confecrat: bot gif thay quha var mareit befoir thay var preiftis, fuld remane ftill
vith thair vyffis, or nocht?It vas fumpart mair
doutfum : and zit the hail Concile of Nice
decernit, that thay fould abftene fra thair vyues : Paphnutius, quhom ze allege for zou
fcheu him felf to be in the contrare opinione
and propofed it to be imbraced be the Concile : bot the Concile did nocht follou his opinione thairin nocht efteming his authoritie
of greit valoure, confidering he vas of the
fect of the Miletianis,and ane fchifmatik,fup-
poife zevald appeir to mak him ane gret man:
Reid Epiphanius quha vas nocht lang eftir
the concile of Nice, and thair ze vil find quhou it is aganis the Canonis, and ordinances
of the Kirk, that thay quha var mareit befoir
thay var preiftis, haue onie companie vith
thair vyuis in tymes cumming, and teftifeis
that gif in onie parte thay do vtheruyfe, thay
do planlie aganis the Canonis,and ordinancis
of the kirk : Bot ze, and zour minifteris vil
be fubiect to na reul, and thinkis it lefum to
do quhat ze pleis.

*M. Quhy may nocht the kirk err alfueil nou, as be-
foir in the Concile of the Ieuis, quha concludit that
our Maifter being innocent fuld nochtuithftanding
de faying, It is expedient that ane dea for the Peopil
And the hail natione perife nocht.*

B. Quhat fubioynis S.Iohne of his fentence
pronounced ?

M. He fpak nocht this of him felf, bot be inftinction

of the halie ſpirit, becaus he vas the hie preiſt of that Zeir.

B. Quhidder than do ze think that the ſentence vas erroneus or treu?

M. *He kneu nocht that quhilk he pronoũced to be the mening of the halie gaiſt.*

B. Ze ſe thairfoir, hou ſure the kirk is, for albeit the perſone be neuer ſo vicious and ignorant, zit hauing lauchfull authoritie the halie Gaiſt vil nocht ſuffer the propir functione, ãd executione thairof to inlaik: By that, thair vas nocht ſua greit promiſes maid to the ſynagoge of the Ieuis, as to the kirk and kingdome of Chriſt, ze it vas foirſpokin that the ſynagoge ſuld be vtterlie aboliſhed, ſua that ſuppois befoir the abolitione of it God, had permitted ſũ errotis to creip in, it had nocht bene aganis the promeis of God: Bot to the kingdome, or kirk of Chriſt, the halie Gaiſt is promiſed euer to aſſiſt, vnto the end of the varld, and that it ſal neuer be ouercummit be hereſie, or onie fals doctrine: vtheruyſe the kirk vald nocht be the treu ſpous of Chriſt, hauing brokin the treuth and couenant maid vith him: And thairfoir ze blaſpheme, aganis the grace of the neu teſtament, quha vil acknauledge na prerogatiue grãced vnto the kirk of Chriſt quhilk befoir vas nocht granted to the ſynagoge of the Ieuis: By that ze derogat aluterlie zour hail doctrine, gif it be treu as ze teache that the kirk may err, becaus na man vil haue aſſurance to follou zour neu kirk of

Ion.16.

Scotlad, considdering as ze confes zour selfis, it may er: And sua ze haue na iust ressone to caus onie man subscryue the confessione of zour fayth: And al that quhilk ze teache is in vaine, considdering zour kirk can gif na assurance of the veritie to onie man, zea in zour kirk ze tak auay al the authoritie of bischopis, quha euer hes bene iudgit to haue had the principal gouernement of the kirk in tymes bypast, and thairfoir gif the kirk may err as ze say, it is maist liclie that zour neu erectit kirk, as being destitute of cheif præ-lattis may maist esilie err, aboue allvther here-tikis that euer hes bene befoir zou.

OF THE ESTAIT OF BI-SCHOPPIS.

CHAP. XXIIII.

*P*Rotest. *Gif the Authoritie of bischopis var grou-dit on the vord of God, and had bene approuit in the primitiue kirk, the bischopis quha ar this day in scotland and namlie the bischoppis of Sanctandrois, Glasgou, and Abirdene vald mentene thair Autho-ritie, and correct the insolence of our ministeris, misk-nauand thair deuitie touard thame as Magistratis, and becaus thay do it nocht, it appeiris that the bis-choppis hes na lauchful authoritie.*

B, Albeit the Authoritie of bischopis (hauing iurisdictione ouer inferiore Pastoris, quha hes na lauchful calling, bot be biscoppis) be sufficientlie

cientlie prouin be the vord of God, as testifeis
S.Paul. [Tak tent to zour selfis, and the hail *Act.20.*
flok ouer the quhilk the halie Ghaift hes
apoyntit zou Bischopis to gouerne the kirk
of God,quhilk he hes conquesed vith his blu-
de]And in the 5.chap.to Timothie spekand of
ane Bischopis iurisdictione, Admit nocht ane
accusatio aganis ane preist,exceptvndir tua,or *1.AdTim.*
threvitnes:And of thair pouar to cal pastoris: *5.*
Lay nocht thy hadis haistelie ypon onie man,
and haue na communicatione vith vther
menis synnis:and to Titus: For this caus haue *Tit.1.*
I left the in Creta, that thou may mend tha
thingis quhilk hes mister of correctione, and
appoynt preistis in euerie toun as I haue ordanit zou to do:zit the Bischopis of Scotland
as ze cal thame,becaus thay loue rather varld-
lie commoditie, and libertie of the fleshe to
marie, than the gloir of God in keiping the
constitutionis of the halie kirk,be quhais mi-
nisterial head thay aucht to haue thair calling,it is na meruel that God of his iust iudgement sufferis thair idiot inferioris callit Ministeris, to be maisteris ouer thame vithout defence of thair dignitie, be ressone it is bot
vsurpit : sua that sence thay ar al enterit in the
scheipfauld of Christ,nocht be the dur,bot be
the midsyd of the house, it is nou cummit to
pas that the ane laboure for the schameful
exterminion of the vther: for euin as the Ministeris ar na lauchful pastoris, and hes neuer
ressauit the imposition of hadis of Bischopis *1.AdTim.*
5.
N

quhairof S. Paul makis mentione: sua the intrudit Bischopis, as thay ar na bischopis, bot fals hypocritis, hes na lauchful authoritie aboue the ministeris, and the Ministeris mekil les aboue thame.

Pr. vald thou than say that the bischopis, gif thay var lauchfullie callit, suld conuocat the ministeris to al assembleis be thair authoritie, and be cheif præsidentis thairin, being lykuyse ordinar iudges in deciding al controuerseis in religione?

B.   Ze verelie : And vald thairfoir haue resolutione of ane dout : gif God sal raise vp in Scotland ane man desyrand disputatione vith onie minister, concerning ane or ma heiddis of religione, quha is abil to cite the testimoneis of the scripture, and sentences of the doctoris to confirme his part of the controuersie: Than I demand gif thair be vithin the realme of Scotland onie Iudge, quha heiring the ressonis of bayth the pairteis, may say to the ane, thou art richt, to the vther, thou defendis ane erroneus opinione, Thairfoir ather of zou man stand at this decreit, and definitione of the treuth: And incaice of disobediéte be authoritie of the halie Ghaist, gráted vnto me, quhairbie I am constitut iudge in this contröuersie , I denunce the disobeyar ane hæretike.

Heir. Smeton tuik on him the disputatione in Paiſlay, in audiēce of the maiſt honorabil the Maiſter of Roß, the lairdis of Caldual, blakhal, Ihoneſtone, Quhytfurd, and ſindrie vtheris.

OF THE IVDGE TO MAK DE-
ciſion of onie controuerſeis of religion, quhilk may aryſe in the kirk of Scotland, and of the iugement of the vord vrytin.

CHAP. XXV.

Smeton.

THair is ane Iudge vithin this realme to vit the vrittin vord and buke of God.

B. I ſay it is maiſt fals that the vryttin vord can be Iudge of al controuerſeis, becaus ane iudge man bayth heir and ſpeke, bot the vryttin vord is bayth deaf ād dume, ſua that it may nather heir the pairteis, nor pronunce the ſentence, quhilk tua thingis apertenis neceſſarlie to the office of ane lauchful iudge: By that, the office of ane iuge is that nocht onlie he pronunce the ſentence, bot put it alſo to execu-tione, that is, that he puneis according to the lauis thame quha be condemnit of onie cry-me, as be death, baniſment, or ſik punitione, bot the vryttin vord hes nocht ſik pouar or ſtrenth, as is maiſt cleir: Thairfoir of neceſſitie ather hæretikis man be vnpuniſed according to the lauis that ar maid aganis thame, or ellis thair man be ſum vthir iudge, by the vryttin

vord:Bot becaus that ze and al vther heretikis
ar condemnit be zour auin consciencis, and
zit vald abstract zour selfis from the lauchful
sentence of ane iudge, ze do veil quhen ze reiect al vther iudge by the vryttin vord, becaus that the vryttin vord vil nather hang
zou, nor burne zou. In the actis of the Apostlis I reid that sum controuersie of religione
did ryse amangis the Christianes in tha dayes,
quha for resolution of the veritie, did nocht
constitute the vryttin vord as Iudge, bot
Act.15. send vp to Ierusalem, to Sanct Petir and
the rest of the Apostlis as pastoris of the flok,
and quik iudges apoyntit be God to gif
deu and lauchful resolutione, be quhais exempil ve ar sufficientlie instructed that in al our
controuerseis, quhilk euer suld occur, for
establishing our conscience, ve suld haue recourse to the successoris of the Apostlis, as
the lauchful iudge to quhom Christ hes promised the assistance of the halie Ghaist to
Ephes.4. the end of the varld. And S.Paul to the Ephe-
sianis testifeis(that doctoris and pastoris ar
apoyntit be god to his kirk, to the effect that
ve be nocht careit auay vith euerie vind of
doctrine)Quhair he apoyntis nocht the vryttin vord iudge, bot the doctoris and pastoris
Deut.17. of the kirk: And in Deuteronô, the Hie preist
vas constitute iudge of al controuerseis of
the lau, that micht fal amang the Ieuis, suppois
thay had al thingis in vryt, that concernit
the sinagoge, als perfytlie at the lest, as ve

haue:And I meruel that ze,quha estemis zour
self to be learned, considder nocht , that the
Lauterianis Zuinglianis, Caluinistis,and Anabaptistis admittis the vryttin vord as onlie
iudge, and zit ze can nocht aggrie amág zour
selfis, euerie ane of zou aledging the vryttin
vord for his pairt , persuading him self that
the vryttin vord aggreis vith that opinione,
quhilk he hes alreddie forgit befoir in his
auin brayn , euin as gif tua men quha var in
cótrouersie about onie mater, vald pas to the
greit bellis of the kirk,and decerne that to be
treu quhilk the bel sould soúde to thair earis,
euerie ane of thame being addictit to his auin
opinione , vald say,that the bel did sound according to his imagination : And sua vald be
na mair resolut be the iudgement ot the bellis,nor thay var befoir: euin sua do ze vith the
scripturis:As for exempil,the Lauterian vil say
maist constantlie,that the scripture iudges for
his pairt,that the treu bodie of Christ is in the
sacrament ioynit vith the breid and vyne.The
Zuingliane vil constantlie afferme , that thair
is na thing in the sacramét bot breid,and vyn,
quhilk ar signes of the bodie and blude of
Iesus Christ: The Cauuinist maist bauld of al
vil afferme , that the vord of god is for him,
that the bodie of Christ is treulie in the lordis suppar, and that ve be certane pilleis , or
ingeynis ar liftit vp to heauin be ane incópre-
hensibil maner: quhat vald ze nou that ane
pure man, quha can nather reid nor vryt , and

N iij

suppoise he could, hes nocht sufficiét literatut
to vndirstand the scripture sould do in this
caice ? I dout nocht bot gif ze be nocht aluterlie obstinat, ze may persaue that he vald be
in ane veray greit perplexitie : and that he hes
na sure moyen quhairbie he may resolue him
self, and consequentlie gif thair be na vthir
iudge by the vryttin vord that Christ hes
nocht sufficiétlie prouydit for his kirk, nocht
leuing in it ane else and infallibil reul, quhairbie euerie ane quha plesis may discerne the
treu religione from the fals, as euerie man in
the day of iudgement man gif compt in particular of his auin religione and fayth. Than
my argument is this, that ve aucht to haue ane
iudge, quha sould pronúce the sentence in sik
maner, that he may put end to al controuerseis, and quhais sentence euerilk ane of the
flok of Christ, hou simple that euer thay be,
may cleirlie vndirstand : bot the vryttin vord
hes neuer zit put end to onie controuersie,
euerie hæretik allegeand it for him self, as said
is , nor zit pronunced the sentence sa cleirlie
that it micht haue bene persauit be euerie
ane: Thairfoir by the vryttin vord, necessailie
thair man be sum vther iudge, as in al com-
moneveil by the lauis that ar vryttin, thair is
sum iudgis apoynted, quha sould haue pouar
to interpretè the lauis, and in al controuerseis
of thame, pronunce thair sentence, and declair the treu mening thairof : vtheruyse na
cótrouersie could euerbe endit: as in the realm

of Scotland gif thair var na Iudge apoynted
for ciuil actionis,and it var permittit to euerie
mã of lau to interpret the lauis, and ordinãces
of the cuntrey according to his auin phanta-
fie,thair vald neuer ane proceſs be endit befoir the day of iudgement. And zit ze vil be
fua ingrate to Chriſt, as to think that he had
les prouidence of his kirk and faluatione of
faulis, for the quhilk he ſched his maiſt precious bluid,nocht prouyding ane ſufficiẽt iudge, for the controuerſeis that micht vpryſe,
nor ane fecular king or prince hes of the Ciuile adminiſtratione of his cõmoneueil. And
for conclufione , ze can nocht deny , bot the
vtyttin vord it felf, may be callit in dout be
heretikis: As the Marcionitis, and Manichæ-
vis denyit the hail auld teftament , vtheris the
tua hinmaiſt epiſtlis of S. Iohne, vtheris the
Apocalypſe : and vtheris, vther pairtis of the
ſcripture:Nou I demãd of zou, quha fal be iud
ge in this controuerſie ? For the vryttin vord
can nocht be iudge, as ze perſaue zour ſelf:
than necefſarlie ze man acknauledge fum
vther iudge: And to enter in particular, Lauter
denyis the epiſtle of S.I ames,quhat argument
haue ze,and al the miniſteris of Scotland, to
conuiĉt him ? For be the vryttin vord ze vil
neuer proue that fanĉt Iames vrait ane epiſtle.
Caſtalio denyis the buik quhilk is callit [Cãti-
ca canticorum] faying that it is ane buke contenand ballatis of luf. Gif onie in Scotland
defendit this opinione,zevald neuer get tham

conuict be the vryttin vord ? zea zour paraclet Theodore Beze , sayis that the Historie of the adulteres in the aucht chaptore of S. Iohne vas eikit to the text, and in the Euangel of S. Luc. thir vordis[quhilk salbe sched for zou]is eikit to the text, quhais sentece gif ze follou nocht, quhou vil ze get him condenit be the vryttin vord?I mycht schau hou Caluin zour maister hes eikit and paired fra monie places of the scripture , and zit be the vryttin vord it is hard to conuict him of sik eiking and pairing: sua I vil gather my argument in feu vordis : The iudge quhilk is appoynted be Christ to his kirk , may iudge of quhatsumener controuersie dois occuir, and condem for hæretikis , quhasoeuer aucht to be condemnit,bot this can nocht be done be the vryttin vord, as is prouin : thairfoir the vryttin vord is nocht the iudge quhilk Christ hes left to his kirk.

Sm. I perfaue of thy anfuer , thou vald refer this Authoritie of decision to the general Concilis, ouer quhom the Paip is præsident as Christus vicar, as the Papistis sayis : Zit the varld is nocht in sik ignorance nou as befoir : for the langagis and diuerse toungis, the philosophie, and al sciencis, ar accuratlie teached, quhairfor thair is na doubt bot ane man natural veil instructed in philosophie, hauing knauledge of the langages , quha hes studeit lang to the text of the scripturis , and red the vorkis of the doctoris, is abil to expone onie paſſage of scripture contening onie quæstione or heid of Doctrine neceſſar for our saluatione.

B. Than supponand zour self to be sik ane
man : gif ane vthir man instructed in tha sam
schuillis, quhair ze learned, als perfyt i al thay
thingis as ze ar, vald cum in Scotland, and
sustene disputatione aganis zou, mentening
ane sentence contrare to zouris, concerning
onie cheif head of religione, according to
zour reul, he vilbe als abil to interpret the
scripture as ze, and al men suld gif als greit
credite to him as to zou: and sua his sentence
being repugnant to zouris, it is necessar that
tua contrare and repugnant sentencis in interpretation of Goddis vord be imbraced
togidder: This is zour neu Theologie, quhilk
ze haue brocht in, in the kirk of Scotland:
To pas forduart, gif ane priuat man, being indeuit vith tha thingis quhilk ze prescryue,
may vith assurance, vithout onie error or de-
ception interpret goddis vord, quhy deny ze
that sam self pouar to the vniuersal Conciles,
in the quhilkis thair is sindrie at al tymes,
quha ar adornit vith sic giftis? or schau me
gif ze can, that euer onie hæresie hes bene finalie extuinguished, bot ather be the authoritie of the Bischop of Rome, or be the general
Concilis, gathered and assembled be him? I
remember that S. Augustine vryttis, hou that
Pelagius the hæretike vas condemnit in the
Concile of Palæstina be sindrie bischopis, bot
at the last quhen he vas condemnit be Inno- *Augusst.*
centius bischop of Rome, he sayis that na far- *epist.* 104.
der iudgemét aucht to be abiddin: Hou var the

Arrianis condemnit, bot be the general Concile of Nice? hou vas Macedonius condemnit bot be the general Concile of Constantinopil? hou vas the Nestorianis condemnit bot be the Concile of Ephesus? hou vas the Eutychianis cōdénit, bot be the Cōcile of Chalchedō? and siclyk of all vther hæretikis: Vil ze be sua bauld as to say that all thir halie fatheris, quha var assembled in the foirsaid Concilis for the extirpatione of erroris var blindit? ze man appardone me gif I say that ze ar rather blindit than thay : Ze I am assurit, quhatsumeuer opinione ze haue of zout self, that ze ar bayth ignorant and blind , as I haif pairtlie schauin befoir , and vil nou schau at mair lenth , ze say that ane man instructed in Hebreu, greik, latene and philosophie, quha hes red the ancient vrittaris , may surelie interpreit the scripture: I deny it maist planelie to zou , and ze and al zour ministeris vil neuer be abil to proue it, or to schau me in goddis vord, that onie sik thing is promised to euerie particular mā quha is indeuit vith sic giftis, and thairsoir all that quhilk ze grounde vpone this vaik fundament, man fall altogidder : Sabellius, Arrius , Macedonius , Nestorius and vtheris var maist learned men, and had red the scriptures veray diligentlie , and zit becaus thay gaue our greit place to thair auin curiositie, thay did fall in heresie, and var Heresiarchis : Zea generalie almaist al thay quha hes bée the beginnaris of hæresie var verie learned men and of gret spirit: vtheruyse thay could nocht haue defendit thair fals opinionis, nor inducit vtheris to follou thame: Bot thir hæretikis according to zour saying, did maist surlie interpret goddis vord, being indeuit vith all tha thingis quhilk ze esteme necessare for the interpretatiõe of the scripture: Nou quhat vil ze do vith ane man that hes nather greik nor hebreu, as sindrie of zour faythful brethrene? quhat reull sall thay haue for thair assurance? or quhou dar thay enter in the office of the ministrie? or quhat assurance can thair flok haue to follou thame? sen thay haue nather hebreu, greik, nor latene, and neuer red the ancient vryttaris, neuer studeit ane vord of Philosophie, bot neu cummit fra keiping of the scheip or the geise, as did Brebbenner and Paul Mephuen: Ansuer vnto me, quhat assurance can sic ministeris haue or thair flok quhilk follouis thame, sen thay ar destitute of al thay thingis, quhilk ze præscryue as necessar for the interpretatiõ of goddis vord? and to mak ãe ẽd to my hail discourse, suppois thay thingis quhilk ze prescryue, help mekil for the interpretatione of the scripture, zit as I haue schauin, thay can nocht gif assurance to onie man that albeit he be indeuit vith thame he may nocht err: I say farder that suppois ane man helpit be the spirit of god, being indeuit vith sic giftis may attene to the richt interpretatione of the scripture, zit that he hes nocht pouar to

command all the varld vndir the pane of fyn
and damnatione to follou fik ane interpretatione, becaus this onlie appertenis to thame,
quha hes iurifdictione in the kirk, and ar
fend be god as his meffingeris vith fik authoritie and pouar that vtheris ar obleift to obey
vnto thame, as Chrift faid to his difcipillis: As
the father hes fend me fua fend I zou, that is
vith pouar and authoritie: Thairfoir all zour
greik and hebreu is in vain , ze quhatfumeuer intelligence ze haue of the fcripture na
man is obleift to trou zou or to imbrace zour
interpretation except that firft ze declair
zour felf to be ane meffinger of God fend be
his authoritie and pouar. Ze vil vith patience
heir this vord onlie, that al tha thingis quhilk
ze præfcryue except thay be conioynit vith
humilitie and cheritie , auaillis lytil or nathing for the intelligence of goddis vord, and
zit ze haue prætermittit thame bayth quhilk
ar principal, ād hes the promeis of the affiftā-
ce of god, quhilk I beleue ze haue done of fet
propofe, becaus ze fe that ze and zour Minifteris hes nather cheritie, nor humilitie amangis zou, bot as ze teache zour felf maift treulie, thair is na thing in zou bot fyn, fua that ze
can not be the velchellis of the fpirit and vifdome of god : as it is vryttin [in maleuolam
animam non introibit fapientia] In ane euil
villie mynd or vickit mī vifdome fal not enter: This is fufficient for the refutatione of
zour anfuere, and albeit I vald grant al thing

Ioan. 20.

to be treu quhilk ze fay, zit ze do bot condēn
zour felfis: For ze can not deny bot befoir
Iohne Caluin and Martin Lauter thair hes bene ane infinit number of doctoris in the kirk
quha hes had the vndirftāding of the toungis,
ftudeit perfytlie in philofophie, ftudeit the
fcriptures verie diligentlie, and red vther ancient vryttaris quhilk preceidit thame, and
zit ze fay that neuer ane of thir vndirftude
the fcriptures, bot that thay var al diffauit: Reid zour Maifter Caluine in his buke de refor-
māda ecclefia: (The ancient vryttaris, fayis he
as Irene. Tertul. Arnob. Auguft. and vheris, fua
fulishlie be the breid hes interpret the bodie
of Chrift, that reffone and the treuth compellis vs to difagrie from thame): Is thair any in
Scotland that dar fay he is better verfit in the
hebreu, greik, and latine tungis, nor vas S.
Hierom? or red the fcripturis mair diligentlie? he hauing turnit thame out of Hebreu in
latine, and fum partis out of greik in latine?
or red mair perfytlie the ancient vryttatis
quhilk had bene befoir him? of quhom S. Auguft. geuis ane teftimonie vryttand aganis
Iuliane the Pelagiane, that almaift thair vas
naEcclefiaftical vrytar nather greik, nor latine
quhilk he had nocht red: As to the ftudeis of
Philofophie, and vther humane fciencis hou
veil he hes bene verfit in thame, it is cleir to
al men, quha reidis his vorkis: and zit ze zour
felfis, fayis that he vas alluterlie diffauit in
the interpretatiō of the fcripture, and reiectis

*Augu. 8.
contra Iu-
lianum.*

Beza in
13. Acto.

it alluterlie : ze zour Paraclet Beze, vrittand
vpone the actis of the Apoftlis pronuncis this
fentéce vith ane greit folennitie and aith faying, I tak god to vitnes and his Angellis, that
the baùldnes of Hierom in thrauing the fcripturis is intolerabil, as in tha thingis quhilk
he vrait aganis Iouinianus, and Vigilátius : Sua
ze may perfaue that ze condem zour felf, gif
the reul of the interpretatione of fcripture,
quhilk ze haue geuin be fure : and gif it be
nocht fure ze condem zour felf in lyk maner :
Sik is the nature of falfet that it aggreis nocht
vith the felf : Nou gif tua Minifteris, quha var
learnit according to that reul quhilk ze pre-
fcryue, be in controuerfie, as for exempil Maifter Patrik Conftant and ze ar in quæftione,
quhidder gif the eftait of bifchopis fuld be in
the kirk or nocht ? euerilk ane of zou, citing
the fcripture for his pairt, quha falbe iudge betuix zou ? For as to the vryttin Iudge, euerilk ane of zou fayis, he hes him for his pairt.
*Sm. Ane of the tua quhilk difagreis vilbe vorthie
of condemnatione, and efter reffoning, he vilbe conuict
of errore.*

B. Bot I pray zou, vil he confent to condemnatione of his auin errore, vnles he be mouit
be the Authoritie of ane Iudge, by the vryttin
vord, or the reffonis of his aduerfare?
*S. I vil efilie grant, that gif onie Minifter fal ref-
fone vith Zou, or ane aganis ane vther, the reft of the
brethrene be monieft voittis, may interpreit the buk
for bayth the pairteis.*

B. ze appeir to forzet that quhilk ze said a
lytil befoir, that the varld is nocht sua blindit
as to follou the decreis of general Concilis, and nou ze vald conſtrain men to follou the decreis of thre or four of zour vain
Miniſteris, ād that thair voittis ſould be acce-
tit as ane certane reul for the definitione of
the veritie, By that ze condem ane vthet
thing alſo quhilk ze affermit befoir, that is,
that ane Miniſter being indeuit vith ſik qualiteis, as ze preſcryuit may eſilie vithout all er-
rour vndirſtand the ſcripture, quhilk gif it be
treu, ſic ane Miniſter can neuer iuſtlie be cōdemnit, he hauand the veritie for him: and zit
it behouis that the ane part be condemnit:
Bot gif Maiſter Patrik Conſtant, ſuppois he
var cōdemnit be the gretaſt part of the voit- *voyces*
tis of zour miniſteris, vald nocht obey al-
ledging euer for him the vryttin vord, quhat
than vald ze do, quha vill haue na vther
Iudge of cōtrouerſie by the vryttin vord? And
quhat gif he haue als monie biſchopis, ad biſchop miniſteris for him, as ze haue miniſteris
inuyaris of the dignitie of biſchopis, for zou?
thair is na reſſone quhy he ſould follou rather
the voittis of zour miniſteris, nor ze the voittis of his biſchopis, and ſua gif ze iuſtlie condem him, he als iuſtlie condemnis zou : And
as vſis to be ſaid in ane commone prouerb,
Ane deuil dois ding another : Bot nocht villing to ſpend tyme in farder refelling of zour
vanitie, I vald propone ane quæſtione to

zou, quhidder gif Chriſt had ane kirk in Scotland quhē Iohne kmnox vas maid ane preiſt, quha had pouar to conſecrat him, or nocht?

S. He had ane kirk hauing ſic pouar, bot it abuſit the ſame.

B. I put the caice than, that ze had bene at that tyme, as ze ar nou, ze vald haue ſaid to that kiık, ze haue pouar to conſecrat Iohne kmnox ane preiſt, bot ze haif abuſit the ſame, hou vald ze haue prouin zour alledgeance?

S. Be the expres vryttin vord.

B. Onie of thame vald haue anſuerit, that ze peruertit the text, as vther lyke hæretikis had done befoir, the controuerſie than ryſing betuix zou and onie of thame, vas thair nocht brethrene quha at that tyme be monieſt voittis, micht haue reconcilit zou'tua in ane ſentence, and exponit the vord treulie for zou bayth?

Sm. I dout gif thair vas onie at that tyme, quha could treulie expone the vord of God.

B. Sen ze confeſs zour ſelf, that than thair var treu paſtoris in the kirk of Scotland, vtheruyſe ze ſuld nocht haue confeſſed that Chriſt had his kirk in Scotland at that tyme, quhne Iohan kmnox vas maid ane preiſt: and affermit alſo a lytill befoir, that in controuerſie vpryſing, be the gretaſt pairt of the voittis theveritie aucht to be eſtablished: Cōſidderīg that all thay paſtoris being aſſembled vald haue pronunced thair ſentence aganis zou, as thay did aganis vther hæretikis, and vald haue

ꝑe ſaid

ue said that ze had nochtvndirstand the vryttin vord, bot thrauin it fra the treu mening
and vndirstanding : hou can ze defend zour
selff bot according to zour auin definitione
ze ar condemnit as ane hæretik? As quhair in
zour ansuere ze say that ze doubt, git thair vas
onie quha could expone the vord of god treulie quhen Iohne kinnox vas maid ane preist,
gif ze doubt quhidder gif in the kirk of Scotland quhilk vas befoir zou, quhilk ze confess
to haue bene the treu kirk of Christ, thair vas
onie mā that could haif interpret the scripturis, quhy is it nocht lesum to me to doubt gif
thair be onie man in zour neu startup kirk,
quha hes pouar to interpret the scripturis? or
quhy dout ze nocht in lyk maner, quhidder
gif that vas the scripture, quhilk the kirk of
Scotland befoir zou appoynted for the scripture? or schau me onie ressone, gif ze can quhy ze doubt rather of the interpretatione of
the scripture, nor of the scripture it self? Gif
ze var veil examinat I seir ze vald dout of al:
bot that ze haue na subterfuge, I propone to
to zou that sam quæstione quhilk I proposed
befoir, gif ze had than callit in controuersie
quhidder gif thair had bene onie in the kirk
of Scotland, quha had pouar to interpret
the vord of God vithout errore? ze defending
the ane part, and the kirk it self the vthir:
And condemning zou be pluralitie of voittis,
ze ar constranit euin according to zour formar definitione, to confess that ze ar iustlie

O

condemnir : or quhat' bauldnes is it to zou to say that the spous of Christ, quhilk ze confessed than to haue bene in the Realme of scotland, to the quhilk the assistance of the halie Ghaist is promised, and doctoris and Pastoris for establishing the veritie, hes nocht pouar to interpret the scripture ? or that ze, quhais vanitie and incostance is knauin to all men haue ane sure & infallibil reul thairof in zour phantastical brayin? ze suld be eschamit of zour impudencie : And gif it be lesum to zou to doubt, gif the kirk of Scotland had pouar to interpret the vord of God, quhy is it nocht lesu to me to doubt gif ze be baptised, and gif ze aucht to be compted in the number of Christiane men? Cheiflie sen ze mak the treu interpretatione of the vord, and lauchful administratione of the sacramentis tua inseperabil nottis of the kirk: gif ze dout of the ane quhy may I nocht dout of the vther? Ze thay bayth being requesed according to zour doctrine, the ane being tane auay, the kirk in nauyse can consist.

SM. *Thou Knauis be decreit of the general Concile of the kirk, quhilk retracted S. Cyprianis sentence of the RebaptiZing of hæretiKis, that hæretikis may baptise.*

B.   Ze suld nocht haue cited ane general Cócile aganis me, sen the varld is na mair in blind nes, as ze said befoir, that it misteris to depend on the decreis of the general Concilis, bot sum plaine testimonie of the vryttinvord:

S.Ioh.16
Ephes. 4.

Or gif ze reſſauit that quhilk hes bene eſtabliſhed be the general Concile, quhy reſſiue
ze nocht al vther thingis quhilk hes bene
eſtabliſhed be thame in lyk maner? Zit I am
nocht ſua illuminat, bot I vil imbrace vith gud
vil the determinationis of general Concilis,
and that hæretikis may bapteiſe : Bot I can
nocht vndirſtand hou this dois aggrie vith
that quhilk ze ſaid a lytil befoir, that the kirk
quhilk cõſecrat kmnox ane preiſt vas the treu
kirk of Chriſt, and that it vas hæretical : except that ane man may be ane treu Chriſtiane, and ane hæretik togidder : Mairouer ze
knau that the ſam kirk quhilk hes determi-
nat that hæretikis may baptiſe, hes determi-
nat in lyk maner, that ynles thay quha ar ſua
baptized, be reconciled vith the treu kirk, the
baptiſme ſal not be valabil to bring thame to
ſaluatiõ: Nou thairfoir I demãd of zou, Quhat
treu kirk vas thair, vith quhom ze micht haue bene reconcilit, by that quhilk reſſauit
Iohne kmnox to be ane preiſt?

OF THE VISIBILITIE
OF THE KIRK.

CHAP. XXVI.
Smeton.

THair *is na dout bot Chriſt had his Kirk at that
tyme, albeit it vas nocht knaum to euerie
man.*

B. Ze cũ nou asvther hæretikis, ſpeciallie the

Donatiſtis did befoir, to ane inuiſibil kirk, quhilk errore is ſufficientlie refuted be S. Auguſtine vrytand aganis thame: And ſiclyk be our ſaluiour in the Euägel of S. Mattheu: [Bot gif he heir zou nocht declair it vnto the kirk] quhilk command na man could obey, gif the kirk var inuiſibil. And gif it had bene than inuiſibil as ze alledge, it had ſeruit na thing at al to thame, quha had bene baptized be hæretikis: becaus thay could nocht adioyne thame ſeluis to ane inuiſibil kirk: and ſua could nocht attene to ſaluatione, nocht being incorporat in the boſum of the kirk. As gif ane Ieu or ane Turk, had bene mouit to imbrace the religione of Chriſt, and to be incorporat intö his kirk, gif his kirk had bene inuiſibil vpone the face of the earth, hou could he haue adioynit him ſelf to it? I meruel gretumlie of zour blindnes, hou ze perſaue nocht that the hail prophecies of the kingdome of Chriſt, vald haue bene in vain, gif his kingdome had bene inuiſibil: for ane prophecie mä be of tha thingis, quhilk may be ſene and perſauit be our ſenſis and experience, vtheruyſe euerie man micht be ane Prophete, and foirſpeke of ane thing to cum: and gif it cum nocht to pas, he micht ſay that it hes cummit to pas in verie deid as he prophecied, bot that it vas inuiſibil, and vnknauin to the varld: thairfoir ze ſe in quhat abſurditeis ze rin zour ſelfis in, be this zour inuiſibil kirk: I vald glaidlie be reſolute of ane quæſtion vith zou, quha vas it to quhō

S. Mat. 18

this inuifibil kirk vas firft reueled? and quha
vas he that firft maid it vifibil to the eais of the
varld?Gif ze fay, to Martin Lauter, or Iohne
Caluin, ze condem zour felfis, becaus that
thay var bayth Apoftatis fra the Catholik
kirk, and that kirk quhilk quhen Lauter began vas inuifibil, remanis zit als inuifibil as
euer it vas, and nocht onlie as ze fay hes bene
knauin to feu men, bot to na man at al. Gif ze
haue red the ancient vryttaris, ze micht haue
fene hou S. Auguftine prouis aganis the Donatiftis, that it is impoffibil that the kirk at
onie tyme be inuifibil, ze euin in the tyme of
the maift feueir and cruel perfecutione of
theAntichrift,it fal remaine vifibil, vtheruyfe
it could thoil na perfecutione. Bot ze vil mak
the deuil ftarkar nor god, and vil that the deuil hes occupeit to him felf al vifibil kingdomes, tounis, citeis, and that he hes left onlie
ane inuifibil kingdome vnto Chrift.

Sm. *Quhy may nocht our Maifter Chriftis kirk be
inuifibil nou, as it vas in the dayes of Elias?*

B. zour argumét is verie vain, the kirk may be
inuifibil,thairfoir it is inuifibil, as gif ze vald
fay, Smeton may be bifchop of Sanctádrois
alfueil as Maifter Patrik Conftant,thairfoir he
is Bifchop of Sanctandrois : I defyre zou to
proue that the kirk vas inuifibil indeid, and
nocht that it may be inuifibil:for ze knau, as
in the fchuillis thay fay comonlie,[a poffe ad
effe non valet confequentia,] this is the firft
fault in zour argument. Nou gif for difputa-

tionis caus I vald grant, that in the tyme of
the particular synagoge of the Ieuis, the kirk
had bene inuisibil, zit Christis kirk may nocht
be at onie tyme inuisibil, fra the tyme he gaue
his Apostlis command, as ve reid in the actis
*Act.*1. of the Apostlis, that thay beginnand at Hierusalem sould preache in al Iudæa, Samaria, and
the far pairtis of the earthe: for lykas the coue
nāt of God maid vith mākynd eftir the flude
of Noe, geuand for ane taikin thairof the
rain bou, sal stay ane vniuersal destructione of
the hail varld nochtuithstāding thair salbe als
greuous synnis cōmittet bē mākynd vniuersa
lie in the latter age, as vas befoir the flude: Euī
sua albeit for the greit synnis of the preistis of
the sinagoge, God had sufferit his kirk aluterlie to be destroyed in the sicht of men, zit
S. Matt. the promise of Christ Iesus saying, (And be-
28. hald I am vith zou at al tyme vnto the end of
the varld] geuād thame ane suir afsistāce taikin
of his ordinar calling ofpastoris be the
onlaying of the handis of the preistheid,
quhairbie the halie ghaist is ressauit: This pro-
meise sal nocht suffer Christis vniuersal kirk
to be at onie tyme inuisibil, quhatsumeuer
crymes be admittit be the pastoris thairof, as
*Esai.*60. is propheceit be Esaias, The portis of the kirk
sal be oppin bayth day and nicht. And be the
*Psal.*80. prophet Dauid. Gif thy sonis leue my lau, I sal
nocht tak auay my mercie from thame, bot
thay salbe as the bricht sone in my sicht : Nou
gif ze pleis schau be quhat argument ze may

proue the kirk of God to haue bene inuiſibil
in the dayes of Elias.

S. *Becaus as ve reid in the bukis of the kingis, Elias*   3. Of the
ſayis lord, thay haue ſlaine thy Prophetis, thay haue   kingis, 19.
brokin doun thy altaris, and I am left alane, quhais   chap.
lyf thay lay vait for.

B. Lyk as ze propone the doubt of Elias, quha
being out of mennis ſocietie, micht nocht vndirſtand, bot be reuelatione quha vorſhippit
God treulie, and quha var idolatouris follouing Baal: ſua I gif zou for ane anſuer, that
quhilk god him ſelf ſubioynis, ſaying (I haue
left vnto my ſelf ſeuin thouſand mé, quhahes   3. *Reg.* 19.
nocht bouitthair kne to Baal) quhavald nocht
haue bene cómendit be ane diuine oracle, gif
thay had bene negligent in goddis ſeruice.
Then I demand of zou quhidder gif ſeuin
thouſand be ane ſufficient number to repre-   *Act.* 1.
ſent ane viſibil kirk, ſeing the elleuin Apoſtlis, electing Matthias in place of Iudas repre-
ſented the kirk viſibil and Catholik? And gif
zour kirk vas inuiſibil, as vas the ſynagoge in
the tyme of Elias, ze ſould haue ſchauin ſeuin
thouſand, quha had nocht bouit thair kneis
to Baal, or at the leſt ane hundreth, or ſeuin-
ſcoir or ſeuin, or at the leſt, ze ſuld haue ſchauin ane For gif the Catholik religion be fals,
ze haue al bouit zour kneis to Baal, and God
hes reſeruit na man to him ſelf at al. Gif ze
had brocht out of the darknes and vildernes
ſum men quha had profeſſed that religione
quhilk ze profes, and quha neuer had onie

communicatione vith vs, than zour sayingis vald haue appeired to haue sum probabilitie, bot sen ze can do na sic thing, ze gif plane testimonie of zour selfis, that zour inuisibil kirk is na thing els bot ane Phátastical dream: And gif onie man vald start vp euin nou in Scotland and teache onie neu hæresie of his auin brayn, gif he var demandit of zou of his kirk, in the quhilk he hes learnit his doctrine, he micht ansuere vith als gret probabilitie as ze do, that his kirk hes euer bene, bot that it hes bene inuisibil: quhat argument can ze be abil to produce aganis him to proue that thair hes nocht bene sik ane inuisibil kirk as he allegis, quhilk ve can nocht be abil to produce aganis zou? And gif it hes bene inuisibil hou haue ze knauin it sua veil? And quhy micht nocht vther men knau it alsueil as ze? And quhy haue ze bene sua inuyous that ze vald nocht schau it to the rest of the varld? Nou to cum to Elias, ze can nocht deny bot Elias him self vas visibil, quhen he maid the complaint. And in Iudæa at that tyme, thair

3. Reg. 22. vas the maist godlie king Iosaphat, quha neglected nocht goddis seruice, and Elias complaint vas onlie aganis Samaria, as is manifest in the text. quhairfoir zour argument prouis na thing at al, becaus it is maist manifest fals, that the sinagoge of the Ieuis vas inuisibil in the tyme of Elias: Bot to zou it is al alyk gif ze dissaue the peopil vith ane appeirance and

colore of the veritie, quhidder ze haue the veritie for zou or nocht.

*sm. Gif ve beleue the Catholik kirk as ve profes
in our beleif ve can nocht se it, becaus our beleif is
of tha thingis quhilk ar not subiect to our sensis.*

B. Be this argument zea beleue not the Byble, becaus ze vil not deny bot it is in lyk
maner subiect to our sensis, ze se thairfoir that
zour argument is of na strenth : For ansuer,
Ve se the Congregatione of thame of the quhilk the Kirk is maid and composed, and zit
ve do not persaue bot be fayth that sik ane
congregatione is callit be god to the inheritance of the lyf euerlesting, gouerned be the
halie spirit in the deu preaching of his vord,
and purgit from syn be the blude of Christ
throuche the mereit of his passione quhilk is
applyit to the membris thairof be the lauchful administratione of the sacramentis:
Thairfoir as in the Byble ve se the buke quhilk is vryttin, bot be fayth ve má beleue that
it is the vord of God quhilk is vryttin in it:
Euin sua ve se the Pastores of the kirk, and
thair flok quhilk is nurished be thame, bot ve
persaue be fayth onlie that thay ar the cõgre-
gatione quhilk is callit be god to the inheri-
ritance of lyf euerlesting as said is. And
thairfoir the visibilitie of the kirk is not repugnant to the article of our beleif, or ellis
ather zour kirk man be zit Inuisibil, or ze vát
ane of the cheif articlis of zour beleif, And in
verie deid gif that be the treu kirk quhilk ze

haue in Scotland,ze deny the article of zour beleif, becaus it is not Catholik according to the mening of the article of the beleif,bot onlie in ane fmal nuke of the varld.

OF THE VNIVERSALITIE OF THE KIRK. CHAP. XXVII.

Smeton

THou vndirſtandis not *in quhat ſens the kirk is callit* Catholik, *for gif thou vndirſtandit as thou vald appeir, that it ſould be ſpred throuch the hail varld ,* Zour Romane Kirk *is not* Catholik, *becaus thair be ma* Paganis, *and* Gentiles *,nor quha profeſſis the fayth of the* Roman kirk.

B. The kirk is callit Catholik for monie reaſonis,quhilk for the ſchortnes of tyme nou I vil ſuperſed, aſſignand to zou ane in ſpecial, becaus it dois comprehend the hail varld, as the hail varld vas promiſed to Chriſt for his kingdome,and inheritance (Dabo tibi gentes .24. hereditatem tuam, & poſſeſſionem, tuam terminos terræ.Oportebat Chriſtum pati, & reſurgere a mortuis, & prædicari in nomine eius pœnitentiam, & remiſſionem peccatorum per omnes gentes. Dominabitur à mari vſque ad mare, & a Flumine vſque ad terminos orbis terrarum.)i.I ſal giue to zou the nationis in hæretage, and the extreme bordoris of the varld in poſſeſſion:It behouit Chriſt to dea, ád ryſe frö the dead,ád pænitence and remiſſione of ſynnis to be præched in his name

Pſ.71.

throch al nationis: And his dominione salbe extendit from the ane sea to the vther, and
from the flude (to vit Iordanis) to the vtter
borderis of the hail earth: And sicly kvther places infinit of the scripture quhairin the obedience of the hail varld is promissed to Christ
be his omnipotent father of heauin: sua that
the Apostlis, and thair succesloris ar send to
subdeu the hail earth vnto the obedience of
Christis kirk, beginnand at Hierusalem vnto
the extreme pairtis of the varld , as he commandit thame to do : Not that the hail varld
sould be al at ane tyme subdeuit to him: bot
becaus his impyre and kingdome being anes
established, it sal neuer decay, bot incresch, ād
dilat it self continualie to the tyme that it haue occupeit the hail varld as vas spokin lang
befoir be al the Prophetis, and as ve se fulfilled alreddie and passand forduart fra day to
day , becaus the Apostlis as thay var commandit be Christ, began to preache the Euangel at Hierusalem, and thaireftir it did incress
and dilate it self throuch inumerabil pairtis
of the hail varld: And eftir the Apostlis had
endit thair course, and seallit the treuth of the
Euangel vith thair blude , thair succesloris in
lyk maner did imploy thair labore for the farder amplificatione of his kingdome: And eftir thame the Pastores quha succedit in thair
places trauellit in lyk maner to inlarge his
kingdome, and hes contiuuet euin vnto our
dayes, in the quhilk ve se the kirk of Christ

largelie amplifeit in the greit cuntreyis of the
Indis, quhair his name vas not acknauleged
befoir: And euin fua it vil increfch to the tym
the hail varld be fubdeuit to him, according to his auinvord: This is ane cleir and manifeft declaratione of the vniuerfalitie of the
kirk, and in quhat fens and mening the kirk
of Chrift is callit Catholik, or vniuerfal confirmed be al ancient doctoris of the halie kirk
collectit of the Prophetis, and gathered of
Chriftis auin vordis. Sua fence zour neu Kirk
of Scotlåd laitlie erected be Iohne kmnox is
not that quhilk began at Hierufaiem, and euer
continuand from tyme to tyme dilated it feif
throuch the hail varld, as is cleir of al hiftoreis, it is manifeft that it can nocht be Catholik:
The mater is fua cleir that I mifter not onie
farder demonftratione , ze being conftrainit
ather to fchau that zour kirk is that felf fam
quhilk euer hes continuer vpone the face of
the earth fen Chrift, quhilk is impoffibil to
zou to do: or ellis that it is not Catholik: Of
this al thay quha ar heir prefent may vndirftand hou lytil ftrenth zour argument hes to
proue zour intent: for the kirk is not callit
Catholik becaus that in ane tyme it is fpred
throche the hailvarld bot in the maner quhilk
I haue declairit befoir. Albeit as S. Auguftine,
Hierome, and vther ancient vrytraris declaris
according to goddis vord: It is vniuerfal at
al tyme in fik maner that it dois comprehend
ane greitar pairt of the varld, nor onie ane

S. Auguft.
de vnit
Ecclefie

Hieron.
côtr: Lu-
cifersanos.

sect of heratikis dois, or the synagogue of the
Ieuis, albeit at al tymes it be nocht sua large as
the infidelis and Paganis: And in this mening
also ze se that the Romã kirk as it is onlie Catholik , this day comprehendis ane greitar
pairt of the varld, nor dois al the synagogis
of the Ieuis, or quhatsumeuer sect of hære- *Aug.lib.3.*
tikis : Thairfoir Sayis S. Augustine that the *contra Do*
Sectis of Hæretikis ar obscure , and onlie in *natist.cap.*
Correris of the varld, in comparesone of the *1.*
vniuersal and Catholik kirk, As ze quha follouis kmnox in Scotlãd, and the follouaris of
Caluine and Beze in Geneua.

*S. Our reformed Kirk is Catholik in that maner
quhilk thou hes declairit and hauing tane the beginning from the Apostlis hes euer continued in the
varld, and dilated it self, sua that it hes bene spred
throche the face of the hail earth, albeit it hes not bene euer manifest to the eais of men, bot in quhatsumeuer pairt of the varld the treu professoris of the name
of Christ hes bene, thair I say our kirk hes bene also,
and is not onlie this day in Scotland bot throuche innumerabil pairtis of the varld, quhair I doubt nor bot
thair is monie quha hes not boued thair knees to
Baal.*

B. Ze ansuere to me euin as the Donatistis
did to S. Augustine, sua I vil vse na vther argumentis to refel the vanitie of zour ansuer,
nor thai quhilk S. Aug. vsed to refel the Do- *Aug.lib.*
natistis: first the propheceis quhilk is var foir- *de vnitate*
spokin of the kirk that it sould be dilated *Ecclef.*
throuch the hail varld, vald haue bene in vain

gif thay had meanit of ane kirk quhilk could
not be manifeslie knauin to the Eeis of men:
Becaus ve could neuer haue assuráce of the fulfilling of onie sik Prophecie, As quhen Daniel

Daniel 2. sayis that the God of heauin sal steir vp to him
self sik ane kingdom quhilk sal neuer be destroyit. And that the kingdome of Christ
sal occupie the hail earth: quhat assurance can
ve haue of this except ve may persaue vith
our eis that Christ hes erectit sik ane kingdome vnto him self? And zit ve can neuer persaue the same gif ve say that his kingdome
comprehendis onlie ane certan numbei of
vnknauin men dispersit on the face of the
earth, as ze say: And hou can ze be abil to conuict the Ieuis that this prophecie foirspokin
of the kingdome of Christ is fulfilled in zour
kirk? for gif ze say to thame that zour kirk
hes euer bene throuch the varld as vas foirspokin of the kingdome of Christ : Thay vil
desyre zou to schau that, quhilk gif ze can
nocht do, as ze profes zour selfis ze can nocht:
Thay vil iustlie lauch at zour fulishnes : As
quhen Daniel foirspake of the impyre of the
Greikis, and the Romane Impyre quhilk sould
be befoir the kingdome of Christ, gif the Roman impyre had neuer bene mair knauin to
the Eeis of the varld, nor zour kirk hes bene,
quha vald euer haue said that the Prophecie
of the Roman impyre had bene fulfilled? or
gif onie man had said it, think ze not that he
vald haue bene iustlie scornit be the hail

varld?Hou than can ze eschaip bot ze expose
zour selfis to be maist iustlie mockit bayth be
the Ieuis and Gentiles?and that ze mak al the
propheceis of the kingdome of Christ to haue bene in vain, gif he had nane vther bot ane
phantastical kingdome quhilk ze imagin to
zour selfis? This is not my argument, bot the
argument of S. August. aganis the Donatistis,
be the quhilk as thay var conuicted, sua ze,
and al hæretikis in the varld ar conuicted:
And to enter in farder consideratione of this
mater, sen ze esteme the Roman kirk to be
the seat of the Antichrist as ze blaspheme, sup-
pó vith zour selfis that thair had not bene sik
ane thing in the varld as theRomane kirkqu-
hen Martin Lauter begane, and imagine vith
zour self that giue ane Ieu had bene present,
ád requirit of Lauter to schau the Propheceis
of Christis kirkbe the quhilk it vas foirspokí
that it suld occupie the hail varld: That the
portis of the kirk sould be oppin bayth day
and nicht: That the princes ád Monarcheis of
the earth suld be subdeuit vnto it: zea the Ro
má impyre it self: that his name sould be louit
and glorifeit in it to the end of the varld: That
it sould neuer be ouercummit be onie vthir
kingdome]to cóuene to that kirk quhilk he
vas to erect í Almanie: quhat vald he haue be
ne abil to haue ansuered? quhat testimonie
could he haue geuí that thatkirk hadcótinued
euer sen Christ? that the kingis and Monar-
chis of the earth hes bene subdeuit vnto it?Or

Ps. 2. &
71.& 102
Esai. 60
& 49.
Daniel. 2.
Mal. 1.
Daniel. 2.

that the impyre of Rome at onie tyme hes
bene obedient vnto it? or that the portis of it
hes bene oppin bayth day and nicht to resaue
euerie man at al tyme? or that in it the name
of Chrift hes euer bene glorifeit? Al men may
eſilie perſaue that he vald haue bene vnabil
to haue maid onie anſuere: As to vs quha ar
propirlie callit Catholikes, ve haue na difficul-
tie in the mater, becaus ve may ſchau maift
cleirlie that al the Prophecies foirſpokin of
the kingdome of Chrift conuenis vnto vs,
and that ve ar his inhæritance: ve ſchau hou
that the kingdome of Chrift began at Hieru-
ſalem according to Chriſtis auin command:
hou that in ane ſchort ſpace it vas imbraced
maift zelouſlie in innumerabil pairtis of the
varld, and euer continualie knauin and ſpokin of vith greit admiration of the hail varld,
hes increſced vnto thir dayis: hou that it did
maift conſtantlie ganeſtād the cruel, and blud
thriſtie Emperoris of Rome, as Nero, Domi-
tian, Diocletian, and vtheris: Hou that in
the middis of thaj perſecutionis it did grou
and increſch miraculouſlie, and at the laſt
brocht in obedience, and ſubiectione the Romane Emperoris as Conſtantinus, and the reſt
of the Emperoris: hou it culd neuer be ouercummit be onie hereſie or ſchiſme: hou the
portis of it hes bene oppin bayth day and
nicht to reſſaue al men: hou in it the name of
Chrift hes euer bene louit, and honorit. Thair-
S. Aug.
epiſt. 166. foir as vryttis ſanct Auguſtine aganis the Donatiſtis

natiſtis ve mak it manifeſt ynto al men that
the kingdome of Chriſt pertenis vnto vs, ſen
ve ſchau that the propheceis quhilk var foirſpokin of it, ar fulfillit in our kirk : As to zou
(as he ſaid in lyk maner aganis the Donatiſtis)
ſen ze can nocht ſchau that thir prophecies ar
fulfillit in zour ſynagogue, ze declair maiſt
cleirlie to the hail varld, that it is not the
kingdome, and inhæritance of Chriſt : And
quhen the Donatiſtis anſuerit to him, that
thay had communicatione vith monie quha
var ſpred throche the hail varld, S. Auguſtine
deſyrit thamе to produce [literas communi-
catorias] that is, thair letteris quhairbie thay
micht ſchau that thay aggreit vith ſik vther
kirkis as thay ſaid var ſpred throche the hail
varld, quhilk becaus thay could not do, thay
var conuicted to be hæretikis, and learis:
be the quhilk argumét ze ar conuicted in lyk
maner, for gif ze vil ſéd throch Spázie, throch
Italie, throuch al Affrik, throuch al Aſia,
throuch the hail Indis, throuch al Germanie,
throuch al Fráce, and the reſt of the varld, ex-
cep it be in ſum lytil nuke, ze vil not get onie
ſik letteris of communicatione. And by that,
thay fra quhom ze vil obtene ſik letteris, ar
bot neu intrudit men, and Apoſtatis from the
Catholik religion, lyk vnto zour ſelfis. And
hes na ſchau of the face of ane kirk, ſen as ſayis
S. Cyprian (Eccleſia eſt plebs ſacerdoti aduna-
ta, & paſtori ſuo grex adhærés,) the kirk cóſi-
ſtis of the peopil vnit vnto the preiſt, and ane

flok adhærent to the auin paſtore , bot amãgis zou thair ar na preiſtis;and thay vith quhõ
ze vald ſeik communication , ar not gatherit
vndir ane paſtore, bot diſperſit lyk vauering
ſcheip vithout onie paſtore:ze albeit ze micht
ſchau this day communicatione vith monie
pretendit kirkis laitlie erectit , zit zour kirk
vald be proui eſilie not Catholik, be reaſſone
Martin Lauter, and Iohne Caluin quhen thay
began could not ſchau communication vith
onie kynd of kirk vpon the face of the earth.
As to vs ze ſe hou eſie it is to ſchau that ve
haue communication vith that kirk quhilk is
ſpred throuche the hail varld : Gif ve vil ſend
to France , to Germanie,to Spanzie,to Italie,
to Pole, to the innumerabil cuntreyis of the
Indis bayth oriental , and occidental, ve vil
find that al the biſchopis and Paſtoris aggreis
in ane doctrine of religion vith vs,and quhaſoeuer hes bene acknaulegit for lauchful biſchopis,and Paſtoris bayth in Aſia, and Afrik
hes maid profeſſione of that ſam doctrine:
Zea in our dayes in the tyme of Adrianus the
ſaxt,biſchop of Rome,the Patriarche of Ale-
xãdria did ſend to Rome,and mak profeſſione of ane fayth vith him . And the Patriarche of Armenia com to Rome him ſelf vith
ane Archebiſchop , and tua biſchopis to acknaulege the biſchop of Rome, and to profes vnitie of doctrine vith him : And in the
tyme of Iulius the thrid the gret Emperore of

Ethiopia send in lyk maner to Iulius the
thrid to haue communicatione vith the kirk
of Rome: and Pius the fourt did constitut ane
Patriarch thair, quha vithin thir feu zeiris
onlie is discessit: The greit Patriarche of Assyria quha hes ane greit number of bischopis
vndir him did cum to Rome for the lyk caus:
And in the tyme of Pius the fourt Abdisu the
Patriarche of the kirkis quhilk ar bezond Euphrates vnto Ind, did cum in lyk maner: And
to præjermit that in the general Concile of
Florence bayth the Greikis, and Armenianis
did al aggrie in the professione of ane fayth
vith the bischop of Rome: Nou presentlie the
greit Emperore of the Moscouitis intraittis
vith Gregorius the threttent, quha is nou leuand, to haif communicatione vith him in
fayth and religione: And thairfoir ze se zour
selfis that amangis thame al quha professis
the name of Christ ve onlie ar callit Catholikis, not onlie be our selfis, bot euin be zou
and al schismatikis: And quhen onie of zou
speikis of ane Catholik, he vndirstandis ane
of thame quha professis our doctrine: For
the quhilk caus sayis S. Augustine, that euin
the name [Catholik] did hald him in the kirk
becaus that kirk euin be the Hæretikis thame
selfis vsed euer to be callit the Catholik kirk,
and gif thay had spokin vtheruyse, na man
vald haue vndirstandin thame: And the ancient father Pacianus vrytand aganis the No-

uatianis sayis (Christianus mihi nomen est, Ca-
tholicus cognomé:) that is my náe is ane Chri
ſtiane, ád my ſurename is ane Catholik, be the
ane ſayis he, I am diſcernit from the Ieuis, and
Paganis, be the vther frō the Hæretikis: Bot
as to zou ze haue na name quhairbie ze may
be diſcernit from hæretikis, ſen ze ar content
ólie to be callit faythful or Chriſtianis, quhilk
al hæretikis dois vſurp vnto thame, ſua ze vant
ane ſurname except ze be callit Caluiniſtis:
or Proteſtaõs: for ze cã nocht vithout extreme
impudencie cal zour ſelfis Catholikes: And
thairfoir al the tyme that euer I vas amang
zou nather red I, nor hard I of ónie man,
the name Catholik: quhil I chanced tó reid
ane Catholik vryttar Dominicus Soto, and
thairfoir in zour beleif, for Catholik ze ſay
commólie vniuerſal kirk, as the head of al the
Proteſtaons Martin Lauter, for the kirk Catholik maid in his Catecheſme the Chriſtian
kirk, quhilk ze do onlie becaus conuicted in
zour auin conſciencis, nather may ze be callit
Catholikis, nather zour neu erectit ſynagoge
the kirk Catholik or vniuerſal.

S. *Thou may nocht be hard to haue onie reaſſoning
in this cuntrey aganis that Religion, quhilk is
confermit be act of parliament.*

B. I abaid ſum vther anſuer of zou, at the
leſt thir gentil men, quha ar heir preſent, I beleue ſalbe skarſlie ſatisfeit: Bot becaus ze ſe
zour ſelf conuict and can gif na anſuer, the
veritie being ſua cleir for my pairt, ze ar con-

ftranit to sklent and mak the act of Parliament ane buclar for zour defence aganis al argumentis: Bot to cum to zour act of Parliamēt, Iohne kmnox, quha vas na paftore bot intrudit him felff in the fcheipfauld of Chrift, About the fpace of xxi zeiris bygane, fchuke loufe all the actis of Paipis, and Emperoris, of Prælattis andkingis maid be continual fuccefs of tyme, the fpace of ane thousād fyue hūdreth and threfcoir zeiris, and zit ze for ane act of parliament, maid nocht be ane king bot ane particular fauorar of zour fect vfurpand the authoritie be zour moyen, vil ftay difputation of onie head of religione at this tyme. Quhairfoir I vil fullie refoluezou of this doubt be the grace of God: I demandit the Erll of Mortone in Dalkeith, quha vas vpone the Cōcile, at the making of the act: Quhat vas confirmit thairby, concerning the religione? For ather it behouit to be(faid I)the treuth of the Bybil, as it is vrittin in the text, or fum certan expofitione thairof, or generallie that, quhatfumeuer the minifteris preachis, or var to preache efteruart, fould be ratifeit, as Goddis vord? gif it vas the treuth of the Bybil, as it is contenit in the text, the act is fuperfluous, becaus thay quha ar callit Papiftis neuer denyit the fam, Albeit the act vas maid to bring thame to ane neu religion, quhilk thair foirfatheres miskneu: Giff it vas onie expofitione of the fam, it aucht ather to haue bene vryttin or prentit: Bot, thair is nather expofitione

P iij

vryttin, nor prented, except sum friuol negatiues, quhilk ar imbraced nocht onlie be the
Ministeris of Scotland, bot be the Ieuis and
Paganis, as that, Christis bodie is nocht vndir
the formes of breid and vyne, That thair is
noch seuin sacramentis & c. For the affirma-
tiuis ioynit heirvith ar al thisteoulie stollin
from the Catholik kirk, Quhairfor said I, it
restis that al quhatsumeuer the Ministeris sal
speke in the pulpit is ratifeit be that Act of
parliament, quhilk is ane vngodlie thing: For
gif the general Conciles of the hail kirk hes
errit, as thay falslie alledge, quhy may nocht
onie particular man of thame, preache erroneus doctrine for the treuth? Nor it is nocht
aneuch that ane minister, being iustlie reprouit be onie of his brethrene, mak ansuer; and
say: Brother quhatsumeuir I teache in the pulpit, is confermit treu be the act of parliamet,
quhairbie ze aucht to dea, as ane transgressore
thairof, becaus ze say thairto be fals, quhilk
the act of parliament confermes to be treu:
My lord Morton ansuerit, that Sanct Augustine vas als vyse ane man, as onie of thame,
quha var on the Concile at the making of
that Act. Quhairfoir lyke as he vrait bukes of
retractation, sua quhen ve find onie act of
parliament sayis he, vranguslie maid aganis
God, and gude reassone, ve vil annul the sam,
and estableis the contrare: And thairfoir zour
actis of parliament euin according to the iudgement of the vittiast of thame that vas the

diuyſaris thairof, can nocht be ane ſure groúd
quhairon onie man may leane his fayth conſidering the materis of fayth at nocht ſub-
iect to onie retractatione, as at the actis of
zour parliament.

OF THE CALLING OF KMNOX
and the fals miniſteris of Scotland.

CHAP. XXVIII.

Sm.

THou art verie blaſphemous aganis that treu paſtore of God Iohne Kmnox, ſaying that he intrudit him in the kirk of God vithout al calling.

B. Gif he had onie calling, it vas ather extraordinar, lyk as had the prophetis befoir
the cúming of Chriſt, or ellis ordinar, quhairbie ane lauchfullie callit paſtore, callis another
be the ſacrament of Ordour, and onlaying of
handis: gif he alledge the firſt kynd, it is neceſſar that he ſchau the viſion of the Angel, vith
the circumſtancis, and haue miracles, leſt the
peopil be ſeducit, or ellis na man is obleiſt to
beleue him: gif he had onie ordinar vocation
I pray zou declair the ſame.

S. He vas ordinarlie callit be the peopil.

B. The peopil is to be commendit, qua geuis
obedient audience to ane paſtore lauchfullie
promouit, bot quhair reid ze in the ſcripture,
that euer ane paſtore vas callit be the multitude? or quha gaue the multitude ſic authori-

1.Tim.4.
1.Tit.1.

S.Ioh.20.

Caluin li.
4.institut.
cap.3.sect.
16.

tie?For I reid that S.Paul ād nocht the peopil callit Titus and Timotheus, quha reſſauit authoritie be the onlayng of his hādis: and that he left Titus in Creta, that in euerie toune he ſould apoynt Biſchopis and preiſtis. And Chriſt in the Euangel of S.Iohne,ſayis, As the leuing father hes ſend me, ſua ſend I zou,that is,as the father ſend mévith pouar and authoritie to ſend vtheris,ſua I ſend zou:that nocht onlie ze may exerceiſe the office zour ſelfis, bot alſo ordane vtheris thairto. This pouar is geuin be Chriſt to the Apoſtlis onlie, and to thair ſucceſſoris, and in nauyſe to the peopil, lyk as euer hes bene practiſed vnto this day. By that, the pouar quhilk is granted to the Miniſteris of the kirk, is nocht ane ciuil or politik pouar, bot heauinlie and diuine,bot the peopil hes na vther pouar bot ciuil or poli tik as is maiſt manifeſt and cleir:Zea Caluine zourMaiſter cōfeſſis that the peopil hes nocht pouar to adminiſtrat the ſacramēt of Ordour, bot that it āppertenis onlie to the paſtoris of the kirk,and the reſſone of this is maiſt cleir, becaus it is ane thing maiſt propirlie apertenand to the gouernement of the kirk to appoynt gude and lauchful paſtoris:Bot the gouernemēt of the kirk appertenis nocht to the peopil,bot to the paſtore,as ye gouernemēt of the ſcheipfauld apertenis not to the ſcheip bot to the paſtore : Quhairfoir gif Iohne kmnox be nocht callit,bot be the peopil,he hes ingyrit him ſelf in the ſcheipfauld aganis the ordi-

nance of God . And albeit I vald grant to
zou that the peopil had pouar to cal onie
man, quhilk is maift fals, zit Iohann kmnox
vald be deftitute of al lauchful vocation,
quhilk that it may be maift manifeftlie knauin to the gentil men, quha ar heir prefent,
I vil demand of zou tua quæftionis :
The ane is to fchau me ane lauchful Magiftrat , or authoritie , that apoynted Iohann
kmnox for ane minifter? For the peopil aganis
the vil of the fupreme magiftrate hes na pouar
nor authoritie to eftableis onie thing , mekil
les , to eftableis ane thing of fua greit importance : to this quæftione ze can nocht anfuer,
Becaus the Quenis Maieftie of Scotlãd, quha
vas than Quene of France, and our fouerane
ladie hir mother, than regent of Scotland, did
bayth ganeftand the vfurpit authoritie of
Iohãnkmnox, and vald neuer approue that he
fould preach in the realme of Scotlãd: And he
violentlie did oppofe him felf vnto thame
bayth: fua he is nocht callit be onie temporal
authoritie quhilk is lauchful , bot intrudit be
the peopil aganis the lauis, and ordinances of
the lauchful magiftrat : The fecund is, quhat
religione profeffed thay, quha apoyntit Iohne
kmnox ane minifter? Gif thay had bene of our
religiõ, thay vald neuer haue apoyntit him: gif
thay var of that fam religion, quhilk he preached, than it is neceffar that fum vtheris fould
haue preched that religione vnto thame, or

he him self befoir he vas callit, ād sua he could nocht be callit be the peopil, or at the lest the first precharis of that doctrine could nocht be callit be the peopil, quhilk is aueuch for my purpose.

Sm. *Quhair thou sayis that Paul left Titus to appoynt Bischopis and preistis, thou art ignorant of the greik langage, quha turnis (Presbyter) to be ane preist, for it is callit, ane eldar.*

B. Albeit the natiue significatione of Presbyter be, that it is callit ane eldar, zit as ve reid ī the Epistles of Ignatius discipil to the Euangelist S. Iohne, Presbyter and Sacerdos in the primitiue kirk signifeit ane thing. Becaus grauitie of maneris, quhilk is speciallie conioynit vith aige, vas requirit in thame quha var consecrat preistis. Siclyk, Erasmus quhom ze vil grant nocht to haue bene ignorant of the greik, translaittis, ϖρεσϐυτείν, be Sacerdotiū. Al the greik authoris, quha vndirstude verie veil quhat ϖρεσϐύτερος vas callit, callis ϖρεσϐύτερος and ἱερεύς bayth ane thing: And S. Hierom quha vndirstude in lyk maner the greik tung, takis for ane thing Presbyter, and Sacerdos, as

Hierom cōt.lucif°. Cyprsa.li. 1. epist. 9. August.d: vnitate Ecclesiæ.

Cyprian, Augustine, and the rest quha hes vryttin in latine, neuer makand mentione of ane Minister. Gif ze sal seik the natiue significatione of euerie vord, onie man may obiect be als gud reassone to zou, that (Minister verbi Dei) sould nocht be callit ane of zour pastoris, bot ane gentil mannis seruand, quhi reidis the chapture of the Bybil at hame, becaus the propir signification of (Minister) is ane seruand. And (verbum Dei) is callit the Byble. Bot nou I pray zou schau me quhat pouar the peopil hes to chuse ane p istore?

S. *Ve reid in the Actis of the Apostlis that thay commandit the multitud of thair disciples to espy out seuin men of gud lyfful of the halie Ghaist and visdome quhom thay micht apoynt diaconis to serue the tabillis.* *Act.6.*

B. Sua may ane Minister desyre the people to search out ane gud and godlie schollar quha may be presented vnto thame, and zit this presentation makis him not ane Minister: Ze may reid in the same Chapture ane lytil eftir, That thir seuin men chosin be the multitude resauit not authoritie of administratione in the kirk, bot be the sacrament of Ordore, and onlaying of the handis of the Apostlis for it is thair vryttin, Thay brocht thame in presence of the Apostlis, and eftir thay had prayit, thay laid thair handis vpon thame. *Act.6.*

S. *Gif thou require ane ordinar calling be onlaying of handis, Iohann kmnox resauit it from Zour Roman Kirk.*

B. Than ze man grant zour Maister Iohann kmnox ane hererik, and Apostat quha maid defectione thairfra, and thaireftir denyit his vocation: Attour that, The pouar of Ordore is not sufficiét to ane man to preache bot he man haue also iurisdictione ouer thame to quhom he preachis, Iohann kmnox resauit neuer sic iurisdictione fra the Roman

kirk to preache in the Realme of Scotland,
thairfoir suppoise he receauit from it the Ordore of preisthead, zit he had na pouar to
preache nor to lauchfullie administrat the sacramentis, finalie ze ar iniureous to Kmnox,
affirming that he hes enterit anothir vay nor
he confessit him self, for he preachit in the
toune of Edinburgh, that gif Esaias,, Hiere-
mias and vtheris var prophetis, he vas ane
prophet lykuyse, and mair nor ane Prophet,
sua that being demandit of the reuerend fa
ther Maister Niniane Vingzet nou Abbot of
Ratinsburgh of his authoritie, he ansuerit
that he vas extraordinarlie callit euin as vas S.
Iohne the Baptist, And this he ansuerit in
publik befoir the people: Bot priuatlie he
scheu him self to be callit in ane vther maner,
that is be gunnis, and pistolis, for in ane conuention haldin be him, Villox, and vtheris of
thair sect, as I vndirstude of ane nobil and honorabil man quha can zit beir vitnes gif I lea
or not, Villox proposed as ane maist vechtie
mater to considder, be quhat vay thay sould
admit thair ministeris, for said he, gif ve admit
thaime be the impositione of handis or onie
vther ceremonie vsit in ordinar calling, the
lyk vil be askit of vs, that ve schau that ve
var admittit to the ministrie vith sik ane
cerimonie, be pastoris quha teached in the
kirk of Scotland befoir vs: Iohann kmnox
ansuerit maist resolutlie, buf, baf, man ye ar

anes entered, lat se quha dar put vs out agane,
mening that thair vas not sa monie gunnis
and piſtollis in the cuntrey to put him out, as
vas to intrud him vith violence: ſua Iohann
kmnox be his auin cófeſſió entered not in the
kiṙk be ordinar vocatione, or impoſitione of
handis, bot be impoſitione of bullatis and
poulder in cultringis and lang gunnis, ſua ze
miſter not to troubil zou farder in ſeiking
out of Iohann kmnox vocatione.

Miniſter. Thair is na dout bot extraordinarlie Io-
kān kmnox vas raiſed vp to ruit out idolatrie out of
this cuntrey, ſua as obſeruit ane of our faythful bre-
threne he vas maiſt iuſtlie callit kmnox (pepulit quia
voce locuſtas) ād be him as be Martin Lauter lykuyſe, Apoc. 19.
that man of ſyn the Antichriſt vas reuelit, quha ſit-
tis vpone the ſeauin hillis in the toun quhilk hes
dominione ouer the hail varld, quhairbie na vther Apoc. 17.
may be vndirſtand except the Paip of Rome. ſic is the
ambitione and corruptione of the maneris of the hail
toune of Rome that it is direẛ repugnant to the lyf of
treu Chriſtiànis. I Knau Zour Germane Papiſtis var
offendit that be the prouidence of God that halie man
ſould be callit λϰmẽ ane lauar for this name is dreuin
from the greik verb λϰω quhilk ſignifeis I veſche, be
reaſone he reneuit the treu doẛrine of the lauar
of regeneration, quhilk befoir vas obſcurit be the Pa-
piſtis.

B. Lyk as the Deuil callit Lucifer ane berar
of licht transfiguris him ſelf in ane Angel of
licht, and playis the Aip to god, his Apoſtlis
dois lykuyſe counterfute the maiſt excellent

of goddis Elect taking to thame selfis names of excellencie, sua Symon Magus vas callit the verteu of god: and Manichæus callit him self the Apostle of Christ makand sum alteraratione in his nameMánichæus, quasi funderet manna, siclyk I micht speik of the Eunomianis, Luciferianis, thame quha var callit καθαροι and vtheris innumerabil, As to the mysterie of zour Maister and prophet kmnox, quhair ze apply his name to the reuelatione of the Antichrist, I think ze micht mair iustlie haue callit him kmnox quasi nox, à nocendo: for he hes bene verie noysum to Christis kirk quha vas his mother, sua that for the desolatione quilk he hes maid in Scotland he may *Apoc. 9.* be callit אבין ἀπολύον, perdens: For in respect of his vil quha had euer in his mouth, [Ruit out, Ruit out]thair vas neuer ane gretar destroyar of policie, lauis, and al thingis befoir buyldit, erectit, ordinit and established the space of threttene hundreth zeiris, lik as the name of Mahometis hes the sam signification *Deut. 29.* a סרס destruere, perdere becaus he destroyit the Christian religiō throuch out al tha pairtis quhilk nou ar vndir the ditiō of the Turk, As to zour vther germane prophet I knau he vrait his name not onlie Martin Luter fra the greik verb λοιω efter the custume of vther Germane prophetis Melanchton, Dryander, Hosiander, quhais fatheris names var blak earth, Aikman, Halieman: bot to declair his singularitie in the bukis quhilk he vrait in

his germane vulgar toung he callit him self
Lauter à lauo, quasi lautor, ane clengear of the
people from the filthenes quhilk thay contracted in the captiuitie of Babylon, for it
pleased him sua to terme the humil obedience of al nationis to the kirk of Christ, zea
he delytit mair to be callit Lauter nor λυπηε
becaus in the germane toung it signifeis pure
and clene: Nou albeit he hes chosin vnto him
self this surname of excellencie his father being callit luder quhilk signefeis dirt in the
Germane toug, or Lutear quasi Luteus, zit Lauter sal haue na caus to complane that I inuie
the excellencie of his name, for sence I haue
this conference in my vulgar toung I sal euer
vnles I forzet my self cal him eftir that name
quhilk he tuk to him self vryttand in his vulgar toung, becaus I knau persytlie sic is the
prouidéce of God, that he turnis thay thingis
to the ignominie of the vickit quhilk thay
think maist glorious: for fra the theme to the
quhilk he referris the deductione of this name
cummis allo (diluuium) quhairbie the varld
vas anes destroyit, sua that as the name ἀπωλύυι
aggreit veray veil to Iohann kmnox, it may
lykuise maist iustlie pertene to Martin Lauter
quha hes destroyit the Catholik religion sua
far as lay in his pouar throuch the hail latine
impyre. Nou to cum to zour obiectione, quhair ze say that nane vthir may be vndirstand
be him quha sittis on the seuin hillis in the
toun quhilk hes dominion ouer the hail varld

Apoc. 9.

Apoc. 17.

except the Paip of Rome be refone of the ambitióne and corruptit maneris of that toune, and that S. Iohne fpeakis of the Antichrift in tha vordis : This obiectione feruis zou for ane commone plaçe in zour preachingis to vithdrau the people from the obedíence of Chriftis vicar in the earth, quhairbie ze fchau maift manifeftlie zour malice and ignorance, *Apoc.*17. for albeit that place of S. Iohne be in verie deid vndirftand of the toune of Rome, zit it feruis na thing to zour propofe, becaus bayth according to the plane vordis of the text, and the interpretation of ancient vryttatis it aucht to be referrit tó the Emperóris of Róe quha maift cruellie did perfecute the kirk of god, and in fpecial the Paipis and hie preiftis of the fame bifchopis of Rome, the fpace of thrie hundreth zeiris fra Nero to Cóftantinus Magnus, during the quhilk tyme al kynd of Idolatrie did ring cheiflie in the toune of *Apoc.* Rome aboue al vther nationis of the varld, *cap.*17.& for the quhilk caus S. Iohne fayis (That the 18. kingis of the earth hes playit the harlat vith hir, and hes drunkin of the coup of hir fornication) becaus that the hail varld vas contaminatvith hir Idolatrie: And as vitnefsis S. Leo bifchop of Rome that fcho vas the mother and maiftres of al error in fic maner, that fcho had ane temple çallit πανθέων .i. quhairin vas al the Idolis of the varld, for as thay fubdeuit euerie natione to thair impyre fua thay brocht the innumerabil Idolis of fua monie diuerfs

uerfs nationis of the hail varld to the foirfaid
kirk of Rome thair to be vorshipped: He sayis
also that the toun of Rome vas drunkin vith *Apoc.17.*
the blude of Martyris, declairing the cruel
perfecution of the Roman Emperoris, be the
quhilk fua exceiding ane greit nûber of Martyris vâr put to maiſt cruel and horribil death,
that skaiſlie burreois could be fundin to ſatisfie thair inquenſibil thriſt of the innocent
blude of the Chriſtianis, as is manifeſt of al
hiſtoreis, and of the louabil memorie of thair
names quhilk ar zit keipit in the toune of Ro
me, and of the covis in the quhilkis thay ſumtyme did lurk to eſcheû a lytil the furious rage of perfecutione and of thair maiſt halie reliques; that almaiſt the hail toun of Rome is
ſanctifeit be the blude of the Martyris: for the
quhilk caûs S. Paul vryttand to the Theſſalonianis, ſayis (Iâm enim myſterium operatur *2.Theſſ.2.*
iniquitatis) for non the hid myſterie of iniquitie dois vork, mening of Nero and vther cruel
Emperoris quha mouit be the ſpirit of the
Antichriſt, quhilk he callis the myſterie of
iniquitie, vas to perſecute the kirk of Chriſt:
And S. Petir him ſelf be reaſſone of the gret *1.Pet.5.*
confuſion of idolatrie of al nationis quha re-
ſortit into Rome callis it Babylon, ſaying the
kirk quhilk is in Babylon ſalutis zou, mening
of the kirk of Rome, as amangis vtheris interpreitis S. Hierom: quhairof zour malice may
eſilie be knauin to the hail varld, becaus ze
deny that S. Petir be Babylon in this place vn-

Q

dirſtandis the toune of Rome, to the effect ʒc
be not côſtranit be exprefs teſtimonie of ſcripture to grant that S. Petir vas in Rome, bot
in the reuelation of S. Iohne be Babylon ʒe
vil haue na thing vndirſtand bot the toune of Rome, albeit ʒe haue na reaſone for
*Apoc.*17. ʒou quhy it ſould be vndirſtand vtheruyſe in
the epiſtle of S Petir nor in the reuelation of
S.Iohne: Heir I haue declarit to ʒou the treu
mening of that place of S. Iohne quhilk ʒe
abuſe. And I ſay farder mouit be gud reaſone
that it can nocht be vndirſtandin of the kirk
of Rome becaus S. Paul him ſelf louit gretû-
lie the Romanis quha had than imbraced the
Chriſtian Religion, and it vas not the kirk of
Rome quhilk did perſecute the Martyris of
the quhilk S. Iohne ſpeikis, bot be the contrare it vas the kirk of Rome quhilk thoillit
the perſecutione of the cruel Emperoris, and
in ſpecial the Papis, quha var almaiſt al Martyris, befoir the dayis of Conſtantinus Magnus: Mairatour al Chriſtian Catholik men
hes euer honorit the kirk of Rome from the
hrit fundation of it in the dayis of the Apoſtlis, to this preſent for thair ſpiritual mother,
as I haue ſchauin to ʒou befoir in my laſt cô-
ference, quhilk thay vald neuer haue done gif
thay had bene of ʒour opinione, or eſtemit
hir to be the hure of Babylon as ʒe maiſt impudentlie blaſpheme: Quhair as ʒe conclud
ʒour obiectione be reaſone of the ambition
and corrupted maneris of the toune of Rôe,

I anſuere to zou according to our Scottis
prouerb, He ſould haue ane hail pow, quha
callis his inchtbour neitie now: And gif I do
not content zou vith this anſuer, S. Hierom
quha vndirſtud the Apocalypſe of S. Iohne
alſueil as ze, vil mak zou anſuer for me: quha
ſpeikand of the toune of Rome vryttis in this
maner (Eſt quidem ibi ſancta Eccleſia, ſunt
trophęa Apoſtolorum & Martyrum, eſt Chriſti vera confeſſio, eſt Apoſtolorum prædicata
fides, & gentilitaté calcata in ſublime quoti-
die erigitur vocabulum Chriſtianum, ſed am-
bitio, potentia, magnitudo vrbis, videri, & videre, ſalutari, & ſalutare, laudare & detrahere,
& tantam hominum frequentiam videre à
propoſito Monachorum, & quiete aliena
ſunt.).i. The treu and halie kirk is in the toun
of Rome, thair ar the taikinnis and triumphis
of the victorie of the Apoſtlis and Martyris,
thair is the treu confeſſion of Chriſt, thair is
the faith quhilk vas preachit be the Apoſtlis,
and the nãe of thã quha pfeſſis Chriſt is daylie
exalted, gentiliſme being trampit vnder fute,
bot ambition, potentnes, the greitnes of the
toune, the deſyre to ſe and to be ſene, to gif,
and tak guddayis, to loue and lak vtheris, and
to ſe ſik ane multitud of men ar not conuenient to the purpoſe of ane Monk, or the trã-
quillitie of ane religious man: Ze ſe thairfoir
that ze ar mair ſkar nor vas S. Hierom, quha
vald not ſeparat him ſelf from communion
vith the kirk of Rome, quhatſumeuer corrup-

tion of maneris he did persaue in sum priuat personis:Bot ze,lyk the Donatistis,vil haue na thing ado vith the kirk of Rome, becaus as ze allege thair is in it sum corruption
of maneris , albeit ze zour selfis euin according to zout auin confession be replenished
vith al kynd of vickitnes.

OF THE ANTICHRIST.

CHAP. XXIX.

Minister.

VE ar not sua ignorant bot ve knau persytlie
that S. Iohne in his reuelatione speaku not
onlie of thingis passed, bot also of thingis quhilk var
beginn and to be compleit quhen he vrait his prophecie, and of thingis to be completit lang thaireftir, and
lykuyse that monie thingis quhilk var spokin of
Rome var fulfillit in the cruel Emperoris: Zit ve affirme maist constantlie that S. Iohne speakis of ane
vther *Antichrist* quhilk vas to inuade the treu
kirk of God ane lang tyme eftir the crueltie of the
infidel Emperoris sould ceise,quhairbie gif ve considder his propirteis aricht ,nane vther may be vndirstand except the Paip of Rome:

B. I grant that by the Emperoris quha ar zit
cummit S. Iohne menis of ane vthir Antichrist quhilk sal inuade the treu kirk , bot
quhair ze alledge that nane vther may be vndirstand except the Paip of Rome, I desyre
zou to produce ane solid reasone to confer-
me zour assertione, vtheruyse al men of gud

iudgement may perſaue hou eſie it is to me
to reiect the ſam, as maiſt fals and vnuorthie
of onie farder improbation. Bot nou to the
end that al mē may vndirſtād quha may iuſtlie
be callit the Antichriſt, I vil propone ſum of
his cheif markis quhilk ar ſetfurth in Goddis
vord, that thairbie ve may knau him and keip
our ſelfis that ve be not ſeducit be his vickit
doctrine: his propirteis contrare vnto thame 1
quhilk we find in Chriſt man be, that he be 2. *Theſſ.*
ane man hauand aſſiſtance of the deuil in al
operation: lyk as the ſeuin giftis of the halie *Eſaiæ.*11.
Spirit reſtit vpone the manlie nature of Ieſus, 2
ſua ſal the ſeuin deidlie ſynnis pryd, auarice, licherie, glutonie, ſleuth, Ire, and inuie regne in
him and his diſciplis: Lyk as the ground of 3
the Chriſtian religione is the confeſſione of
S. Petir, that the ſone of the leuing God is cú- *Mat.*16.
mit in the fleſhe, ſua ſal the principal but
quhairat he ſal ſchut be to deny Chriſtis cú- 1. *Ioh.*2.
ming in the fleſhe, and the hail vorkis done 4
be verteu of his incarnation: Lyk as in
Chriſt vas puritie of doctrine vithout onie 1. *Pet.*2.
error and godlines of lyf, Sua in the Antichriſt ſal be ane denyal of al doctrine befoir
eſtablished, and ane Maſs of al erroris befoir
códénit maiſt impudētlie teached for treuth,
and contempt of al gud commandimentis
and godlie lyf, zea ane prouocation to al im- *S.Mat.*
pietie: Lyk as be the Conſil of Chriſt his diſci- 19.
ples left thair vyſis, and thay quha var vnma- 5
reit villinglie leuit chaſt al thair dayis, that

thay micht indeuor thame selfis haillelie to
the seruice of God, Euin sua the Antichristis
disciples be his consile sal think thame selfis
maist vnhappie gif thay haue not vyfis, not
uithstanding thair estait and aige sal be repugnant to sik mariageis as thay sal desyre, For
Daniel.11 Daniel testifeis that the hart of him and his
disciples sal be brunt vith the lust of vemen:
6 Lyk as Christ began his preaching in the treu
kirk of God, be planting the doctrine quhilk
vald haue bene the caus for the quhilk Hierusalem sould haue standin for euermair, gif
the induellaris thairof had resauit it: Euin sua
2.Thess.2. the Antichrist sal sit in that kirk be making
the peopleApostatis, quhilk befoir acknau-
leging the lauchful pastore vas the treu Hierusalem or kirk of God, and nou be defectiō
is maid the seat of the Antichrist, quhairof vil
inseu gret desolatiō ād ane suddane ruine: Lyk
7 as Christ promised that the zettis of hel mening
Matt. 16. thairbie error and fals doctrine sould not pre-
uale aganis his kirk, bot his halie spirit sould
gyde hir ī al treuth to the end of the varld, sua
sal the Antichrist teache the plane contrare,
to the ēd it may be collectit that Christ vas ane
deceauer makand ane fals promeiss, for he sal
preache that the hail kirk hes imbraced monie headis, of erronious doctrine : Lyk as
8 Christis kingdome had ane smal beginning
Act.1. at that tyme quhen the varld in verie deid vas
in greitast blindnes, and thaireftir grouis quhil it haue occupeit the hail varld, Euin sua the

Antichrist vil maist impudentlie affirme that the hail varld vas in blindnes befoir his cumming, and persuade his disciples that obstinatlie thay thoil the dead for mentenance of his errotis, quhilk obstinatnes paintit vith the colore of patience vil seduce monie, and be thocht falslie miraculous proceiding of the Spirit of God, and mak thame quha vil be seducit, be ane blind and inordinat zeal becum inraged to persecute the treu Christianis maist extremlie, quhil he haue dilated his poysone vniuersalie, that is quhil he haue in al pairtis quhair the kirk is, professed ennimeis to the same, laboring for hir destruction: bot quhen it is at the heicht it vil left onlie thre zeir and ane half, quhil as be the contrare to the gret cófort of the treu Catholikes, Christis kingdome being anes at the heicht sal left for euermair : Lyk as Christ descendit of the tryb of Iuda, and vas reueled quhen the Impyre of Rome vas resauand incress and maist florishing: Euin sua the last Antichrist be operation of the deuil sal be generat of the seid of Dan, quhen the Impyre of Rome salbe sua imminished that it sal skarslie haue the maiestie of ane impyre, quhilk be the preaching of the Antichrist vil resaue gret hurt : for he and his disciples vil be maist desyrous to eiect lauchful kingis, Princes Dukis, Lordis and haue thame selfis placed in thair roumes albeit be hypocrisie thay vil labor to clok the same and appeir to seik na les: first vndir pretence of li-

S. Paul 2. Thess. 2.

Apoc. 11.

Daniel. 7. 6

Gene. 49.

2. Thess. 2.

Q iiij

bertie bringand kingis and princes subiect to
the Impyre of Rome from obedience to the
same, to the effect that thaireftir euerie ane of
thame may be the mair esilie ouerthraui: Lyk
as Christ vas præfigurat in the auld lau be tua
beastis commonlie, sua S. Iohne in his reuelation bringis in tua beastis for compleitting of
the bodie of the Antichrist, calling ane of thame ane blasphemous beist absolutlie, quhair-
Apoc. 13. bie is signifeit ane professit Apostat and infidel, the vther ane beast hauing tua hornis lyk
the lamb, and zit notuithstanding spekand as
dois the dragon, quhairbie he signifeis ane Pa
triarche of Hæretikis quha albeit he prætend
the mantenance of fayth and lauchful calling
zit in effect he aggreis vith the formar beast,
quhilk S. Iohne callis the vorshipping of the
Apoc. 13. vther beast: And that quhilk is spokin be S.
Iohne of the beast vith the seuin headdis and
ten hornis, may be vndirstandin not onlie of
the vitious Emperoris of Rome quha did per-
secut the primitiue kirk, bot also of the last
Antichrist: for the headis signifeis diuers Hæ-
resiarchis and Maisteris of fals doctrine. The
hornis signifeis the assistance of temporal
pouaris quhairbie thair impietie is defendit:
Apoc. 17 And thir as S. Iohne sayis, resauis pouar at ane
hour vith the beast: for lyk as thay quha ar
Ministeris deput to preache in the kingdome
of the Antichrist dispossessis lauchful preistis
and Bischopis: Euin sua temporal men infe-
ctit vith thair pernicious doctrine vil think

thame seltis inferior in spirit and courage to thair brethrene, vnles thay lykuyse eiect temporal Magistratis metenaris of the treu religioͦ,as Kingis, Quenis, Dukis and Erlis,occupeand violentlie thair roumes, for the quhilk caus S.Iohne callis thame not kingis, bot hauing pouar as kingis: Lyk as S.Iohne declairis his cumming be the lousing of ane vyld beast,sua he vil not be eschamit to cal him self ane vndatonit beast quhilk may not be ouercumit: And his kingdome vilbe at the heicht quhen the deuil sal be loused, quhilk laxation vil be knauin be vniuersal vitkitnes, and infidelitie almaist throuch the hail varld,vith exceiding gret feir to profes Christis doctrine, and the sacrifice of his bodie and blud callit the Mess: Sik as is this day in Scotlad,and Ingland quhairin is ane viue image of the kingdome of the Antichrist,quhairin gret desolation may be sene in the halie places, and gret persecution of the treu Catholikes:For in the Antichristis kingdoͤe abhominabil hurdome vil be placed in the kirk for he preasthead, and Sodomitical syn as bougrie,incest, and adulterie vilbe honorit as Mariage: He is callit the beast vpon quhom the hure sittis, that is be quhais doctrine the Authoritie of the hure aboue the kirk is approued:For as Christis doctrine admittis nane of the feminine kynd to beir reul in the kirk,sua the disciplis of the Antichrist vil promoue not onlie Bairnis, and Idiotis bot Vemeͤ also in place of bis-

Ibid.

Mat.24.
Dan.12.

Matt.24.
Apoc.11.

2.Tim 2.

chopisād hie preiſtis: for of ane in tha cútreyis quhair the Antichriſt ſal be beſt obeyit Sanct Iohne ſpekis maiſt planelie in his reuelation
Apoc. 2. [Permittis mulierem Hiezabel quæ ſe dicit prophetiſſam, docere, & ſeducere ſeruos meos, ſcortari, & edere ex iis quæ ſimulachris immolantur, & dedi illi tempus vt reſipiſceret à fornicatione ſua, & nõ reſipuit,] .i. Thou ſufferis the voman Hiezabel quha ſayis that ſcho is ane prophetiſs beríg office in the kirk, to teache and deceaue my ſeruandis, and play the harlat and eat of tha thingis quhilk ar offerit to Idolis, ād I haue geuin hir tyme to repent from hir fornication and harlatrie, bot ſcho hes not done pœnitence : And agane
Apoc. 18. (Quantum glorificauit ſe & in deliciis fuit, tátum date illi & tormentum, quia dicit in corde ſuo, conſideo Regina, & vidua non ſum, & luctum neutiquam videbo) .i. Sua far as ſcho hes exaltit hir ſelf and leuit in ryattouſnes, geue hir als gret torment and murning, becaus ſcho ſayis in hir hairt, I ſit ane Quene in my throne, and I ſal not ſe murning or lamenta-
10 tion: As Chriſt honorit the father of heauin,
Apoc. 13. ſua ſal the Antichriſt and his diſciplis honor the Deuil of hel as onlie vorkar of al thingis: for he vil teache that notuithſtanding the grace of Chriſt it is impoſſibil to reſiſt the ſuggeſtionis of the Deuil, or that onie mã hes pouar to do vtheruyſe nothe dois: he vil maiſt blaſphemouſlie affirme that al the vorkis quhilk the treu Chriſtianis dois mouit be the ſpirit

of God ar the vorkis of the Deuil, ād that God
dois al the miſcheif quhilk is vrocht be him
and his diſciples, this is the vorshipping of the
dragon quhairof S. Iohne ſpeikis in his reuelation: As Chriſt is conſiderit in propir perſo- 11
ne quhō al faythful men vorshippis for thair
God, being bayth God and man: And lykuyſe
in his myſtical bodie quhilk comprehendis al
his diſciples in vnitie of ſpirit concerning doctrine and maneris: Sua may the Antichriſt be
cōſiderit in his bodie natural ād myſtik, to the
quhilk al thay apertenis quha ather imbraces
fals doctrine ōlie, or ar of vitious lyf ōlie vith 2.Tim.4.
cōtinuāce, or Ioynis thir tua togidder vithout Iudæ ep.
repētance: for the quhilk caus not onlie aucht Apoc.11.
thay thingis to be attribut to the gret Antichriſt quhilk he in propir perſone performis,
bot thaythīgis alſo quhilk ar performet be his
diſciples in his name and be imitation of him
eftir his death, euin to the aucht generation:
As S. Auguſtin vrait of Arrius that his pane in
hei vas not definit befoir the tyme that his Apoc.17.
hæreſie come to the heicht, and vas alluterlie
extinguished: This menis S. Iohne vryttand,
in this maner, [Videntes beſtiam quæ erat &
non eſt, etſi eſt) .i. ſeand the beaſt that vas and
is not, albeit he be: and, (Quinque ceciderunt,
vnus eſt, alius nondum venit, & cum venerit,
oportet ipſum breue tempus manere, & beſtia
quæ erat & non eſt, & ipſe 8.eſt, & de nūero 7
eſt, & in interitū vadit:) .i. fyue ar deſtroyir,
preſēdie thair is ane, anevthir is not zit cūmit,

and quhen he cummis, he man byd ane schort tyme, and the beast quha vas and is not, is the aucht, and zit nothuithstanding he is of the number of the seuin headdis: for this differé-ce and opposition is to be markit cheiflie, that quhair Christ is onlie ane head: In the kingdome of the Antichrist thair sal be mo-nie, quhilk ar signifeit quhylis be the number of tua, quhylis of thrie quhylis of ten, and sik vther numbris quhilk ar expressit in the re-uelation of S Iohne: For ane gret number of Deuillis sal adioyn thame selfis inseparabillie in al operation vith men of vain, curious and ambitious spiritis quhairbie thay vil mak thame abil to do thay thingis to the gret ad-miration of ignorantis quhilk passis the na-ture of man: Thir ar lykuyse the fals miraclis quhairbie simple people geuin to the libertie of the flesh, and fleing trauel vil be seducit and maist miserabillie deceauit: Sua that the cum-ming of the Antichrist vil be at that tyme qu-hen be the negligence and slugagenes of the lauchful Pastoris, al kynd of iniquitie aboudis, and the deuillis sal possess men vith sik force and vehemencie as in the primitiue kirk the Apostlis var possessit be the halie spirit: Zit nothuithstanding the multitude of sa mo-nie contrarious headdis amang the disciples of the Antichrist, he vil find out and chuse ane Name quhairbie he vill distinguish his disciplis from al vtheris, common to thame al, quhais signification gif it be veil obser-

1. Cor. 8.
1. Timo. 2.
Apoc. 13.
Apoc. 16.
Apoc. 9.
2. Thes. 2.

Zacha. 11.
Matt. 24.

netvil be directlie repugnát to the significatió
of this vord (Chrift) as it is the name of our
faluiour, and as from it al treu vorshipparis of
God ar namit Chriftianis: And albeit at the
beginning he vil prætend ane gret humilitie
and luf of goddis honor, zea haue participatió
of tha facramentis quhilk var inftitut be God,
and reuerence the vord of god, and declair
him felf ane maist vehement ennimie to al
Idolatrie, to the effect that as Chrift him felf
hes foiruarnit vs, he may feduce, gif it be poffibil, euin the elect, and thame quha as thair
confciéces dytis thame feiris God vnfézeitlie:
Zit in hairt he vil be fua proud that he vil not
onlie contén al fupré pouaris and Magiftratis
bot alfo craif thay thingis to be attributit vnto
him, quhilk ar propir to God onlie: for S Paul
vryttis to the Theſsalonianis (as I faid befoir) that ane greit defection from the Roman
impyre fal be befoir the cumming of the
Antichrift, faying, vnles firft thair be ane defection (mening not onlie from the fayth bot
from the impyre of Róe alfo) And that má of
fyn be reueilet quha is ane Aduerfar exaltand
him felf aganis al thame quha ar callit God,
or vorſhippit as hauing Diuin pouar, fua that
he fal fit in the kirk of God vantand him felf
as gif he var God: Nocht that he fal erect ane
kirk of neu, and dedicat it to the feruice of
god, for his trauel vil be beftouit mair on dóue
cafting nor erecting: Bot becaus be eiecting
lauchful Paftoris (quhilk S. Iohne menis be

*Hippolit
in orat de
confum.
mundi.*

Matt. 24.

*2. Petr. 2.
Iudas epi.
canon.*

2. Theſ. 2.

the seaging of the halie citie) he vil place his auin abominatiõ in Hierusalem that is in that kirk quhilk befoir the imbraceing of the pernicious doctrine of the Antichrist, vas the temple of God quhen the people acknauledgit for thair Pastor him quha had lauchful vocation: He is callit maist iustlie ane aduersar becaus as obseruis Tertullian: Al Hæretikis in quhom the spirit of the Antichrist dois regne vsis euer to destroy and not to buyld, to improue and not to confirme, to doubt and not to gif credit, to ganesay and not to aggrie vith vtheris quha præceidit thame, and finalie to propone na doctrin propir to thame selfis insafar as thay disagrie from the Catholik kirk, except it be negatiue: And as testifeis the ancient and Godlie father Hippolitus the onlie defence of the disciples of the Antichrist quhen thay fal in disputation vith the treu Christianis vil be, that mouit be sik prætencis as he vil forge to obscure the veritie, thay deny al thingis quhilk ar brocht aganis thame: for the quhilk caus in the letteris of the name of the last Antichrist not onlie may ve find the number sax hundreth, saxtie sax, as vitnessis S. Iohne: bot also as Hippolitus supponis monie vthir names expressand sindrie of his condicionis, and contenand lykuyse the foirsaid number: Amangis the rest ve may find expressit be the letteris of his name his great seal quhilk is the verb (Ἀρνῦμαι.) and fra it ane propir name also de-

Tertul. de præscript. Hæret.

Hippolitus orat. de consum. mundi.

Apoc. 13.

ducit contenand the foirſaid number exactlie
aſit is reuelit be S. Iohne quhilk may be Ἀρνῦμε
for ſua it aucht to be vryttin and pronunced
(Ἀρνῦμ, or Ἀρνῦ) ſua that the ſound of (μ) and
(ε) be ſkairſlie perſauit: For declaration heirof the halie father Hippolitus vryttis in this
maner [Sigillum illius tam in fronte, quàm
in dextera manu eſt Calculus χξϛ. At vt opi-
nor, neque enim certo ſcio permulta reperi-
untur nomina quæ numerum illum habeant,
ſed dicimus fortaſſe ſcriptúrā illius ſigilli eſſe
(Ἀρνῦμαι) .1. Nego: Nam antea quòque hoſtis
ille, nobis aduerſarius opera miniſtrorum ſuo-
rum .1. idololattarū Chriſti Martyres hortan-
tium, Negato aiebat Deum tuum crucifixum:
Tale erit, tempore illius honeſtatis omnis
oſoris ſigillum, dicens, Nego creatorem cæ-
li & terræ. Nego baptiſma, Nego adoratiōe
à me Deo præſtari ſolitam] 1. The ſeal of the
Antichriſt quhilk his diſcipillis ſal reſſaue bayth in the foirhead and richt hand, is ſignifeit
be the letteris of his name, quhais number be
calculatiō extendis to ſax hundreth ſaxtie ſax:
Bot as I ſuppon, nather knau I perfytlie, thair
be monie names compoſit of the letteris of
the name of the Antichriſt quhilk contenis
the number ſax hundreth ſaxtie ſax :
Bot peraduēture ve may ſay that his great ſeal
is ſignifeit be ane vord compoſed of the letteris of his name quhilk is (Ἀρνῦμαι) and ſignifeis I deny: For befoir this tyme alſo, this our
auld ennimie be the trauel and diligence of

A 1
P 100
N 50
O 70
Y 400
M 40
E 5.
ῦμα χξϛ
666.

his ministeris to vit the Idolateris exhorting
Christis martyris, said maist impudentlie, Deny that thy God vas crucifeit : Siclyk at that
tyme quhen the Antichrist in propir persone
ane haittar of al honestie sal appeir, this sal be
ane singular taikin quhairbie he may be knauin, becaus he and euerie ane of his disciples
sal euer haue in thair mouth ane stif denyal of
al veritie, saying, I deny that God hes sik pouar that he micht haue created the heauin and
earth : I deny that Baptisme hes onie strenth
to purge men from thair synnis : I deny the
maner and custume quhairbie befoir I vsit to
serue god : Zea not onlie, Ἀρνέμε bot Ἀρνέμαι also the verb, is in ane certan maner the name of
the Antichrist expressand that infidelitie quhilk be operation of the Deuil sal be impré-
ted in the hairt of him and al his Disciples, lyk
as he ingrauit it in the hart of Eua seduceand
Gen.f.3.   hir in Paradise, saying, Non moriemini .i. Ze
sal not dea. As be the contrare Amen, qu-
hais significatiō is plane repugnant to Ἀρνέμαι,
is in ane certan maner ane of the names of
our saluiour Iesus Christ, as vitnessis S. Iohne
Apoc. 3.   in his reuelation, Hæc dicit Amen testis fide-
lis et verus, principium omnis creatur æ : This
sayis (Amen) the faythful and treu vitnes, the
beginning of al thingis created : And as in the
kirk of Christ al Prayeris, al Benedictionis,
al Thākisgeuīg, al Articlis of fayth al Propheceis concerning goddis promises, al treu in-
terpretationis, and leasōnis of halie scripturis
al apoynt

al apoyntment al couenantes of God vith his
people, ar concludit, confermit, and seallit be
Amen, signefeand Est, Verū Est, etiam. As S. *S. Paul*
Paul interprettis this mysterie vrytand to the *2. Cor. 1.*
Cor. (Nā Dei filius Iesus Christus qui inter vos
per nos prædicatus est per me et Syluanum,
ac Timotheum, non fuit, (Etiam, & Non)sed
(Etiam) per ipsum fuit : quotquot enim pro-
missiones Dei, per ipsum sunt(Etiam), & per
ipsum (Amen)Deo ad gloriam per nos). 1. For
Chtist the sone of god quha vas preachit a-
mangis zou be me and Syluanus, and Timotheus vas not(Zea and na] bot vas(Zea)onlie,
For al the promisses quhilk God hes maid be
him ar(Zea)that is be him thay ar ratifeit, and
be him thay ar(Amen)that is thay ar cōfirmed
be Goddis gret seal (Amen) that be vs the
gloir may redound vnto God. Be the cōtrare
the Antichrist vil end al the mystereis of his
iniquitie vith Ἀρνῦμαι Nego, Non, Non est verum: 1. Na, It is not sua, I deny that euer onie
sik thing hes bene.] And his Ministeris vil cō-
clude al thair sermonis vith denyal of tha
thingis quhilk befoir be the spirit of God hes
bene approuit, and confirmit : As al the propir articlis of thair beleif vil be negatiue contenand plane contradiction to al treu fayth :
And finalie thay vil deny the fulfillīg of goddis promishes maid vnto his kirk Catholik,
Zea euin that quhilk vith ane aith God the
father maid vnto his sone Iesus Christ , that *Psal. 109.*
the preisthead and offering of Christis bodie

and blude vndir the formes of breid and vyne, quhilk be the kirk is callit the Mess, sal not cease vpon the face of the earth vnto the end of the varld: Becaus the Antichrist and his disciples vil indeuoir thair hail trauel to the abolishing of this sacrifice, as vitnessis the halie prophet Daniel: Quhairfoir in the name *Daniel.12* of the last and gret Antichist ve sould maist diligentlie obserue gif ve find be the letteris thairof not onlie his number 6 6 6. expressed bot also his gret seal Aϛῦμαι. Nou to mak application of tha thingis quhilk I haue spokin of the Antichrist in general: lyk as s. Iohne inducis tua beastis to compleit the bodie of the Antichrist, Euin sua thair ar tua horribil beastis acknavledgit be the kirk Catholik throuch the hail varld for notabil persecutaris of Christis kirk: The ane is Mahometis in the greik impyre, the vther Martin Lauter in the latine impyre: For lyk as the letteris of euerie ane of the names of thir compleittis exactlie the number of the Antichrist, euin sua it is maist esie to apply to euerie ane of thame al the propirteis of the Antichrist quhilk I haue befoir rehersit: For thair is na doubt bot Mahometis hes bene, and is ane verie notabil ennimie to the kingdome of Christ, quha had for ane of his parentis ane Ieu as treu and faythful men reportis, and ascryuit vnto him self tha thingis quhilk ar piopir to the halie Ghaist, lyk as al the rest of the propirteis of the Antichrist may be maist esilie accomodat

The number of the name of Mahometis the first of the tua beastis.

M	4	0
α		1
ȣ	7	0
μ	4	0
ε		5
τ	3	0
ι	1	0
ϛ	2	0

Sũma. χξϛ or 6 6 6.

Apoc.13.

vnto him. Martin Lauter is the vther beast in quhais name alſo this number is compleit, And that ve ſould nocht doubt bot he is the vther beaſt, be the prouidence of God in his auin vrytingis he callis him ſelf ane beaſt, Saying. *Vos Papiſta ab anteriori parte, vos tumultuoſi à poſteriori, vos Diaboli ab omni parte incitate, venamini, exagitate alacriter, verā habetis ferā ante vos, iacēte Lutero ſalui eſtis & victoriā obtinuiſtis .i.* Ze Papiſtu, Ze troubilsū men, Ze deuillis befoir me, behind me, and on al ſyd ſet on me, cal me forduart, and hunt me, Ze haue befoir Zou ane verie beaſt, gif luter be ouercummit Ze ar ſaif and haue obtenit the victorie : Quhat beaſt meanit Lauter of in this place, except of that ſerpent be the quhilk the Antichriſt is ſigniſeit in the ſcripture ? As he declairit maiſt planelie of him ſelf quhen he firſt begane to impugne the fayth, that the Catholik kirk ſould find him Ane edder in the hie vay, and ſerpent in the rod bytād the hors houis that the rydar may ſal bakuart : Quhair of I can collect na vther thing bot as God mouit Cayphas to ſpeik prophecie quhilk he vndirſtude not, ſua he hes mouit Martin Lauter albeit in general termis, and obſcurlie to apply this prophecie to him ſelf as deſcendit of the tryb of Dan, lyk as verie monie Ieuis mareis vith the Germanis, quhilk myſterie vnles be inſtinction of God he had confeſſed it him ſelf, vald haue bene vtheruyſe vnknauin to the varld. He vitneſſis be manifeſt vryt that he exaltit him ſelf aboue al diuī pouar, ſaying,

Margin notes:

The nūber of the name of the vther beaſt Martin Lauter.

M	3	0
A		1
R	8	0
T	1	0 0
I		9
N	4	0
L		1 0
A		1
V	2	0 0
T	1	0 0
E		5
R	8	0

Summa
χ ξς or
666.
Apoc.13.
Genes.49

Ioann. 13.

Rectum permanere oportet quicquid ego scripsi, aut docui, etiam si per hoc totus mundus in ruinam abire debeat .1. It is necessar, that, that thing be estemit richt quhatsumeuer I haue vryttin or teachit, albeit it sould be the caus of ruine to the hail varld: And,

Lauter in lieb. contra statum Ec- clesiæ. *Ego verò neque Papæ, neque Imperatori, sed ne An- gelo quidem de cælo doctrinā meam amplius submit- tere iudicandam volo, sed quoniam de ea certus sum, per eam iudex esse volo non modò hominum, verum- etiam cunctorum Angelorum: Vt si quis doctri- nam meam non acceptauerit, saluus esse non possit, quia Dei est, non mea, idcirco & iudicium meum Dei quoque est non meum: .1.* I vil nather submit my doctrine to be iudgit be the Paip, nor be the Empe- ror, nor be onie Angel of heauin, bot becaus I am assurit of it: be it I vil be iudge not onlie to men, bot to al the Angellis of heauin, sua that gif onie man resaue not my doctrine, he may not be saif, becaus my doctrine is goddis doctrine, and my iudgement is al- so Goddis iudgement: And agane. *Ea autem certi- tudine & fiducia tentandum nobis est quod præ- stituimus, vt non modo totius mundi iudicia pro fo- liis leuibus, & summis aristis habeamus, sed & ar-*

Lauter de abroganda Missa. *mati simus in morte contra portas inferi, quinetiam aduersus iudicium tentantis Dei pugnare, & cum Iacob contra Deum præualere, mundi enim voces occlussis auribus vtcumque etiam infirmiores contem- nere possunt, at conscientiam quis occludet, ne Satha- nam, ne Dei iudicium sentiat? .1.* Ve man essay to performe that quhilk ve haue tane in hand vith sik assurance and confidence that ve not onlie esteme al the iudgementis of the hail varld als licht as the le-

uis of the treis, or caff quhilk is blauin auay vith the
vind, bot that ve inarme our selfis also aganis the
feir of Death and hel quhilk god threatnes for tran-
sgreßion, and that ve may preuail euin aganis the
iudgement of God quhen he temptis vs as did Iacob:
For as to the commune sayingis of the varld, thay qu-
ha ar bot sumpart mair vaik , may be closing thair
earis, neglect the same: bot how bauld man he be
quha closis his conscience that he nather persaue the
accusationis of the Deuil, nor iudgement of God aga-
nis euil doing? Quhair (be abuſing the place of
ſcripture in the quhilk to declair ane hid myſterie of the victorie of the ſeid of Iacob, it is
ſaid that Iacob did preuail aganis God , as he
abuſit the exemple of Abraham to proue his
Euangelical ſentence , Si non vult vxor veniat
ancilla) he ſchauis maiſt planelie that he vil
eſſay gif he may to caus leaſingis preuail aganis the treuth , hæreſie aganis the Catholik
fayth and the Deuil aganis God. Martin Lauter (quhilk is requyrit in the Antichriſt) vas
conceaued of the Deuil not onlie as tuiching   *Vide Lin-*
his carnal generation, ſence as monie faythful   *dani dialo-*
men teſtifeis of him, he vas gottin be ane de-   *gum.*
uil in ane zoung mannis liknes, bot alſo concerning his ſpiritual generation be coopera-
tion of his auin fre vil , he confeſſis him ſelf   *Laut. libr.*
that be geuing place to the argumentis of the   *de Miſſa*
Deuil brocht aganis the Meſs , quha oftymes   *angulari.*
valkinnit him, and gaue him conſale to vryt
for abolishing of the ſame : and proponit vnto him the titil of his buke de abrogáda Miſſa

Dan. 14. (quhilk Daniel foirprophecied to be the
cheif but quhairat the Antichrift fal fchuir) He
become fua gret ane Prophet, as efteruart he
vas eftemit to be amangis the Germanis, and
conceaued ane exceiding gret hetret aganis
the Roman kirk: For gif the maift bleffed
Virgin Marie be ear and fayth, geuing credite
to ane gud Angel, vithout coniunction vith
man, conceaued Chrift Iefus, quha become the
father of monie fonis fpiritual: Quhy micht
not Martin Lauter lykuyfe vithout coiunctió
vith vomã, be geuing credit to the Deuil his
father, becum the Antichrift? quha hes begottin the Zuinglianis, Oecolampadianis,
Anabaptiftis, Suenkfeldianis, Amfdorfianis,
Caluiniftis, Puritanis, kmnoxiftis, al the Antichriftis, and Proteftaons of our dayis vith innumerabil fik vther viperis, and fyrie ferpétis
quha be inftruction of thair father Martin
Lauter, hes oppinit vp the hid myftereis of his
neu Euãgel, obtrudãd for Goddis vord al pefti-
lent hærefeis befoir condemnit be the kirk,
As of Symon Magus, Marcionitis, Blaftus, Arrius, Macedonius, Manichæus, and al vtheris
Apoc. 13. quhilk S. Iohne fignifeis in his reuelation
quhen he fayis that the head of the beaft quhilk befoir vas cuttit of, vas hailled agane, and
his vound curit: For thir hæretikis quhill as
thay condem al general Conciles, of neceffi-
Staphy. de tie thay man approue al hærefeis condemnit
Lauteran. be thame: Zea fum of this gret Antichriftis
concordia. difciples as Dauidgeorgius ane Glaifin vricht,

faidT hat he vas the treu Meſſias promiſed to
the Ieuis: Rotmánus ane vthir of his diſciples
denyit that Chriſt vas borne or reſauit humane nature of the Virgin Marie : And Leidan
ane vthir Miniſter , to counterfut Dauid, vas
choſin king be his follouaris. And albeit thair
be ma nor threſcoir of cheif Maiſtris of Sectis quhilk var diſciples to Martin Lauter, zit
for the name(Catholik) be the electiõ of thair
Maiſter thay haue ane common name, quhais
ſignification is directlie repugnant to the name of Chriſt: for thay ar callit Proteſtaons
from making Proteſta°n aganis the Decreittis of the Paip and Emperor of Rome, deſ-
chargeing onie diſputation or imbraceing of
onie doctrine concerning the verteu of indulgencis befoir ane day, quhilk be thame
vas apoyntit for diſputatiõ of the verteu thair
of,eftir that be Martin Lauter, Legatus indul-
gétiarum vas ſend agane to Rome out of Ger
manie, vithout the ſiluer quhilk he com for,
quhairuith the kirk of S. Petir in Rome
micht haue bene repairit . As rhe hiſtoreis of
the beginning of the troublis of Germanie
bearis record: For inſafar as the vord Chriſt
ſigniſeis anoynted to vit king , Preiſt, and
Prophet, quhilk aggreit not onlie to Chriſt
Ieſus in propir perſon , bot alſo to al thame
quha var, or is to be lauchfullie promouit to
ſik offices,ſua that thayvar in plenitude in the
Paip and Emperor repreſentãd Chriſtis hieaſt
dignitie vpon the face of the earth,It follouis

R iiij

neceſſarlie that thay quha receauit thair name becaus thay maid Proteſtaͦn aganis the decreitis proceidíg from the lauchful authoritie of Kingdome Presthead and Prophecie inioy the name of the Antichriſt, and that al the Proteſtaons ar Antichriſtianis: For confirmation, Martin Lauter intitulat ane of his bukes (Contra duo cæſaris mandata) and ane vther (contra ſtatum eccleſiæ): And ane of his diſciples in the Ile of Britannie, kmnox intitulat lykuyſe the blaſt of his ſeditious trumpat, (Aganis the regiment of yemen:) It is mair hor manifeſt hou the Proteſtaons hes reiectit al kynd of anoynting or Chriſme, for hetret of the vord Chriſt quhilk is the name of our ſaluiour: and ſould be lykuyſe aboliſhed according to the principal groundis of thair doctrine : For gif the Proteſtaons in Scotland var mouit be gud reaſon to turne [kyrie eleyſon in lord haue mearcie on me] and, Amen, in Sobeit, thay had als gud reaſon to haue Changit (Ieſus in ſaluiour, and Chriſt or Chriſtus in anoyntit) And it ſould haue lykuyſe bene changit in vther vulgar toungis and lágages: Martí Laut. be his auin iudgemét alſo is conuict to haue ſochtin directlie aganis Chriſt: Becaus in al his diſputationis, vrytingis, and preachingis aganis the biſchop of Rome, he laborit for na vther thing, boͻ for the aboliſhing of the Authoritie of the Paip in quhais perſone and authoritie he acknauledgit Chriſt Ieſus as head and reular of the

kirk: As is manifeſt of his auin vordis, eüin eftir he had maid defeſtion frō the kirk of Rome : [*Quare beatiſſime pater proſtratum me pedibus*
tua beatitudinis offero , cum omnibus quæ ſum , &
habeo, viuifica , occide , voca , reuoca , approba, re-
proba vt platuerit : vocem tuam, vocem Chriſti in te
præſidentis agnoſcam, ſi mortem merui , mori non
recuſabo . 1. *Quhairfoir maiſt bleſſed father I caſt my*
ſelf befoir the feit of ʒour halines vith al quhat-
ſumeuer I am, or haue, quickin me, ſlay me, cal on me,
bring me from the propoſe quhilk I vas at as ʒe pleis ,
I acknaulege ʒour vord for the vord of Chriſt, quha
ſpeakis and beris reul ouer the kirk in ʒou: Gif
I haue deſeruit the death , I vil not refuſe to dea:
Quhairfoir al men of puiſſance infeſtit vith
the poyſonit Antichriſtian doſtrine of Martin
Lauter, ſould feir leiſt the Deuil hauing ful
pouar ouer thame, vſe thame as inſtrumen-
tis to performe the reſt of the vickitnes of
the Antichriſt: for gif I vald vſe particular application of al the reſt of the propirteis of the
Antichriſt thay may al be maiſt conuenientlie
accommodat vnto him And his diſciples, onlie except that the meſour of impietie begun
be him is nocht zit fullie accompliſhed : And
to prætermit vther Antichriſtian condicionis
inſinit as that thay contemn the maner hou
thair foirfatheris vorſhippit God: And ar capital ennimeis to the continual ſacrifice of
the kiſk : Al the diſciples of this monſtrous
beaſt Martin Lauter, dois put ſik fœlicitie in
the luſt of the fleſch that in auld men quha

Lauter
epiſtola 2.
ad leonem
10. Papâ.

Dani. 11.

Dani. 12.

to the iudgement of the varld according to thair vou leuit chaift to the tyme thay var me-kil mair nor threfcoir of zeiris, and had al-maift the ane fut in the graif, the fpirit of for-nicatione and adulterie enterit vith fik inor-dinat luft that fkarfelie could it be quenshit ather be vyf or hyre vomã: I micht produce for exemple that renegat and periurit preift fchir Iohã kmnox, quha eftir the death of his firft harlat, quhilk he mareit incurring eter-

S. Paul 1. Timot. 5.

nal dãnatiõ be breking of his vou ãd promifs of chaftitie: quhẽ his age requyrit rather that vith tearis and lamentatiõ he fould haue cha-ftifed his flesh ãd beuailit the breaking of his vou, as alfo the horribil inceft vith his gud-mother in ane killogie of Hadintoun: zit notuithftanding, heauing laid afyd al feir of the panis of hel, and regarding na thing the honeftie of the varld, as ane bund fklaue of the Deuil, being kendillit vith ane inquenf-hibil luft and ambition, He durft be fua bauld to interpryfe the fute of Mariage vith the maift honorabil ladie my ladie Fleming, my lord Dukes eldeft dochter, to the end that his feid being of the blude Royal, and gydit be thair fatheris fpirit, micht haue afpyrit to the croun. And becaus he receauit ane refufal, it is notoriouflie knauin hou deadlie he haited the hail hous of the Hamiltonis, albeit being deceauit be him traittorouflie it vas the cheif vpfettar, and protector of his hærefie: And this maift honeft refufal could nather ftench

his luſt nor ambition, bot a lytil eſtir he did
perſeu to haue allyance vith the honorabil
hous of Ochiltrie of the kingis M.auin blude,
Rydand thair vith ane gret court on ane trim
gelding, nocht lyk ane prophet or ane auld
decrepit preiſt as he vas, bot lyk as he had bene ane of the blude Royal, vith his bendis of
taffetie feſchnit vith Goldin ringis and precious ſtanes : And as is planelie reportit in the
cuntrey, be ſorcerie and vitchcraft did ſua al-
lure that puir gentil voman, that ſcho could
not leue vithout him : quhilk appeiris to be
of gret probabilitie, ſcho being ane Damo-
ſel of Nobil blud , And he ane auld decrepit creatur of maiſt baiſ degrie of onie that
could be found in the cuntrey : Sua that ſik
ane nobil hous could not haue degenerat ſua
far , except Iohann kmnox had interpoſed
the pouar of his Maiſter the Deuil, quha as
he transfiguris him ſelf ſumtymes in ane Angel of licht: ſua he cauſit Iohann kmnox appeir ane of the maiſt nobil and luſtie men
that could be found in the varld : Bot not to
offend zour earis langar vith the filthie abhominationis of Schir Iohann kmnox, and
to returne to tha thingis quhilk ar common
to the ſect of the Proteſtaons, lyk as S. *Apoc.13*
Iohne deſcryuis the Antichriſt to haue ane
blaſphemons mouth aganis god , his ſanctis,
and halie tabernacle quhilk is his kirk Catholik, Euin ſua the blaſphemeis ar maiſt hor-
ribii quhilk thir grishopperis and maiſt noy-

sum serpentis the sonis of Martin Lauter spe-
uis out of thair venemous mouthis, maist impudentlie defending the sam, as gif thay var
headdis and articlis of healthsum doctrine: sik
as ar thir.

1. Calu. lib.
2. inst. ca. 7

1. That God may do na thing by the established ordor of the varld.

2. Calu. li.
1. inst. ca. 13
sect. 23. &
Bez. acōtra
Hessusiū.

2. That the secund person in the Trinitie is
nocht the sone of God: becaus the sone taikis his
substance of his father, and the secund persone
takis not his substance from the first, bot hes his
substance of him self and na vther persone.

3. Cal. lib.
1. institut.
cap. 13.

3. That the halie Ghaist takis nather his substance of the father, nor zit of the sone.

4. Mat-
thias Zarē-
sis test. Co-
clao in Ge-
nealogia
Laut.

4. That the trinitie of personis in ane Godheid is bot ane Phantasie.

5. Lucas
sternbergē-
sis.

5. That the trinitie is to be estemit na vther
thing bot triceps Cerberus.

6. Similie
lauteria-
nis i prussn-
land vide
Cocl. in ge-
nealo. laut.

6. That thair is not onlie ane God: bot thrie.

7. Matthi-
as Illyric⁹.

7. That ὁ λογος in the beginning of the Euangel of S. Iohne signifeis nocht the secund persone in diuinitie.

8. That murtheraris, adulteraris, theüis, and traittoris ar effectuouslie mouit be God and constrainit to commit sik crymes, and finalie that al thingis cummis of absolut necessitie: and that God is the author of al syri.

8. Al the protestaöis aggreis on thisblasphe mous head of Antichri stiä doctriē 9. Cal.li.2. inst.cap.21. num. 5. & lib. 8. de prædestina. Et in cap.1. Genes.

9. That God hes created men to that end that he may puneis thame for euer.

10. That Christ vas nocht borne of the virgin Marie.

10. Rotmä laut. disci- pulo art. 9.

11. That Christ quhen he vas ane bairne vas ignorant, and gaid to the scuil to learne vith vther bearnis.

11. Swideli nus lauterä nus.

12. That Christ is composed of the substance of God, and of flesch, and of Spirit, and of thrie increated elementis.

12. Michael Seruetus, & Cal.discip. teste Caluï lib.2. inst. ca. 14. sec.5

13. That Christ vas nocht the sone of God, be- foir he vas borne of the virgin Marie.

13. Idē test. eod. Caluin ibid.

14. That Christ vas nather God nor man.

14. ibid.

15. That Christ vas ful of Grace nocht that he had onie grace inhabitant into him, bot be- caus the father fauorit him gretumlie..

15. Brent. Hömil. 12. in Ioannē.

16. Caluin lib. 4. inst. ca.14. sect. 4. Beza in sua Antithesi.

16.   That the vordis of consecration of the bodie, and bluide of Christ, pronunced on the breid and vyne is vitchcraft and incantation of the Deuil, quhairof consequentlie it follouis that Christ vas ane vitch and inchantar, becaus he pronuncit thir vordis first vpon the breid and vyne for consecration of the sam, and commandit that thay sould be pronunced in lyk maner for consecration of breid and vyn in his bodie and blude vnto his cumming agane to iudgement:

17. Caluin lib.2. inst. cap.16.sec. 10. & 11. & in harmo.

17.   That Christ pronunced vpon the Croce the vords of Desperatiõ, and that he vas cõdemnit to hel, and tormentit be the Deuillis thairin.

18. Musculus Auth. Stap. de Lauteran. concordia.

18,   That Christ nocht onlie as man, bot in his diuin nature also deed vpon the Croce.

19. Hosiãder lauteri discipulus.

19.   That in our iustification ane pairt of the diuin substance of Christ is conioynit vith our substance, and thairbie ve resaue ane substantial or essential iustice throuch Christ Iesus.

20. Al the Ptotestãns aggreis on this blasphemie.

20.   That Christ hes institute and left vs ane Religion vithout al lau quhilk ve ar obleist to obey and fulfil, and vithout al sacrifice and preasthcad.

21. *That na Christian man is obleised, to keip the ten commandimentis.*

21. Lauter serm. de Moyse.

22. *That thair aucht nocht to be onie distinction of temporal magistratis in heichar or laichar degrie.*

22. Mützerus Lauteri discip.

23. *That Christianis aucht nocht to resist, or fecht aganis the Turk albeit he be ane cöiurit ennimie to the name of Christ.*

23. Lauter art. 34.

24. *That al vse of armore is deuilishe.*

24. Rotm. art. 4.

25. *That the communion of Sanctis consistis in this, that it is lesum to euerie man to raif his nichtbouris geir.*

25. Quintinus pikardus teste Cal. cötra lib.ca. 21.

26. *That it is lesum to euerie man to tak his hyre voman and ly vith hir, quhen his vyf refusis.*

26. Lauter lib. de voto & cötinët.

27. *That it is the estait of innocencie, and treu regeneration, nocht to mak onie difference betuix gud and euil, bot to imbrace al thingis alyk.*

27. Anton. Coppinus teste Cal. ca. 18. cöt. lib.

28. *That al thingis quhilk ar spokin of the Deuil, and syn, ar bot mere imaginationis and phantaseis.*

28. Anton. Copp. test. Calu. lib. cont. liber: cap. 1.

29. Al the protestaont aggress on this blasphemie.

29. That Christ is not our redemar in sik sort that he destroyis our syn, and in verie deid delyueris vs from the bondage thairof, becaus that syn being anes contracted, remanis in vs continuallie.

30. Zuing. de Baptismo.

30. That the zoung Childrene contractis not original syn be natural generation and propagation of Adam, and that in thame thair is na thing vordie of condemnatione.

31. zuing. de baptis.

31. That monie men var saif and attenit vnto the kingdome of heauin vithout fayth in Christ quha vas to be reuelit, as Numa, Cato, Scipio and vtheris.

32. Lauter art. 16.

32. That the mair ane man repent him of his syn, he synnis the mair greuouslie.

33. Laut. art. 31. & Calu. lib. 2 instit. cap. 14. sect. 19

33. That in euerie Gude vark done maist excellentlie, euerie iust mã, zea euin the Martyris deing for confession of the name of Christ, dois deserue æternal damnation.

34. Rotmã test. Calu. lib. ψυχο̄. παυχία.

34. That the saul deis vith the bodie, or sleipis quhil the day of iudgement.

35. Al the Protestaons.

35. That thair aucht nocht to be onie distinction of pastoris in heichar or laichar degrie in the kirk of Christ Iesus.

36. That

36. *That the kirk of Christ may be sua ouer-thrawin, that na man may be knawin throuch the hail varld for the space of monie hundreth zeiris, makand oppin profession of the name of Christ.*

36. Al the protestaos.

37. *That the Euangel of Christ vas neuer treulie preached in Germanie, France, Scotland, and Ingland, quhil Martin Lauter, Caluin, and kmnox var raised vp, to publeis ane vord vnknauin to the hail varld befoir thame. And the Quein of Ingland to be prophetiss, and hie schopreist or head of the kirk, hauing pouar to decyd all controuerseis of Religion.*

37. Al the Ministeris of Geneue Germanie, Scotland, and Ingland.

38. *That the treu doctrine of Iustification vas neuer Knauin to the hail varld, vnto the tyme Martin Lauter reueled the sam.*

38. Vilgägus in lib. de bonis, & malis Germaniæ

39. *That eftir the Apostlis, na man had the treu vndirstanding of the mysterie of the lordis Suppar, befoir Iohan Caluin.*

39. Beza in vita Caluini.

40. *That ane hyre voman may gif absolution to onie person alsueil as ather preist, or Paip.*

40. Lauter de captiuitate babylonica.

41. *That thay repugne to God quha apoyntis*

S

41. Rotmä art. 5.

Pastoris to haue reul ouer certane places, quhil as thay sould ryn continuallie from ane place to another, as did the Apostlis.

42. *Lau-* | 42. *That the people aucht to be instructed nocht to feir excommunication, nor gif obedience vnto thair prelatis.*
ter. art. 24

43. *Quint* | 43. *That thair is na resurrection of the bodeis pikardus.* | *to compeir in iudgement.*
teste Caluino. lib.
côtra liber.
cap. 3.

Vith vther impudent blasphemeis innumerabil aganis the omnipotêt pouar of God, and the halie Angellis and Sanctis in heauin, quhilk I abhorr to reherse trimbland quhen I think on thame: For mair detestabil, and ma in number, can nocht be deuysit be al the vickit spiritis in hel, than Martin Lauter and his disciples proponis for healthsum doctrine.

Nou to cum to the gret seal of the Antichrist Ἀϱϱναϛ, and Ἀϱϱϻε, quhilk is sould be expressit be the letteris of the name of the Antichrist contenand his number sax hundreth, saxtie sax: Ve find the letteris of thame bayth in the name of Martin Lauter, to-wit. A.r. n. u. m. a. i. or, A.r.n.u.m.e. sua that Ἀϱϱϻε is not onlie composed of the letteris of his name bot also côtenis the sam núber sax hundreh saxtie sax, as I haue alreddie declarit at lenth quhen I proponit the proprieteis of the Antichrist in general: The force and strenth of this verb

M A A
a Ἀ ϱ
r ϛ ·
t ν ν
i μ μ
n a ϛ
L ι.
a χ ξ5
u
t
e
r.

Æʀƞαι is lykuyse ingrauit in the haittis of al the protestaons, And is thair onlie refuge, quhen thay ar preissed be the vecht ather of solid reasonis, or authoritie: For thay deny al the traditionis of the Apostlis, al the custumes of the halie kirk, al the sentencis of the doctoris quhairbie thair hereseis ar conuict, the force and strenth of the sacramentis, the verteu of grace throuch Christ be the operatione of the halie ghaist in vs, the continual sacrifice of the bodie and blude of Christ vndir the formes of breid and vyne, quhilk is the cheif vork of the Antichrist, as vitnessis the halie Prophete Daniel. Quha denyis that it is *Daniel 11* lesum to Christianis to haue the image of Christ, and his glorious Mother for remembrance, bot eftir the exempil of Iulianus Apostata hes trampit thame vndir futt, and in place thairof, hes erected Abhominatione, substituting thair auin heretical imagis, as in oppin markat the imagis of the tua bougouraris Caluine, and Beze ar sauld in Geneua, sua that he is nocht compted ane gud Christiane, that hes nocht thair images at thair bed headis, or befoir thair burdis: Siclyk for the Ecclesiastical historie of Christis halie sanctis, that abhominabil sodomeit, and filthie beist Beze, (quha learned his religione at Priapus, as he confessis in his lyf, that his vif vas the caus, quhy he passed out of Pareise, scho being mareit vith ane vther housbād) is nocht eschamit to haue dedicat to ane maist nobil king, ane

S ij

buke contening ane rabil of imagis, conioy-nád vith fals traittouris to god and man, treu Chriſtianis, as gif thair micht be communione vith the ſonis of licht and belial, thairby intyſing ignorant peopil to mair groſe and deuillish idolatrie, nor euer the gétilisvar polluted vith befoir the cúming of Chriſt, quhilk is ane maiſt craftie inuétione of Sathane quha vndir pretence of deliuerance from idolatrie, blindis the miſerabil flok thairin. To this cheif heid Αϵἴϭμαι or Nego ve may cal the hail articlis and confeſſione of thair negatiue fayth, and al thair expoſitionis of ſcripture be contrare ſentencis, of the quhilk I think expedient to ſubioyne certaine of the principal-lis, quhair vpone the Proteſtaôs groúdis thair ſaluatione: and firſt of al ſay thay.

Ve deny al traditionis of the vniuerſal kirk quhilkis at onie tyme hes bene reſſaued befoir the cumming of Lauter and Caluine.

Ve deny al lauis, and determinationis of general Concilis, quhilk the hail varld hes reſſaued befoir vs.

Ve deny al ordour, and policie that euer hes bene eſtablished in the Kirk of god befoir the dayes of Iohne Caluine.

4 *Ve deny that the Euangel hes bene treulie prechhed, or that Chriſt hes had onie viſibil kirk vpone the earth thir monie hundreth ʒeiris.*

5 *Ve deny al thingis, quhilk ar nocht expreſlie vrittin in the ſcripture, and ve deny monie bukis, of the ſcriptur it ſelf, quhilk the vniuerſal kirk befoir hes reſſaued for canoniKis, as the bukis of the Macha-*

beis, of Iudith, Hester, Tobias and vtheris, and as to
thame quhilk ve reſſaue for Canonikis, ve deny monie pairtis of thame insafar as thay ar nocht conforme to our doctrine laitlie reuelit to the varld be Lauter and Caluine: As.

6 Quhair it is vryttin in the halie ſcripture *Luc.1.*
that na thing is impoſſibil to God.

Ve afferme the contrare and ſayis, that monie thin-
gis ar impoſſibil to God, becaus he may nocht be pre-
ſent in the ſacrament of the altar, nor tranſſubſtan-
tiat the breid in his bodie, as the Papiſtis ſayes.

7 Quhair it is vryttin that Chriſt vas borne *Matth.1.*
of ane virgine. *Ve affirme the contrare, that he vas*
nocht borne of ane virgine, bot that ſcho vas corrupted *Beza cō-*
in hir birth, as ſayis our paraclet Theodore de Beʒe. *tra Bren-*
tium.
8 Quhair it is vryttin that our ſaluiour Chriſt *Epheſ.4.*
deſcendit into hell eftir his deth. *Ve affirme the*
contrare that he deſcendit nocht into hel eftir his
deth, bot onlie vas in deſperatione befoir his deathe.

9 Quhair it is vryttin I beleue the halie Ca-   *Matt.18.*
tholik kirk. *Ve affirme the contrare. I beleue nocht*
the halie Catholik Kirk, becaus the definitionis thai-
rof, doctrine, and ceremoneis ar to be reiected.

10 Quhair it is vryttin that the kirk is the *1. Timo.3.*
pillar, ād groūdſtaone of the treuth. *Ve afferme*
the contrare, that the kirk is nocht the pillar, nor
groundſtane of the treuth, becaus ve teache, that the
vniuerſal kirk may err, and imbrace fals doctrine.

11 Quhair it is vryttin I ſal be vith ʒou to *Matt.28.*
the end of the varld, *Ve affirme the contrare, I ſal*
nocht be vith ʒou to the end of the varld, for the Spi-
rit of Chriſt hes left the hail kirk in idolatrie, thir

monie hundreth зeris bypaſt.

S. Ioh. 16. 12. Quhair it is vryttin I haue monie thingis
to tell зou, quhilk ze may nocht beir at this
tyme. *Ve affirme the contrare, I haue na vther thing
to tel зou, becaus the Apoſtlis lernit na thing efter
the cũming of the halie ghaiſt quhilk thay had nocht
learned befoir of Chriſt.*

2. Cor. 8. 13 Quhair it is affermit, I beleue the cõmu-
nione of Sanctis. *Ve affirme the contrare I beleue
na communione of ſanctis, beaus the ſanctis quhilk
ar in heuin hes na communicatione vith vs, and can
nather do vs gud nor euil, and ſalang as ve ar on erth
ve ar na ſanctis being roplenished vith al kynd of
vickitnes and adhominatione.*

Math. 9. 14 Quhair it is vryttin I beleue the remiſſiõ
of Sinnis. *Ve affirme the contrare becaus thay
ar neuer remitted vnto vs, bot abydis continuallie fixed in our hairtis.*

S. Ioh. 3. 15 Quhair it is vryttin, Except ane man be
regenerat be the valter and be the ſpirit, he
may nocht enter in the kingdome of heuin.
*Ve affirme the contrare albeit ane man be nocht rege-
nerat be the valter and be the ſpirit, зit he may enter in the kyngdome of God: becaus ve teache that infantis deing vithout baptiſme, ar ſaif be the fayth of
thair parentis.*

Act. 19. 16 Quhair it is vryttin, that thay quha var
baptized be ſanct Iohne, reſſaued eſtiiuart the
baptiſme of Chriſt. *Ve affirme the contrare vith
our Maiſter Caluine, and ſayes that thay reſſaued
nocht the baptiſme of Chriſt, becaus the baptiſme of
Iohne, and Chriſt vas alane, and na difference*

betuix thame.

17 Quhair it is vryttin that Petir and Iohne be the onlaying of handis or the sacrament of confirmatione, gaue to the samaritanis baptized, the grace of the halie spirit. *Ve affirme the contrare, becaus ve vil nocht acknauledge Confirmatione for ane sacrament.*   *Act.8.*

18 Quhair it is vryttin Ressaue the halie ghaist, quhais synnis ze forgiue ar forgiuen to thame. *Ve affirme the contrare, becaus the Apostlis and thair successoris, hes na pouar to remit synnis.*   *S.Ioh.20.*

19 Quhair it is vryttin: Do fruittis vordie of repentance. *Ve affirme the contrare, do na fruttis vordie of repentance, vtheruyse it behouit vs to grant satisfactione vith the Papistis.*   *S.Mat.3.*

20 Quhair it is vryttin redeme thy synnis vith almous deiddis. *Ve affirme the contrare, that nather almous deiddis, nor vther gud vorkis seruis onie thing for to obtene remissione of synnis.*   *Daniel. 4.*

21 Quhair it is affermit that the Angelis reioysis mair for the repentance of ane synnar, nor for 99. iust men. *Ve arffirme the contrare that the Angellis reioyses nocht for the repentance of ane synnar, becaus thay knau nocht quhidder it be treu or senzeit, nather heir thay our prayeris, vtheruyse thay vald haue ouer lang luggis.*   *S.Luc.15*

22 Quhair it is vryttin, quhatsumeuer ze louse in the earthe, it sal be loused in heuin. *Ve affirme the contrare, becaus gif ve grant this, ve vil be compellit to grät in lyk maner, that the kirk may bayth inioyne penance, and lyk uyse relax the same,*   *S.Mat.18*

quhilk *is na vther thing, bot to estableis the indul-*
gencis.

23 Quhair it is vryttin that Iudas Machabæus causit offer Sacrifice for the deid, and that
the prayer for the deid, to the end, thay may
be releued from thair synnis, is ane halie and
godlie exerceis. *Ve affirme the contrare, and denyis*
the bukis of the Machabeis to be canonikis, as is said
befoir, becaus ve reiect praying for the deid, and pur-
gatorie as Papistical.

Mach. 2.
chap. 12.

24 Quhair it is vryttin I propose to the lyf
and death, gud and euil, chuse to thy self the
ane, or vther. *Ve affirme the contrare, becaus gif*
this var treu, it var necessar that man had fre vil, to
chuse gud or euil, quhilk is repugnant to our refor-
med doctrine, quhairbie ve teache that al thingis
cummis of absolute necessitie.

Deut. 30.

25 Quhair it is vrytin that the zoke of Christ
is licht, and that his commādimentis ar nocht
hauie. *Ve affirme the cōtrare and sayis, that his Zok*
is nocht licht, bot verie hauie, and that it is impossibil
to vs, to keip his commandimentis.

S. Mat. 11

S. Ioh. ep. 1
chap. 5.

26 Quhair it is vryttin, ze se thairfoir that
ane man is iustifeit be vorkis, and nocht be
fayth onlie. *Ve affirme the contrare; that ane man*
is iustifeit be fayth onlie, and nocht be vorkis.

S. Iac. 2.

27 Quhair it is vryttin that God is nocht
iniust that he vil forzet zour gud vorkis. *Ve*
affirme the contrare, that it apertenis nocht to the iu-
stice of God to recompanse gud vorkis, and that nocht
onlie he is nocht iniust, quhen he forZettis our vorkis,
bot that he dois ane benefeit to vs thairbie, al our vor-

Heb. 6.

kis being bot *ſyn*, and vorthie of condemnatione.

28 Quhair it is vryttin, that euerie man ſal be preſented befoir the tribunal ſeat of Chriſt to reſſaue according to that quhilk he hes done in this varld, ather gud or euil. *Ve affirme the contrare, and ſayis that na man ſal reſſaue according to his vorkis, becaus our vorkis deſeruis na thing at goddis handis in the varld tocum:*   2. Cor. 5.

29 Quhair it is vryttin, he quha is borne of God, ſynnis nocht, becaus the ſeid of God remanis in him. *Ve affirme the contrare, and ſayis, that he quha is borne of God, ſynnis continuallie, ʒe that quhatſumeuer he dois is ſyn, and iniquitie.*   S. Iohn. 1. epiſt. cha. 3

30 Quhair it is vryttin that the cheritie and loue of God, is zet and poutit in our hairtis. *Ve affirme the contrare, that thair is na cheritie in vs, vt heruyſe ſen iuſtice, and cheritie ar al ꝗne thing, ve vald be conſtrainit to grant inherent iuſtice, and nocht imputatiue onlie.*   S. Paul. Rom. 5.

31 Quhair it is vryttin vork zour ſaluatione vith feir, and dreddor. *Ve affirme the contrare, and ſayis, haue na feir at al, bot be als aſſurit of ʒour ſaluatione, as that God is in heuin, and gif ʒe doubt thairof, ʒe can nocht be ſaif.*   S. Paul. Philip. 2.

32 Quhair it is vryttin be S. Paul, I am giltie of na thing, and zit for that, I haue na aſſurance of my Iuſtificatione. *Ve affirme the contrare that ve ar giltie of monie execrabil crymes, and ʒit ve ar aſſurit of our iuſtificatione.*   1. Cor. 4.

33 Quhair it is vryttin that god intyſis na man to euil. *Ve affirme the contrare vith our maiſter Caluiue that God mouis, and impellis men to ſyn,*   S. Iam. 1. Caluin li. 1. inſtitut. cap. 18.

1.Tim. 2. *as the efficient caus thairof.*

S.Mat.19 34 Quhair it is vryttin that god vil that euerie man be saif. *Ve affirme the contrare, and sayis that he vil nocht that euerie man be saif, bot that he hes created almaist al men, except ane feu nomber, to the effect he micht condem thame eternalie.*

S.Mat. 19. 35 Quhair it is vryttin gif thou vilbe perfyte, sel al quhilk thou hes and gif to the pure. *Ve affirme the contrare, and sayes that it apertenis nocht to the perfectione of the euangel to mak professione of pouartie.*

S.Matth. 26. 36 Quhair it is vryttin this is my bodie quhilk is geuin for zou. *Ve affirme the contrare and sayis, that it is nocht his bodie.*

37 Quhair it is vryttin My fleshe is verie meat, the breid quhilk I sal gif is my fleshe, S.Ioan.6. quhilk salbe geuin for the varld. *Ve affirme the contrare and sayis that the breid quhilk he gaue to his Apostlis, in his latter suppar, vas nocht fleshe, vtheruyse it behouit vs to confes the transsubstantiatione of the breid in Christis bodie.*

Genes.14. 38 Quhair it is vryttin that Melchisedec offerit breid and vyne, he being the preist of the maist hie God. *Ve say the contrare that he offerit neuer breid nor vyne, vtheruyse ve vald be constrainit to grant the Mess, quhilk is amang the Papistis, to haue bene præfigurat be the sacrifice of Melchisedech.*

109 Psal. 39 Quhair it is vryttin of our maist halie saluiour, and redemptor Iesus Christ, Thou art ane preist for euer eftir the ordore of Melchisedec. *Ve affirme the contrare thou art nocht ane*

preiſt for euer eſtir the ordour of Melchiſedec : becaus
thou hes na perpetual ſacrifice eſtir that ordour, quhilk may be offered in thy kirk, to the end of the
varld.

40 Quhair it is vryttin lat al thingis be do- 1.Cor.14.
ne amangis zou vith ordore and honeſt diſcipline. Ve affirme the contrare, and ſayes that in adminiſtratione of the ſacramentis na honeſt, and lauchful ceremoneis aucht to be keiped for the deu reuerence of the ſamyn, and that amangis Paſtoris of the
kirk thair is na ordour, bot that thay ar al alyk in
pouar, and authoritie: and that the miniſteris in exteriore apparel, ſould be in na thing different from the
peopil, and that our kirkis ſould haue na external
ornamentis, as vas amangis the Papiſtis, bot that thay
ſould be tyrred that the licht of the Euangel may
enter the mair eſilie in thame.

41 Quhair it is affermit gif thou be ſeik cal S.Iam.5.
for the preiſtis of the kirk and be oynted vith
oyle in the name of the lord, that prayer being maid for the thou may be releued from
ſyn. Ve affirme the contrare, Albeit thou be ſeik,
thou ſould nocht cal for onie preiſt in the kirk, and
that thov ſould nocht be oynted vith oyle in the name of the lord, vith prayer conioynit, for heirbie thou
may obtene na remiſſione of ſynnis, vtheruyſe extreme vnctione vald be ane ſacrament, quhilk is aganis
the actis of Parliament.

42 Quhair it is vryttin that mariage is ane Epheſ.5.
greit Sacrament in Chriſt and his kirk. Ve
affirme the contrare that it is na ſacrament nather
gret, nor ſmal, bot onlie ane contract betuix man and

voman, as vther contractis of bying and selling.

Rom. 7. 43 Quhair it is vrittin that the voman is subiect to the lau of hir housband salang as he leuis. *Ve affirme the contrare and sayis that scho is nocht subiect thairto, bot scho may marie another, albeit hir housband be alyue : vtheruyse our diuorcementis in our reformit kirk vald haue na place.*

1. Cor. 7. 44 Quhair it is vryttin, he quha mareis his dochtir, dois veil, bot he quha mareis hir nocht dois bettir. *Ve affirme the contrare, and sayes, that scho quha keipis hir virginitie, dois nocht bettir, nor scho quha mareis, and that mariage is als acceptabil to God as virginitie, vtheruyse ve vald nocht haue brocht Virginis out of thair closteris, and mareit thame on monkis.*

1. Timot. 5 45 Quhair it is vryttin that zoung vidouis, quha var consecrat to the seruice of the kirk incurris damnatione quhen thay marie, be breking of thair first promeis. *Ve affirme the contrare, and sayis that sik promises maid to keip Chastitie ar superstitious, and aucht nocht to be keipit : And that thay incur na damnatione, vtheruyse it had bene vnlesum to frere Martine Lauter to haue mareit ane Noue, and to monie of our faythful brethrene to marie in Scotland, quha befoir had maid vou of chastitie, quhen thay var monkes, and freris, as dene Iohne Vynrame, frere Craig, and sindrie vtheris.*

1. Timot. 3 46 Quhair it is vryttin that ane bischop, or superintendent sould be bot the housband of ane vyf, or anes mareyt. *Ve affirme the contrare, that albeit he be tuyse mareit he may veil aneuche be ane superintendent, vtheruyse ve vald condem Iohän*

Kmnox, *the laird of Dun, and sindrie vtheris of our reformit* kirk.

47 Quhair it is vryttin that Christ said to S. *Math.16.* Petir, Thou art ane Rok and vpone this Rok I sal buyld my kirk. *Ve affirme the contrare, Thou art necht the Rok, and vpon the I vil nocht buyld my kirk, vtheruyse he vald haue bene heid of the Kirk, and sua the Kirk vald haue bene ane möster hauing tua heiddis.*

48 Quhair it is vryttin, Neglect nocht the gift *1.Timot.4* of prophecie, quhilk thou hes ressaued be the onlaying of the handis of the preistheid. *Ve afferme the contrare, thou hes nocht the grace or gift of prophecie be the onlaying of the handis of the preisthead, becaus ordour quhairbie it sould be ressa-* Caluin *uit is nane of our sacramentis, and in this poynt ve* lib.4. *in special Ministeris of Scotland sayis that our mai-* instit.cap. *ster Caluin hes sklentit, quha grantis it to be ane treu* 14.sect.20 *sacrament.*

49 Quhair it is vryttin that the halie spirit hes *Act.20.* apoyntit bischopis to gyde ād reul the kirk of Chrst. *Ve afferme the cōtrare, becaus in ane reformit Kirk sic, as ouris, thair sould be na bischoppis ād ve Mi nistres ar equal to ony of the Bischopis, or rather superio ris, sua that ve may excōmunicat thame quhēve pleise.*

50 Quhair it is vryttin, that Christ hes left *Ephes.4.* doctoris and pastoris to his kirk to the end of the varld. *Ve afferme the contrair, and sayis, that, at the lest, thir tuel hundreth zeiris bygane, thair hes neuer bene ane treu doctore nor pastore in the kirk, quha hes bene knauin to the varld, bot that thay haue bene al Papistis as Augustine Hie-*

rom, *Basil*, and vtheris.

2.Pet.3. 51 Quhair it is vryttin, that S.Paul hes vryttin monie thingis difficil to be vndirstand.

Ve affirme that he hes vrittin na thing difficil to be vndirstãd, and that soutaris, tailzeouris, ãd skynnaris may vndirstand him veil aneuch.

Rom.13. 52 Quhair it is vryttin, That euerie man sould be subiect to his magistrat. *Ve especiallie Ministeris of Scotland affirme the contrare, that he sould nocht be subiect to his magistrat, ãd thairfoir ve gaue cousal to impresone the Quenis maiestie of Scotland in Lochlevin, and to tak armore aganis hir Maiesteis mother, quhilk ve defend to be agreabil to our Euangel, and professione.*

Breiflie gif I sould mak rehersal of al the notabil sentécis of the halie scripture quhilk the Protestaons interpretis in this maner be manifest contradictionis, I sall find na thing in thair mouthis quhen halie scripture is proponit to thame, Bot that the contrare thairof is trew, and that all thair doctrine is groúdit vpone Αριϑμοι, And thay deprehédit tobe the sonis of the Antichrist, quhilk beS.Paul is callit ane aduersar, becaus his hail studie and trauel consistis nocht in affirming bot denying, nocht in illustratione of hid treuth, bot impu-

2.Thes 2. gnatione of the manifest veritie, nocht in buylding, bot destroying, nocht in cómending the godlie antecesloris, and follouing thair furstoppis, bot in proud contempt, and reiectione of thair doctrine, sentencis, and maner of leuing: Sua that to this head Αριϑμοι

in lyk maner pertenis al thair anſueris, quhen
ſoeuer thay fall in diſputatione : For ʒif ane
teſtimonie of the expres vrittin vord in the
neu or auld teſtament be brocht aganis thame, thay thraw it efter thair auin phantaſie,
or ellis denyis it alluterlie. Gif the vniuerſall
conſent of the doctoris be allegit, thay anſuer
that the doctoris var bot men, as gif thay var
goddis or angellis: Gif ane traditione of the
Apoſtlis be brocht aganis thame, thay deny
that ve aucht to beleue onie thing, as perte-
ning to ſaluatione quhilk is nocht expreſlie
vrittin in the neu and auld teſtament.

OF THE DEV OBEDIENCE
quhilk treu Chriſtian men aucht to the
hie preiſt and Chriſtis vicar vpon
the face of the earth.

CHAP.   XXX.

M.

THair be ma propirteis of the Antichriſt quhilk
aggreis to the Pape of Rome nor onie vther, for
he vil that men fal doune befoir him, and kis his feit
as gif he var god quhil as Petir refuſit ſik honore: for
quhen Cornelius as ve reid in the Actis of the A-
poſtlis fel doune at his feit, Petir raiſed him vp be   Act.01.
the hand ſaying: I am ane man als veil as ʒe ar: Mairatour he ſettis him ſelf furth for god, quhil as he
vil bind mennis conſciencis be his lauis and conſtitu-
tionis aganis the libertie of the Euangel quhilk ve
haue cleirlie reiueled to the varld.

B. Sence it is maiſt treu quhilk the poet ſayis,

(qui tacet confentire videtur)he quha keipis
his peax appeiris to confefs that quhilk is
fpokin : I perfaue that conuict be zour
auin confciéce ze confefs my formar demó-
ftratione necefsar, fua that Mahometis and
Martin Lauter ar the tua beiftis, quhairof
mention is maid in the reuelatione of Sanct

Apoc. 13. Iohne to compofe ane bodie of the Antichrift: As to the obiectionis quhilk ze bring
aganis the Paip,thay ar verie friuol : And firft
ze appeir to misknau quhairin confiftis honor, and the differencis thairof: For it dois
confift in humiliatione of the mynd according to the knaulege of the præeminence of
him aboue vs,to quhom it is exhibit: Sua as
to the vtuart actione and cerimonie,it may be
ane quhilk is exhibit to God,and his creaturis quhilk he hes apoyntit to haue præeminé-
ce aboue vs: as ve fal done on kneis , ve dif-
couer our headis,ve bek befoir god, and onie
vardlie prince.Quhairfoir fence that outuart
cerimonie hes bene vfit fa monie zeiris in
Rome for declaratione of the reuerence quhilk alChriftianis aucht to the Paip or heich
preift infafar as he is Chriftis vicar and legat
on earth:Ze may put zour mynd to reft albeit the Italianis and auld Romanis learne not
the Cerimoneis of courtafie at zou, quha ar
ennimeis to al ciuilitie: And gif Chrift hono-

*S.Iohn.*13 rit his Apoftlis and S Petir fua that he vefchit
thair feit, quhy reproue ze thame quha kiffis
the feit of him,quhom thayknau to be placed
be god

be God in the Chyre of Petir? Zea the Getiles
instructed be the lau of nature onlie, gaue fik
reuerence to thair heich preist, as is manifest
of Plutarch defcryuad the maneris of the ancient Romanis, quhilk is fufficient to codem
zour inciuilitie quha refufis to do the lyk
reuerence to the treu vicar ane lieutennent of
Chrift vpone the face of the earth, as al obedient Chriftianis hes done fen the dayis of S.
Petir vnto this prefent : For the quhilk caus
the Ethnik Emperoris as Diocletianus be æ-
mulatione of the rite and cerimonie quhilk
thay perfaued amangis the Chriftianis in honoring of thair heich preist, var mouit to promulgat ane lau that al men aknauleging the
Emperoris authoritie, for declaration of the
obediéce and honor deu vnto him, fould kifs
his feit. As to the place of fcripture quhilk ze
alledge, Dar ze reproue the godlie man Cornelius that he did caft him felf at S. Petiris feit?
Or gif ze dar not reproue him, as ze dar not,
quhy reproue ze vs becaus ve do the lyk to
the treu fucceffaris of Petir? Sanct Petir anfue-
red indeid that he vas ane man, and commandit Cornelius to ryfe vp, geuand vtheris ane
exemple of humilitie, and lattand Cornelius
alfo vndirftand that the difciplis of Chrift as
concerning thair auin priuat perfonis, defyris
na fik honor to be exhibit vnto thame, bot
that quhatfumeuer honor be geuin vnto thame, it redoud vnto Chrift: And zit Cornelius
did bot his deuitie, As quhen ane nobil man

T

sittis doune on his kneis befoir the kíg albeit
the king say that he is ane man lyk him, and
caus him ryse and speik to him, zit he dois bot
his deuitie in doing sik honor and reuerence
to the king. As to the secund pairt of zour obiectione gif S. Paul gaue cómand to the Chri-
Rom.13. stianis to obey the lauis of infidel príncis maid
for ciuil gouernement not onlie for feir, bot
for conscience befoir God : Hou mekil mair
aucht ve as obedient sonis to obey the consti-
tionis of our spiritual fatheris and pastoris
maid for our veil, according to the command
of S.Paul, [Obedite præpositis vestris & sub-
Heb.13. iacete eis, ipsi enim peruigilát quasi rationem
reddituti pro animabus vestris:].i.Obey zour
reularis and pastoris, and submit zour selfis
vnto thame, for thay vatch for zou, and ar to
gif compt for zour saulis? And S. Paul teachis
maist plálie that Christianis aucht not ólie to
obey the lauis quhilk the pastoris settis furth
in the name of Christ as propirlie callit the
Iau of God, bot thay constitutionis in lyk maner quhilk thay propone for the profeit of
the commonweil, As quhen he vsis sik ane
forme of speiking (Præcipio ego non domi-
1.Cor 7. nus)it is not the Lord quha geuis this cómád,
bot I gif this command. And gif men in hairt
and conscience ar not obleist to the obseruatione of the Ecclesiastical lauis and constitutionis , quhat is the caus that ze constrain the
People to obey the inuentionis of zour headles assembleis, and compellis thame incaice

thay difobey, to ftand bairfuttit in fekclayth
fa monie fondayis in tyme of zour preachingis ? The Anabaptiftis quhais doctrine is na
thing ellis, bot fum conclufionis neceffarlie
inferrit of zour groundis, becaus obediéce to
the lauis of Princis is cōtrar to the libertie of
this neu Euágel quhilk be the Proteftaons is
reuelit to the varld, collectis that in the temporal eftait thair fould be na kingis, fence al
chriftianis ar equal: And zeMinifteris in Scotland ryd als neir thame as ze may, As is manifeft of the blaft of the trúpet, vryttin be Iohán
kmnox zour firft prophet, quhair he laboris
to proue that vemen may haue na lauchful
authoritie to beir gouernement in onie commonweil, quhairof it follouis neceffarlie that
the king of Scotland king Iames the Saxt can
haue na titil to the croune: fen he can haue na
richt to it bot onlie be the Quenis Maieftie
his Mother : This is lykuyfe maift euident of
Maifter George Buchananis buk (Of the richt
of the kingdome of Scotlád) That the people
fould chufe him to be king quhó thay think
maift vyfe and abil to tak on him the gouer-
nemét of the cútrey: Quhairbie, gif onie man
fal enter in deu confideration of the mater, he
vil efilie vndirftand that al thir thingis var
done to fulfil the promeiff of fchir Iohann
kmnox to the Erl of Murray, quhom he deceauit in S. Paulis kirk in Londone, bringand
him in confait, that God had chofin him extraordinarlie as ane Iofias to be king of Scot-

land, to ruit out Idolatrie, and to plant the
licht of his neu Enangel, quhair thay conuenit in this maner, That the Prior of Sanct An-
drois Erl of Murray fould mentene the neu
Elias aganis the Preiftis of Baal, (for fua blaf-
phemouflie he namit the preiftis of Chrift Iefus) And the neu Elias, fould fortifie the neu
Iofias, be procuring the fauor of the people
aganis Iezabel, blafpheming maift impudentlie the Quenis M. To this end tédit al his railling and zouris aganis the Queuis g. euer calling hir Iezabel, mening heirby that ze vald
haue hir and hir feid ruited out: quhil as be
the contrare ze ftylit the Erl of Murray, the
gudeIofias quha vald caus the rafch bufs keip
the kou: And to perfuade the people that he
micht be reable air to his father, ze preachit
euer vnto his death that promeifs of mariage
vas lauchful mariage, fupponand that his father promifhed to marie his mother, for na
vther propofe, bot that thair fould be na hin-
derance to the promotion of him vnto the
kingdome: And eftir that be zour moyen he
had bene chofinking, ze vald haue thocht that
ze had als fufficiét pouar to depoife him agane, as ze had to promoue him: fua that al zour
doctrine tendis to that end, that ze acknaulege na fuprem Magiftrat nather fpiritual, nor
temporal, bot that ze onlie haue pouar to cōmand euerie man in the cuntrey, of quhatfü-
euer degrie or eftait he be.

OF THE TRADITIONIS VNI-
uersalie resaued be the kirk Catholik.

CHAP. XXXI.

Minister.

TO *quhat propos seruis the obseruation of the lauis, traditionis, and ceremoneis institute be the Paip, sence al thingis ar expreslie vryttin in the neu and auld testament, quhilk ve sould beleue as perte-ning to saluation?*

B. I vil be the grace of God proue maist eui-dentlie that al thingis ar nocht expreslie vryt-tin in the neu and auld testament quhilk ane Christian man sould beleue als fermlie, as the Euangel: sua that zevil be constrainit to grant that monie thigis aucht to be beleuit, quhilk ar nocht expreslie vryttin in the Canonik bu-kis of the scripture : As Sanct Paul him self **S. Paul.** teachis vryttad to the Thessalonianis, 1. Stad, 1 and keip al thingis quhilk ze haue learned **2. Thess. 2.** ather be vord or vryt: And in the actis of the Apostlis, By al the disputationis of Sanct Paul, and the rest of the Apostlis, quhilk ar nocht ·   **Act. 16.** expreslie vryttin. 2. Ve reid that the Apostlis 2 quhen thay passed throuch al citeis teachand, Thay gaif to thame quha var conuertit to the fayth, the Decreis, ad Ordinacis of the Apost-lis, and Preistis of the kirk, to be obseruit be thame. 3. Ve man beleue that infantis sould be baptized, quhilk is nocht expreslie vryttin. 3.

4 4. Ve man beleue that thir bukes of the neu, and auld teſtament quhilk ar canonik, hes authentik authoritie, and ar altogidder vithout errore, dytit be the halie Ghaiſt ſpeikand in the Apoſtlis, and vther halie men the vryttaris thairof. 5. That the tuelf Artiklis of the beleif var dytit be the halie Ghaiſt ſpekand in the Apoſtlis. 6. Ve reid in the Euangel of S.

5

6
Matt.26. Mattheu that Chriſt and his diſciples, eftir his latter ſuppar ſang ane Hymn, quhilk being proponit to vs, ve aucht to beleif, albeit it be nocht vryttin in the neu or auld teſtament.

7 7. Ve aucht not onlie to beleue the expreſſ vordis of the text, bot alſo the mening of the ſpirit of god quha dytit the ſame: as for exẽple, quhatſumeuer Sanct Luk being requyrit, vald haue ſpokin be inſtinction of the halie ſpirit, for vndirſtanding of thir vordis (This is my bodie) aucht to be beleuit be ane Chriſtian, quha peraduẽture vald haue vryttin ane tracteis for the vndirſtanding of thir vordis, and the hid myſtereis cõtenit in thame, mair prolixe nor his hail Euangel. 8. In the laſt chapter

8 of the Euangel of S. Mattheu Chriſt geuis command to his diſciples, to teache al nationis tha thingis quhilk he had commandit thame, and zit ve find nocht al thir thĩgis expreſlie vryttin. 9. It is mair nor manifeſt that nane

9 of the Apoſtlis, nor Euangeliſtis propoſed to comprehend al tha thingis, in thair vryttingis quhilk ſould be fermlie beleuit be Chriſtianis, bot as vryttis S. Auguſtine, and vther an-

cient doctoris to mak ane buke contening
ane admonitione to thame, that befoir had
beleuit concerning the mysterie of the incarnation of Christ, of his lyf, and deathe: Thairfoir thair ar monie thingis concerning the
iustificatione of man. 10. The number of the 10
sacramentis, and thingis requesit to the administratione of euerie ane of thame. 11. The 11
communione of sanctis, 12. Ordoure and dis- 12
cipline of the kirk: 13. the obseruatione of the 13
Sōday and festual dayes, presigurat be the Sabaoth day, and vther halie dayes in the auld
lau, vith monie vther siclyk headis that can
nocht be schauin expresslie in Euangelistis,
and the Epistles: quhilk eftir var vryttin onlie
be certane occasionis, and nocht to comprehend in thame al the mystereis of our fayth: S.Ioan.16
And thairfoir the halie Ghaist is promised to
assist Christis kirk vnto the end of the varld, Augu.I.
for the quhilk caus S. Augustine vryttād aga- cōt. Cresc.
nis Cresconius grāmaticus, sayis that the scri- cap.33.
pture in ane certane maner geuis vs ane resolutione of al quæstionis, becaus in tha thingis
quhilk it contenis nocht expresslie, it geuis vs
command to pas to the kirk, quhilk vil gif
vs ful resolutione of al: 14. Siclyk al antece- 14
dentis necessar, al consequentis, and conclu-
sionis necessarlie collectit, vith vther circum-
stancis, ar of als gret vecht, as thay thingis quhilk ar expresslie mentionat. 15. And albeit the 15
buke vryttin var perished, the kirk vald
nocht decay, lyk as Christis kirk vas plan-

tit amang the gentiles befoir the vrytting
of onie of the Euangelis , and Epiſtles :
16 16 Quhair as ve beleue the halie Catholik
kirk,ve ar bund to beleue fermlie all tha thingis, quhilk the halie Catholik kirk reſſauis
17 to be treu, and expedient for inſttuctione. 17
Iohne. 16. In the Euangel of S. Iohne, Chriſt ſayis vnto
his diſcipillis: Mair atour I haue monie thingis to tell zou , quhilk ze may nocht beir at
this tyme, bot quhen the ſpirit of treuth ſal
cum,he vil teache zou al veritie:Of the quhilk
teſtimonie it is manifeſt that monie thingis
nocht vryttin expreſlie, ar referrit to the ſe-
creit ſuggeſtione of the halie ſpirit quhen ty-
18 me ſal require. 18 Quha is ſua far by reſſone
as to affirme that al the preachingis, adhorta-
tionis, admonitionis, diſputationis, and formes of prayeris of the Apoſtlis at expreſlie
vryttin? quhilk gif thay var offerit vnto vs,or
reuelit be the halie ſpirit to the ſucceſſoris of
the Apoſtlis, and be thame proponit to vs,ve
aucht fermlie to beleue. S. Paul in the thrid
Epheſi. 3. of the epiſtle to the Epheſianis vryttis. 19
19 [ze haue hard of the diſpenſatione of the
grace of God , quhilk vas geuin to me for
zour caus, becaus be ane reuelatione he maid
the myſterie knauin to me (as I vrait in ſeu
vordis befoir , of the quhilk , quhen ze reid
thame, ze may vndirſtand my knauledge in
the myſterie of Chriſt) quhilk in vther aiges
vas nocht knauin to the ſonis of men ,] this
Epiſtle is nocht extant, and zit ve ſould nocht

doubt bot the halie spirit vorking in the hartis of Pastoris, succeidand vnto S.Paul reue-
lis the same thingis in lyk maner. 20 And in ²⁰
the Epistle to the Hebreuis quhair he vryttis *Heb.6.*
eftir this maner [Quhairfoir leuing the doctrine appertenand to thame quha ar zit rude in
the knauledge of Christ, lat vs pas to perfectione, not laying agane the groud of repentance from dead vorkis, and of fayth in god,
of the doctrine of baptisme, and the impositione of handis and rysing of the dead, and
eternal Iudgement:) Of the quhilk vordis it
is manifest that thay had bene instructed befoir of thir commone places, and zit ve find
na large explicatione thairof expreslie vrittin:
S.Paul makis mentione of 21.Excommunica- 21
tione, of the quhilk thair is na tracteis contening the forme thairof in the scripture: Ve 1. *1 Heb.*
reid i the scripture of nyne ordoris of Angelis, 2. *Iudæ ep.*
tó vit ¹ Angeli 2. Archangeli. 3 Virtutes 4 Prin 3. *Ephe.*1.
cipatus, 5. Potestates, 6. Dominationes, 7. 4. *Ephe.*1
Throni, 8 Cherubin, 9 Seraphin, of the quhilk 5. *Eph.* 1.
ve haif na cleir declaration, quhilk nochtuith- 6. *Eph.*1.
standing gif it be offerit to vs, ve aucht ferm- 7. *Colos.*1.
lie to beleue : 22. And for confirmatione of 8. *Psal.*17.
this, I micht produce zou the testimonie of 9. *Esa.*6.
the hail ancient fatheris quha in onie aige hes *Irænæ. cō-*
florished in the kirk of God, As Irene, in *tra Valent.*
the thrid buk aganis the valentinianis, and *Tertu. de*
thrid chapture : of Tertullian in his buke de *corona mi-*
corona militis, of Augustine in his Epistlis to *litis.*
Ianuarius : of Basile in his buke de spiritu *Aug. epist.*
180.
Basilius de
spiritu Sāc.
ca. 37.

sancto, chap. 37: of S. Ierom in his buke aganis the Luciferianis, and vtheris: Quhairfoir it
is manifest that al thingis ar nocht expreslie
vryttin in the neu, and auld testament, quhilk
ane gud and obedient Christian man aucht
to beleue als fermlie as the text of the scripture: And to cum to zour particular doctrine, * 1 Ze beleue, that al man soulde persuade
him self assuritlie that he is predestinat to
lyf eternal quhilk is nocht expreslie vryttin
in the neu, or auld testament: 2 Ze beleue that
the sacramentis ar onlie seallis of the mercie
of God, and geuis na grace, quhilk is nocht
expreslie vrittin; 3 Ze beleue, that the infantis
of infidellis aucht nocht to be baptised, quhilk is nocht expreslie vryttin, 4 ze beleue
that quhasoeuer is baptizet, quhatsumeuer
4 synnis he haue committed, calling to memorie that he is baptized, thairbie obtenis remissione of thame al, quhilk is nocht expres-
5 lie vryttin: 5 Ze beleue that it is Iesum to ane
man to put auay his vyf ad marie another, qu-
6 hilk is nocht expreslie vryttin, 6 ze beleue that
it is Iesum to Mōkis to marie Nunnis, quhilk
7 is nocht expreslie vryttin. 7 Ze beleue, that
quhasoeuer persuadis him self, that his synnis
ar forgiuen, thay ar forgiuen to him, quhilk is
8 nocht expreslie vryttin: 8 Ze beleue, that in
the in suppar, ve ar treulie lifted vp to heauin,
and that ve ressaue Christ al, bot nocht all
that quhilk he is, according to zour Maister
Caluinis doctrine, quhilk is nocht expreslie

Hierom.
contra Lu-
cife.

*

Sindrie he-
addis of
doctrine
quhilk the
protestaons
beleuis vi-
thout the
varräd of
the express
vryttin
vord.

vryttin : 9 Ze beleue that zour kirk hes bene 9
thir monie hundreth zeiris inuisibil, quhilk
is nocht expreslie vryttin : 10 Ze beleue that 10
ze ar extraordinar Prophetis send to reforme
the kirk, quhilk is nocht expreslie vryttin : 11 11
Ze beleue vith zour maister Caluine , that
God hes created men to condem thame eternalie, quhilk is nocht expreslie vryttin : 12 Ze 12
beleue, that god nocht onlie permittis syn,
bot mouis men to syn, and is the caus thairof , quhilk is nocht expreslie vryttin : 13 13
Ze beleue that Christ thoillit The paines
of ane condemnt man in his saul, quhilk
ir nocht expreslie vryttin. 14. Ze beleue 14
that na sin is imputed to zou, hou horribill
crymes that euer ze commit , quhilk is not
expreslie vryttin : 15 ze beleue that thair be 15
bot tua sacramentis onlie, côtrare the vniuersal kirk sen the dayes of the Apostlis, quhilk
is nocht expreslie vryttin.16.Ze beleue Calui- 16
nis lang institutionis , and resauis the lea-
singis of his catechisme teaching thame pu-
blictlie on sondayis eftir none as gif thay
var the oracles of the halie Ghaist , quhilk at
nocht vryttin in the Bybil. 17. Ze beleue 17
nocht that Christ descendit into hel in verie
deid,bot that thay vordis signifeis onlie the
anguish of death quhilk he sufferit in spirit
quhen he cryit (my god, my god quhy hes
thou left me?)quhilk is nocht expreslie vryttin. 18. Ze beleue that ze sould nocht fast on 18
frydayis eftir the custume of the kirk , bot

vpon fondayis in contempt of the kirk, for
the quhilk ze haue na varrand in the expefs
18 vryttin vord. 18. Ze beleue al zour preachingis, and prayeris quhairin aganis al cheritie ze
craif the confufion of Nichtbouris, quhilk ar
not expreflie vryttin. Ze beleue al the formes
19 of baptizing, 19 Mareing, 20. of Making re-
20 pentance in fekclayth, 21. of Apoynting Pa-
21 ftores, 22. of Adminiftratiõ of the lordis fup-
22 par, as ze cal it, 23 of Excommunication and
23 eiedtion of men out of zour kirk, and focie-
tie quha var neuer in it : Thir and monie
vther he addis alfueil of dodtrine as adtis
of zour general affembleis (quhilk ze fuffer
not to cum to licht, incaice zour vanitie
be lachin at be the hail varld) ze vil neuer be
abil to fchau in the fcripture , and zit ze
imbrace thame maift obftinatlie as gif thay
var the vord of God, fua ze condemn zour
auin felfis be reiedting the traditionis of
the kirk, and faying that ze beleue na thing
bot that quhik is expreflie vryttin.

M.   *I think the vnuorthie to quhõ I fould mak an-*
fuere , quha ar not efchamit to defend that rabil of
traditionis quhilk the Papiftis vfis , fen God him felf
Deut. 12. *hes fpokin,that quhilk I command the, do it onlie, na-*
ther eik onie thig, nather diminife from the fame: ãd
iĩ the reuelatione of S. Iohne,gif onie man eik or pare
Apoc. 22. *from thir vordis , God fal bring on him al the plagis*
quhilk ar vryttin in this buke . And thay vorf-
Math.15. *hipe me in vane teachãd the dodtrines of men : Be thir*

places and sindrie vtheris lyk vnto thir I find that Zour traditionis ar reiected as the inuentionis of men.

B. Thir ar zour gret gunnis quhairbie ze vse to attonishe the simpil and ignorant peopil, quhilk being considerit a far af, appeiris to haue gret strenth, bot being neirar examinat ar fund vithout onie force at all. And to cum to the first place of scripture allegit be zou, I knau that zour Maister Caluine vndirstandis it of the lau of Moyses, and that na thing sould be eikit nor parit from it, quhilk expositione gif ze imbrace, ze man reiect al vther thing by the lau of Moyses, quhilk efteruart hes bene vryttin, as the Prophetis and vthir halie bukes, euin as did the Samaritanis quha mouit be the sam argument ressaued onlie the fyue bukes of Moyses, and reiected al the rest of the scripture: ze man reiect the neu testament, and quhatsumeuer hes bene vryttin be the Euangelistis, and Apostlis, in the quhilk monie thingis ar bayth eikit to the lau of Moyses, and parit from it, althocht Caluine vald dissemble the mater, as gif nathing var in the neu testament quhilk is nocht in the auld. For quhatsumeuer tergiuersatione he find, he vil be constranit to grant that monie thingis ar commandit in the neu testament quhilk var nocht commandit in the auld, and monie thingis forbiddin in it, quhilkis in the auld testament var commandit, or ellis Iohan Caluine and al zour faythful brethrene sould

be circumcidit as var the Ieuis according to the lau of Moyſes. This expoſitione thairſoir being reiected as maiſt vane and repugnant to goddis vord, The mening of this place of ſcripture is, that nathing aucht to be eikit or parit from the vord of god, quhairin al Catholiques aggreis vith zou, and this is nauyſe repugnant to the traditionis : becaus the quæſtione is nocht betuix zou and thame quhidder gif onie thing ſould be eikit to the vord of god or parit from it : bot quhidder gif tha thingis onlie apertenis to goddis vord quhilk ar vryttin? Sua gif ze vald haue ſaid onie thing to the purpoſe, zeſould haue ſchauin ſum plane teſtimonie of the ſcripture, that thair is nathing apertenād to goddis vord, bot that onlie quhilk is vryttin, quhilk nather haue ze done, nor can be abil to do: Zea the ſcripture teachis
„ vs the plaine contrare, Stand and keip the tra
„ ditionis quhilk ze haue reſſaued ather be vord
S. *Paul.* or vryt , be the quhilk vordis S. Paul lattis vs
i.*Theſſ.*2. to vndirſtand that the Theſſalonianis and al vtheris quhaſoeuer ſtandis in the treu religiōe aucht to keip the traditionis of the kirk , albeit thay be nocht vryttin , and thay quha reiectis the foirſaid traditionis ſtandis nocht in the veritie bot ar fallin from it : Hou than can ze excuſe zour ſelf, bot ze haue fallin al from the veritie ſen ze vil obſerue na traditione? The ſecund place of Scripture in the reuelatione of S. Iohne aucht to be vndirſtand in lyk maner that na thing aucht to be eikit or

parit from his Prophecie, and nocht that na
thing aucht to be beleued or reſſaued for the
vord of God, bot that quhilk is in this prophecie, vtheruyſe ve vilbe conſtrainit to re-
ieƐt al the reſt of the neu teſtament, ſua al men
may eſilie vndirſtand hou far aganis the mening of the ſpirit of God, ze vſe ſic places of
ſcripture in zour ſermonis for to diſſaue the
ſimpil peopil. Nou to cum to the thrid
place quhair Chriſt obieƐted to the Phariſæanis, thay vorſhip me in vane teachand the traditionis of men: ze peruert it in lyk maner, ſen
it is maiſt manifeſt of text, that tha ar callit
the traditionis of men quhilk ar repugnant
to goddis vord, as quhair God commandit to
honore the parètis, the Phariſæanis did com- *Mat. 15.*
mand the plane contrare, to negleƐt thair parentis and mak offeringis vnto God of tha
thingis quhairuith thay ſould haue ſuppleed
thair parentis indigence, quhairin thay con-
trauenit expreſlie Goddis commandiment.
Bot the Ieuis had ſum treu traditionis amangis thame vithout the quhilk thay could not
attene to the perfyte intelligence of the ſcripture, in the quhilk is Moyſes did inſtruƐt the
ſeuintie eldaris quhom he did apoynt to gouerne the peopil quhairof ze may reid Hila- *Hilar. in*
rius gif ze pleis vryttand vpone the ſecund *Pſal. 2.*
Pſalme, and vther ancient vryttaris bayth
befoir Chriſt and eftir him. And this traditione vas na lytil caus that the ſeuintie
interpretoris quhilk vas ſend to Ptolome

the king of Egypt to tranflate the Bybil out
of the Hebreu in Greik, did fua perfytlie aggrie in al poyntis, that albeit thay var feparat
ane from another, zit as monie vryttis, thair
vas nocht famekil as ane vord in difference
amangis thame, quhairin thay had ane fpecial
affiftance of the halie fpirit, being helpit be
the traditione quhilk from hand to hand thay
had reffaued from Moyfes. And the caufe of
fa monie fectis amang the Ieuis as var the Sad-
duceanis, Pharifæanis, Effianis, Hemerobapti-
ftis, and vtheris, vas, becaus thay interpreit
nocht the fcripture according to the tradition
of the eldaris, bot according to thair auin
Matt. 23. phanthafie. Thairfoir Chrift gaue command to
obey thame quha teached in the Chyre of
Moyfes, vndirftanding be the Chyre of Moyfes, the pouar of teaching according to the
maift certane reul and traditioe that vas geuin
be Moyfes, quhilk quhen thay folloued, thay
teached maift found and healthfum doctrine,
euin as nou amangis the Chriftianis, thay quha interpretis the fcripturis according to the
traditione geuin be the Apoftlis, and euer obferuit in the kirk, thay teache maift healthfum
and foleid doctrine, and thay that follouis
nocht the faid traditione, bot thair auin phā-
tafie as ze do: thay teache erroneous and per-
uerfed doctrine, and hes neuer conftancie nor
ftabilitie in onie thing, bot fallis ordinarlie
out of ane condemnit and pernicious errore,
in ane vthir mair dangerous: And thairfoir
the

The ancient fatheris be this reul vsed euer to conuict hæretikes, As did Irenæus the Valentinianis, Tertul.the Marcionitis, Sanct Basil the Eunomianis, S. Hierom the Luciferianis, and S. Augustine the Donatistis, becaus that thay ressaued onlie the vordis of the scripture, and vald nocht ressaue the interpretatione of thame according to the traditione of the kirk. The quhilk traditione S.Paul callis the Reul of fayth,saying latvs nocht depairt from *S. Paul.* theReul of fayth,that ve may al say ane thing. *Philip.3.* And to the Cor. For ane final resolutione of *I.Cor.11.* ane controuersie, he proponis as ane maist certane and infallibil vay of decisione,the maner and Custume of the kirk. And sua quhasoeuer follouis thisReul, that is the traditione of the kirk in the interpretatione of the scripture, he can nocht in onie vyse vauer from the richt intelligence, and mening thairof.

For the quhilk caus sayis Tertulliane that S. Paul passed vp to Hierusalem to the rest of the Apostlis,to the end that he micht aggrie vith thame in thisReul of fayth. And the caus that ze,and al thay quha professis neu doctrine thir dayes,ar fallin is sa monie erroris, and sua discrepant ane from another,is, becaus ze haue nocht follouit this reul in the reiding of the scripturis, and vndirstanding of thame, bot zour auin phantasie, and inuentionis of zour auin braine.

V

OF THE OBSERVATIONE
of the festual and halie dayis.

CHAP. XXXII.

Minister.

Bot the mater vil appeir mair euident gif ve
sal enter in particular consideratione of the traditionis of the Papistical kirk, for thairin supersti-
tiouslie ar obseruit ane greit number of halie dayis
aganis the command of God, Remember that thou
keip halie the sabaoth day, Sax dayis sal thou labour,
sua that gif ve labour not on euerie day of the oulk,
except the sonday, ve brek this commandiment: And
S. Paul vryttis aganis the obseruatione of the halie
dayis maist planelie: [I feir leist I haue bestouit my
trauel on zou in vain, for ze obserue dayis and zeiris,
And siclyk I micht proue vtheris zour traditionis
to be plane repugnant to Goddis vord and commandimentis, as the Making and vorshipping of Imagis,
the Inuocation of Sanctis, the Honoring of deid menis
banes, the Ganging in pilgramagis and monie vtheris
quhairof ze sould be eschamit.

B. The treu mening of the commād of God
quhilk ze thrau for establishing of zour hæresie, is that thay sould not labour vpone the
sevint day: As to the sax vthir dayis it is permitted to thame to labour gif thay pleise, bot
it is not commandit that thay labore, as ze
falslie allege aganis the plane vordis of the
scripture, cōsidering the Ieuis had monie fes-

Exod. 20.

Gal. 4.

tual dayis by the Sabaoth, As the feistis of the *Leuit. 23.*
Pasouer, of the First fruitis, of the Tabernaclis *Deut. 16.*
and sindrie vtheris, quhilk var lang to reherse,
zea sum feastis thay obseruit hail aucht dayis
throuch out, and zit notuithstãding brak not
Christis commandiment concerning the keiping of the Sabaoth day : quhairof it is maist
euident, that ze vraist the scripture to ane sini-
strous mening: for gif the Ieuis keipit the feast
of the Pasouer vith ane gret solennitie in remembrance of the temporal benefeit, quhilk
thay resaued, to vit deliuerance from the bodelie seruice and bondage of Pharao, hou mekil mair sould ve obserue Pasche day in memorie of the deliuerance of mankynd from
hel, be the resurrectione of our saluiour Christ
Iesus ? sen as testifeis Sanct Paul tha thingis
quhilk var proponit to the Ieuis in ane obscu- *1. Cor.10.*
re schaddou and figure onlie, ar offerit to vs
in treuth and veritie, [Lex continebat vmbrã *Heb. 10.*
futurorum bonorum, non ipsas imagines re-
rum:] .i. The lau contenit the schaddouis of
tha thingis quhilk vat to be reuelit, and not
the propir images, and formis of the thingis
thame selfis. As to the secund reasone quhilk
ze vsit in zour obiectione, lyk as al the headdis of zour doctrine quhairin ze disagriefrom
the Catholik kirk, calland it Papistical, ar auld
condemnit hæreseis, sua in this poynt ze follou the futstoppis of the Manichæuis, for as
testifeis Sanct August. thay obiectit this place *Aug. epist.*
of scripture aganis the Catholikes of that *119.*

aige, becaus thay keipit the halie dayes : to
quhom he anſuerit that Sanct Paul ſpeakis
not of the halie dayis dedicat be the hail kirk
to Goddis ſeruice for memorie of his benefeittis, bot of the ſuperſtition of the Gentiles,
quha beleuit that ſum dayis of thair auin nature var vnhappie for ane coniunctione of
noyſum planetis or ſtarres, and becaus this, or
that planet vas in ſik ane hous of the heauin,
quhilk opinionis var maiſt vain and impro-
fitabil. The Manichæanis obiectit lykuyſe
that the Chriſtianis eftir the cuſtume of the
Getiles obſeruit (ſolſtitia and Æquinoctia) becaus the Chriſtianis keipit halie the Natiuitie
of the lord, and Paſche day, of the quhilk the
ane befel in the ſolſtitial of vynter, and the
vthir eftir the æquinoctial of the ſpring tyme: To quhom Sanct Auguſtin anſuerit that
the Chriſtianis obſeruit not thir ſeaſonis mouit be the ſuperſtition of the Gentiles, bot be
the command of Chriſtis halie kirk, quha
apoyntit thame halie for rememberance of
the exceiding gret benefeitis quhilk redoudit
to the hail varld of Chriſtis Natiuitie and Re-
ſurrectione. For defence of this louabil cuſtume of the vniuerſal kirk in keiping of the halie dayis S. Ignatius quha vas S. Iohne the
Euangeliſtis diſcipil and ane halie martyr
vryttis to the Chriſtian people, that thay keip
halie the feſtual dayis, and vther diſtinctionis
of tymes, and meattis inſtitute be the halie
Apoſtlis and kirk Catholik, ſaying, (Feſtiuita-
tes ne ſpernite, quagrageſimam ſeruate, conti-

*Ignat. epi.
4. ad Phil.*

net enim exemplar conuersationis Domini-
cæ)that is to say. Lichtlie not the halie dayis,
keip the halie tyme of Lentern, becaus it
contenis ane exemplar of the conuersation
of the lord: And S. Cyprian in monie of his
epistlis commandis that the dayis vpon the *Cypr. epi.*
quhilkis the Martyris disceissit be diligentlie *69.*
obseruit, that thair dayis anniuersar or returning be zeirlie course may be dedicat to the
seruice of God, and thankisgeuing for thair
victorie: For the quhilk caus immediatlie estir
the decess of the Apostlis, The kirk constitute
in Rome Notaris to collect and register the
Actis of the Martyris: S. Augustin also for defence of the treuthvrittis aganis Adimátus the *Augu. co-*
Manichæan in this maner. (Nam & nos quo- *tra Adi-*
que Dominicum diem, & Pascha celebramus, *mantum.*
& quaslibet alias dierum festiuitates, sed quia *cap. 16.*
intelligimus quò pertineant, non tempora
obseruamus, sed quæ illis significantur temporibus). i. for ve obserue also the Sonday, Pasche
day, and quhatsumeuer vthir halie dayis, bot
becaus ve vndirstád to quhat end the keiping
of thame vas institute, ve keip not sik tymes
samekil, as tha thigis quhilk at signifeit be sik
tymes. And in ane vther place(Popul°Christia- *Augu/l.*
nus memorias Martyrum religiosa deuotione *lib. 20. co-*
cócelebrat ad excitandum imitationem, & vt *tra Fau-*
meritis eorum consocietur, atque orationi- *stum.*
bus adiuuetur:). i. The Christiane people celebratis the memorie of the Martyris vith
ane Godlie deuotion, ta moue thame selfis to

imitation and follouing of thair gud lyfis, and
that thay may haue folloufchip and participation of thair merites, and be helpit be thair
prayeris : And this vniuerfalie in al aiges hes
bene keipit be al Chriftianis to this day : And
is obferuit not ólie be vs quha ar Catholikes,
bot alfo be the Lauterianis in Germanie, be
the Zuinglianis in Sueishland, and be zour
nichtboutis in Inglád:fua that in this head ze
difagrie from al Chriftiã people in the varld,
mouit onlie be auarice as appearis , becaus ze
think it hurtful to zour gayn ád profeit gif ze
abftene from laboure vpone onie day by the
fonday, quhilk is alfo verie euil keipit amangis zou : And zit zour foirbearis quha obferuit al the halie dayis verie diligentlie, had als
gret veith and aboundance of al thingis, as ze
haue : And euin as thay did imploy thame felfis vith gret liberalitie to the honoring and
feruice of God , fua God did beftou his giftis
the mair liberallie vpone thame: Bot ze think
al tyme tint quhilk ze imploy in Goddis feruice , for the quhik caus God fédis fik dearth,
skairfnes, and hungar amangis zou, quhairof
yithout al doubt ze ar the cheif and principal
caus be tranfgreffion of the halie dayis, quhilk
calamitie gif the people reuenge not vpon
zour felfis, thay vil reuenge it vpon zour bairnis gif ze leif onie behind zou: And gif thay
fend thame not to the Gailzeonis, at the left
thay vil fend thame to Candie, to the effect
fua nobil ane cuntrey be not contaminat be

sik ane vnhappie and adulterous generatione,
quhilk peraduentur vil cum to pas sonear
nor ze beleue, sua that Dene Iohne Durie vith
his tua pistolatis, his lang gún and bricht mur-
reon may be thair captane general, to the
quhilk office he is mair meit nor to disput of
the hid mystereis of the Christian fayth: (Ane
fuil sumtymes may be ane prophet). As to the
vthir headis of treu religione concerning the
vse of Images, the Inuocation of Sanctis the
Honoring of the reliques, and Ganging in
Pilgramagis, I vil distingueis thame seueralie,
and speak of euerie ane of thame apairt.

OF IMAGIS.

CHAP. XXXIII.

Protestaon.

Q Vhat sayis thou than anent the vorshipping of
Imagis, seing the command is geuin be Exod.20.
God him self, thou sal mak na grauin
image?

B. Gif euerie command of God var tayne
eftir the outuart schau of the vordis, ād nocht
in the treu mening, thair vald monie thingis
appeir to be commandit vnfructfullie, as for Math. 5.
exemple, Gif thy richt hand hinder the cut it
of, and cast it in the fyre. Quhairfoir this commandiment concerning Imagis is nocht to
be sua vndirstādin, as gif God disalloued ima-

V iiij

ges altogidder in his kirk, and the vse thairof
bot that he forbiddis the Ieuis, quha var verie
bent to sik idolatrie, as thay had sene amang
the gentiles, to mak imagis beleuand thame
to be verie leuand Goddis, or to represent
God, as hauing the figure of onie thing ather
in heauin or earth: And thairfoir Moyses, quhé
he forbad to mak onie image, as kir, in quhat
liknes God had appeirit vnto thame? Declairing his mening to be that thay sould mak
na image, for the representatione of God, as
gif God had the figure of onie thing, quhilk
had appeirit vnto thame.

P. *Bot God alluterlie forbiddis to haue onie imuges*
in his kirk, for he, quha is ane incomprehensibil spi-
rit, may nocht be represented in ane material image.

B Zour assertione is manifest fals: becaus gif
God had alluterlie forbiddin images, he had
cómáditMoyses to breke this cómádimér, quha be his directione maid in the kirk of the
Ieuis, the imagis of tua Cherubinis, quha ar
Angellis in heuin : quha maid also the brasin
serpent in the vildernes : Salomon lykuyse
maid the images of tuel oxin, berand the brai-
sin sea, quhilk be thingis in the earth : ze can
nocht say, that God hes bene repugnant to
him self, or that he hes commandit tua contrare thingis: And thairfoir necessarlie ze man
confes that in the first command he did nocht forbid al erecting of images in his kirk,
bot onlie the erecting of onie image, quhilk
sonld represent god in onie figure sik asve per-

Exod. 25.
Num. 21.
3. Reg. 6.

faue in thingis in heauin or earth: I anfuere to
zou thairfoir, vith the ancient vrytar Tertullian aganis the Marcionitis quha denyand the
haill auld teftament, amangis vther reffonis *Tertul. lib*
propofed this, That the God of the auld tefta *2. contra*
ment vas repugnant to him felf, forbiddand *Marcio.*
Moyfes to mak onie image, and eftir commandand to mak the braifin ferpent, and the
Cherubinis: He anfueris to thame that thay
vndirftand nocht the command, becaus thay
confidder nocht the end quhairfoir god forbad to mak onie image, quhilk vas that he
onlie fould be vorshippit as God, and that na
image fould be maid to the quhilkhis honore
fould be geuin, for the quhilk ëd he cömandit
neuer onie image to be maid, bot onlie for fü
certane figne, or reprefentatione, as the braifin
ferpent vas commandit to be maid: And he
addis thairto, that gif it vas lefum to the lenis
to mak the braifin ferpent for the fignificatione of Chrift, hou mekil mair is it lefum to
mak the image of Chrift? Zea Petrus martyr *Petrus*
ane man of zour auin feôt confeffis, that it is *Martyr in*
lefum to mak the images of Chrift, the Virgi- *c. 8. iudiciū.*
ne Marie, and vther Sanôtis for ane halie reprefentatione of thame: And amãgis the Lauterianis zour brethrene, as ze cal thame, ze
knau in quhat honore is the image of the
Crucifix: And gif ze vil confidder the reffone quhairfore god forbad Moyfes to mak
Imagis, it vas becaus thair could na image be
lyk vnto god: bot fen the fecund perfone of

diuinitie hes tane flesshe lyk vnto ouris, and is becummit man, ve may màk ane image lyk vnto his humane nature: And thairfoir the caus for the quhilk God forbad Moyses to mak onie image, hes nocht place aganis vs, quhen ve mak the image of Christ, or of his Sanctis, as lang afoir the learnit vrytar Tertullian did teache. And I vald demàd zou, gif it be aganis the lau of nature, or nocht to mak imagis? Gif ze say that it is aganis the lau of nature, ze condem zour selfis, quha makis the imagis of Caluine, Beza, and vther heretikis: gif it be nocht aganis the lau of nature, it can nocht be euil of the self, bot onlie infafar as it is referrit to sum euil end : Bot the Catholiques makis al imagis for ane gud and godlie end, that is for remembrance of Christ, of his bitter Death and Passion, and that thairbie ve may vorship and honore him: Thairfoir suppois it had bene forbiddin to the Ieuis to mak onie images, it follouis nocht that it is forbiddin to vs, becaus as concerning the commandis of the auld lau, ve ar onlie obleist to that, quhilk is of the lau of nature, be the quhilk it is nocht forbiddin to mak onie image as said is, and sua Christ him self being demandit of the Ieuis, quhilk vas the first cōmand of the lau, he Ansueris nocht that the first vas, thou sal mak to thy self na grauin image, bot thou sal loue thy lord God vith al thy hart, vith al thy mynd, vith al thy pouar: This is confirmit be the hail antiquitie, for

Tertul. lib 2. cont. Marcio.

Math. 22

as teſtifeis monie ancient vryttaris S. Luc. him ſelf maid certane images of our Ladie, quhilk ar pairtlie keipit to this day: And Nicephorus teſtifeis that Chriſt did ſend his auin image to Abagar[9] the kíg of Edeſſa: ád the hemorrhoiſſa, quha vas hailit, quhair of thair is mentione maid in the Euangel, did erect ane image vnto Chriſt, quhilk na man reprouet, vnto the tyme of Iulian the Apoſtat, quha pullit it doune ád placed his auin image thair, quhilk vas ſtrukin done vith the thundir: Athanaſius vryttis, hou that the Ieuis throuche hetret of Chriſt, perſed his image, and hou the blude did ſpring out of it, be the quhilk miracle tha Ieuis var conuertit to the fayth: Metaphraſtes vryttis, hou that Siluſeter Biſchop of Rome, ſcheu to Conſtantinus Magnus the imagis of Petir and Paul, quha be ane reuelatione in liknes of ſik imagis, had appeirit to Conſtantinus Magnus befoir: And S. Auguſtine de conſenſu Euangeliſtarum teſtiſeis, hou the cuſtume of the Roman kirk vas that the images of S. Petir and S. Paul vſit to be payntit beſyd the image of Chriſt : S. Chryſoſt in ane oraeſon maid of ane Martyr Miletius , is vitnes alſo, hou that the image of the ſaid Martyr, vas reuerentlie keipit be the Chriſtianis: Gregorius Nicenus makis ane lág diſcourſe of the image of Abrahame , and the immolatione of his ſone Iſaac, hou it mouit his hairt to teiris and compaſsione. And Damaſus in the lyf of Conſtantine vryttis,

Metaphra in vita luca. Theod. lector in collecta. li. 1. cap. 14. Niceph. li. 5. cap. 14. Niceph. li. 2. c. 7. Euſeb. lib. 7. cap. 14. Sozom. li. 5. cap. 20. Athanaſ. in lib. de paſsione imag. chriſti.

Metaphraſtes in vita Silueſtri.

Augu. de conſenſu euangeliſtarum.

Chryſo. in oratio. De Miletio.

that he did offer vnto the kirk ane image of Christ maid of gold, and the imagis of the tuelfe Apostlis in siluer. And Theodoret descryuand the lyf of the halie man Simeon, testifeis that the Christianis in that age, vsit to haue his image in thair housis: Procopius, and Nicephorus testifeis also, quhen the toune of Edessa vas seagit be Cosdroas the king of Perse, and almaist tane, hou that the Christianis quha had keipit the image of Christ quhilk he had sed befoir to Abagar the king of Edessa being desparit of al vther remedeis, did bring furth that image, quhairbie al the interpryssis of thair aduersaris var ouercummit: And to cum to our auin Ile, quhen Augustine vas send be the Bischop of Rome to conuert Ingland to the fayth, as vitnessis the maist lerned Beda, for his baner he vsit olie the signe of the Croce and the image of the Crucifixe: As the Emperor Constantinus Magnus monie hundreth zeiris befoir did, as vitnessis Eusebius, to quhom the Croce did appeir in the air, quhen he vas to fecht aganis the tyrann Macentius, vith this inscriptione, In hoc signo vinces, And this hes bene the signe of al Christian men, quhairbie thay haue bene knauin, and discernit from the Ieuis and infidellis, and vrocht sumtymes miraculous vorkis: Thairfoir sayis the maist ancient Tertulliane, Befoir al our actionis ve vse to mak the signe of the Croce vpone vs: The lyk testifeis al vther an-

Damasus in vita Siluestri.
Theodo. in vita Simeonis.
Nicephor. lib.18.c.16
Beda li.1. cap. 25.
Euseb. in vita Constantini.
Tertul. de corona militis.

cient vryttaris, fua ze may perfaue that ve do
na thing in this poynt, bot that quhilk is
conforme to goddis vord, and to the vfe, and
practeife of the vniuerfal kirk befoir vs.

Pr. *The imagis quhilk var vfit in the Kirk, var*
the caus of horribil Idolatrie, and thairfoir fould Reg.4.ca.
haue bene brokin, eftir the exempil of the gude king 18.
Ezechias, quha deftroyit the braifin ferpent, qu-
hairof thou makis mentione, quhen it vas the caus
of Idolatrie.

B. This is ane commone place, qnhairfra ze
collect fophiftical argumentis: from the abufe of ane gude thing to deftroy it alluterlie,
and the richt vfe thairof: Be the fam argument ze may collect that the fone, and the
mone fould haue bene tane out of the firma-
ment, becaus thay var vorshippit be the gentiles as goddis : And ze may collect that
zour merchandis fould nocht pas to burde-
oufe to bring hame vyne, becaus it makis
monie of zour headdis diffie : And monie
vther ficlyk collectionis micht be maid als
gude as zouris, quhilk vald not be verie pro-
fitabill to the commonweil : For this argument from abufe feruis mair, to proue the
contrare conclufione, becaus it follouis veil:
Imagisvar abufit, thairfoir thay ar gude in the
felf, for that quhilk is euil be abufe onlie, of
neceffitie man be gude being veil vfed. As to
the fimilitude of the braifin ferpent, it makis
nathing for the mentenance of zour errore,
becaus the richt vfe of it feruit for ane tyme

onlie, to vit falang as the peopil remaning in
the vildernes, var ftangit bethe fyrie ferpentis:
Quhairfoir the richt vfe thairof ceiffing, efter
thay had entered in the land of Chanaã, It vas
iuftlie deftroyit, becaus the peopil offerit in-
cens to it, follouand the exempil of the Idolatrous nationis: quhil as be the contrare, ze neuer hard that onie Chriftiane offerit to ane
image: And gif onie fik abufe had bene cõmit
ted, it aucht to haue bene tane auay be publik
authoritie eftir diligent infpectione and con-
fideratione of the mater, ãd nocht be the peopil, as ze haue done : I reid that ane thoufãnd
zeir fyne ane Serenus Bifchop of Maffilia be
fik ane zeal as ze haue , did brek doune
fum imagis : Bot Gregorius the firft , Bifchop of Rome reprouit him maift fchar-
plie that he had done by his deutie, and that
neuer onie bifchop befoir him had interpry-
fit onie fik thing: Bot ze appeir to attribute les to men nor ze do to doggis quha hes
na participation of reafon , for ane dog can
difcern betuix ane hair and the image of ane
hair : be reafson he vil rin to tak ane hair
gif he fe hir, bot albeit he fe payntit, the maift
viue image of ane hair that can be deuyfit, he
vil not moue him out of his place : And zit
ze vil that men be fua daft , that thay can
nocht difcern betuix ane man, and the image
of ane man.

*Prot. Bot quhil as the Papiftis in thair kirkis in
tyme of prayeris behalding thair Idolis and imageſ*

Gregor.
lib.9.
epift.9.

fel doune on thair kneis, vithout al doubt thay var Idolateris.

B. Sence ane Idol is that propirlie, quhilk being nathing, is reprefentit to be fum thing: or that quhilk reprefentis the thing that is nocht: ze can not cal the Images of the Crucifix, of the Virgin Marie, of al the Apoftlis and Sanctis, Idolis, vnles ze beleue that thair vas neuer fik ane thing as Chrift crucifeit, as the Virgin Marie, as the Apoftlis, and Sanctis: For it follouis necefsarlie, The Image of Chrift crucifeit is ane Idol, thairfoir Chrift vas neuer crucifeit: This is the hid vennum quhilk lurkis in the hairtis of the blafphemous Proteftaons quhen thay cal the imagis that ar in the Chriftian kirkis, Idolis. Bot to zour obiection: Thay var na mair Idolatoris quhen entering in the kirk of God, and be infpection of the Imagis being brocht in memorie of onie benefeit refauit of God, thay fel doun on kneis to gif thankis, and craif grace in tyme cumming, nor ze reiding zour prayeris vpon zour bukes vryttin, hauand zour ene fixed vpon the Paper at idolatoris: Sua that thay ar maift ignorant and deftitut not onlie of fupernatural grace, bot of natural wit alfo quha grantisthe vfe of the bukis vryttin in the kirk of God, and refufis the vfe of imagis, quhilk thing the Deuil perfytlie foirfau quhen he mouit his minifteris to burn al the bukis and monumentis of the Doctoris, lyk as be thame he deftroyit the imagis, to bring the miserabil people in obliuion of the thingis signifeit thairbie : The Anabaptistis ar les blindit in this poynt, nor the rest of the Antichristian Protestaons, for thay refuse the vord vryttin and vse thairof, lyk as thay haue done the images, ād lukis for reuelationis out of heauin : Becaus the vord vryttin and images hes sik affinitie in thair substance, vse, and end, that nane can be deuysed mair : for gif I vald compair euerie thing requeset to the ane, and to the vthir, this vil appeir maist manifest. Becaus in the bukis vryttin, the matet quhairof thay ar maid cōmonlie is paper, ane artificial thing inuentit be the brayn of man: In the imagis correspondent to this, is ane quhyt val, biggit be ane Craftis man: To vryt the bukis, is requirit ane scrib or craftis man learned to vryt vith pen and ink, quha be letteris (quhais formes var also excogitat be the brayn of man) trauelis to expres the images and memorialis of thingis done, as he hes treulie consauit thame in his mynd, that be representation invryt thay may estiruart be callit to our memorie, as for exemple he vryttis the hail historie of the passion of Christ: To ane scrib vith pen and ink, is correspōdent ane paynter vith his pinset and coloris, quha drauis the images of tha sam thingis vpon ane quhyt val correspondent to the paper, for the sam vse, and end : Nou gif ze quha ar learnet at the schuillis be nocht ane Idolater becaus ze behald the Paper as

requesit

requesit to bring zou in memorie of Chriſtis
Paſſion, and al the circumſtancis thairof: Quhy ſould the ignorāt pleuch mā, quha als perfytlie be help of the payntrie deſcryuis the
hail Paſsion of Chriſt, as ze deſcriue the ſam
be zour buk vryttin, be comptit ane Idolater
becaus he fallis doune on his kneis to rander
thākis to God quha hes inſpyrit his hairt vith
remembrance of tha thingis quhilk ar repre-
ſentit be the paintrie? For he vorſhippis na
mair that thing quhilk he behaldis nor ze dó
the buke: Gif the Images hes bene abuſit, ſua
vas, and is, the buk vryttin abuſit mair miſe-
rabillie, and vith gretar loſs of ignorant ſaulis:
Becaus al heretikis thrauis the ſentencis of the
buke for eſtablishīg of thair erroneoꝰ doctrine, to thair auin perdition: Quhairfoir as the
vſe of Imagis ſeruis mekil for edification and
inſtruction of the vnlearned people, ſua thay
labore to bring the people to Atheiſme, quha
refuſis to haue thame in thair kirkis and priuat houſis: For gif Theodor Beze vas mouit to
compaſſion be inſpection of the imagis of his *Beza in*
Apoſtat brethrene, as he teſtifeis of him ſelf: *lib. Iconū.*
think ze it not als reaſonabil, that be inſpection of the image of Chriſt being iuſt and Innocent put to maiſt ſchameful death for our
ſynnis, vé be mouit to beuail our auin faultis
and rander him thankis for ſua gret ane benefeit? Quhat man is ſua mad that vil think
that is vas leſum to Theodore Beze to paynt
the Imagis of fals, traittorous, and deceatful

X

hæretikis, and vnlesum to treu Catholikes to
haue the images of Chrift reprefentit as he
vas ane bairne in the armes of his glorious
Mother the virgine Marie : And lykuyfe of
Chrift Crucifeit, as be his paffion on the croce he triumphit ouer the Deuil and al his Apo-
ftat Angellis, he abolifhed death and reconci-
liat the varld to his father of heauin ? Thair is
na man in his richt vit quha behalding onie
image trampit vndir fut, vil not efilie collect
that the perfone reprefentit thairbie is con-
temnit : Bot albeit Beze defyris rather to behald the images of Audebert quhom he bou-
grit, and Candida vith quhom he committit
Adulterie, nor of the virgin Marie the mother
of the leuing God, quha redemit the varld, and
of Chrift Iefus hir fone quha deed to mak fatisfaction for our fynnis, zit I think gude to
propone to zou thair images, that ze may có-
fidder vith zour felfis hou lytil difference is
betuix paynting and vrytting, fence thay ferue
bayth to ane propos.

OF THE INVOCATION.
OF SANCTIS.
CHAP. XXXIIII.

X ij

Bot Ze ar not content to haue the images of the virgine Marie and the sanctis, vnles Ze cal vpon thame for support, quhil as the inuocatiō of Sanctis is vnlesum: becaus it is vryttin, thay can not cal vpon him in quhom thay beleue not, *Bot Christian men beleuis not in the Sanctis: thairfoir thay may not cal vpon thame.*

Rom. 10.

B. This zour argument, be abusing the halie scripture, is collectit out of ane vther sophistical place callit in the schuillis [Homonymia] to detene ignorāt people in blindnes: for inuocation is tane tua maner of vayis, first for the incalling of the author of grace, quha may according to his omnipotent pouar, mak help of na thīg: of the quhilk S. Paul speakis in this place be zou allegit, and this is propir to God onlie: Vtheruyse it is tane for requesting of thame quha ar membris of ane kirk vithvs, to mak vs support be praying vith vs to God, that ve may obtene our petitione in the name of Christ Iesus onlie mediator betuix God and man: quhilk inuocation is commandit vs, insafar as euerie membir of Christis kirk sould request ane another for mutual prayer, gif it be possibil.

M. Ve may require mē leuād vpō the face of the earth to pray for vs, becaus thay ar membris of ane kirk vith vs, bot ve aucht not to require thame quha ar deid

*Hieron. cō
tra vigi-
lantium.*

B. Sanct Hierom tuelf hundreth zeiris sensyne ansuerit to zour argument, That gif the Martyris ād halie men quhē thay vat vpō the face of the earth, and subiect to the infirmitie

of thair bodeis and fyn, as vther men, micht
impetrat fua monie thingis from God, hou
mekil mair being in heauin delyuerit from al
fyn, and crounit vith gloir and immortalitie
may thay obtene quhatfumeuer thay ask?
And gif Sanct Paul being in this varld did
pray fua feruentlie for al tha people quhilk
he conuertit to the fayth of Chrift, is it liklie
that quhen he is in heauin, he vil cloife his
mouth, and forzet thame al aluterlie?

Quhairfoir it is plane infidelitie to doubt that
the halie Sanctis may heir our petitionis, fen
thay haue the fruitione of God, and acknau-
ledgis al thingis quhilk thay defyre to knau
côcerning vs : And hauand Cheritie, and loue
touardis vs, as S. Paul teftifeis, that fam felf *1.Cor.13.*
Cheritie man moue thame bayth to defyre to
acknauledge our eftait, and in lyk maner to
help vs : vtheruyfe thay vald haue les cair of
vs, nor the Riche glutone, quha vas condem- *Luc. 16.*
nit to hel, had of his brethrene: And thair Che
ritie vald auail vs na thing at al, quhilk is ane
blafphemie: Quhair ze fay that theSâctis apertenis nocht to the bodie of Chrift, it is ane
manifeft blafphemie, for Chrift hes nocht tua
bodeis, bot ane : fua neceffarlie the fanctis of
heauin apertenis to his bodie, quhilk is his
kirk : as amangis vtheris S. Auguftine in his   *Aug. de*
bukis of the Citie of god, and aganis Fauftus   *ciuitate*
Manichæus fchauis maift manifeftlie : Sua be-   *Dei, &*
ing membris of ane bodie vith vs neceffarlie   *côtra Fauf*
thair man be fum communicatione betuix vs   *tum.*

X iij

and thame, And as euerie membir is helpful,
and profeitful to vtheris, fua it is neceffar
that thay being the maift cheif and principal
membris, be alfo maift profitabil and helpful vnto vs: Thairfoir Chrift hes declaret
be monie miracles that fik prayer vnto
the fanctis is plefand vnto him. S. Auguftine
Augu. in
lib. de cura in his buke de cura pro mortuis agenda, maift
pro mortuis planelie teftifeis hou that quhen the toune of
agenda. Nola vas feagit be the Gothis and Vandalis, Felix quha vas fumtyme bifchop of that
toune apperit vpone the vallis of the toune,
Nicepho. and defendit it. Nicephorus, and vther hi-
lib. 12. ca. ftoriographoris vryttis hou that Theodofi-
39. us the Emperore in al his troublis vfit to haue recourfe to S. Iohne, ãd hou that in the bat-
tel, quhilk he had aganis Maximus the tyrã,
quha inuadit his impyre, S. Iohne apperit vnto him in the nicht, and did forfchau the
victorie quhilk he vas to obtene aganis his
Nazian. ennemie. Gregorius Nazianzenus teftifeis,
in oratione hou that Iuftina ane halie voman being allu-
de Cypria. rit to fyn be vitchcraft, did cal vpone the help
& Iuftina. of our Ladie the mother of god, and be hir in-
terceffione did ouercum al the tentatione of
the deuil: I micht cite zou monie vther lyk
teftimoneis of the antiquitie quhairbie ze
micht vndirftand that this hes bene the Doctrine quhilk euer hes bene profeffed in the
kirk of Scotland fen the beginning, as ze
zour felfis can nocht misknau, hou that in
the tyme of S. Hierom, Vigilantius vas con-

demnit for ane Hæretik, becaus he denyit the *Hiero. ad*
Inuocatione of Sanctis, as is manifest in the *Riparium.*
buke of S. Hierom aganis him: Thair vas
sum in the age of Tertulliane, quha defendit *Tertull.in*
that sam self hæresie, aganis quhom Tertulli- *Scorpiaco.*
ane for defence of the veritie vrait ane buke
quhilk he callit Scorpiacum, as testifeis also
S. Hierom: sua ze, and al vtheris quha defendis this errore, var condemnit in zour foirfatheris befoir ze var borne.

M. Gif the Angellis and Sanctis of heauin micht
heir our petitionis, that thairby thay var mouit to
pray for vs, it var necessar that thay kneu the
secreitis of our hairtis, quhilk is propir to god
onlie.

B. Albeit God be onlie searchar of the secreit-
tis of the hairt, zit it follouis nocht that the
Angellis may nocht knau the sam : Becaus
that quhilk aggreis to God onlie be nature,
aggreis to the Angellis be participatione, and
special gift of God : For the quhilk caus our *Matt.19.*
saluiour Christ callis God onlie gude, albeit ze
vil nocht deny, bot the Angellis quhilk fel
nocht vith Lucifer ar gude also. That the Angellis, and lykuyse the Sanctis depairted, quha ar callit be our saluiour Christ ressonand *Matt.22.*
aganis the Sadducæis ἰσάγγελα, knauis the secreitis of our hairtis, it is manifest in the *S. Luca 5.*
Euangel of S. [Luc.I say vnto zou that thair
salbe gretar Ioy in heauī for ane synnar repē-
tand, than for nyntie nyne iust men quha
hes na mister of repentance:] gif than the An-

gelis, and Sanctis reioyfis for the repentance of ane fynnar, thay man knau quhidder
the fam be vnfenzeit or nocht: And fence the
firft pairt of Repetance confiftis in the dolore of the hairt, to vndirftand quhidder this be
hypocritall, or proceiding from the loue of
iuftice, thay man knau the maift hid fecreitis
of the hairt : And gif the Propheittis be reuelatione of God kneu tha thingis quhilk
var to cum monie hundreth zeiris eftir, zea
did penetrat fumtymes the hairtis, and cogita-
tionis of men, as ze may reid of Elias, and Elifæus, hou can ze deny that to the Sanctis,
and Angelis of heuin quha ar indeuit vith
gretar illuftrationis, nor euir at onie tyme var
the Prophetis, or mortal men in this earth?
And gift ze, quha ar miferabil men on the
earth, knau that the Angelis ar in heauin, and
in fælicitie, thay hauad ane mair perfyt cogni-
tione, man knau in lyk maner that ze ar in
miferie: or ellis ze vil attribute vnto zour felf
farder knauledge of the eftait of thame quha
ar in heauin, nor thay haue of zour eftait, quhilk is ane blafphemie : Than fen thay can
nocht misknau that ve ar in miferie, as thay
misknau nocht bot thir bodeis fal ryfe vpone
the latter day, and that the day of iudgement
is not zit cumed, and that the number of thair
brethrene is nocht zit accomplished, bot monie of thame ftryuand in this vaill of miferie,
albeit it var granted to zou, that thay kneu
nocht our thochtis, zit being in that place

Reg. 4.
ca. 5.6.

quhair thay micht help vs, louing vs, ad vndir
standing that ve ar in miſerie, thay vald nocht
deſiſt to pray for vs : As ze, ſuppoiſe ze be in
Scotlad, zit ze pray for zour brethrene i Frace,
albeit ze penetrat nocht the thochtis of thair hairtis: And gif it vas leſnm to willox,
kmnox, and ſum vtheris of the Miniſteris quha profeſsis vitchcraft and ſorcerie, to cal vpo
the deuillis, and reſaue thair ſupport as did
Craig quha be his auin confeſsion reſſauit
ane purſe ful of Gold fra ane blak dog paſ-
ſand throuch Italie, quhilk vas ane great occa-
ſio quhairbie he vas mouit to reioyſe for licht
leing of his Coule, and tak him to the Mini-
ſtrie : Quhy ſal it nocht be leaſum to vs to
cal vpon the halie Anglis of heauin and
Sanctis of God? Sen at the leſt thay may al-
ueil heir vs and knau our deſyris as the deuil
did ather heir willox and kmnox, or Knau the
deſyre of Gold and Honoris kendillit in the
hairt of the Apoſtat Craig, quhen he ſend him
ane purſe be ane of his Apoſtat Angelis in
liknes of ane blak dog: to ſignifie that be geuing obedience to the ſecret ſuggeſtionis of
the deuil hevas to becu ane odious tyk barking aganis al treuth, aganis the authoritie of
Chriſtis veilbelouit ſpous the kirk, and halie
ſanctis quha ar nou in heauin, denying lykuyſe the reuerence quhilk treu Chriſtianis exhibit to thair reliques as the ve ſchellis of
the halie Ghaiſt , for confirmation of thair

fayth concerning the ryfing agane of thir fam self bodeis vpon the day of iudgement.

OF THE HONORE THAT
in the Catholique kirk vfis to be exhibit to the reliques of the Sanctis.

CHAP. XXXV.

Minifter.

THinKis thou it nocht ane fuperftitious thing to tuiche deid mennis banes and to abyd thairbie onie benefeit of health, or onie fik thing, as the Papiftis ar accuftumed to do in thair kirkis?

B. Gif this be fuperftitione, the Chriftianis euin in the Apoftlis dayes hes bene fuperftitious, as quhen thay did put thame felfis in the fchaddou of S. Petir, as ve reid in the actis of the Apoftlis, and quhen thay caused the naipkinnis, ãd mutfchis of Paul to be brocht to thame, that be the tuiching of thame thay micht be delyuerit from thair difeafis: confidering thair is na les force in the reliques of Petir nor vas in his fchaddou, and thair is na les force in the reliques of S. Paul, nor vas in his naipkinnis and mutfchis. By that, gif this had bene fuperftitione, God vald neuer haue approuit it be fa monie miracles, as he hes done, quhairof ze may reid S. Auguftine in the tuentie tui buke of the citie of god, quhair amangis vtheris he fchauis hou beand prefent in the toune of Millen, the reliques of the halie MartyrisGeruasius, and Protasius var fund, and hou that ane blind man did tak his naipkin, and tuiche the said reliques, and hauing put it to his eyne, vas incontinent restorit to his sicht: The lyke he schauis of ane blind voman quha hauing brocht certane flouris to the reliques of S. Stephane and hauing put thame to hir eyis, vas incontinent restored to hir sicht. S. Hierome in his buke aganis Vigilantius declairis at lenth, hou that thay quha ar possessit vith the deuillis, quhen thay cum befoir the reliques of the Martyris, ar delyvered: And in lyk maner ve reid of the halie bischop Marcellus, quha passed to Ingland to refel the heresie of Pelagius, hou quhé ane blind voman vas presented to him, he did tuiche hir eyis vith certane reliques quhilk he bure vith him, and scho thairbie recouered hir sicht: Theodoret in his buke de curandis græcanicis affectionibus, geuis sufficient proue thairof, and hou that the Chiistianis, be the miracles quhilk ordinarlie var done be the reliques of the Martyris, vsed to confirme the treuthe and veritie of the Christiane religione, becaus that euin the Martyris, quhen thay appered to be ouercummed and vincused, var maist starke, and did voik euin miraculous vorkis, to the quhilk argument the Gentiles had na vther thing to say, bot that sik voikis var done be the craft, and subtilitie of the deuil, as amangis vtheris testifeis Sanct Hierom

Hierom. contra Vigilátium.

Theod. lib. 8. de curädis græcanicis affectionibus.

Hieron.cõ
tra Vigi-
lantium.
aganis Vigilantius. The Gentiles, sayis he, Por
phyrius, and Eunomius, sayis that al thir thingis ar done be the illusione of the deuiles, quhais futstoppis ze ar nocht eschamed to fol-
Petrus
·Martyr
in 18. Ind.
lou: zea Petrus Martyr zour great Prophete to-
stifers that he can nocht deny that sik miracles sindrie tymes hes bene done, bot that
God permitted thame to be done for to diffa-
ue and begyl men be thame, euin as God var
ane deceauer lyk Petrus Martyr, quha, gif he
had bene in the primitiue kirk, vald haue ad-
ioyned him self to the Gentiles, and Infidelis
aganis the Christianis, in denying the force
and strenth of sik miraclis, as the Christianis
vsed for ane cheif confirmatione of thair
fayth.

*M. Ze may cloike the mater as Ze pleise, Zit I se na
vay quhairby Ze may eschaip the crime of Idolatrie,
quha vorshippis deid mennis banes.*

B Ze schau zour self to be ane Ieu, Samari-
tane, or ane Gentile that makis sik ane obiectione to me, considering ze can nocht mis-
Hieron.cõ
tra Vigi-
lantium.
knau the ansuere, quhilk S. Hierom gaue to
Vigilantius in the fame verie caus, quhen Vigilantius callit him and al vther Catholiques
Idolatouris, becaus thay vorshippit deid mennis banes : Sayis S. Hierome, daft man, quha-
euer amãgis the christianis hes vorshippit deid
mennis banes ? ve vorship nocht, sayis he,
the reliques of the Martyris as godis, bot ve
honore thame as veschellis, and tabernaclis in
the quhilk the spirit of god did vmquhyl mak

refidence, and quhilkis ar to be honorit be
God him felf vith gloir and immortalitie: and
zit ve honore nocht the banes of the deid, becaus the martyris ar nocht deid bot leuisvnto
God, he nocht being the God of the deid, bot
of the quik, as he fayis him felf: And gif in *Matt. 22.*
the auld teftamēt the Ieuis had in fua great ho
nore the Ark of the teftament, and the propi-
tiatoure, onlie becaus that God in ane fpecial
maner vfed to declair his prefence in fik places, hou mekil mair aucht ve to haue the haliè
reliques of the Martyris, quha hes bene the
verie templis of God, in honore and venera-
tione? as euer al treu Chriftian men hes had
befoir vs: quhairof ze may reid S. Hierome
in the faid place, hou that Conftantinus Magnus the Emperour, caufed tranfport the reliques of S. Andro, S. Luke, and S. Timothie to
Conftantinopil: Arcadius caufed tranflate the
banes of the Prophet Samuel out of Iudæa
to Thracia: Theodofius zoungar commandit *Georgius*
that the reliques of S. Chryfoft. vith al honore *Alexādri.*
fould be tranfportit to Conftantinopil: and *nus.*
Theodoret teftifeis, hou that al the peopil of
Conftantinopil vith great honore did pas befoir the faid reliques in Bofphorus, as gif thay
had bene on the land, and conuoyed thame *Theodorét*
to the toune of Conftantinopil, vith torchis, *lib.5.ca.36*
and lampis: Thairfoir S. Auguftine prouokis *S. Aug.*
the Gétiles to fchau that the fepulture of Ro- *de Ciuit.*
mulus vas keipit in fua great honore, as Chri- *Dei.*
ftianis fchauis the fepulturis of the Martyris to

haue bene keipit. And S.Hierome vrittand to Marcella, ve haue in honore the sepultures of the Martyris, and ve tuiche our eyis vith thair halie reliques, and kissis thame vith our mouthis: And Amianus Marcellinus quha vas bot ane Gentile, testifeis in his historie descryuand the persecutione of the Christianis in the toune of Rome, hou that the Gētiles vsed to cast the bodeis of the Martyres in the flude of Tyber, to the end that the Christiane mē sould nocht honore thame. The lyk ve reid to haue bene done in sindrie vther places, be the infidelis as be king Lisinius in Sebaste ane toune in Armenia, and vtheris. Ze Iulian the Apostat, as vitnessis Cyrillus in his bukis aganis him, obiected to the Christian men, that nocht onlie thay vorshippit Christ, bot aganis his command, thay honorit the reliques of the Martyris, quhairof ve may considder quhais futstoppis ze follou in dishonoring and burning the halie reliques of the Martyres, that is of the maist vickit infidelis, and cruel Apostatis: Quhat gif Sanct Hierome var leuand in thir dayes? Quhat sadnes and desolatione vald he haue to se tha thingis done be thame quha callis thame Christiane men, quhilk he deplored sua mekil to se done be the maist vngodlie and barbarus peopil in the varld, vrytād in this maner [Capti Episcopi, interfecti Presbyteri, subuersæ Ecclesiæ, ad Altaria Christi stabulant equi, Martyrum effossæ reliquiæ, vbique luctus, vbique gemitus?

Hiero. ad Marcellā.

Amianus Marcellinus.

Basilius de 40. Martyribus.

Cyrillus in lib. contra Iulianum.

Hieron. ad Heliodorum.

quot monasteria capta? quot fluuiorum aquæ humano sanguine mutatæ sunt? The bischopis ar tane, the Preistis ar slayne, The kirkis ouerthrauin, hors ar stabillit at the altaris of Christ, the Reliques of the Martyris ar delued vp, ouer alquhair thair is dolore, ouer alquhair murning: hou monie abbayes ar tane? hou monie fludis of valter ar changit in mennis blude?

M. Ze ar nocht content to honore Zour reliques, except that Ze cleyth thame with gold, and precious staones, and in the mentyme Ze lat the pure quha ar the quik membris of Christ dea for hungar.

B. Gif ve reid in the auld testament that the Ark and the propitiatore var sua richelie appareled, hou can ve doubt bot the reliques of the Sanctis, quhilkis ar the verie tabernacles of the halie spirit, sould be estemed vorthie of al apparel? zea of greatar nor the pouartie of man may attene to, sen God him self is to adorne thame vith the gift of gloir and immortalitie? Bot ze, as ansuerit sumtymes S. Hierom to Vigilantius, ar verie soriful that thay ar not castin in the middinis, or coueritvith sect clayth: as Iudas the traittour vas sorie that Christis feit var oynted vith sua pretious ane vnguent: Sua ve do na thing bot that, quhilk the kirk of God hes euer done befoir vs, as Sanct Hierom and vther authoris dois testifie. And Sozomenus vryttis hou that Pulcheria Augusta did couer the reliques of the fourtie Martyris vith ane maist pretiouscouer

Lib.9.hist. cap.11.

ture. And ze zour selfis cleythis zour vyuis
vith silkis and veluot, quha ar nocht sua precious veschellis of the halie Ghaist, and zit ze
esteme nocht zour selfis idolateris . Quhair
ze say that the pure in the mentyme ar naikit
ze appeir to tak Iudas pairt aganis Christ,
quhen he said that the oyntment vith the qu-
Matt.26. hilk Christ vas oynted micht haue bene sellit
and geuin to the pure folk: Zea ze haue sellit in verie deid al the precious ornamentis
of the reliques of the Martyris in the Realme
of Scotland, bot the pure folk ar mair naikit
nor euer thay var.

*M. Bot thinkis thou it nocht ane vaine thing to
licht lampis and vax candillis befoir the reliques of
the Martyres in fair day licht, the sone schynad mair
cleirlie nor onie candil, and to bring flouris quhair
vith thay may be buskit.*

B. Theodoret in his aucht buke de curandis
Theodoret græcanicis affectionibus, ansueris to zour ar-
lib.8. de gument, quhilk vas obiected to him be the
curandis
græcanicis Gentiles, that ve licht the candelis befoir the
affectioni- reliques of the Martyris, nocht that thay haue
bus. mister of licht, bot for professione, and protestatione of our fayth , to testifie that the
sanctis ar in the eternal licht of gloir and immortalitie : And S. Hierom vryttand aganis
Vigilantius quha maid the lyk obiectione to
him, ansuerit also, that the Christiane peopill
vsed to licht candellis and lampis befoir the
reliques of the Martyris, for declaratione of
the loue and zeal quhilk thay beir vnto thame
The

The quhilk zeale, he doubtis nocht, bot is acceptabil vnto God, as vas the zeale of thame quha did put thame selfis in the schaddou of Sanct Petir, and vas hailled from al thair diseasis: And thairfoir for ane halie significatione and professione of fayth, quhen the Euangel is red, sayis he, ve vse to licht Torchis, for to declair that the Euangel is the licht of the varld : And in Christiane mēnis buriallis as testifeis Gregorius Nazianzenus, Torchis and lampis vsed euer to be lichted, for ane demōstratione that thay pas to that licht quhilk surpassis the vit and vndirstāding of man: Bot ze, as sonis of darknes, heaue na vil of licht, according to the saying of our saluiour, (he that dois euil heattis the licht,) and thairfoir ze gloir sua mekil, in zour inuisibil kirk, becaus it hes neuer sene the licht, thir thousand and fyue hūdreth zeiris bypast, and depairting from this varld ze vil nocht that at zour burialis torchis be lichted, to mak protestatione that ze pas to that place, quhair thair is na licht at al, bot ane maist feirful horrore, darknes, and obscuritie vithout confort. Quhair as ze obiect that the Catholikes buskis the reliques of the Martyris vith flouris, ze appeir to haue cōsauit ane inquensibil anger aganis the halie reliques, considering ze vil that na kynd of ornament at al be granted vnto thame, nor zit thatve do onie thing quhairbie ve may declair our loue and affectione touardis thame : For the flouris signifeis the sueit and

Gregorius Naziāz.

Y

precious sauore of thair gude vorkis befoir God., quhilk ve alfo profes quhen ve adorne thame, and valkinnis our felfis thairbie to follou thair futft oppis, and halie exemple. Thairfoir Sanct Hierome vryttand of Nepotianus, louis him that he vas accuftumed to apparel the kirkis of theMartyris vith flouris, vith the branchis of the treis and vther fik ornamentis : And Sanct Auguftine vryttis of ane blind voman quha brocht flouris to the reliques of Sanct Stephane, quha efter fcho had tuiched his reliques vith thame, be tuiching hir auin eyne vith the fame, vas reftorit to hir ficht agane : quhairot ze may efilie vndirftand, that God vald nocht haue confirmit and approuit the deid of this voman be fua greit ane miracle, gif it had miflykit him. Bot ze ar foriful that famekil as ane floure fould haue bene applyit to onie halie vfe, or fignificatione, follouing the futft oppis of zour foir father Iudas.

Hiero. ad Heliodorum.

Aug. 21. e ciuitate Dei. ca. 8.

OF THE PILGRAMAGIS.

CHAP.   XXXVI.

Minifter.

THe people vas gretumlie abufit be the honoring of Zour reliques, infafar as vithout onie cōmēdation of Goddis expreß vryttin vord, Pilgramagis to the kirkis and grauis of Zour Martyris var inioynit to the ruid and ignorant people, as gif God var nocht alyk potent in al place, and his pouar of virking mi-

raclis var limitat tö tha pairtis önlie quhair Zour Sanctis var bureit.

B. Infafar as na man can be abufit be doing of that onlie quhilk apertenis to his deuitie, the people vas nauyfe mifufit be the reuerence quhilk thay buir to the reliques of the Sāctis,as the maift precious vefchellis of Goddis maift halie Spirit, to quhais honor al reuerence exhibit befoir the reliques of the Martyris, did redound: And it var lang to reherfe al the teftimoneis of fcripture quhairbie Pilgramagis ar gretumlie commendit, lyk as the myfterie thairof is verie great,declairing hou fyn is the caus quhy ve pas from God, and that it behouis vs to fuftene trauel and pane,gif ve fal returne to Goddis fauore agane.For the thrie kingis ar gretumlie commēdit in the fcripture, quha come out of the far pairtis of the Eaft,to viffie our faluiour Chrift Iefus at his natiuitie vith offerandis : In lyk maner the Quene of Saba, quha vifeit Hierufalem to heir the vifdome of Salomon. Siclyk our halie faluiour Chrift commendis the Pilgrammage of Naaman the Syrian, to Elifæus the prophete, be quhom he vas hailed of his leprofie, Albeit monie in Hierufalem quha var neirar hand, deed in thair feiknes: And al the Ieuis vfit to mak ane folemne Pilgramage to the toune of Hierufalem,as is cleir in Goddis vord. Ve misknau nocht that God is ouer al, and that his infinit pouar is nocht limitat to onie certane place, bot may

Matth.3.

S. Luc.4.

4. Regü 5.

Y ij

vorke equallie in al places, zit it hes pleifed
his infinit vifdome, and fapiéce to fchau mair
fingular vorkis in ane place, nor ane vthir:
as ane fpecial grace vas promifed to thame
quha fould pray in the kirk of Hierufalem,
quhilk Salomon in hallouing of the fame did
craif of god befoir: And Daniel being in
the captiuitie, quhen he prayed to God, he
turnit his face touart the kirk of Hierufalem:
And Heliodorus quhé he vas ftrickin doun af
his horfe be the Angel of God, vas compellit
to grant to Antiochus his Maifter, that thair
vas fum fpecial verteu and puiffance of god,
quhilk did remaine in that kirk. Lykuyfe
quhen the Ieuis prayit befoir the ark of the
teftament, and the propiciatoure, God did
declair to thame mair miraculous vorkis, nor
he vfit to do in vther places. S. Auguftine
vryttand to the clergie, and peopil of Hippona, fchauis hou that God be his infinit vifdome, dois vork fum thingis in certane places,
quhair the Relictes of Martyres, and vther
halie men be, that he vorkis nocht in
vthir places: The quhilk thing, he fayis, pertenis onlie to ane myfterie of his infcrutabil
vifdome, fua that ve can nocht comprehend
the reaffone heirof: For the quhilk caus, he
fchauis vnto thame, hou that he had fend tua
of his auin houfe, quha var diffamed of ane
verie horribil cryme, in Pilgramage to Nola
in Iralie, quhair the bodie of S. Felix vas
keipit: To the effect that God micht declair

Regum. 3.
cap. 8.

Macha. 3.
cap. 3.

Anguft. in
Ser. ad Po-
pul. Hippo.

his iudgement in that place, quhidder gif
thay var innocent of the said cryme or nocht:
He addis thairto, that being in Millen him
self, ane man vas brocht befoir the reliques
of the Martyris, to sueir gif he had commited
ane certane thift, or nocht, quha vas constrainit euin aganis his vil to confes his thift:
And eftiruart concludis in this maner, that
euin as al giftis ar nocht geuin to euerie Sanct
in this varld, bot sum hes the spirit of healthe,
sum the spirit of prophecie, and sum, vthir
giftis, sua eftir thair deathe, God dois certane vorkis be sum, quhilk he dois nocht be
vtheris, quhairof ze may reid in the said Author at mair lenth.   And in the tuentie tua   *Aug. 22.*
buke of the citie of God in the aucht chap-   *de ciuit dei*
teur he vryttis, hou that ane zoung man, and   *cap. 8.*
zoung voman Callit Paulus and Palladia quha
had fallin in ane paralysie, and trimbling of
al thair membris, be reassone of thair motheris malisone, come in pilgramage to his toune
of Hippona quhair he vas bischope for the
tyme, And in sicht of the hail peopil,
be intercessione of S. Steuin, var hailed.
Sidonius Apollinarius vryttis to S. Hiero-   *Sidonius*
me hou that he had copleit his pilgramage to   *lib.1. Epi.*
Sanct Petir and Paul, and that thairbie he had *6.*
obtened his health. And S. Hierom him   *Hierom.*
self vryttis to Marcella, that it var almaist im- *ad Mar-*
possibil to him to compt al the learned and   *cellam.*
halie men, and vemen, quha sen the ascen-
sione of Christ, hes cummit in pilgramage to
                    Y iij

Hierusalem: He testifeis mairouer, that euin from our Ile of Británie, thay quha var maist halie and deuoit, could nocht be content vith thame selfis, quhil thay had bene in Hierusalem, and adorit Christ in that place in the quhilk he vas crucifeit for the saluatione of man: S. Chrysost. in his 32. homilie on the Epistle to the Romanis, schauis quhat deuotione he had to pas to Rome to se the halie chainis quhair vith S. Petir and Paul var bund, and to humil him self befoir the bodeis of the halie Martyris. Eusebius in the sext buk and elleuint chapteure reherses the lyk of the ancient vryttar Origenes, quha desyrit to pas in Pilgramage to Rome. Basilius in his homilie of the fourtie Martyris, exhortis al men to pas vnto thame, that hes mister of quhatsumeuer thing: God sayis he, vil refuse na thing to the Martyres, quha hes sched thair blude for him: Theodoretus in the lyf of Simeon geuis the caus, that mouis halie men to pas in Pilgramage, quhilk is ane treu and ardét loue: For thay sayis he, quha loues onie man, at blythe to se the places quhair he hes remanit, or quhair he is bureit, or onie thing that apertenis to him: And siclyk in his aucht buke de curandis Græcanicis affectionibus, quilk is almaist al of this argument, quhair he declaris, hou that innumerabil peopil hes obtenit health be the intercessione of the Martyres, and halie men to quhome thay did mak thair Pilgramage, quhairof sayis he, the testi-

Chrisost. Homi. 32. in Epist. ad Romanos.

Eusebius lib. 6.

Basil. Homi de 40. Marty.

Theodo. in vita Simeonis.

Theodo. 8. de curta- gne: affect.

moneis ar maist euident and cleir, be the markis, quhilkis thay quha hes obtenit sic healthe, hes left in the kirkis of the Martyris, as
Imagis of the membris, quhilk hes bene restorit to health: And as tuiching domestik
exemplis thair be zit, ane hundreth treu and
faythful men in the vest of Scotlád, quha can
beir gude recorde of the profeit of that Pilgramage, quhilk the peopil maid to S. Ni-
nian of Gallouaye, suppois ze quha ar rude
and ignorant of al that, quhilk hes bene
befoir zou, leaning onlievpone zour auin vane, and phantastical Iudgement, esteme maist
fulishlie, nocht vithout greit iniurie of God, ád
his halie Sanctis, sik thingis to be superstitious. Thair vas sum four hundreth zeiris syne
quha condemnit the ganging in Pilgramagis,
as ze do, quha var iudged to be hæretikis, be *Petrus clu-*
al the Doctoris, and learned men of that aige, *nia lib. 2.*
as amangis vtheris vitnessis the maist halie *Epist. 2.*
man S. Bernard, and Petrus Cluniacensis, Te-
stifeand that the vniuersal kirk hes euer approuit the vse of sik Pilgramagis as maist halie and profitabil, ze that God dois vork monie thingis mair miraculouslie be his Martyris and Sanctis eftir thair deathe nor he did
vork be thame quhen thay var on lyffe: To
schau, as vryttis the maist learned Theodoret
in the same buke quhilk vas cited befoir, that
the vord of God be the quhilk he promised
to his Apostlis, and seruandis, that the varld
could nocht be abil to vincuse, or ouercum

thame is maist certane and treu, becaus that euin quhen the lyf is tane fra thame, thay ar mair michtie and potent, nor euer thay var befoir, and vorkis sua miraculous vorkis, that euin thay, quha put thame to deathe var constrainit to confes the vord of God to be treu, that is, that the Martyris and seruandis of god, can nocht be vincused, or ouercummit. Bot ze, gif ze considder veil, quha takis auay sua glorious vorkis of the Martyris, sa far as lyis in zour pouar, ze vald mak god ane lear. Monie hundreth zeir befoir S. Bernad thair vas sum Heretikis callit Eustachiani quha reprouit the vniuersal kirk, be reassone of the Pilgramagis, ad assembleis quhilk the Christiane peopil vas accustumed to obserue in the kirkis of the Martyris, quhilk Heræsie vas incontinent condemnit in the Concile Callit Gangrense, sua that in this poynt, as in monie vtheris, ze haue onlie reneuit auld, and condemnit hereseis, and maid ane mass of thame al togidder: As Of SimonMagus, denying gude vorkis, and that ve ar iustifeit thairbie: of the Marcionitis, denying the distinctione of ordoris in the kirk: of the Nouatianis, denyig the sacramentis of Pænitence, and Confirmatione: of the Manichæanis denying the frie vil of man: of the Aerianis denying the praying for the deid, and offering of the sacrifice of the Mess for thame, and the keiping of fasting dayes apoyntit be the kirk: of the Noetianis, affirmand that quhasoeuer beleuis

as ze do, nochtuithſtanding thay be deſtitu-
te of gude vorkis, that thay may be ſaif, as the
Noetianis teached of thair fayth: Of the Eu-
ſtachianis, denying the Pilgramagis vnto the
halie places, quhair the reliques of the Martyris ar : Of the Pelagianis, teaching that the
baitnis ar ſanctifeit in thair motheris vombe,
ád that Baptiſme is nocht neceſſar to thame: of
Iouinianus affirmand na difference to be betuix Mariage and virginitie, and that it is leſum eſtir the vou of chaſtitie to Marie: Of Vigilantius that ve ſould nocht pray to the Sanctis, nor honore thair reliques: Of Berengarius
affirmand that thair is onlie ane ſigne of Chri
ſtis bodie in the ſacramēt: And of monie vtheris that hes follouit eſtir, as of Viclephe Huſſ
and vtheris, condemnit be thame quha euer
hes bene eſtemit for lauchful doctoris and paſtoris in the kirk, as be Irene, Iuſtine Martyre,
Arnob, Cyprian, Nazianzenus, Baſil, Auguſtine, Ambroſe, Hierom, and vtheris. This is the
ſome of my conference vith the Miniſteris,
quhairin I haue diſſembled na thing of the
force of thair argumentis, as al men, quha vas
preſent, vil teſtifie: As to my pairt, becaus it var
tedious, and our prolixe to reherſe al the reaſ-
nis quhilk I vſit for defence of the treuth the
tyme of my impreſonement, being content
to haue ſchortlie tuiched thir principal and
cheif headdis, I deſyre maiſt erniſtlie euerie
mā, as he louis his auin ſaluatione, to cōſidder
of quhat ſpirit, the reformatione (as the Mi-

Concilium Gangréſe cap.20.

Aug. de pcc. merit. & remiſſ. li.1.cap.11. Aug.hæ-reſ.82. Hiero. ad Ripariū.

Lāfrancus iu lib.cōtra Berenga-rium.

nifteris callis it)of that deformit kirk in Scotland hes proceidit : quhilk gif he do vithout
affectione,I dout nocht bot he fal cleirlie perfaue that al the mifcheif,thift,facrilege,adul-
terie,inceft,cōtempt of God,violating of his
lauis,and commandimentis, mutther of fpiritual magiftratis,ād paftoris , Be felling thame
in priuat ftreittis vndir filence of nicht , Ca-
ftīg of rottin eggis ād al kynd of filthe at thame in oppin mercat,ʙe banifing,imprefoning
and harling thame on fleddis,ʙe tramping the
memoriallis of al religione in gurtaris,be rug-
ging doun of kirkis,be fpulezing of Abbayis
be transferring the ornamētis and rentis thairof to the vphalding of huris, ignominious
vagabundis,or at the left men vithout al verteu,hes proceidit thairof:Sua that gretar Ab
hominatione may nocht be lukit for, at the
cumming of onie vtherAntichrift heireftir.As
to the Sacramentis,quhilk Chrift hes inftitute
as ordinar menis, quhairbie grace neceffar for
the fpiritual, and temporal eftait in general,
lyk as the oynting of Preiftisfor fpiritual re
generatione: The marcing of men and vemen
for procreatione of Childrene:The pmotio-
ne of fuperioris for regiment,ād gouernemēt:
And ficlyk ordinar menis, quhairbie grace
neceffar to euerie particular mannis faluatione is geuin be God,vfand the adminiftratione
of ane anoynted Paftore, ar pairtlie vilfullie
reiected as Cōfirmatione,Repentance, and ʙx-
treme Vnctione:Pairtlie in vord granted, and

in verie deid annullit, as Baptifme, and the
Sacrament of the Altar . For the quhilk caus
monie regardis nocht quhidder thair Childrene be baptized, death approching, or nocht:
Thay cum to thair cōmunione as to ane hun-
taris bankat: Gif thay fal in deidlie fyn, thay
abyd continuallie in the net of the deuil, vithout remiſſione of the fame, for reiectig the
ordinar mene of abſolutione: The pure peopil
deis lyk doggis vithout confort, nather vil
the Miniſteris dengzie thame felfis to viſſie
thame, Albeit thay vil ryd xx mylis for hoip of
ten Crounis to viſſie ane lord, that gif he haue
leuit al his dayes faythfullie in the feir of God,
thay may troubil his conſcience vith controuerſeis of diſputationis, quhidder gif the Angellis prayeris be profitabil for vs or nocht?
Thair is na thing hard out of thair pulpittis,
bot blaſphemie aganis God in lauchfullie promouit Paſtoris, and princes, to bring thePe-
pil in fuſpitione, that the neu teſtament of
our faluiour, is the inuentione of the Paip,
lyk as thay blaſphemouſlie fpeke of his Sacrifice, and Canonis of the Apoſtlis. Gif onie
man feiring God, conſidering thair beginning
and conferring the famyn vith hæreſeis condemnit in our foirfarheris dayes, offer thame
diſputatione: Thay trauel be al menis to feik
his lyf, fua that thay appeir nocht the murtheraris of him: As be experience I knau of my
felf, aganis quhom, thay, lyk fals traittorous
learis, as I tak god to yitnes, Inuenit thingis

quhilk I neuer thocht, concerning the honore of the kingis Maieſtie, nocht vorthie of re-
herſal, quhairbie thay laborit my ruine, transferring the caus from profeſſione of religione
to leſe Maieſtie, and treaſſone, as thay vald
haue callit it : Bot zit the eternal God, quhạ
neuer fruſtrat onie, that vnfenzeitlie beleuit
in him, in deſpytt of thair rage, hes preſeruit
me from danger bayth of bodie and ſaul. God
of his mercie grant the Peopil of the hail
cuntrey grace to vndirſtand, that lyk as the
Miniſteris began vith ane fals promeis, to vit
that the peopil ſould haue thair teindis frie,
ạnd the teacharis of the Proteſtaons ſould gang in ſik ſimpil pouartie, as did the Apoſtlis,
ſua thay may knau that the leſingis hes na
meſure, fund out be thame, quha hes ſucceidit to thair leing father kmnox : And lykuyſe
perſaue the hid abhominationis, quhilk lurkis vndir thair negatiues : For gif the Paip of
Rome, quha euer hes bene Preſident to Chriſtis kirk ſen his aſcenſione, be thocht the Antichriſt, It follouis conſequenlie that nather
Chriſt hes ane kirk, nather zit hes cummit in
the varld, ſeing as thay teache be inſtinctione
of Sathan, and contempt of God, that his
kirk hes bene inuiſibil : The reiecting of the
halie dayes, quhilk vas inſtitute be the Apoſtlis, tendis to na vther thing, bot ane obli-
uione, and forzetfulnes of al the Ioy, that al
mankynd hes obtenit be the cúming of our
ſaluiour, ád the neglectíg of ſik ſolicit honore

Ignat Ep. 4 ad Phi-lippenſes.

of his halie name, as had our foirfatheris, quhõ
God blissed in thair dayes vith al spiritual, and
temporal benefeittis: Quhairfoir to the effect
the Rottin frutes of thair deformatione may
be zit mair manifest to the hail varld, I vil
subioyne ane comparesone of the treu religione befoir professed in Scotland, vith this
diabolical hæresie, quhilk being offerit to me
be the Author, efter I had endit This my conference, I thocht gude to subione as maist
pertinent to the sam effect and purpose.

THE DIFFERENCE, COM-
paresone, and change from the treu Catholique fayth, to the neu deformed religione.

C H A P.   XXXVII.

1   A Ne change is maid from ane religione quhilk ze had, *Vnto monie diuerse
and contrarius sectis*, and formes of maist damnabil
hæresie: from ancient: *Vnto neu:* from vniuersal,
and commone, *to priuat, and singular:* from that
quhilk had the vniuersal consent of zour selfis at hame; togidder vith al Christian nationis of Europe. *Vnto that, or thame, in the quhilk
nather zour selfis ar ag greit, nor onie monarchie Christian agreis vith zou.*

2   Ane change from ane religione gouernit
be the iust monarchie of our saluiour Christ,
his Apostlis and thair successoris, *To ane mon-*

struous policracie of ſa monie headis as thair be vſur-
pit Miniſteris, Ʒe of vemen headis, Childrene head-
dis, and popular headdis, as thocht thair var als mo-
nie Goddis, as thair be abſolute Princes, and as gif it
var lauchful to haue als monie diuerſe formes of go-
uernement in the kirk of God, quhilk can nocht be
bot ane, as ve may haue ſeueral policies, in Ciuile
kingdomes be thay neuer ſua monie.

3 Ane change from that quhilk vas planted
be godlie Apoſtlis, mentenit be the aſſiſtance
the halie Ghaiſt, and men of gude conſciencis,
Vnto this quhilk is foſterit, be vſurparis of princes
pouaris.

4 Ane change from that quhilk maid fiſcha-
ris Apoſtlis, *vnto this that makis Biſchopis, Ab-*
botis, Prioris, Archidiaconis, monkis, preiſtis, perſo-
nis, vicares, freris, and religious Nonis, to becum periu-
rit Apoſtatis, and foirſakaris of that Chriſtiane and
godlie fayth, quhairunto thay gaue thair ayth befoir
God, and his halie kirk.

5 Ane change from praying for ſaulis according to the vord of God, and cuſtume of the
halie kirk ſen the dayes of our ſaluiour, *To con-*
demning the lyf and ꞇōuerſatione of our prædeceſſoris
vnto hel, be the verie inſtinctione of Sathan : From
geuing of almous, *To diſſoluing of hoſpitallis :* Frō
creiping in conuentis, *To bragging in courtis:*
From vouing of Chaſtitie, *To mareing of Mon-*
kis: From conſecrating virginis, *To vedding of*
Nunnis, From promiſing pouartie, *To profeſſed*
vſurie : From volontar obedience, *To obſtinat*
arrogance : From faſting on fiſhe dayes, *To gor-*

manding fleshe on frydayes, and the halie tyme of len-
tearne: From vatching and praying, *To sleiping*
in the kirk: From kirk mēnis praying, *To layitt*
mēnis preaching: From sermonis by doctoris, *To*
vemēnis lecturis: Frō ressoning, *To railling:* From
reuerence speche , *to fulishe lauching at al halie*
thingis : From remembring on Sanctis, *To bur-*
ning thair imagis : From going in Pilgramage,
To hanting of harlattis: From penance of Pardo-
nis, *To dissimulat fayth, and presumptione :* Frō ve-
ping for vickitnes , *To lauching at syne :* From
scrupil of euil doing in smal thingis, *To gloir of*
mischeuous dealling in materis of gretast vecht and
importance.

6 Ane change from that religione quhilk
condemnit al erroris, *Vnto this quhilk mentenis*
al herefeis, sua that na heresie is thair of auld condem-
nit, quhilk is nocht nou amang Zou reneuit, and pro-
fessed maist impudentlie.

7 A change from that religione quhilk acceptit and imbraced Christ, his Apostlis, and
thair ordinar successoris head of the general
kirk, *To this quhilk hes imbraced ane inuisibil kirk*
vithout knauledge of Christis authoritie in onie
lauchful superior vpone the face of the earth: Albeit
it tuik the fundamēt from the kirk of Ingland, qu-
hais first frute of religione vas to place, in the Chyre
of Petir and feminine, head as gif onie vomā be peruer-
fion of the ordore and lau of nature, micht haue su-
premacie and iurisdictione ouer the kirk of our sal-
uiore, As head, paip, heich preist or Apostle, *as Prophet,*
or Patriarche, as Archebischop, or Bischop, *as* Abbot, *or*

prior, *as* person or *Vicar*, *as* preist, clerk, or *spiritual magistrat* and pastore quhatsumeuer.

8 *Ane religione of negatiues, a religione of leis, a religione of periureis, a religione of fleshlie and licetious libertie, a religione that leidis to lousues, and al dissolute lyf*, *a religione that of scripture*, *denyis sindrie hail volummes, that of text it self, corruptis places infinit*, *and vntreulie translaittis the rest; that sould decyd onie questione or controuersie.*

9. *Ane religione that lewis Zou na scripture at al, quhen sa monie bukes ar denyit, sua monie places corruptit*, *and changit, sua monie textis falslie translated, and sua monie haretical glossis*, *and expositionis put thairvpone.*

10 *Ane religione that Falsifeis the fatheris, sklanderis the doctoris, beleis the paipis*, *beleis the Emperoris*, *beleis the practeis of the kirk, and al histoteis, that testifeis the treuth of thingis past.*

11 *Ane religione that callis Christ in the sacrament ane idol, that callis the onlie sacrifice of the Christian kirk, idolatrie: that professis it to be sin to beleue that the Euangel is treu, saying. This is my bodie, my fleshe is verie meat, or that fasting, praying, almous, vouis, or vther gud vorkis dois pleise, or appese his vrayth, albeit thay proceid from special grace, throuche Christ Iesus our saluiour: That teachis Christiane fayth ta be fals doctrine, and thair auin fals, arrogant, and abhominabil haresie to be the treu fayth of Christ, albeit it be repugnant thairto in al poyntis.*

12 *A religione that teachis the cheif outuard sacrifice, and honore to God*, *that euer vas vsit quhair Christis name vas pfessed, to be idolatrie: that teachis*
                                                                        sacrilege

sacrilege,inceſt,and the vilful ſlauchter of ſacred,and unoyntit perſonis , to be verteuous deiddis , acceptabil to God,and that teachis the auld,cõmone, and knauin vay of ſaluatione,to be the hie vay to damnatione I'tal it thairſoir be inuicibil conſequentis a religione that turnis darknes into licht,that teachis hel to be heuin,and God him ſelf to be the deuil of hel.

13 Ane change from ane religione , quhairin fayth,hoip,cheritie,fidelitie,abûdance of gude vorkis, gud diſcipline , ordour , famous , and vorthie renoune in al proceidingis did abûde, *To this, quhairin exces of vengeãce,laik of fayth,vehement miſcheif,miſtruſt in nichtbourheid , inſidelitie of kinred, and acquentance, inſatiabil auarice in ſteid of prudent liberalitie dois regne.*

14 Ane change from reuerence bering to the day of the birth of our ſaluiour Chriſt,his cruel Paſſione,michtieReſurrectione,and glorious Aſcenſione , faſting , praying, abſtening from mechanict labour , and doing al gud turnis quhilk may procure the mercie of God touart thame,*To ane blind and miſordorit forme of religione,that makis abhominatione thairof,and confoûdis thir feyſtis vith vther dayes apoyntit to mechanict laboris : quhairhie it may be eſilie collectit , that thay , and thair ſect ar the maiſt affectionat diſciplis of the Cheif Antichriſt , becaus thay haue laborit be al meinis to put the bleſſed monumentis of Chriſtis benefeittis out of the memorie of thair miſerabil auditoris.*

15 Ane change from ane veil ordorit religione, quhairin euerie eſtait yas knauin ſeueráliẽ

be his Ecclesiastical apparel, *To ane neu fund,* *headles, and cõfused rabil. of vitles Bischopis inarmit* *vith tua handit suordis, in steid of blissingis, and* *feiding of thair flokis: quha ather compellis thame to* *pay doubil teindis, to garneis thair vnsauorie mules* *that beiris thair Croces, and bringis furth vther smal* *conspiratoris aganis the kirk of God, or ellis to delu-* *ge, and leue the grounde voyd, and red to thame selfis:* *And breiflie sik confusione that na stranger, except he* *be of continual conuersatione vith thame, can discer-* *ne betuix the popular, and vsurpit estait of the daft* *Abbotis, gukkit Prioris, guseheaddit Personis, asin* *vittit Vicares, and the pretland Prebendaris, for hou-* *soeuer the headles Parochinaris be inclynit, sua is he* *also, that he may be estemit ane gude follou, and na* *thing different fra the commone sort.*

16 Ane chãge from that, quhais peopil aluays pænitent, and reddie auaittand vpone the calling of God, had participatione of the sa-crament of Christis bodie and blude befoir thair departure out of this lyf, at the hour of death: *To this quhilk hes prescryuit, and limitat* *certane tymes to the mocking of Christ, and abusing* *his peopil, vndir the pretext of administratione of the* *said sacrament, falsifeing that scripture, as al vtheris,* *quhilk Christ our saluiour expreslie hes left vs, for* *ane sufficient and maist plaine testimonie of his lat-* *ter vil.*

17 Ane change from a religione, quhais Pa-storis addicted thame selfis, and thair actionis onlie to the kirk, the veilbeloued spous of Christ, and for his saik bure al honore, and re-

uerence thairunto, *Vnto this quhais vnlauchful Ministeris neuer anoynted, nor ressauit in spiritual societie quhatsumeuer, castis auay the foirsaid spous, and vith palliardise and al kynd of harlatrie abusis the sacred and halie place.*

18 Ane change from that quhais anoynted Bischopis, and Preistis in presence of God and halie kirk auoued chastitie, and leued continent lyuis, *Vnto this quhais vsurpit Bischopis, apostat Preistis, and palliard Ministeris, professis procreatione of adulterous childrene, and monie of thame piuralitie of harlattis, falslie callit vyuis.*

19 Ane change from that quhilk vas spred throuche the varld at first, and euer sence mētenit by the vryttin gospellis, and epistles of treu Euangelistis, and vndoutet Apostlis, *Vnto this quhilk by hargabusis, and pistolattis of armit suldartis of the Antichrist is intrudit, and mentenit eueriequhair.*

20 Ane change from that quhilk vas serued be the ministrie of thame, quha had bene brochtup in learning, ordour, and obedience. *Vnto this, quhais fals prophetes ar maid of Tinklaris, schocloutaris, soutaris, broustaris, skinnaris, tailzeouris, glaisin vrichtis, and professoris of mechanict artis, of the baisaist qualitie, and maist mischeuous conditione, that could be fund amang the vnreulie peopil, becaus the honestar sort vil nocht accept the vocatione.*

21 Ane change from that, quhilk throuche cheritie contenit men vithin the boundis of pietie, iustice, temperance, and verteous

Z ij

exerceisis , *Vnto this quhilk by ane solisidiane presumptione first induces in man lousnes of lyf, rudnes
of maneris, vyldnes of lukis, pryd of speiche, hautenes
of gesture , and ane ruffiane lyk rusching vnto al vy-
ce, nixt thaireftir vnto atheisme, barbarisme, or Mahometis fayth at the leist.*

22 Ane change from that, quhilk by na pe-
naltie constrainit onie man to leue the fayth,
or religione, quhilk he imbraced, *Vnto this quhilk by feir of authoritie, priuat actis of parliament,
maid in tyme of Ciuile dissensione , commandiment of
commissionaris, banesing from the cūtrey, vith souer-
tie nocht to returne , by bandis , infinit vexationis, a-
merciamentis, baratrie , depriuatione from lewingis,
and offices, inuy of the cūtrey, putting out of the court,
displesour of the king, Tinsal of landis, confiscatione
of guddis, personal impresonment, by sindrie deathis
schort and violent , tormentes of hungar , compelling
men be vord or deid, mair, or les to fal from the fayth,
quhairin thay var baptized.*

23 Ane change from that quhilk by ancient,
general , and godlie lauis corrected onlie thame that vald haue departed from it , quhen
thay had first freylie professed the same , *Vnto
this , quhilk by neu, priuat, and vsurpit, vranguse
lauis, contrare al ressone punises, impresonis, oppres-
sis, and makis pure thame quha neuer acceptit , nor
allouit the same .*

24 Ane change from abounding in Riches
spiritual, and temporal, *To this quhilk aboundis
in riches, and hes nather of thame bayth, from cre-
. . . . discredite in seal, and obligatione.*

25 Ane change from voluntar repentance, *To compelling, and prouoking a reddie vay to do the lyk or rather varse, quhen thay loue men for committing of al kynd of impietie, aganis God, his halie kirk and the lauchful authoritie of supreme magistratis.*

26 Ane change from that, quhais first frutes var to rin in vildernes, to forsaik the varld, and al feliciteis of this miserabil fleshe, *Vnto this quhais first fructis var to spulzie Christ our saluiour of his spiritual kingdome, demolish kirkis, to mak Nonis, and freris spulzie thair closteris, the voued men to rin auay vith harlattis, the professed men to steil auay temporal mennis vyues, and dochteris, and to caus thame spulzie thair housbandis, and fatheris.*

27 Ane change from that, quhilk keipit zour vomankynd in al vomanlie grauitie, *To this that leidis the zelous imbracearis thairof vnto al glaikrie:* From that quhilk teached thame madinlie schamefastnes, *To this that teachis thame to be eschamit at na thing. And hes drauin thame,* frô sobrietie, *To vanitie,* from cleynnes be veschĩg, *To vnsauorie painting:* From being the exemplis of modestie to al nationis, *To be patronis of al lichtnes and instabilitie of vit :* From sobir lukis, *To licht eyne :* Frô sad, and ciuil speking, *To bauld babling quhatsumeuer, lest thay sould seme ignorant:* From vorking, *To playing :* From spairing, *To spending :* From bukis of prayer, *To ballattis of luue :* From occupeing beiddis, *To brydling thair heiddis :* From veiring of Christis Croce and image, *To behalding of thair auin dissimulat*

Z iij

viſage: From threid, ſeyme, ād neidil, *To danſe at the feidil*: From blushing to heir of mariage, *To lauching to heir of loue* : From the bondage of mariage vith ane, *To the libertie of Mareing manie*, From a decent feirfulnes conuenient to thair kynd, *To ane vndecent hardines* : From modeſt, and pudict behauiour cumlie for vemen, *Vnto mair nor a manlie audacitie , in vord , deid , and al vther ſort planlie repugnant to al halines of lyf , and the qualiteis of ane profitabil vyf.*

28 Ane change from ane brydil aganis ſyn, *To ane ſpur, and exempil of al iniquitie* : From that quhilk feirit mē to do euil, *To this quhilk ſtayis men to do veil , leſt thairbie thay be thocht Papiſtis:* From that quhilk by hoip of Goddis reuard, inuited men to do gud varkis, *Vnto this quhilk be hoip of mannis auancemēt, alluris men to miſcheif:* From conſcience in ceremoneis , *To defy ſacramentis:* From contritiône of hart for ſyn, *To induratione of hart in al abhominabil vickitnes:* From confeſſion of ſyn be mouthe, *To conceling of ſyn by aithis* : From ſeiking to ſatisfie for ſyn , *To the doubling of ſyn vpone ſyn.*

29 Ane chāge from ſeyndil ſuering, *To oppin, manifeſt , and vſual periurie , vith blaſpheming of Goddis halie name* : From vniuerſal treuth , and fidelitie ane touardis another, *To cōmone diſcredite be febil fayth, vord, and vryt:* From feiting to lie, *To plane, and accuſtumit impudēcie:* From building of Chapellis, *To doun pulling of kirkis* : Frō erecting of altaris, *To ouerthrauing of Abbayes:* From honoring the ſanctuarie , *To Prophaning*

she fam vith al kynd of licherie, filth, gun, and geng-
zie, smythis, maisonis, fals decreittis, murther, buche-
rie, stabling of horse, ky, scheip, and suyne, vith infinit
pollutionis horribil to be rehersed, as manifest testimoneis of the kingdome of the Antichrist, and his
abhominabil desolatione.

30 Ane religione that euerie quhair generalie is
first apprehendit, maist zeloustie imbraced, and vehe-
mentlie mentenit be the leudast of conditione, the
maist vitious of maneris, the maist contentious, vn-
quiettast, and varst of conuersatione, Inchaptaris, Ne-
cromātiaris, mischāt mensleyaris, and manifest adulteraris, quhairof, lat euerie mannis priuat experience
gif testimonie, that may remember the first precharis
of this doctrine, the principal, and maist feruent discipillis thairof in Scotland, or ellis quhair in euerie toune, citie, village, Parochin, and houshald.

31 Finalie, Ane change is maid from a religione quhais imbrecearis Christ blessed vith al
kynd of requesit benefeittis bayth spiritual,
and temporal Vnto this quhais imbrecearis, God hes
plaged befoir the eyis of the varld vith schameful tormentis, befoir thair suddane, and odious deathe : hes
diminisit thair rentis, for tending to augment thair
dominionis, vith spiritual benefices : And for testimonie that he vil haue his decreit performed vpone
that generatione, he hes tane from diuerse, and the
maist special of thame al hoip of birth, of neir, or
lauchful airis, to succeid to the samyn : Or gif be his
visdome he haue sufferit thame zit on lyf, ather thay
ar retened vithout dignitie, out of memorie, and of na
reputatione, or ellis extreme abiect, quhil God haue his

iuſt iudgemènt pourit on thame, for thair fatheris faltis, and t hair auin perſeuerance in the ſam vickitnes. God of his infinit gudnes grant thame knauledge of thair impietie, and grace to returne to the boſume of the Catholique kirk of Chriſt Ieſus, the natural ſone of the leuing and maiſt heich God, to quhome, vith the Father, and halie Ghaiſt in vnitie of Godheid, be al honore, glorie, and praiſe, for nou and euer. Amen.

Becauſ the ſones of Iſrael hes foirſaikin thy *3. Reg.ca.* couenant, thair aduerſaris hes brokin doun *19.* thy altaris, and perſecute thy Prophetis.

Zit,

In the dayis of tha kingdomes, the God of heauin ſal raiſe vp ane kingdome, quhilk ſal neuer be ouerthrauin, and that his kingdome *Dan. 2.* ſal nocht be geuin to ane vther people, bot it ſal ouercum, and put at vndir al thir kingdomes, and it ſal ſtand for euermair.

Exurgat Deus, & diſsipentur inimici eius.

FINIS.
Deo gratias.

THE MATERIS OF
CONTROVERSIE QVHILK
ar intreated in this confe-
rence ar thir.

SI quis videtur inter vos sapiens esse in hoc sæculo, stultus fiat vt sit sapiens: sapientia enim huius mundi, stultitia est apud Deum.

Gif ony man amang zou appeir to be vyse in this varld, let him be ane fule, that he may be maid vyse in verie deid: for the visdome of this varld is folie in the sicht of God. S. Paul. 1. Cor. 3.

Elegi abiectus esse in domo Dei mei magis, quàm habitare in tabernaculis peccatorum.

I haue chosin to be repute abiect and contemptible in the hous of God, rather nor to duel in the tabernaclis of the vicked. Psal. 83.

FINIS.

Imprentit at Pareis, the first day of
October, The zeir of
God, 1581.

APPENDIX

The vther t'Audebert: Zit Candida nei-die
Vald BeZa haue hail scho is so gre-die:
And Aude-bert vald BeZe haue hail
So couetous is he for to pre-uail.
Bot I vald so thame baith imbrace
To be al hail vith baith in a place
Hir vith hir cunt, him vith his erß,
And I betuix vith ane stif terß:
　Zit th'ane sould I prefer indeid
Bot ô how hard a thing is neid!
And sen the ane man be preferd
My fore-quarters sal be con-ferd
To Aude-bert for Bou go-rie
The cheifest of my vo-luptie
Bot Candida gif scho com-plaine
I sal hir cunt Kiß laich a-gane.

Siclyk Caluin vas markit vith the flour de-
lise vpone his schuldir for the horribill syn
of Sodomie : And this is the halines of zour
kirk , quhairin ze gloir , reprouing euer the
auld Romane kirk (in the quhilk sa monie
halie mē andMartyris hes florished) of sik cry
mes quhilk ze can nocht be abill to proue:
and albeit zour accusatione var treu; it seruis
na thing to zour purpose.